CW01238954

Translation and Censorship in Different Times and Landscapes

Translation and Censorship
In Different Times and Landscapes

Edited by

Teresa Seruya and Maria Lin Moniz

Cambridge Scholars Publishing

Translation and Censorship in Different Times and Landscapes
Edited by Teresa Seruya and Maria Lin Moniz

This book first published 2008 by

Cambridge Scholars Publishing

15 Angerton Gardens, Newcastle, NE5 2JA, UK

British Library Cataloguing in Publication Data
A catalogue record for this book is available from the British Library

Copyright © 2008 by Teresa Seruya and Maria Lin Moniz and contributors

All rights for this book reserved. No part of this book may be reproduced, stored in a retrieval system, or transmitted, in any form or by any means, electronic, mechanical, photocopying, recording or otherwise, without the prior permission of the copyright owner.

ISBN (10): 1-84718-474-X, ISBN (13): 9781847184740

TABLE OF CONTENTS

List of Illustrations viii
List of Tables ix
Acknowledgments x
Foreword xi

CHAPTER ONE
TRANSLATION & CENSORSHIP IN PORTUGAL:
THE LONG NIGHT OF *ESTADO NOVO*

Foreign Books in Portugal and the Discourse of Censorship in Portugal in the 1950s 3
Teresa Seruya & Maria Lin Moniz

Faulkner and the Portuguese Censorship 21
Ana Teresa Marques dos Santos

Forbidden Images of Portuguese Colonialism: a Translation of a Book by C. R. Boxer.. 30
Gabriela Gândara Terenas

Shakespeare Surveilled by Salazar: Anatomy of a Censorship's Story 47
Rui Pina Coelho

Shakespeare and the Censors: Translation and Performance Strategies Under the Portuguese Dictatorship.. 61
Fran Rayner

Censorship(s) and Contradictions: the "Draw" (1971/72) of Witkiewicz's Play The Mother... 74
Christine Zurbach

Who is Holding the Blue Pencil? A Visit to Intralingual Translation in the Portuguese Theme Park "Portugal dos Pequenitos" 84
Alexandra Assis Rosa

CHAPTER TWO
TRANSLATION & CENSORSHIP IN SPAIN:
PHILOSOPHIES, IDEOLOGIES AND SELF-CENSORSHIP

Translations of German Philosophy into Spanish and Censorship 103
Ibon Uribarri Zenekorta

Un Bergman "a la Española" 119
Glòria Barbal

(Para)Translated Ideologies in Simone de Beauvoir's Le deuxième sexe:
The (Para)Translator's Role 130
Olga Castro Vázquez

*Pseudonyms, Pseudotranslation and Self-Censorship in the Narrative
of the West during the Franco Dictatorship* 147
María del Carmen Camus Camus

The Danger(s) of Self-Censorship(s): The Translation of 'Fuck'
into Spanish and Catalan 163
José Santaemilia

Censorship and the Self-Translator 174
Helena Tanqueiro & Patrícia López López-Gay

*The Francoist Censorship Casts a Long Shadow: Translations
from the Period of the Dictatorship on Sale Nowadays* 184
Cristina Gómez Castro

CHAPTER THREE
TRANSLATION & CENSORSHIP: DO DIFFERENT LANDSCAPES
& TIMES CALL FOR (DIS)SIMILAR CONSTRAINTS?

Censorship in Brazil: the Case of Clube do Livro 199
John Milton

Translation and Censorship in Communist Czechoslovakia 215
Jaroslav Špirk

*Censorship in Translation and Translation Studies
in Present-day China* 229
Nam Fung Chang

Language Planning in Turkey: a Source of Censorship on Translations... 241
Hilal Erkazanci

Ukraine: Translating the Wars 252
Natalia Olshanskaya

CHAPTER FOUR
TRANSLATION & CENSORSHIP: REVISITING PAST CONSTRAINTS
AND ASSUMPTIONS

*Morality and Poetic Theorizing as Censorship Strategies:
The Translation of* Heroides *by Miguel do Couto Guerreiro
(1720 - 1793)* 265
Maria dos Anjos Guincho

*Censorship and Self-Censorship in English Narrative Fiction
Translated into Spanish During the Eighteenth Century* 289
Eterio Pajares

Iberian Censorship and the Reading of Lazarillo *in 19th Century
Portugal* 298
Rita Bueno Maia

Self-Censorship in Victorian Translations of Hans Christian Andersen... 308
Viggo Hjørnager Pedersen

Contributors 319

Index 327

LIST OF ILLUSTRATIONS

Fig. 2-1: Censorship file 1497/43 115

Fig. 2-2: Distribution of the 191 authors in the sample 151

Fig. 2-3: Distribution of the 141 pseudonyms in the sample 155

LIST OF TABLES

Table 1-1: Approved and banned books according to language 9

Table 1-2: Approved and banned books according to subject 9

Table 2-1: Catalogue of censorship files (Kant) 115

Table 2-2 125

Table 2-3 126

Table 2-4: List of the 80 Spanish authors who used a single pseudonym .. 153

Table 2-5: The three pseudonyms shared by more than one author 154

Table 2-6: The 24 Spanish authors who used two or more pseudonyms.... 154

Table 2-7: Main usages of the lexeme *fuck* in the BNC (adapted from McEnery & Xiao 2004) 164

Table 2-8 165

Table 2-9: Main usages of the lexeme 'fuck' in *Bridget Jones's Diary* and *Bridget Jones: The Edge of Reason* (1999) 166

Table 4-1 299

ACKNOWLEDGMENTS

I would like to thank

- The members of the Scientific Committee of the Conference: João Almeida Flor, João Ferreira Duarte and John Milton, for their careful reading of the many paper proposals;

- The members of the Organising Committee: Maria Lin Moniz, Inês Espada Vieira and Isabel Chumbo, for their valuable contribution to the success of the Conference;

- The members of the Scientific Committee of the Proceedings, for their hard work in the selection of papers to be published in this volume: Maria Lin Moniz, John Milton, Raquel Merino and José Miguel Santamaría;

- The Portuguese Catholic University (Lisbon) and its Centro de Estudos de Comunicação e Cultura [Research Centre for Communication and Culture Studies], for having provided the most adequate facilities;

- Cambridge Scholars Publishing, for their interest in the Conference and the publishing of this volume.

Teresa Seruya,
President of the Conference
2007

FOREWORD

> Translation as a teleological activity *par excellence* is to a large extent conditioned by the goals it is designed to serve, and these goals are set in, and by, the prospective receptor system(s). Consequently, translators operate first and foremost in the interest of the culture *into* which they are translating, and not in the interest of the source text, let alone the source culture.
> —Gideon Toury

1.

The topic of censorship linked to translation is by no means unexpected, if one takes into consideration the "novelty claim" Gideon Toury has attached to the role played by any translation in its target system. Semiotically speaking, "translation is as good as initiated by the target culture", due to "a certain deficiency in the latter", which always "entails some change [in it], however slight (…)" (Toury 1995: 27). Beyond the mere introduction of the target text, this change also stems from the fact that translation "tends to *deviate* from [the] sanctioned patterns [of the target culture], on one level or another (…)" (*Ibidem*: 28).

Censorship in Translation Studies (in general, as well as in Portugal) has not so far been assigned the importance it deserves. It was this lack of attention to a less well-known chapter of the discipline that encouraged the organization of the Lisbon Conference on "Translation and Censorship. From the 18th Century to the Present Day". Some relevant and very fruitful research has been carried out in Spain by the project TRACE, which has published several books on censorship of literature, theatre and films during Franco's dictatorship. Another important contribution to the visibility of the subject was the Forli conference (University of Bologna) on "Translation in fascist systems: Italy, Spain, Germany" (April 2005)– where Portugal was left out, for lack of information on the part of the organization, although the Portuguese dictatorship was the longest in modern Europe (1926-1974). On the other hand, only recently and slowly has Translation Studies gained an international dimension in this country.

After the call for papers for the Lisbon Conference (early Spring 2006) two other related events were announced, one in Arles and the other at the University of São Paulo (Brazil), within the convention of the ICLA– International Comparative Literature Association (Summer 2007), not to mention the very recent publication of the first book on the topic, which includes a theoretical introduction and several case studies from various contexts and media, but again with no interest in Portugal (Billiani 2007).

Enlarging the historical and geographical scope of the topic was one of the main goals of the Lisbon Conference. Just by looking at the history of translation in Europe can we state that censorship goes along with this history. The chapter concerning the Bible translation alone shows how censorship could, at times, turn into official murder–in only one decade influenbiased by(1536-1546) John Tyndale and Étienne Dolet were sentenced to death because of their translational work. On the other hand, however, translators themselves are not innocent agents in the whole process of translation. A striking example of censorship exerted by the translator upon the author can be found in the French translator Nicolas Perrot d'Ablancourt's justification for cutting and altering his source text by Lucian (1706; *apud* Lefevere 1992: 35-37). The difference between the two examples is surely one between life and death. This is why the concept of censorship has to be defined in such a way as to avoid being either too broad, and hence possibly mixed up with manipulation (which translation as rewriting is in some way), or too narrow as it is used when referring to institutionalized censorship (e.g. in fascist and communist systems). As it often happens when an object is observed from a close viewpoint, our conference has indeed contributed to make clear how diverse and complex the many faces of censorship are, and how they range from the selection of the text/film to be translated, the stage G. Toury names "culture planning" (Toury 1999), to several forms of self-censorship.

2.

Our call for papers prompted a wide response from several continents and countries, dealing with different contexts and times. The papers now approved for publication also reflect this diversity, although the Iberian presence (first two chapters) is more visible than others.

CHAPTER I is an almost complete novelty in the topic (see Seruya 2006). It introduces the official censorship to of translations during the Portuguese dictatorship. **Seruya & Moniz**'s study is a follow-up of a paper delivered in Graz (2005) dealing with banned translated literature mainly in the 1940s. The present study moves forward to the 1950s and begins with the political and cultural characterization of the decade. Its scope was enlarged to foreign books, since they were approved or banned by the Censoring Commission having their prospective translation in mind. A quantified analysis of several aspects of the *corpus* precedes a presentation of the most common arguments for the ban (propaganda, sexual morality, speculation, discomfort in relation to National Socialism and democracy, among others). They can be regarded as a sort of *mise en abîme* of the prevailing ideological values of that time.

Following this more general approach, **Ana Teresa Santos** presents a case study on the censorship of W. Faulkner's *Sanctuary* (1931), whose first translation into European Portuguese was published in 1958, after the Brazilian one had been banned. Santos discusses several passages of the 1958 text, where much of the sexual violence and perversion present in Faulkner's realistic novel is deleted. The Portuguese readership would have to wait until 1973 to read a full version of the source text.

Criticism to Salazar's overseas policy was one of the regime's taboos. The case presented by **Gabriela Terenas** deals with the banned Brazilian translation (1967) of Charles Boxer's *Race Relations in the Portuguese Colonial Empire, 1415-1825* (1963). About twenty works by this famous specialist in Portuguese Studies were translated after 1928. Terenas reconstructs the whole controversy about the book and the context of its translation and prohibition, which has to do not only with expressed doubts about Salazar's statements on the good principles of Portuguese colonization and its support by some Portuguese historians, but also with the Brazilian political and cultural context at the end of the 1960s.

Theatre is an activity prone to attract the censors' attention, due to its public setting. And indeed it was kept under surveillance since 1927 through a specific censoring commission, the General Inspectorate of Theatres. **Rui Pina Coelho** writes about the eleven Shakespeare plays staged in Portugal between 1927 and 1974, informing about the circumstances and agents involved in each performance/ translation, including the ordeals with the referred commission. Special attention is given to *Anatomia de uma História de Amor* [*Anatomy of a Love Story*], an adaptation of *Romeo and Juliet,* which was eventually approved, although with cuts. The performance (Lisbon, 1969) included a video projection dealing with the events of May '68, as well as some Brechtian techniques introduced by the director and actress Luzia Maria Martins. Coelho comes to the conclusion that the introduction of the Portuguese public to the Epic Theatre and to political theatre "was made under the veil of Shakespeare's *Romeo and Juliet*".

Shakespeare is also the main subject of **Fran Rayner**'s study, although her main goal is to advocate the collaboration between Translation and Performance Studies, since only the conjunction of both uncovers the full context of a production. She analyses two cases from the 1960s, Rebello's *Dente por Dente* [*Measure for Measure*] (1964) and Monteiro's *O Amansar da Fera* [*The Taming of the Shrew*] (1967). Although it is clear that censorship did have major implications in the two performances, they, on the other hand, represent significant attempts to modernize the Portuguese theatrical repertoires. Another important conclusion relates to the bureaucracy of censorship: it was sometimes "brutal", but also "incoherent and awkward".

In her paper, **Christine Zurbach** discusses the interaction between translation and censorship as cultural practices within the target culture, more precisely the Portuguese theatrical life of the 1970s. Having been chosen for the season of 1971-1972, Witkiewicz's play *The Mother* was to be staged in March 1972, but it was eventually banned, although the Portuguese translation was published in the same year, together with the documents relating to the banning of the performance.

Finally we learn about a very typical institution of Salazar's *Estado Novo*, the theme park for children "Portugal dos Pequenitos", in Coimbra, built as a nationalist promotion and propaganda of the Portuguese colonial empire. **Alexandra Assis Rosa** analyses the area called "Overseas Nucleus" with its eleven overseas provinces. In some cases, the visitor is introduced to them through "two generations of plaques", the most recent of which was rewritten after 1974 for ideological reasons. This phenomenon of intralingual translation is then discussed in its relation with censorship, by both the colonial supporters and their revolutionary successors.

CHAPTER II is dedicated to Spain. It starts with **Ibon Zenekorta**'s new line of research within the TRACE project. Its novelty stems not only from its subject–the translation of philosophy–but also from the implicated source language, German, (so far TRACE had focused on English-speaking theatre, cinema and narrative). Zenekorta mentions the difficulties in the institutionalisation of modern philosophy in Spain, because it was seen as a challenge to religion as "an ideological framework for social realities". The reception of modern German philosophy could thus be considered a modernizing force in Spain between 1850 and 1936. In 1939 it was no longer a priority of the new regime. The study gathers information about translations of German philosophy under Franco. The author describes the methodology used to deal with, and to contextualize and interpret, the results obtained. The reception of I. Kant is his main focus, but Marx and Nietzsche are referred to as well. He also comments on the censors' opinions about several translations of Kant.

Glòria Barbal introduces us to the Francoist censorship of Ingmar Bergman's *The Seventh Seal,* a film that drew the censors' attention, due to its religious themes. It was the catholic priest Staehlin who introduced Bergman into Spain. According to the available sources, he must have played some role in the final dubbing presented to the Spanish audience. Barbal gives and comments on examples of censorship taken from the VHS version she had access to.

Different approaches to translation must prove adequate to the particular case under observation. **Olga Castro Vázquez** explains, in an incisive introduction, why scholars have been paying more and more attention to ideology in Translation Studies, refusing taken-for-granted notions such as the view of the translator as a neutral bridge or as an invisible or objective agent. Her position is particularly adequate to her case study, the English and Spanish translations of Simone de Beauvoir's *Le deuxième sexe,* the "first landmark in the modern feminist upsurge". Her *corpus* is extended to encompass translations in the USA and the Anglophone world, as well as Spanish-speaking Latin America and Spain. The concept of "paratranslation/ paratranslator" (Garrido) proves particularly fruitful as, besides the translator, it includes in the analysis other agents such as sponsors, patrons and editors, all sharing the responsibility in the final product.

The common interest of the two following papers is self-censorship. **María del Carmen Camus** extends the practice of self-censorship to all literary production during Franco's dictatorship, but her specific purpose is to study the use of pseudonyms as a form of self-censorship. Her *corpus* consists of the translations/translators and pseudotranslations/ pseudotranslators of the narrative of the West ("Westerns") under Franco. Attention is drawn to the international phenomenon of the use of pseudonyms in the popular novel circulating in a mass-market. Different kinds of censorship (political, economic, governmental) are commented on and illustrated.

The translation of sex-related matters is prone both to censorship and to self-censorship, since what is at stake is "not only grammatical or lexical accuracy". **José Santaemilia,** who has recently edited a book on the subject (*Gender, Sex and Translation. The Manipulation of Identities,* 2005), presents us with a thorough analysis of the translation of the word "fuck" into Spanish and Catalan in both Bridget Jones' novels by Helen

Fielding, by pointing out some interesting differences between the two languages of the same country.

Self-translation (or auto-translation) is a recent topic in Translation Studies and has much in common with adjacent areas such as Comparative Literature or the Sociology of Literature. **Helena Tanqueiro** and **Patricia Lopez-Gay** are members of the research group AUTOTRAD (University of Barcelona). In their study they focus on self-censorship within self-translation, defined as "limitation or censure that one imposes on oneself when the self-translator is translating from one culture into another". Their example is Jorge Semprún's translation of *Federico Sanchez vous salue bien,* but they also refer to the book *Picolo Karma,* by Carlo Coccioli, an Italian writer living in Mexico.

Finally we learn how some editors keep on editing censored translations after the restoration of democracy in Spain. **Cristina Gómez Castro** describes the context of these practices in narrative but also in some films. People were not aware of the fact until a journalist denounced it as late as 1991. Her two main examples of how changes imposed by censorship survived the years are Mario Puzo's *The Godfather* and W. Peter Blatty's *The Exorcist.*

CHAPTER III introduces a more international dimension in the analysis of censorship procedures. **John Milton**'s case study on Brazil's first book club founded in 1943 (under the dictatorship of Getúlio Vargas) starts with broader information about institutional censorship in different periods of the Brazilian history in the 20th century and with an overview of the story of Clube do Livro as a publishing house. He then gives examples of different forms of censorship in works by, among others, Rabelais, Dickens, Gorki and Charlotte Brontë. These forms include elimination of scatological elements, of political references and of descriptions of racial characteristics.

From a Latin American dictatorship we move on to a former European communist dictatorship. **Jaroslav Spirk** writes about the censorship of translations and translation theory in communist Czechoslovakia from 1948 to 1989. Following a brief overview of the major historical events in the given period, translations from English, French, German, Russian, Spanish and Portuguese into Czech are considered. The paper also deals with the issue of censorship as accounted for by the Czechoslovakian theorists of translation, Jirí Levý and Anton Popovič.

It is not common to have access to credible, firsthand information about China. **Nam Fung Chang**'s paper describes the ways in which state censorship operates in present-day China. Two main areas draw the censors'attention: anti-Marxist and anti-China sentiments, and explicit descriptions of sex, including moral taboos, such as extra- and/or premarital sex. Examples are drawn mainly from Hilary Clinton's *Living History*, Mandla Langa's short story "A Gathering of Bald Men", Vladimir Nabokov's *Lolita*, and David Lodge's *Small World*. Chang also addresses other questions such as the censors' identity, how far censorship is admitted, and how state control is exerted on publishers subject to different pressures: the translational requirements of completeness and faithfulness, the market norms of competition, the satisfaction of public demand (consumers and their economic power) and the official ideology, backed up by the power of the state.

The repression of heteroglossia is another sub-topic that eloquently illustrates both "the polymorphous nature of censorship" and "its slipperiness when applied to translations" (Billiani 2007: 3). **Hilal Erkazanci**, drawing on Bourdieu and Bakhtin, studies her topic within the political act of language planning in Turkey, where it aims to silence non-standard language varieties in favour of linguistic purism. She analyses the discourses on standard Turkish, how they influence translational strategies and act as an implicit censoring apparatus for the translators who deal with heteroglossic texts and are thus led to internalise standardisation. Her examples are drawn from Turkish translations of Cockney dialect and from the Scottish novel *Trainspotting* by Irvine Welsh.

One of the many covert heads of the hydra of censorship is presented to us by **Natalia Olshanskaya.** Her case study is the Ukrainian edition of the newspaper *Weekly Mirror*, which is published in Ukrainian, Russian and English. Drawing on Bourdieu and H. Paul Grice, she analyses how certain subjects such as the war in Iraq or the outcome of the 2004 elections in Spain (linked to the bombings in Madrid and the withdrawal of the Spanish troops from Iraq) undergo different forms of censorship depending on whether the translations are packaged for American and Western audiences or for Eastern European readers. Besides the most common practices of deleting phrases, sentences, paragraphs, and even blocks, she also comments on, and illustrates, other forms of censorial mechanisms aimed at the manipulation of meaning through subtle changes in vocabulary and grammar. Information transfer from the East to the West and from the West to the East is thus involved in a fabric of power relations, whose aim is to attract mass readership and win their support.

CHAPTER IV presents four case studies from the European history of censorship in the 18th and 19th centuries. **Maria dos Anjos Guincho** scrutinizes the translation of Ovid's *Heroides* by the Portuguese writer, translator and physician Miguel do Couto Guerreiro (1720-1793), following an informative description of the state and Church bodies that exerted censorship in Portugal since the 16th century. She also discusses the blurred frontiers between censorship and self-censorship: writers and translators, who were well acquainted with the behaviour and arguments of the different political and religious censors, would willingly introduce all sorts of changes into the source text, for their main goal was to get their work published. Such cases can be labelled as self-censorship. On the other hand, though, as in the case of Guerreiro, they would not give up their moralizing duty, and so the question of manipulation and ideology in translation is also addressed by Guincho.

Eterio Pajares's paper addresses the same period (Enlightenment) and, because it is about 18th century Spain, it refers to similar censorship levels. In fact, novels in Spain were submitted to the double filter of government and Inquisition. The genre of the (foreign) novel was particularly prone to mistrust, as it was linked with the corruption of customs. Pajares's examples are taken from the English narrative fiction: Fielding's *Joseph Andrews* and Edward Young's *Selected Works*. Censorship by the Church, or the Inquisition, had other purposes and sometimes surprising results, as in the case of sexually related matters. As an illustration of Iberian convergences, Pajares also analyses how the translator can become a conscious/unconscious collaborator with the censors, so as to achieve the final goal of being granted *imprimatur*.

Rita Maia's main interest is the Portuguese reception of the picaresque novel *La vida de Lazarillo de Tormes y de sus fortunas y adversidades*. A few years after the first edition, the novel was banned in Spain. Expurgated versions circulated later. Maia analyses a few Portuguese translations of the 18th and 19th centuries, some based on censured Spanish versions, others having French as the source language (1838, translated by António José Vilale), which, considering the source context of the *belles infidèles,* also accounts for its many versions.

Although censorship was officially abolished in England in 1695, the requirement of decorum, that eventually led to self-censorship, never ceased to be active in many contexts. An eloquent example is the translation of literature for children. This is the main focus of **Viggo Pedersen**'s study, which concentrates on Victorian translations of Hans Christian Andersen. He draws on examples from the two best-known translators of that time, Caroline Peachey and Henry Dulcken. Both the author and his translators never suffered persecution from public authorities, but the literary climate in 19th century Britain and in Denmark did not allow freedom of expression

This volume aims to bring a significant contribution to the knowledge about translation and censorship in very different geographical and time contexts. In a very obvious manner this topic confirms how right Toury is in viewing translation as a teleological activity. It becomes very clear how censorship goes hand in hand with translation, not only in dictatorial regimes or in a distant past, but also nowadays, and in countries deemed as democratic. This set of studies also discusses different forms of censorship, thus attempting to clarify a concept that is far from being unequivocal.

Lisbon, November 2007
Teresa Seruya

CHAPTER ONE

TRANSLATION & CENSORSHIP IN PORTUGAL: THE LONG NIGHT OF *ESTADO NOVO*

FOREIGN BOOKS IN PORTUGAL AND THE DISCOURSE OF CENSORSHIP IN THE 1950S

TERESA SERUYA,
UNIVERSIDADE DE LISBOA
CECC – UNIVERSIDADE CATÓLICA PORTUGUESA, PORTUGAL

MARIA LIN MONIZ,
E.S.PALMELA/ CECC – UNIVERSIDADE CATÓLICA
PORTUGUESA DE LISBOA, PORTUGAL

Abstract: This paper is part of a larger project dealing with translation and censorship during the Portuguese dictatorship. As regards the 1950s, we start with some historical and political information about the decade (known as "the *lead* years"), followed by a description of the members and the procedures of the Censoring Commission, in collaboration with the political police and the post office. Global information about the books read by the Commission is also given. The main goal of the paper is to analyze speech regularities in the discourse of the censors, which gives a vivid idea of the prevailing ideological values of the regime, especially regarding propaganda, sexual morality, philosophical attitudes (speculation, realism) and the democratic access to books. These were the main fields where books were banned.

1. Introduction

This paper is a follow-up to the German version presented at the Conference "Translation and Interpreting as a Social Practice" held at the University of Graz in 2005 (Seruya 2006: 317-328). Both papers are part of a wider research about translated literature under the dictatorship that governed Portugal for 48 years (1926-1974). The listing of these translations is almost compiled whereas the project *Intercultural*

Literature in Portugal (1930-2000): A Critical Bibliography is taking shape.

The paper presented in Graz focused mainly on the 1940s. Now we move forward to the 1950s. Considering that the percentage of literary books, among the total amount of foreign books submitted to the Censoring Commission, is quite low, we have decided to enlarge the scope of the study and include foreign books. This can be justified if we bear in mind that the decision of approving or banning a book was clearly a decision about its *circulation* and hence about its prospective translation. Other reasons, however, motivate us: if quite a lot has already been said and written about the censorship of national literature, very little is known about the banned or approved foreign literature (Azevedo 1999). We will present a systematised and quantified study of the latter. We also intend to bring to light, and therefore make credible, the study of the real procedures of Censorship, though we are fully aware that part of the whole circuit has still to be reconstructed, namely as far as before and after the judgement of the Censoring Commission is concerned, that is, how did the political police (*PIDE–Polícia Internacional de Defesa do Estado*) or the post office (*CTT–Correios, Telégrafos e Telefones*) find out about *the* books? What did actually happen to the censored copies? This question is related to another one that we consider relevant: what was the real reach, the real efficacy of the ban–since it cannot be compared, in terms of visibility and public impact, to the censorship imposed on plays or films, not to mention the press?

Another purpose is to look more closely at the texts of the reports, i.e., at the argumentation and lexicon of the reader/censor and the decision-taker, whose opinions not only were often dissimilar but were sometimes antagonistic, in order to identify and analyse speech regularities.

2. Political and cultural characterisation of the 1950s: from the "*Iron* years" to the "*Lead* years"

As demonstrated in relation to the 1940s, it seems possible to delineate an identity in relation to the 1950s, which followed the so called "*Iron* years" and the enforcement of António Ferro's "Spirit Policy".[1] Not

---

[1] "Ferro" means literally "iron". "Spirit Policy" [Política do Espírito] was the name given by Ferro himself to his cultural policy as head of the propaganda office (1933-1949). As a very talented journalist and intellectual coming from the Portuguese Modernism, Ferro (1895-1956) defended a nationalist art supported by

irrelevant was the fact that, once Ferro's efforts to attract writers and artists to the regime had failed, he was dismissed by Salazar himself in the early 1950s, with no public justification (Ó, *apud* Rosas 1994: 454). Moreover, Salazar deplored the lack of national artistic talent:[2] "we don't have nowadays famous painters or architects who have won converts, and both the theatre and the literary production have not been able to enlarge their horizons" (Garnier *apud* Ó, *Ibidem*).[3] His will to change would even allow friendly relationships with his political opponents, as long as they were talented, even if they were "enemies of the regime" (*Ibidem*). The subsequent events, however, would contradict such statements, since the directors of the propaganda office (*SNI–Secretariado Nacional para a Informação*), for example, were "career bureaucrats or men without any close connections with the leading members of the intelligentsia", who "did nothing but manage current affairs and stifle all the initiatives taken by Ferro" (*Ibidem*).[4] According to the art historian José Augusto França, one of the milestones of the decade was also the shock caused by the appointment, by Francisco Leite Pinto, the Minister of Education, of the painter Eduardo Malta to succeed the late Diogo de Macedo in the administration of the Contemporary Art Museum (França 1991: 485s).

Among other outcries, that shock was materialised in a petition, signed by 200 personalities in the fields of art and literature of the time, from multiple ideological and aesthetic sectors. Moreover, the publishing of this petition was forbidden by the Censorship (*Ibidem:* 597).

In political terms, this decade had also its own identity. Reference books eloquently qualify this decade as the "Lead years" (1950-58). This expression refers to the apparent political calm plodding since 1949, when the regime, through the outcome of that year presidential elections (Carmona vs. Norton de Matos) achieved the reestablishment of "order" in "the streets" and of "peace in the minds", after a ruthless police action (Rosas 1994: 408). In other words, once the oppositions were defeated and

---

the state, aiming at the improvement of the aesthetic taste of society and of the people and helping to create a favourable atmosphere for all artists (see Ó 1999).

[2] All quotes originally in Portuguese, either from the bibliography or from the censorship reports, are our own translation. For the sake of readability, English glosses will be used in the text and the majority of Portuguese quotes will be included in footnotes. This applies to all the papers included in this volume.

[3] "Não possuímos hoje grandes pintores nem arquitectos que tenham feito escola e tanto o teatro como a produção literária não conseguiram alargar os seus horizontes."

[4] "burocratas de carreira ou figuras sem contactos sérios no meio intelectual [que se] limitaram a gerir e deixar morrer as iniciativas encetadas por Ferro."

disbanded, once the apparent unity was re-established, and under the effects of the "cold war" context, the "grey and apparent almost apolitical drowsiness of a monotonous life" was restored in the country (*Ibidem:* 503).[5] On the other hand, as stressed by Rosas, as a result of the Western support not only to the foreign policy but also to the dictatorship itself, Salazar's regime "seemed even to gain a certain political and ideological arrogance"[6] achieved through a vigorous revival of the "anticommunist, corporative, catholic, nationalist and ultraconservative" discourse, expressed by the regime's jargon (*Ibidem*).[7] One of the most significant *corpus* for the study of this "regime jargon" is precisely the discourse of the censors working at the headquarters of the Censoring Commission. As we will see, their speech regularities allow us–and this is a good starting point–to consider the performance of the Commission as a sort of *mise en abîme* of the prevailing ideological values.

The 1958's presidential election, associated with the phenomenon known as the "Delgado's earthquake", signals "the beginning of the end of Salazar's regime" (*Ibidem*: 523).[8] Among other phenomena revealing the accumulated tensions under the mentioned "apparent calm" are the well-succeeded students' strikes in December 1956 and January 1957. On the other hand, due either to the internal division of the opposition, or to the "rather soft" attitude of Trigo de Negreiros leading the Home Office, there is a less severe intervention of the political police (Rosas 1994: 518). Furthermore, the new emigration surge and the industrial development at that time have also contributed to "a certain pacification of social tensions" (*Ibidem*).[9] In short, when evoking today the year of 1960 and the assault upon the ship *Santa Maria*, commonly known as the "Dulcinea operation", or 1961 and the beginning of the colonial war, we can, undoubtedly, draw the historical and political boundary lines of the 1950s.

---

[5] "modorra cinzenta e, à superfície, quase despolitizada de uma vida sem surpresas."
[6] "parecia mesmo retomar certo arreganho político e ideológico"
[7] "anticomunista, corporativista, católico, nacionalista, ultramontano"
[8] In the end of his already mentioned book on *A Arte em Portugal no Século XX (1911-1961) [Art in Portugal in the 20th Century (1911-1961)]*, José Augusto França depicts the greyness of this decade, at least in political terms. The columns of the graph refer to "political facts", "cultural facts", "artistic facts" and "art abroad". In the 1950s, the only political facts which are mentioned are the integration of Portugal in the UNO in 1955 and, in 1958, the referred campaign for the presidential elections lead by Humberto Delgado (França 1991: 616-620).
[9] "para um relativo abrandamento das tensões sociais"

3. The study *corpus* and the procedures of the Censoring Commission[10]

It is worth noting here that the most relevant legislation concerning Censorship was produced in the 1930s and 1940s (see Rodrigues 1980 and Ó 1999). In fact, it was in 1944 (Decree no. 33454, February 23) that the Censorship became officially an organ of political training and propaganda. The Censoring Commission was part of the SNI which, in turn, was under the direct supervision of Salazar. The 1950s did not bring relevant legislative changes to the procedures of the Censoring Commission, whose members were mainly Army officers.[11]

However, what really arouses our curiosity, the big question, is the starting point of the process, i.e., how and how systematically did PIDE and CTT know about the books? Some answers were found while reading the reports: books displayed or visits to bookshops (Sá da Costa and Bertrand in Lisbon), where the title/topic and/or the cover of the book could be decisive. The procedure of the CTT can only be explained by the violation of private mail, following instructions given to the Post Office clerks concerning suspicious signs: either the source (publishing houses,[12] countries), or the receiver. In some cases, not many in the 1950s though, the name and address of the receiver are specifically mentioned in the report, often names with no public relevance. Sometimes, in spite of being forbidden, the book was allowed to be delivered to the receiver (for example, *La Chine ébranle le monde* by Jack Belden or *Au pays de Staline*

---

[10] We have decided not to publish the names of the censors, according to the archiving principles of the National Archives (IAN/TT – Instituto dos Arquivos Nacionais/Torre do Tombo). This applies to all Portuguese papers included in this volume. Besides, we believe that a personal identification would not be relevant for the study, although some differences in their discourses can be outlined. The general impression, however, is that the censors were a rather homogeneous group, which is not surprising either.

[11] For the common civilian, this double loyalty of the Armed Forces is very interesting. On one hand, there were officers performing censorship, a role played by the military since the 1926 *coup d'état*, which put an end to the First Republic (1910-1926), but on the other, it was also high-rank officers who played leading roles in important episodes of opposition against the Salazar's regime. It is enough to remind Admiral Quintão Meireles, the candidate of the conservative opposition to the 1951 presidential elections, General Norton de Matos, Humberto Delgado, Henrique Galvão, etc.

[12] The censor of Vera Panova's *Serioja* wrote with his own hand on the report: "'Les Éditeurs Français Réunis' is considered a communist publishing house" (R5973/57–see footnote 13)).

by Fernand Grenier). There are some intriguing cases, however, since they should not have been included in the commonly censored themes (politics, religion, sex and morality). Thus, why did the CTT send for censorship Anacreonte's *Odes* (R5410/55),[13] or works by Sofocles and Euripedes (R5415/55), Racine (R5414/55), B. Constant (R5411/55) or a book like *Le premier amour du monde* by Fulton Sheen? The latter was quite certainly a case of suspicion aroused by the title as well as a display of ignorance about the author. It is a "Book by a well-known Catholic priest (...), a work of the highest morality and Christian postulate. Therefore, harmless." (R5578/56).[14] Or why was *Memorias Posthumas de Braz Cubas* [*The Posthumous Memoirs of Bras Cubas*] by the Brazilian author Machado de Assis also intercepted by the CTT (R5085/53)? A totally absurd case is the didactic work by Dorothy Bussy, *50 Nursery Rhymes*, dealing with morphology and phonetics of the English language, eventually approved.

So, how did the Censoring Commission have access to the books? Foreign books were mostly provided by PIDE or confiscated by the CTT. There was a new agent, however, in 1953, the Customs Services. Books originally written in Portuguese (either from Portugal or Brazil) were "presented" for censorship, i.e., publishers, as well as authors themselves, sent their books for approval. Books in Portuguese or Portuguese translations were quite often "requested" for censorship. One single case of report was registered (1951) and in another case (1959) it was the Commission that bought the book. One book in 1952 and two books in 1954 were offered to the Chairman of the Commission.

We can say that the Commission worked hard, since *about* 1897 books (we say *about* as a large number of reports is missing) were read during the whole decade: about 469 in Portuguese; 996 in foreign languages (mostly French, Spanish and Italian); 268 Portuguese translations and 159 Brazilian translations. 1957 accounts for the highest number of books read by the Commission (274), whereas the lowest number was registered the following year (111).

Analysing the percentage of approved and banned books, we can draw the following tables:

---

[13] Such references shall be read as: Report number/ Issueing Year; the book titles will be reproduced as they appear on the reports; when in Portuguese, they will be translated; all quotations from the reports are our translation.

[14] "Livro de um ilustre sacerdote católico (...) obra da mais alta moral e apostolado cristão. Sem inconveniente, portanto."

	Approved	Banned
National literature	35%	12%
Literature in French	33%	58%
Portuguese translations	20%	7%
Brazilian translations	7%	10%
Literature in Spanish	3%	7%
Literature in English	2%	4%
Literature in Italian	-	2%

Table 1-1: Approved and banned books according to language

It is no surprise that the largest percentage of books read by the censors were in French, either originals or translated texts, considering the long tradition of French language and culture hegemony by that time.

What subjects/books were submitted to censorship? We divided them into "Literature/Culture", "Politics/Ideology", "Moral/Sex", "Religion", "Didactics" and "Other" (sociology, medical sciences, monographs, etc.). Although there are no clear boundaries among these types, we were able to confirm that literature, politics and moral/sex related matters were thought to be the most inconvenient and labelled as "social dissolution" subjects.

	Approved	Banned
Literature/ Culture	50%	38%
Politics/ Ideology	15%	32%
Morals/ Sex	3%	18%
Religion	5%	2%
Didactics	1%	-
Other	26%	10%

Table 1-2: Approved and banned books according to subject

Who were the censors? We cannot say that 100% of them were Army officers because some reports do not mention any rank or name. Only five can be considered as members of the permanent body of censors throughout the decade. Other members, however, had a regular activity for several years, while others had a reduced or occasional participation. In general terms, we can say that there was a regular group of about twenty censors.

The predominant ranks were lieutenant, captain, major, lieutenant-colonel and, by the end of the decade, colonel, seemingly due to promotions occurring in the meantime. Only in 1959 did we find a report signed by a second-lieutenant.

From their reports, we can infer that they were quite diligent in their work. Some books were approved provided that some excerpts/whole pages (thoroughly listed) were removed. Their arguments also reveal deep knowledge of political and/or philosophical issues. This contradicts somehow the common idea that they were dull. It is also important to bear in mind that most of them could read French, English, Spanish, Italian and German, an ability displayed by only a minority of the Portuguese population of that time.

4. Assessment criteria of the Censoring Commission

- There were no authors or themes to be *a priori* and categorically rejected. Each case was special. For example, subjects as the URSS and Stalin, or authors as Gorki, Pitigrilli, Sartre, Camus, Bertrand Russel and Brecht, could be either banned or approved; there is, however, an interesting exception: surrealism and its authors (Aragon, André Breton) were always firmly banned.
- Several factors were taken into consideration, such as the image of the regime (Colette),[15] the fact that certain topics were already known through the press, or that the author was a classic, well-known in Portugal (Balzac, Dostoievsky, Gorki, Hemingway), which incidentally did not prevent some of their books from being banned.
- The pronouns "we"/ "us" were used very often when expressing judgements and opinions in order to convey the idea of a

---

[15] Colette's *Chéri* was banned in 1950 because it contained "much pornography and illustrations". Fifteen years later the book was again presented for censorship, but the ban was then cancelled (6/5/1965), not only because times were more "daring in the field of immorality", but also "considering she is a very famous writer, a member of the Goncourt Academy and of the Royal Academy of Belgium, to whom the French government paid homage through an official funeral." [atendendo a que se trata de uma escritora consagrada, membro da Academia Goncourt e da Academia Real da Bélgica, a quem o governo francês prestou especial homenagem promovendo-lhe funeral oficial.] (R 4484/50)

harmonious and homogeneous social whole, whose spokesmen and guardians were these censors.

5. The most common arguments for the ban

- Propaganda (proselytise, apology)

This label, in both a qualifying and a disqualifying sense, is attributed to a very large number of books, mainly of French origin and dealing with any topic concerning the URSS (in a few cases concerning China), regardless of its content: historical, biographical (Stalin, Trotsky) or philosophical and doctrinal. The same argument was applied to literary writers like Paul Éluard (R5215/54) and Pablo Neruda (R5273/55), or even to a volume of *New Russian Short Story Writers* [*Novos Contistas Russos*], a 1942 edition. In 1953 this book was reassessed and banned because its authors were "communists" and the short stories "were written according to the dangerous and propagandistic doctrine of Bolshevism" (R5071/53).[16]

Propaganda proper was of course not objectionable–the censors could not ignore that they themselves were working in a propaganda department. The objection had to do merely with its purpose: it is understandable that PIDE would confiscate a book entitled *Ainsi fut assassiné Trotsky*, by Sanchez Salazar and Julien Gorkin. Nevertheless, the book was eventually approved because it revealed the "ferocious persecution set upon Stalin's enemies abroad". The book was, therefore, "in a certain way, of anticommunist propaganda" (R4322/50),[17] hence the favourable decision regarding its circulation.

- Sexual morality, social dissolution doctrine

After the political and ideological arguments, and quantitatively speaking, is not only the literature considered pornographic but also everything taken as offensive in the light of Christian morality, regarding marriage, homosexuality, adultery and divorce (but concerning women alone), sexual satisfaction, birth control. Only one case of sexual morality associated with racism was found: the reader/censor of *La maîtresse noire*,

---

[16] "estarem escritos nos moldes da doutrina perigosa e de propaganda do bolchevismo."
[17] "a perseguição feroz a que são submetidos no estrangeiro os inimigos de Estaline", [sendo, portanto,] "de certo modo, um livro de propaganda anti-comunista."

by Louis-Charles Royer writes: "immoral and demoralising novel about a white man's life, de-civilised, dehumanised and demoralised by the lust of his sexual intercourse with African indigenes" (R6190/58).[18]

It is worth listing the expressions and the most frequent verdicts:
- "excerpt of indisputable immorality (but of disgusting debauchery)" (R4345/50);[19]
- "voluptuous descriptions of women" (R4408/50);[20]
- on *Caras Pintadas* [*Painted Faces*] by Pitigrilli: "it is full of social dissolute thoughts and narrations, not suitable especially to young people" (R4613/51);[21] "series of pictures and descriptions of the greatest sensuality and unimaginable voluptuousness and lust" (R5052/53);[22]
- on *La saison chaude* by Jean Claudio: " immoral novel with descriptions of arousing love scenes" (R5041/53);[23]
- on *A Reabertura do Paraíso Terrestre* [*The Reopening of the Earthly Paradise*], by Clément Vautel: "The whole book is full of great immorality and debauchery" (R5136/54);[24]
- on *Guide international de l'amour*, by Louis-Charles Royer: "I think it has to be banned because it is absolutely lewd (...) and a real guide to sensuality" (R5173/54).[25]

In fact, the title of this section is quite pertinent: the senses and the instinct, expressed in sex, had to be restrained, for the disruption of "our common moral sensibility" could, in fact, "dissolve" the political order (R5186/54).[26]

An eloquent epitome of the censors' thought can be expressed by the justification for the ban of the reference book *Capaz ou Incapaz para o*

---

[18] "romance imoral e desmoralizante da vida de um branco des-civilizado, cafrealizado e desmoralizado pela voluptuosidade das suas relações sexuais com indígenas africanas."
[19] "passagem de autêntica imoralidade (mas de nojenta lubricidade)"
[20] "descrições voluptuosas da mulher"
[21] "está cheia de pensamentos e de narrações dissolventes, especialmente para a juventude"
[22] "colecção de quadros e descrições do maior sensualismo e voluptuosidade e lascívia imagináveis"
[23] "romance de ficção de baixo fundo moral, com descrição de cenas amorosas excitantes"
[24] "Leitura toda ela de grande imoralidade e devassidão."
[25] "Julgo de proibir por ser absolutamente luxurioso (...) e um verdadeiro breviário do sensualismo."
[26] [pois que o desregramento da] "nossa habitual sensibilidade moral" [podia de facto] "dissolver" [a ordem política].

Casamento [*Apt or Inapt for Marriage*], a Brazilian translation of a medical book by Th. H. van de Velde:

> This book is of the same kind of so many others that Brazil has exported to our country. Given the misleading label of science or prophylactic circulation, they escape from the police intervention. Sexual pedagogues do know that what is essential is not to draw people's attention to sex-related issues, but to deflect it. Knowing the evil around us is not enough to avoid it (...) (R 6055/57).[27]

Besides the clear norm about sexual education, it is worth mentioning the true knowledge that censors had about the book market, as far as the circulation of Brazilian books in Portugal, either originals, or translations, was concerned. They were also aware of the deceiving techniques used to escape their own control (such as the scientific nature of a book).

- Realism (a stigmatizing judgement, meaning, in this *corpus*, "how things really are")

Let us look at some examples. Of *Duelo ao Sol* [*Duel in the Sun*] by Niven Bush it is written: "it contains several highly realistic excerpts (...) nevertheless, I raise no objection to its approval" (R 4364/50);[28] of *Les femmes que j'ai aimées*, by Casanova: "The description is so realistic that reading it is unsuited to under-aged people and makes the book immoral" (R 4433/50);[29] or of *Les dames galantes* by Brantôme (i.e. Pierre de Bourdeille): "Highly realistic prose, sometimes ignoble when it describes particular scenes of wedlock" (R 5038/53);[30] of the Portuguese translation of Guy de Maupassant's stories *O Prazer* [*The Pleasure*] "free and ultra-realistic literature" (R5464/55).[31] The obvious association of realism with immorality reveals the purpose of imposing an unreal, fanciful, alienating

---

[27] "Este livro é do género de tantos outros que o Brasil tem exportado para o nosso país e que, dado o rótulo especioso de ciência ou vulgarização profiláctica escapam à acção da polícia. Na pedagogia sexual sabem os educadores que o essencial não é chamar a atenção para assuntos da sexualidade, mas desviá-la. Não basta conhecer o mal para ele ser evitado (...)"
[28] "tem várias passagens muito realistas (...) mas mesmo assim não vejo inconveniente na sua autorização"
[29] "A descrição é tão real que a sua leitura é imprópria para menores e torna o livro imoral"
[30] "Prosa realista ao máximo, por vezes ignóbil quando aborda passagens particulares da vida conjugal."
[31] "literatura livre e ultra-realista"

image of the world, which always plays an important role in the political agendas of dictatorships. The argument of "realism" has, moreover, to do with different types of readership.

- "Elites" or "the learned " vs. "the many"

This dichotomy was the only label used in relation to what was displayed in the bookshop windows and to decide about the circulation of a foreign book or its translation. About *Deux essais sur le marxisme* by Jean Marchal, it is written: "The bookshops are allowed to fulfil their customers' orders but not to display them publicly in their shop windows" (R 5450/55).[32] The argument clearly shows that the cultural gap existing in the country is acknowledged and even supported by the authorities. There is also a real condescending and patronising attitude towards the learned, the "scholars" and the educated people in general, who are considered "strong-willed and not easily influenced" (see reports on Enrique Jardiel Poncella, R4335/50, R4336/50), whereas the "illiterate masses" are "particularly inclined to a thoughtless absorption of the ideas expressed" (R 4894/53).[33] There lies the danger because "you cannot restrict the sales to elites alone" (R4915/53).[34] Nevertheless, quite often the book is approved because it is written in French (it was the case of J. P. Sartre's *Nekrassov* (R5830/57), i.e., only accessible to a happy few, but there are also cases where the subject seemed intolerable to the censors: *Une femme à hommes* by Christian Carel "could be approved considering its reduced circulation on account of being written in French" (R5705/56).[35] However, it was morally unacceptable on account of "too much realism", a good reason why it was eventually banned.

The taboo of homosexuality associated to the idea of scandal, indecency and disease is also worth mentioning. Such assessment of homosexuality was also applied to possible readers, with the exception of medical doctors (obviously included among the scholars). Consider the

---

[32] "Autorizadas as livrarias a satisfazerem os pedidos de encomendas dos seus clientes, mas não à exposição pública nas vitrinas."
[33] "particularmente predispostas a uma absorção não raciocinada das ideias expostas." This report concerns the French translation of Calvin B. Hoover's *La vie économique de la Russie Soviétique*.
[34] "não se pode limitar a venda só a elites." This report concerns the banned Brazilian translation of Harold J. Laski's *Reflexões sobre a revolução da nossa época* [*Reflexions on the revolution of our time*].
[35] "pode ser autorizado atendendo à sua pequena expansão por estar escrito em francês."

following written about *Les homosexuels*, a French translation of *The Homosexuals, as Seen by Themselves and Thirty Authorities* edited by Aron M. Krich (1954):

> One cannot say the book is really pornographic but the topic is absolutely indecent (...). The first part is useless and only introduces the reader to the disgusting mind of the homosexual. The second part is undoubtedly intended to give the book a cultural semblance, of dubious usefulness, since it can only be of any interest to the medical class (...). Considering, however, that once the book is displayed on the shelves of bookshops it will be at everyone's disposal and that its acquisition will be lustfully wished by all the morbid minds eagerly seeking scandalous readings, it is my opinion that the book should be banned. (R 5743/56)[36]

- "Speculation"

The argument of speculation becomes particularly interesting on account of the dual manipulation of the concept, i.e., it is used either to ban or to approve. Even concerning a hot subject in the Portuguese society like the Freemasonry and its relationship with Catholicism, we can read the following about the French translation of *Franc-Maçonnerie et Catholicisme* by Max Heindel:

> I think this small book is a mere philosophical or historical or scientific speculation. If a true catholic reads it, there won't be any harm. If an indifferent person reads it, it won't give him/her any arguments to change his/her indifference. If an unlearned person reads it, it won't bring him/her any further culture. Therefore: I don't see any reason to ban or suppress it, taking into consideration the essentially speculative philosophical character of the book. (R 4665/51)[37]

---

[36] "Não se pode dizer que a obra seja propriamente pornográfica mas o assunto é absolutamente escabroso (...) a primeira das duas partes (...) não tem qualquer utilidade e apenas põe o leitor em frente da mentalidade ascorosa (*sic*) do homosexual (*sic*). A segunda parte quer sem dúvida dar ao trabalho um aspecto cultural, de interesse duvidoso, dado que a coisa só pode interessar à classe médica (...) Tendo, porém, em atenção que, posto o livro nos escaparates das livrarias ele fica à disposição de toda a gente e que a sua aquisição será gulosamente desejada por todos os espíritos mórbidos ávidos de leituras de tipo escandaloso, sou de parecer que a obra seja proibida."

[37] "Julgo a obrinha de pura especulação filosófica ou histórico-científica. A um católico que bem o seja, não lhe fará mossa lê-la. A um indiferente não lhe dará argumentos para alterar a indiferença. A um inculto, não lhe trará cultura. Portanto:

The Banquet by Kierkegaard also belongs to the good speculation, the "pure philosophical speculation" (R 4921/53). But there is bad speculation as well, the kind of speculation related to ideological and political issues, which might prompt critical attitudes towards dictatorships. Thus, in relation to *L'univers concentrationnaire* by David Rousset, where the Nazi concentration camps are mentioned, it is written that "maybe it is not politically convenient to remind such camps, for reasons that have to do with speculation (...)" (R4723/52).[38] In other words, to preserve the historical memory of National Socialism, as stated above, causes discomfort. But there is still a third content related to the theoretical and doctrinal Marxist thought. About a French edition of selected texts by Babeuf, for example, we can read that "this book is an historical analysis of one of the men of the French Revolution, Babeuf. However, the third part is presented as a speculation of a communist theoretician, therefore aiming at spreading communist propaganda. That is why I think that the circulation of the book should be forbidden" (R4275/55).[39]

- Discomfort in relation to National Socialism (NS) and democracy and to war

This feeling follows the discourse of the 1940s and shows how the defeat of NS was so unwillingly digested. In relation to the translation of *A Small Village Called Lidice* by Zdena Trinka, the report refers objectively to what happened in Lidice as well as in Oradour, but most probably the reason for the ban was another type of fear, the "references to communistic propaganda, largely speaking about a world government of all nations" (R4867/53).[40] If criticism is aimed at democracies, then "there is no harm in its circulation". Such is the case of the translation *Has Democracy Collapsed?*, by Jean Bayle, who "makes a brief study about the countries governed by democracies, focusing on their drawbacks and

---

não vejo razões para proscrição ou impedimento, dado o carácter da obra, essencialmente ou especulativamente filosófico."
[38] "não será conveniente politicamente a lembrança de tais campos, por motivos que se prendem à especulação (...)"
[39] "Este livro é uma análise histórica de um dos homens, Babeuf, da revolução francesa (*sic*), no entanto, na III parte é apresentado em especulação de um teórico comunista, assim julgo que esta obra tem um fim político de propaganda comunista, pelo que acho que deve ser proibida de circular."
[40] "Porém, há também referências a propaganda comunizante, falando-se muito num governo mundial de todas as nações."

limitations (...)" (R4863/53).[41] In fact, might one think that the Portuguese regime subscribed the humanist and pacifist post-war consensus one would be immediately disappointed when reading about *L'enseigne de Gersaint*, by Aragon, that "the 13 first pages consist of an apology of the concept of humanity overcoming the concepts of Fatherland and Nationality. The book also conveys loose morbid defeatism and plenty antimilitarist and pacifist ideas of communist influence (...)" (R5208/54).[42] In other words, it is clearly advised to subdue the NS, allegedly based on international policy, but the truth was that the defeat of NS could not help disrupting the establishment and that the strong Germanophilia of the 1940s had not receded. So, the French translation of *Kaputt*, by Curzio Malaparte, "a vigorous opponent of fascism", was considered unsuitable by the censor because it didn't seem "appropriate to bring again to light facts that should be forgotten in the context of the current international politics" (R5481/55).[43] This is one of the few cases of a clear ban concerning the translation, although the French text has been considered "tolerable".

Pacifism and antimilitarism are uncomfortable issues due both to the Cold War context and to the important role the Armed Forces played in the support of the regime. Such was also the case in the countries under Soviet influence, like the German Democratic Republic. This discomfort would reach famous books like Hans Hellmut Kirst's trilogy *08/15*, translated by José Saramago (never mentioned in the censorship reports). The translation was considered "good" from the literary point of view, but "unsuitable in case it could damage the reputation of the Armed Forces in any non-communist country" (R5789/56)[44]. The first volume of the trilogy (*The War*) is considered "antimilitarist". It was feared that those who were not "convincingly aware of reality" could lose their "respect for the military institutions" (R5789/56). The French translation of John Dos Passos *Terre élue*, confiscated by the CTT, was object of the same kind of

---

[41] "estudo sucinto dos países governados por democracias, focando os seus inconvenientes e deficiências (...)"

[42] "as 13 primeiras páginas consistem numa apologia do conceito de humanidade, antepondo-se, ou melhor: sobrepondo-se ao de Pátria e de Nacionalidade. Também por toda a obrinha andam soltos um derrotismo mórbido e fartas ideias antimilitaristas e pacifistas de marca comunistóide (...)"

[43] [não parece ao censor] "presentemente recomendável trazer outra vez à superfície factos que as actuais conveniências de política internacional aconselham a deixar esquecer."

[44] "mas inconveniente se contribuir para o desprestígio das forças armadas de qualquer país não-comunista"

reasoning (R6006/57). If in other cases, such as Zola (R4284/50), Balzac (R4286/50), or Hemingway (R5154/53), the argument of the "great author" prompted authorisation, in the case of Dos Passos the fact that he was "a renowned writer all over the world for his deep knowledge of sociology and psychology"[45] was easily overlooked. His flaws, however, are closely examined and listed, thus the book should be banned on account of the "patent immorality, the communist mystic he reveals and intends to disseminate, and the anti-war attitude he assumes" (R6006/57).[46]

6. Conclusion

There is no way to be absolutely sure about what happened to the foreign books that PIDE, CTT, bookshops or other unidentified sources sent to the Censoring Commission. It seems, however, that they were prospective translations, since some reports clearly forbid their circulation in Portuguese language as was the case of *La Ciociara*, by Alberto Moravia, whose translation, requested by the publishing house Portugália, was denied (R6257/58); on the other hand, to approve or ban the "dissemination" or the "circulation" of a foreign book conveyed nothing but the political meaning that the very existence of Censorship could impart to that decision, having in mind that the book could reach a wider readership. A single reader or anyone included in the category of the "learned ones" wasn't regarded as a dissemination agent of the forbidden fruit.

We can say that the arguments expressed in the reports show that there was a relationship between translation and democratisation of the access to literature in a broad sense. This was a relationship of fear in psychological terms, which was then, in political terms, put into practice through repression. Translations were feared because they were "available to those belonging to the less learned classes, who might be exposed to harmful effects by reading them" (R4803/52)[47] or, as another censor writes, "since

---

[45] "um escritor mundialmente considerado, com profundos conhecimentos de sociologia e psicologia"
[46] "pela imoralidade que revela, pela mística comunista que revela possuir e da qual pretende fazer propaganda e pelo anti-belicismo que manifesta (...)"
[47] "ficam ao alcance das bolsas que correspondem às camadas menos cultas e para quem a sua leitura pode ser prejudicial"

the book is available to a large number of people, I think it should be banned" (R4335/50).[48]

In addition, there were some topics considered undesirable by the regime, such as Darwinism and death penalty. This is clearly illustrated in the following extracts from the Commission's judgment on *La Selección en el Hombre*, an Argentinian translation of Havelock Ellis's book, and on the French translation *Cellule 2455. Couloir de la mort*, by Caryl Chessman, respectively:

> Although the books of this collection have a scientific basis, they all aim to develop and spread the materialistic orientation of young people–which is one of the characteristics of the communist training. Of course they meet the scholars' needs and they fit in their libraries. However, they should not be available to the general public or sold in cheap editions (…). (R 4803/52)[49]

> (…) allow its acquisition by the scholars who are interested in it. In fact, reading this book may have dire consequences for the pure and simple minds of adolescents, or for the "predisposed", potentially imbalanced minds. Therefore, in my opinion, it should not be allowed to be freely sold and its translation is of no use, since those who, on cultural grounds, may find it a source of study and meditation, can read it in its original language or in already existing translations. (R5618/56)[50]

The final decision about this book was: "I totally agree with the judgement of the Assistant-Director and so its translation *will not be allowed* (*sic*) and neither will translations in Portuguese published in

---

[48] "como o livro é acessível ao grande número, julgo de proibir"

[49] "As obras desta colecção, embora de fundo científico, visam todas o desenvolvimento e propaganda da orientação materialista da juventude–o que constitui uma das facetas da preparação comunista. É claro que servem aos estudiosos e estão bem nas respectivas bibliotecas. Não devem, contudo, ser vulgarizadas e vendidas numa tradução barata, ao alcance das bolsas que correspondem às camadas menos cultas e para quem a sua leitura pode ser prejudicial."

[50] "(…) autorizar a sua aquisição aos estudiosos interessados. Com efeito, em mentalidades puras e simples de adolescentes, ou nas de "predispostos" porque desequilibrados em potência, a leitura da obra poderá produzir frutos de malefícios extremos. Sou, portanto, de opinião que não deverá ser permitida a venda livre nos escaparates e que não interessa a tradução, visto que, para todos os que nele podem encontrar matéria de estudo e de meditação, por força da sua cultura, podem fazê-lo na língua de origem ou nas traduções existentes."

Brazil be permitted in our country" (R5618/56).[51] This and many other examples illustrate the Commission's opposition to a book condemning death penalty.

We can conclude that the restrict sphere of the foreign book censorship clearly illustrates the antidemocratic agenda of *Estado Novo*: it was forbidden to become familiar with more crude or unpleasant aspects of life (**realism**), to think and discuss about possible worlds (**speculation**), to let senses and instinct play their role (**sexual moral and social dissolution literature**), to read about adverse regimes and ideologies (**propaganda**). Almost at a twenty years' distance, the words of the fascist politician Hipólito Raposo are still true when he referred to Portugal as "the famous Republic of Il-lusitania" (1940).[52]

References

Azevedo, Cândido de (1999) *A Censura de Salazar e Marcelo Caetano*. Lisboa: Caminho.

Costa Pinto, António (1991) "The Literary Aspirations of Portuguese Fascism", in *Fascism and European Literature/Faschismus und europäische Literatur,* ed. S.U. Larsen and Sandberg, Bern a. o.: Peter Lang, 238-253.

França, José Augusto (1991) *A Arte em Portugal no Século XX (1911-1961),* Lisboa: Bertrand Editora.

Ó, Jorge Ramos do (1999) *Os Anos de Ferro. O Dispositivo Cultural durante a 'Política do Espírito' 1933-1949,* Lisboa: Editorial Estampa.

Rodrigues, Graça Almeida (1980) *Breve História da Censura Literária em Portugal*, Lisboa: ICLP (Biblioteca Breve).

Rosas, Fernando (1994) *O Estado Novo* (*História de Portugal,* dir. José Mattoso, Vol.7), Lisboa: Editorial Estampa.

Seruya, Teresa (2006), "Zur Koexistenz von nationaler Kultur und internationaler Literatur unter dem *Estado Novo* Salazars", in Michaela Wolf (ed.), *Übersetzen–Translating–Traduire: Towards a 'Social Turn'?*, Wien, Berlin: Lit Verlag, 317-328.

---

[51] "Dou a minha inteira concordância ao parecer do Sr. Director Adjunto e assim *não será permitida a tradução* [sublinh. *sic*] no nosso país, nem a entrada nele de traduções em língua portuguesa editadas no Brasil."
[52] *apud* Azevedo 1999: 24 ff. The meaning of the adjective "fascist" in the Portuguese context of the time is very well explained in Costa Pinto 1991.

FAULKNER AND THE PORTUGUESE CENSORSHIP

ANA TERESA MARQUES DOS SANTOS,
CÁTEDRA GIL VICENTE - UNIVERSITY OF BIRMINGHAM, U.K.

Abstract: In this study the case of the 1958 translation of William Faulkner's *Sanctuary* into European Portuguese is used to access some of the ways in which mechanisms of censorship operated in Portugal during the dictatorial regime.

The case of this novel, whose title refers us to the religious framework Faulkner so often works within, is particularly relevant for my purposes since it is, according to the critic Michael Millgate, a book which was notorious for its "violence, physical realism and sexual perversion"–all of them non-ideological aspects that were nonetheless bound to cause a negative impression on the censors, working "to protect" the country's moral values. I look at specific parts of the novel which are likely to be more problematic in terms of what was considered unacceptable, both in terms of language and content, and identify the strategies used by the translator to overcome restrictions imposed by censorship. This analysis allows me to argue for the role of censorship not only as a means of delaying the arrival of the novel in Portugal but also as a reason for its first retranslation.

William Faulkner's *Sanctuary*, first published in the United States in 1931, was translated three times into European Portuguese: in 1958 by Marília de Vasconcelos, in 1973 by Fernanda Pinto Rodrigues and in 2001 by Ana Maria Chaves. The first two translations were both published by Editorial Minerva, while the 2001 text was published by Publicações Dom Quixote. As I hope to show in this paper, the first translation of this novel, notorious for its "violence, physical realism and sexual perversion", in Michael Millgate's words, is a text whose sexual references were extensively manipulated, sometimes to the point of deletion. Censorship, regulating Portuguese artistic expression from the beginning of *Estado Novo* and, more specifically, during the time of publication of the two first translations of *Sanctuary*, might not only have been the reason why it took so long for this novel to be translated in Portugal, but it was also the reason why a first retranslation of the book was made.

On 11th October 1953, one of the censors signed censorship report number 5090 concerning *Santuário* by Lígia Junqueira Smith, published by Instituto Progresso Editorial, S.A. in S. Paulo. This was the first Brazilian translation of the novel, which was published in Brazil in 1948, and one of the first Faulkner translations to appear in that country. The censor's conclusions after having read the Brazilian translation were as follows:

> The whole book is based on a sinister, raw description of vicious environments–houses of prostitution, alcohol smugglers, etc.–and is reproachable due to its perversion, sadism and depraved amorality.
>
> In order to advise or determine the strict prohibition of such a book one would not even need to consider the violation or rape scenes, described with vicious sophistication.[1]

This prohibition of the Brazilian translation was prompted by the Portuguese postal services (CTT) which are mentioned in the report as the "origin" ("proveniência") of the book. The collaboration of these services with PIDE (the political police) was indeed crucial for the thorough control of the Portuguese book and cultural market. As Cândido de Azevedo explains:

> As far as imported books and other sorts of publications were concerned, Censorship also had the support of control structures that PIDE permanently kept there, in collaboration with the administration of the Post Office and with the help of Post Office employees, who were nominated specifically to fulfil that role. In fact, PIDE did the same thing in Customs, with cooperation from *Guarda Fiscal*. It was also responsible for listening to amateur radiobroadcasts. (Azevedo 1999: 77)[2]

---

[1] "Todo o livro, escrito à base de uma sinistra crueza na descrição de ambientes viciosos: prostíbulos, contrabandistas de alcool [*sic*], etc., é condenável, pela sua perversão, sadismo e amoralidade depravada.
Nem seriam precisas as cenas de violação ou estupro, descritas com vicioso requinte, para aconselhar ou determinar a rigorosa proibição de tal livro."

[2] "[n]o domínio dos livros e outras publicações importadas, a Censura dispunha ainda do apoio das estruturas de controlo que a PIDE–em colaboração com a administração dos correios, CTT, e com o concurso de funcionários dessa empresa especialmente nomeados para o efeito–, mantinha permanentemente nos correios centrais. Aliás, a PIDE desempenhava idêntica tarefa, em colaboração com a Guarda Fiscal, nas Alfândegas, tal como se encarregava dos serviços de escuta aos postos radioamadores."

Brazil, and the colonies in general, were obviously a privileged form of access to books whose publication was forbidden in Portugal. We find another expression of the importance of the "Brazilian connection" in Francisco Lyon de Castro's words, the founder of Publicações Europa-América, which published the first Faulkner translated novels in Portugal. He implicitly refers to Brazil when explaining the idea that he had, back in the 1930s, to create a new publishing house:

> I came back to Portugal in 1936. I was returning with the idea of working in the area of Culture, importing and distributing publications and books that would contribute to the enlightening of the population and the increasing of its cultural level.
>
> Being a strong antifascist militant […] I was aware, and still am, of the fact that Culture would be an essential element for the democratisation of our country, which is why I thought that it was crucial for Portugal to obtain books, newspapers, magazines, etc., from Europe and America, especially South America–where, at the time, there were already excellent publishing houses–, and also from USA and even England, which would contribute towards the cultural development of the country, towards the information that our people were lacking, and consequently, towards the changing of the political situation we were living. (Azevedo 1999: 527-29)[3]

This situation establishes a clear parallel with neighbouring Spain and the important role that Spanish-speaking South American countries, namely Argentina, had for the Spanish book market during Franco's regime. The influx of South American translations of Faulkner into Spain was decisive for the intellectuals of that country:

---

[3] "[…] regressei a Portugal em 1936. Vinha com a ideia de exercer uma actividade profissional no domínio da Cultura, de importar e distribuir publicações e livros que contribuíssem para o esclarecimento e a elevação do nível cultural da população.
Convictamente militante antifascista [...], eu tinha a consciência, que ainda hoje subsiste, de que a Cultura constituiria um elemento fundamental da democratização do nosso país, e por isso pensava que era indispensável para Portugal que pudessem aqui chegar, vindas da Europa e das Américas, sobretudo da América do Sul – onde existiam já naquela altura excelentes editoras - , mas igualmente dos EUA e da própria Inglaterra, livros, jornais, revistas, etc. que contribuíssem para o desenvolvimento cultural do país, para a informação de que o nosso povo carecia e, por conseguinte, para a alteração da situação política em que nos encontrávamos."

There was nothing in the bookshops, everything was either sent or offered as a present. I can only think of Enrique Canito, besides Guillermo de Torre or Luis Torres, who were all abroad, having some works of Faulkner. (Gullón quoted by Bravo, Bravo 1985: 31)[4]

One translation in particular proved very popular in Spain. In Maria Elena Bravo's words, Jorge Luís Borges's 1940 translation of *The Wild Palms* "se leerá mucho en España, así como el resto de las traducciones realizadas en Argentina durante el decenio de los años cuarenta" [would be extensively read in Spain, as would the remainder of the translations done in Argentina during the 1940s] (Bravo 1985: 24). According to James Meriwether, "Argentina and Spain have occasionally shared the same translation [...] Portugal and Brazil share a language but not [...] any Faulkner translations" (Meriwether 1972: 125). While Spain was effectively reading the South American translations, PIDE, CTT and the censors prevented the Brazilian *Sanctuary* from reaching the Portuguese readers. This measure is likely to have contributed to the long lack of interest in *Sanctuary* on the part of the Portuguese publishers: France and Spain published their first translations in the early 1930s but in Portugal the first *Santuário* was published in 1958, one decade after the Brazilian text. Indeed, why would anyone risk trying to publish the translation of a book whose subject and setting alone seemed to fall within the censor's criteria for rejection?

Part of the repugnance created by what Faulkner himself considered to be "the most horrific tale" he could conceive (Faulkner 1993: 323) comes from the treatment of the sexual aspect, associated with violence, corruption and perversion, and expressed on the one hand by the threefold theme of rape, impotence and voyeurism introduced by the pair Popeye/Temple, and on the other hand, the subject of incest, belonging to Horace Benbow's story. Although the rape is, arguably, the nuclear moment of the text, determining the fate of all central characters, Temple, Popeye, Horace, Goodwin, Ruby and also Tommy, the reader is never explicitly told that it had happened. When, in chapter thirteen, it does take place, the reader merely knows that "something" is happening to Temple, as we first see her and Popeye at a distance, via the omniscient narrator's voice, and then hear the thoughts that go through Temple's mind while she dissociates herself from the scene. This is conveyed mainly by the tenses chosen by Faulkner. Marília de Vasconcelos's tenses, however, avoid the

---

[4] "En las librerías no había nada, todo era a base e envíos o de regalos. Sólo recuerdo a Enrique Canito, aparte de Guillermo de Torre o Luis Torres desde el extranjero, que tuviese alguna obra de Faulkner."

assertion that something actually happened and both "Something is going to happen to me" and "Something is happening to me!," taken from Temple's thoughts, are translated as "vai suceder-me qualquer coisa" (Faulkner 1993: 102 and Faulkner (Vasconcelos) 1958: 94). The latter prevents the reader from accompanying (albeit at a distance) what is happening to Temple. In fact, the deletion of the present tense enlarges the detachment between the reader and the plot and, moreover, it weakens the force of not only the moment, but also of Temple's hopeless anguish and, ultimately, of the reader's terrible intuition–that she was probably being raped.[5]

The suspicion is confirmed when, in the following chapter, references are made to the fact that Temple is bleeding. In the majority of cases, Vasconcelos manipulates the reference, at times even deleting it altogether:

> He took her arm.
> "It's all over the back of my coat," she whimpered. "Look and see."
> "You're all right. You'll get another coat tomorrow. Come on." They returned to the car. (Faulkner 1993: 323)

> [...] ele pegou-lhe no braço. Voltaram para o carro. (Faulkner (Vasconcelos) 1958: 126)

Later, when Temple is already in the brothel where Popeye has taken her, the madame tries to calm her down. While in the English text we read:

> "Now, now," Miss Reba said. "I bled for four days, myself. It aint nothing. Doctor Quinn'll stop it in two minutes, and Minnie'll have them all washed and pressed and you wont never know it. That blood'll be worth a thousand dollars to you, honey." (Faulkner 1993: 145)

> - Vamos, vamos–ia dizendo Miss Reba.–Isso não é nada. O Dr. Quinn é capaz de estancá-lo num instante. (Faulkner (Vasconcelos) 1958: 129-30)

However, Vasconcelos is not consistent and in other moments her text will make a reference to the hemorrhage similar to Faulkner's and the other translations, as for instance when "feeling her secret blood" is translated as "sentindo correr o sangue do baixo-ventre" (Faulkner 1993: 138 and Faulkner (Vasconcelos) 1958: 124-5). A close analysis of the

---

[5] Critics have often demonstrated how the nightmarish quality of this passage in particular is achieved and developed almost from the beginning of the book. See, for instance, Reed 1973 and Guerard 1998.

different examples that can be found in the text suggests that the more explicit the reference, the more reluctant Vasconcelos's text is. Her difficulty does not lie in the reference to the blood flowing, but rather in the contextualisation of that reference in a way that it relates more clearly to the possibility of rape.

The bleeding is the strongest hint leading to that hypothesis but, obviously, Temple's physical and emotional description also has a role to play. Here too Vasconcelos tones down the allusions made: "Began to scream", for instance, becomes "sentiu-se bastante aflita" (Faulkner 1993: 138 and Faulkner (Vasconcelos) 1958: 124-5) and whenever a reference is made to Temple's underwear, the translator chooses a superordinate form for it. This is consistent throughout the text and even before Temple and Popeye have met, we find "final squatting swirl of knickers" translated as "num esvoaçar final de roupa interior" (Faulkner 1993: 28 and Faulkner (Vasconcelos) 1958: 28).

A common superordinate form in Vasconcelos's translation is "baixo-ventre," which in one instance contrasts with the 1973 "sexo" and the 2001 "entre pernas" (Faulkner 1993: 145; Faulkner (Vasconcelos) 1958: 129; Faulkner (Rodrigues) 1973: 101 and Faulkner (Chaves) 2001: 130). The following example not only illustrates another instance of the occurrence of that expression, but also shows how Vasconcelos's text excludes references to sexual intercourse:

> He returned the slipper slowly, looking at her, at her belly and loins. "He aint laid no crop by yit, has he?" (Faulkner 1993: 41)

> [...] ele devolveu-lhe o sapato, com os olhos a mirarem-lhe o ventre e as coxas. - Ainda não pariu, pois não? (Faulkner (Vasconcelos) 1958: 39)

Here, Vasconcelos avoids explicitness firstly by translating "loins" as something very different, "thighs" ("coxas") and secondly by changing the focus and the subject of the action the feeble-minded Tommy refers to. As she eliminates the agricultural metaphor, an important element reinforcing Tommy's rusticity,[6] the translator avoids referring to the sexual intercourse and mentions its result, "parir" ("to give birth"), instead.

Contradicting what the deleted and toned down references mentioned above might have led us to expect, Vasconcelos does not manipulate in the same way the elements concerning Popeye's physical impotence and voyeurism:

---

[6] See Brown 1998 for an analysis of this character's speech.

Minnie said the two of them would be nekkid as two snakes, and Popeye hanging over the foot of the bed without even his hat took off, making a kind of a whinnying sound. (Faulkner 1993: 258-9)

Minnie contou que enquanto os dois se beijavam, Popeye, inclinado aos pés da cama, sem mesmo tirar o chapéu, se punha a fazer uma espécie de relincho. (Faulkner (Vasconcelos) 1958: 226-7)

While the 1958 reader is aware of Popeye's impotence and perversion in general terms, the weakening of the force of expressions like "nekkid as two snakes," and the consequent blurring of details, indicate that much is left unsaid. Vasconcelos, unlike her colleagues, does not allow her readers to identify the objects used by Popeye to overcome his handicap. In fact, the most important single element deleted in her version of *Sanctuary* is one of those objects–the corncob Popeye has used to rape Temple.

Although the assault is referred to much earlier in the book, Faulkner chose to postpone revealing the corncob until chapter twenty-eight, merely thirty pages before the end of the novel. Such a disclosure is then made implicitly, during another man's trial (Goodwin's), as part of the charges he is accused of. At that moment of the text, the corncob is mentioned, twice, but not articulately linked with the rape and those are the instances when Marília de Vasconcelos also mentions it. However, when immediately afterwards the corncob is explicitly alluded to as the object with which Temple was raped, the translation deletes it: "I saw her. She was some baby. Jeez. I wouldn't have used no cob" is in Portuguese "Eu vi-a. Bonita garota." And also: "Do to the lawyer what we did to him. What he did to her. Only we never used a cob. We made him wish we had used a cob" reads "Façamos ao advogado o que fizemos a ele. O que ele fez à rapariga" (Faulkner 1993: 294-6 and Faulkner/ Vasconcelos 1958: 258-60).

The references to the corncob that Vasconcelos has chosen to delete are, arguably, the two most crucial ones, since they finally and very unambiguously identify it as the object used in the dreadful assault. A parallel can thus be established with the deletion of the allusions to Temple's bleeding considered previously: both types of references are excluded only when they represent explicit indications to what they are ultimately about.

Apart from the consequences that this has for the understanding of the plot in general, the allusions to the corncob also have a direct effect upon the characterization of Popeye (and Temple): the terror quality, mainly of a sexual nature, associated with this character in the other texts is here considerably understated. Likewise, the omissions and toned down references identified in the context of Temple's rape and immediate reaction to it, also allow for a characterization of her which is radically different from the one available in the retranslations of the same novel.

All of these aspects explain why Minerva decided to publish a retranslation of Faulkner's text only fifteen years after the first translation. The implicit aim behind this decision is discreetly and succinctly stated on the cover page of that pocket size edition, where, in small print we can read: "texto integral" (full text). In terms of the references considered above, Fernanda Pinto Rodrigues's choices can be easily contrasted with Vasconcelos's, because, at the other end of possible approaches to the text, Rodrigues often uses strategies such as clarification and explicitation. She also repeatedly resorts to the use of exclamation marks, emphasizing the character's emotions. However, the details of her strategies and the differences between the intervention of censorship in 1958 and in 1973 will have to wait. Important for now is mainly to note that every reference of a sexual nature deleted in the 1958 translation is present in the 1973 text, and all the vaguely implicit allusions are much more clearly available to the reader.

Such a comparative perspective of the 1958 translation, emphasizing its "failures," could lead to a criticism against which Peter Fawcett has advised:

> There can be no question of a blanket condemnation of translators who are forced by the translation commissioner or by overwhelming cultural pressures to betray the original work by excluding the reader of the translation from the choices made in the source text. (Fawcett 1995: 186)

At this moment it is not possible to determine to what extent the manipulation of the 1958 text was a result of self-censorship or, for instance, a consequence of the interference of the translation commissioner, but the fact that the book was indeed published, five years after the "rigorous" banning of the Brazilian text and more than two decades after the publication of the Spanish and the French ones, is an obvious sign that it conformed to the strict constraints paternalistically put in place and thoroughly controlled to defend and preserve the regime's moral values.

References

Primary Sources

Faulkner, William (1993) *Sanctuary*, New York: Vintage International (Random House), (1st edition 1931).
—. (1958) *Sanctuary* (translated by Marília de Vasconcelos), Lisboa: Editorial Minerva.
—. (1973) *Sanctuary* (translated by Fernanda Pinto Rodrigues), Lisboa: Editorial Minerva.
—. (2001) *Sanctuary* (translated by Ana Maria Chaves), Lisboa: Publicações Dom Quixote.

Secondary Sources

Azevedo, Cândido de (ed.) (1999) *A Censura de Salazar e Marcelo Caetano: Imprensa, Teatro, Televisão, Radiodifusão, Livro*, Lisboa: Caminho.
Bravo, Maria-Elena (1985) *Faulkner en España–Perspectivas de la Narrativa de Postguerra*, Barcelona: Ediciones Península.
Brown, Calvin S. (1988) "*Sanctuary*: From Confrontation to Peaceful Void", in Harold Bloom (ed.) *William Faulkner's Sanctuary*, New York, New Haven, Philadelphia: Chelsea House Publishers, 27-52.
Fawcett, Peter (1995) "Translation and Power Play", in *The Translator* 1 (2): 177-191.
Guerard, Albert J. (1988) "*Sanctuary* and Faulkner's Misogyny", in Harold Bloom (ed.) *William Faulkner's Sanctuary*, New York, New Haven, Philadelphia: Chelsea House Publishers, 63-80.
Meriwether, James B. (1972) *The Literary Career of William Faulkner. A Bibliographical Study*, Columbia, South Carolina: University of South Carolina Press.
Reed Jr. & Joseph W. (1973) *Faulkner's Narrative*, New Haven and London: Yale University Press.

Forbidden Images of Portuguese Colonialism: A Translation of a Book by C. R. Boxer

Gabriela Gândara Terenas,
Universidade Nova de Lisboa, Portugal

Abstract: This paper analyses the complex relationships between translation and censorship in the case of the Portuguese translation of *Race Relations in the Portuguese Colonial Empire, 1415-1825* (1963). The book, which is listed amongst the publications whose circulation in Portugal was forbidden during the Salazar/Caetano regime, was written by the British historian C. R. Boxer (1904-2000), a well-known Lusophile and a specialist in Portuguese studies. His works were widely read both in Portugal and in Brazil, where the first translation was published. The essay investigates the possible reasons why the censor decided to ban public access to C. R. Boxer's book and reveals the complex series of circumstances in which the translation was undertaken and published.

"Ich kann nicht anders."
—C. R. Boxer

1. Introduction

In 1963, the Clarendon Press published a book by the eminent British historian and specialist in Portuguese Studies, Charles Ralph Boxer (1904-2000),[1] entitled *Race Relations in the Portuguese Colonial Empire, 1415-*

---

[1] Charles Boxer joined the Lincolnshire Regiment in 1923, after attending Wellington College and the Royal Military College. He was wounded in the Second World War and served in the British Army until his retirement in 1947 with the rank of Major. During this period he visited Japan, China, Manchuria, Korea and the Dutch colonies in Asia. In 1945 he married Emily Hahn. After leaving the Army he became a Lecturer in Portuguese at the University of London (1947-1951 and 1953-1967), and he was offered the *Camões* Chair by King's College. Between 1951 and 1953 he taught the History of the Far East at the

1825.[2] It brought together a series of three lectures Boxer had given at the University of Virginia in November 1962. In his preface the author explained that the lectures had been published exactly as they had been delivered, with the addition of footnotes to provide further clarification where it was thought useful. (Boxer 1963: V). Taken together, the three lectures, entitled "Morocco and West Africa", "Mozambique and India" and finally "Brazil and the Maranhão" offered a critical study of Portuguese colonization in the three regions, principally in the 16th and 17th centuries. Boxer's critique was founded on three premises which were particularly sensitive issues for the *Estado Novo* regime: firstly, the Portuguese belief in the superiority of the white man and the consequent discrimination against colonized peoples; secondly, the prevalence of illicit relations between settlers and the native women; and, finally, the existence of racial prejudice allied to religious intolerance.

As it happens, of the twenty or so works by Charles Boxer which were translated into Portuguese after 1928, the translation of this book is the only one listed as having been forbidden during the Salazar/Caetano regime (Comissão... 1981: 22). Whilst the reasons for banning the book can quite easily be understood upon reading it, the controversy which arose and the context in which the translation and subsequent prohibition occurred are less straightforward. Let us begin with the reasons which would have led the censor to ban the book. Right at the beginning of the first essay on Morocco and West Africa, Boxer not only questioned the fundamental principles upon which the regime based its claim to its overseas territories, but also quoted Salazar on the matter and went as far as to doubt the veracity of the dictator's statements:

> As most of you probably know, it is an article of faith with many Portuguese that their country *has never tolerated a colour-bar in its overseas possessions*[3] and that their compatriots have always had a natural affinity for contacts with coloured peoples. In a recent interview with Life

---

School of Oriental and African Studies. In 1957 he was elected member of the British Academy and in 1968 was appointed Emeritus Professor of Portuguese at the University of London. Boxer was Professor of European Expansion Overseas at Yale between 1967 and 1972, the year in which he was appointed Emeritus Professor of History at the same University. He was Visiting Professor at the University of Indiana (1967-1979) and was awarded Honorary Doctorates by the Universities of Utrecht (1950), Bahia (1959), Liverpool (1966), Hong Kong (1971) and Peradeniya (1980).
[2] Henceforth the book will be referred to as *Race Relations*.
[3] All underlining is the responsibility of the author of this paper.

Magazine,[4] Dr. Salazar affirmed: "These contacts *have never involved the slightest idea of superiority or racial discrimination*... I think I can say that the distinguishing feature of Portuguese Africa–*notwithstanding the congregated efforts made in many quarters to attack it by word as well as by action*–is the primacy which we have always attached and will continue to attach to the enhancement of the value and the dignity of man *without distinction of colour or creed*, in the light of the principles of the civilization we carried to the populations who were in every way distant from ourselves." (Boxer 1963: 1)

Charles Boxer maintained that Salazar's arguments were not always backed up by historical documents; hence the explicit aim of the three lectures to show that the true situation had undoubtedly been more complex and that "race relations in the old Portuguese colonial empire did not *invariably* present such a picture of harmonious integration", that Salazar wished his readers to believe (Boxer 1963:2). The Portuguese (in Boxer's opinion) had almost always endeavoured to affirm the white man's supremacy and had seldom made any effort to understand other peoples, especially those of African origin (Boxer 1963:14, 40). Although the Portuguese Crown had often legislated against discrimination against coloured people, the real situation differed greatly, especially in the case of appointments to more senior military, government and even ecclesiastical posts (Boxer 1963:5-6). Charles Boxer argued, moreover, that local authorities in the overseas territories had often been guilty of racial prejudice against negroes, mulattos and mestizos (Boxer 1963: 70-73, 31). Furthermore, he argued, as the slave trade developed, there was an increase in the number of expeditions and wars between the tribes of the interior, with the objective of capturing slaves for the Brazilian plantations and mines, whilst, at the same time, the conviction, widely held by the Portuguese settlers, that the negroes were virtually irrational and inferior beings and therefore justifiably enslaved, became more deeply rooted (Boxer 1963:29).

Obviously, to question the truth of Salazar's arguments was sufficient reason, in itself, for the book to be banned. To do this when the war in Africa, which had aroused fierce opposition in many countries to Portugal's "aggressive colonialism", had already started, was a real insult to the regime. In fact, the United States, as well as certain European

---

[4] The author was referring to the American magazine *Life*, to which Salazar had given an interview published under the title "An Exclusive Talk with Portugal's Enigmatic Salazar. Dictator on the Defensive", no. 18, May 4th 1962, pp. 94-95, 98-99, 100B, 102, 105-106 and 108.

nations such as Great Britain, which were coming to the end of their decolonization processes, and which had previously tolerated, if not fully accepted the regime, now raised their voices to protest against the conflict between the Portuguese armed forces and the independence movements. The prohibition of the book could readily be explained, therefore, by Boxer's frontal attack on Salazar and the ideology which, according to the regime, justified the Colonial War. However, as mentioned previously, the bitter controversy in the Portuguese press concerning the publication of *Race Relations* and, above all, the context in which the translation and the subsequent prohibition of the book took place, are far less straightforward. It is precisely the circumstances which surrounded these events which I now propose to examine more closely.

2. The Controversy: Boxer, Cortesão and Salazar

Whilst Charles Boxer justified most of his arguments with recourse to Portuguese documentation from the 16th, 17th and 18th centuries, which he considered credible, [5] he was, on the other hand, openly critical of certain Portuguese 20th century historians (and even some from the 19th century). And towards the end of the book he concluded:

> In Brazil, as in Portuguese Asia and Portuguese Africa, *Negro, Preto,* and *Cafre*, were all pejorative terms, often synonymous with *Escravo*. […] *if I have dwelt in these lectures on the dark rather than on the bright side of Portuguese colonization in past centuries*, it has not been with the object of suggesting that they behaved worse than other European nations would have done in the prevailing circumstances. *I only wish to show that sweeping generalizations like the following recent pronouncement by Dr. Armando Cortesão* [6] *must be taken with a pinch of salt*: 'The Portuguese

---

[5] Ironically, it should be noted that the vast majority of the references he quotes, both of ancient and coeval sources, were by Portuguese authors, such as D. Francisco de Almeida (1450? -1510), João de Barros (1496-1570), Padre José de Anchieta (1534-1597), Diogo do Couto (1542-1616), Padre Manuel Severim de Faria (1609-1655), Joaquim Heliodoro da Cunha Rivara (1800-1879), Visconde de Paiva Manso (1831-1875), Luciano Cordeiro (1844-1900), Padre Serafim Leite (1890-1969), A. A. Banha de Andrade (1915-1982), A. Teixeira da Mota (1920-1982) and particularly António de Oliveira Cadornega (? -1690).

[6] A scholar, cartographer and historian, Armando Cortesão (1891-1977) was, like his well-known elder brother, Jaime Cortesão, an opponent of the Salazar regime. Forced into exile in 1932, as a consequence, he lived in London between 1935 and 1946. Charles Boxer had met Armando Cortesão in Portugal in 1926, and they were soon to become very close friends. In the early days of Cortesão's stay in

never had any preconception of race or of colour. They always dealt with and still deal with Christian fraternity towards all, whether they are white, black, swarthy or yellow!' *This statement, though made in perfect good faith, is not the truth, the whole truth, and nothing but the truth.* (Boxer 1963: 120-122)

It was precisely this direct reference to Armando Cortesão, together with the implicit criticism of Portuguese colonial policy which triggered off the controversy in the Lisbon daily, *Diário Popular,* between 27th December 1963 and 25th January 1964. The controversy has already been thoroughly examined, not only by Boxer's biographer Dauril Alden (Alden 2001: 365-397), but also by J. S. Cummins and Luís de Sousa Rebelo (Cummins & Rebelo 2001:233-246), amongst others (Ramos 2005:189-212). I do not propose to analyze the dispute itself in this paper but rather to attempt to assess how far the controversy acted as a form of what I would term "propaganda censorship". The *Diário Popular* classified Charles Boxer's book as "insidious" from the outset, publishing a series of five articles by Cortesão, who, according to the newspaper, "masterfully dissected" the thesis of the "former Lusophile" (Anonymous 1963:1). The paper dutifully reported on the repercussions of the articles amongst the Portuguese *intelligentsia*, printed Boxer's riposte in a single article on 24th January 1964 and finally called an end to the debate with the publication of the Portuguese Professor's "remarkable" counterargument. After the controversy in the press any attempt to translate Charles Boxer's book in Portugal would have been inconceivable and the dispute thus acted as effective *a priori* censorship against any possible translation in Portugal.

3. Censorship and Translation

Although the listing of books prohibited by censorship provides only the title of the book in Portuguese and the author's name, omitting both the

---

England, Boxer helped him to get a salaried post. However, in 1952, having somehow reconciled himself to the Salazar regime, Cortesão returned to Portugal to take up the Chair of Cartography at Coimbra University. To a great extent, it was the onset of the war in Africa which led a number of Salazar's adversaries to feel obliged to align with the regime behind the banner of the nation's integrity. Boxer's source was *Realidades e Desvarios Africanos. Discurso proferido na Sociedade de Geografia de Lisboa, quando da Sessão de Encerramento da Semana do Ultramar em 9 de Junho de 1962* (Lisboa, Sociedade de Geografia de Lisboa, 1962, pp. 30-31).

date and the place of publication as well as the name of the translator and the publisher, there could be little doubt that the book which had been banned in Portugal was the Brazilian translation of *Race Relations*, published in 1967. The difficulty was how to obtain proof.

Firstly, as far as I was able to ascertain, no other translation of the work into Portuguese had been published before 1977. Furthermore, I was fortunate enough to discover a document in the archives of the Torre do Tombo, dated 13th August 1970, originating from the *Serviços da Censura*, which proved that it was, indeed, the translation of *Race Relations*, published in Rio de Janeiro, which had been forbidden. The document is Report no. 8855 and it reads as follows:

> This book seems to have, as its only purpose, a wish to destroy everything good we have ever done in the Overseas Territories. This objective, which can already be anticipated from perusal of the back cover, is patent throughout the whole book, but *most particularly in the 20 pages of the "Prologue for Brazilians", in which everything we have done is denigrated,* and where only certain figures are presented for a certain ends, and in which the reasoning is false and erroneous conclusions are reached!
>
> All over the world there has always been a great difference between what is legislated upon and what, *principally far away*, is actually carried out! It is true that there have been many things in which people have behaved badly, or exaggerated, or failed to comply with issued instructions, but to take advantage of this to negate so much that is good and unique in the Overseas Territories, is revolting. *The real intention is to deny any historical justification for our presence in the Overseas Territories, but even this fails because we do not aspire to perpetuate Portuguese sovereignty in the Overseas Territories, but merely to defend parts of what is ours!*
>
> *Reading the Prologue is enough to conclude, in my opinion, that the sale of this book should not be authorized.*" (R8855/70: 1-2)[7]

---

[7] "Este livro parece ter, como única finalidade, o desejo de destruir tudo o que de bom, e desde sempre, fizemos no Ultramar. Essa finalidade, que já se antevê na contracapa, está bem patente em toda a obra, mas *muito especialmente nas 20 folhas do "Prólogo para Brasileiros", em que se procura denegrir tudo o que fizemos,* em que se apresentam só determinados números e para determinados fins, em que se fazem raciocínios falsos e se tiram conclusões erradas!
Em todo o Mundo sempre houve uma grande diferença entre o que se legisla e o que, *principalmente muito longe*, se cumpre! É certo que muitas coisas houve em que se procedeu mal, se exagerou, se não cumpriram as determinações emanadas, mas que se lance mão disso para negar o muito de bom, e até de único, que se fez no Ultramar é revoltante. *O que se pretende, verdadeiramente, é negar qualquer justificativo histórico para a nossa permanência no Ultramar,*

Having thus reached the conclusion that the book attacked the ideological foundations of the *Estado Novo*'s Overseas policy, the censor chose to concentrate his attack on the synopsis and, above all, the preface, which, it was alleged, supplied false statistics concerning public health, illiteracy and the economic situation of Portugal. In an attempt to defend the Portuguese government's military intervention in the Overseas Territories, the censor underlined the difference between the law and its implementation, which Charles Boxer discussed in his book, and revived the argument which had been employed since the 19th century concerning the "historic rights" of Portugal, and, in so doing, blatantly missed the point of Boxer's thesis. It seems quite likely that he did not take the trouble to read the whole book, but had probably heard about it at the time of the controversy in the press, a few years earlier. This document illustrates a form of *a posteriori* censorship which was common practice at the time. In this case, the objective was not to force the translator to omit certain parts of the text, but rather to prevent the Brazilian translation from being distributed in Portugal, which the regime would have been unable to do otherwise.

In view of the above it is worth examining the context in which the Brazilian translation was published, beginning with the repercussions of the Boxer *versus* Cortesão controversy in Brazilian academic circles.

4. Boxer in Brazil: Echoes of the Controversy

Charles Boxer had been well-known in Brazil for many years and several of his works had been translated there before *Race Relations* was published. Indeed, he had been variously described as "an old admirer of Brazil", "a legitimate representative [of the] [...] tradition of English historiography" and "a specialist *par excellence* in the history of the Portuguese colonial world" (Chacon 1967: 27).

Boxer knew the Brazilian academic world well and especially one of its most distinguished representatives at the time, Gilberto Freyre, who had dedicated his book *O Luso e o Trópico*,[8] which had been published in

---

mas até nisso se falha pois que não se pretende "perpetuar o domínio Português no Ultramar" mas apenas defender parcelas do que é nosso! Basta ler o Prólogo para se concluir, em minha opinião, que não deve ser autorizada a venda deste livro em Portugal."

[8] In *O Luso e o Trópico*, Freyre referred to Boxer in rather complimentary terms: "*O historiador inglês Charles Boxer, numa das suas melhores páginas de síntese do que foi a acção portuguesa no Oriente de 1500 a 1800*, salienta terem-se os Lusos deixado influenciar na sua arte pelos estilos asiáticos de decoração de

1961, at the beginning of the war in Africa, to the British historian. The volume was a compilation of several of Freyre's essays based on his theory of Luso-Tropicalism, which identified an intrinsic ability in the Portuguese to settle in tropical areas and to mix easily with the indigenous peoples, so creating harmoniously integrated, multiracial societies. Not surprisingly, Freyre's theory provided the scientific support for the official line during the *Estado Novo* regime, particularly as regards the supposed absence of racism. In essence, the doctrine of Luso-Tropicalism was to provide an argument for the regime to justify Portugal's continuing presence in Africa (Freyre 1961:33-61; Alexandre 1999:391-394; Moreira 1964). In January 1964, however, immediately after the controversy with Cortesão, Freyre was to turn against Boxer, attempting to belittle him as a historian and accusing him of being an enemy of Portugal (Alden 2001:386). Charles Boxer chose not to confront the Brazilian sociologist and in his article in defence of the book, which he published again in the São Paulo journal *Revista de História* (Boxer 1964:405-408), he merely refuted Cortesão's categorical statements, without referring to Freyre.

---

cerâmica e de móvel; pelos seus tapetes e tecidos; pelas sedas e porcelanas; e que vários objectos de arte oriental foram por eles trazidos do Oriente para as áreas por eles ocupadas na África e na América. […] *modernos historiadores europeus–um deles o inglês Charles* Boxer–afirmam da Misericórdia estabelecida na capital do Oriente português desde o século XVI, para socorro de viúvas, de órfãos, de pobres, dos velhos, de enfermos não só lusitanos e cristãos como de autóctones e mestiços e indivíduos não só de outras raças como de outros credos–que *nem os Holandeses, nem os Ingleses, nem os Franceses tiveram nas suas colónias orientais organização que, no género, se aproximasse em amplitude e em eficiência da fundada na Índia pela gente lusitana.*"
["The English historian Charles Boxer, in one of his best pages of synthesis regarding the Portuguese presence in the Orient between 1500 and 1800, points out that the Lusitanians had allowed their art to be influenced by the Asian styles of ornamentation in ceramics and furniture; by their carpets and textiles; by silk and porcelain; and that they brought several pieces of Oriental art from the Orient to the areas they occupied in Africa and America. […] modern European historians, amongst them the Englishman Charles Boxer, say of the Misericórdia, which had been established in the capital of the Portuguese Orient since the beginning of the 16th century to aid widows, orphans, the poor, the old and the infirm, not only Portuguese and Christians but also native peoples and mestizos as well as people of other races and of other creeds, that neither the Dutch or the English, nor the French, possessed an organization in their Oriental colonies which, of its kind, came close in scale and efficiency to that which had been founded in India by Lusitanian folk."] (Freyre 1961: 205, 262)

5. The Brazilian Political and Cultural Context in 1967

The controversy in the Portuguese press, Gilberto Freyre's involvement and the advent of the military dictatorship in Brazil all came together to produce a highly complex set of circumstances which were to influence the translation of Boxer's book. Whereas there is every likelihood that the controversy between Cortesão and Boxer attracted the attention of the Brazilian academic world to the work, on the other hand Freyre's criticism (he sympathized with the Brazilian military regime) and the censorship of books, which had by then been introduced, probably led potential publishers to hesitate about proposing a translation.

After the military coup of 31st March 1964, somewhat surprisingly, the right-wing dictatorship did not immediately move against what was viewed as leftward-leaning cultural production and until 1968 a rather paradoxical truce prevailed. (Schwarz 1992:62). Elio Gaspari coined the term the "sham dictatorship", to describe the period and it also became known as the "soft dictatorship" or "Dita branda", as opposed to the "*Dita dura*" or "*ditadura escancarada*", the "out and out dictatorship" or the violent, hard-line version which was to follow (Gaspari 2004), especially after the introduction of the repressive legislation known as "Acto Institucional No. 5" on 13th December 1968.

Although it is true that the "*Dita branda*" period, together with the cultural heritage of the previous twenty years of democratic life created a climate conducive to the translation of Boxer's *Race Relations,* the awareness that the regime was becoming more repressive may have led the publishers to think twice about translating a book which, first and foremost, questioned the "highly thought of" theory of Luso-Tropicalism and, indeed, the very identity of Brazil. The translation and publication of *Race Relations* was not only a calculated gamble, therefore, but also a decision deliberately guided by an element of caution, as the prologue demonstrates. Before addressing the preface, however, I would like to turn my attention briefly to the Brazilian translator and the publisher.

6. The Brazilian Translator and the Publisher

Elice Munerato, the translator of the Brazilian edition of *Race Relations,* was a radical feminist and a frequent contributor to the opposition press, and later becoming a filmmaker of some renown.[9] It is

---

[9] Elice Munerato also translated *A Massa Cinzenta* (Rio de Janeiro, Editora Artenova, 1973, from the original *Gray Matters* by William Hjortsberg) and was

conceivable that the publisher's choice of translator and Munerato's interest in doing the translation can be explained by the importance which Charles Boxer devoted to women throughout his book, emphasizing the way in which they had been subjected to different kinds of discrimination due to racial prejudice.

The translation of *Race Relations* was published as part of the "Biblioteca Tempo Universitário", a series belonging to the publishing firm of the same name, which specialized in scientific works for research purposes and was supervised by an advisory board of distinguished academics. The same series included translations of the writings of Heidegger, Sartre and Lévi-Strauss, amongst others. Identified, perhaps, as a threat to the regime because of its avant-garde policy, the publisher's offices were targetted by a bomb attack in 1968, which destroyed them completely.

7. "Prologue for Brazilians": the Author of the Preface

Taking into account the repercussions in Brazil of the controversy, Gilberto Freyre's critical review, the political and cultural situation when the translation was published and the profiles of the publisher and the translator, it is hardly surprising that it proved necessary to precede the text with an introduction which partially camouflaged Boxer's true message. For this reason, Vamireh Chacon's [10] preface to the Brazilian

---

one of the main contributors to the magazines *Opinião* and *Pasquim,* which were opposed to the military regime and its official policy. In the former publication, which was considered to be the most influential voice of the alternative press in Brazil during the seventies, Elice Munerato wrote the following articles between April 1975 and March 1976: " Feminista até certo ponto", "Uma frágil linha de acção social", " Os problemas dela", " Elas terão centro de estudo", "Mais um debate delas", "Dois pesos e duas medidas", " Um (falso) jornal feminino" and "Carmen da Silva e a arte de ser mulher", the latter article in collaboration with Branca Moreira Alves. The articles deal with the social and professional problems faced by Brazilian women and the idea of Feminism in Brazil. In 1982, in collaboration with Maria Helena Darcy de Oliveira, she published *As Musas da Matiné* (Rio de Janeiro, Rioarte), a study of female participation in full-length feature films in Brazil, which includes the analysis of the female characters in the same films.

[10] A specialist in Political Science, Vamireh Chacon was born in 1934 in Recife. He has directed the Department of Political Science at the Universidade de Brasília, has been a visiting Professor at several American, German and Portuguese Universities, and is a member of the Academia Pernambucana de Letras. He has received a number of literary prizes, amongst which the Calouste

translation can also be seen as a form of *a priori* censorship, within the context of the reception of the work in Brazil. Fully aware that the translation might face the risk of being apprehended and destroyed like so many other works at the time, the publisher took the precaution of inviting a preface writer who was capable of deceiving the censors as to the book's real content and scope. Chacon's curious introduction, which was entitled "a Prologue for Brazilians", was successful in meeting the publisher's requirements without jeopardizing his own reputation. To this end he employed three cunning and successful strategies: in the first place, he based his arguments on the (supposedly) exceptional character of Portuguese colonization in Brazil; secondly, he devised an unusual chronological division of the History of Portugal and Overseas Expansion; and finally, he chose to deal exclusively with Salazar's dictatorship, making no mention whatsoever of Brazil's military regime. The preface began with a series of brief but revealing statements:

> O Brasil é criação dos brasileiros.
> Portugal não repetiu na África o êxito que lhe é atribuído no Brasil: eis a principal lição deste livro do Professor C.R. Boxer.
>
> [Brazil is the creation of Brazilians.
> Portugal did not repeat in Africa the success which was attributed to it in Brazil: this is the principal lesson of this book by Professor C.R. Boxer.]
> (Chacon 1967: 9)

Vamireh Chacon argued that Boxer's "serene", "objective" and "non-aligned" book ought to be viewed as a song of praise, albeit of an indirect kind, for the construction of a Brazilian identity, for which the Brazilians, not the Portuguese, could feel proud.[11] Whilst Chacon recognized

---

Gulbenkian Prize of the Academia Portuguesa de História. Considered one of the foremost specialists in the History of Ideas in Brazil, in January 2005 he was awarded the title of Emeritus Professor by the Universidade de Brasília. His publications include: *História dos Partidos Brasileiros: Discurso e Praxis dos seus Programas* (Brasília, Editora Universidade de Brasília, 1981); *Gilberto Freyre: uma Biografia Intelectual* (Recife, Editora Massanga/ São Paulo, Editora Nacional, 1993); *A Construção da Brasilidade: Gilberto Freyre e a sua Geração* (Brasília, Paralelo15/ São Paulo, Marco Zero, 2001); or *O Futuro da Lusofonia* (São Paulo/Lisboa, Verbo, 2002).

[11] As Antero had argued long before, at the Conferências do Casino, in a lecture entitled "Causas da Decadência dos Povos Peninsulares nos Últimos Três Séculos", Chacon also attributed the cause of decadence of the Iberian nations to the Council of Trent.

Portugal's legacy from the period before the Counter-Reformation (Chacon 1967:29), i.e. the Portugal of the Discoveries, he, as a Brazilian, saw no reason to identify with Portugal after the mid-sixteenth century. Thus, he argued, what had happened in Portugal's African territories was in no way comparable with the Portuguese presence in Brazil. Chacon further argued that until the mid-nineteenth century, before the "Scramble for Africa" and the struggle between the European powers for African territories, Portuguese colonization was characterized by a sincere attitude of miscegenation, which, in total consonance with Freyrean doctrine, left its mark on pre-independent Brazil and was to become a feature of its identity. On the other hand, Portugal's policy regarding its African territories had changed completely when Cecil Rhodes's plan, which, in the final analysis, led to the *Ultimatum* of 1890, became known.[12] The failure of Liberalism in Portugal,[13] the awareness of the country's

---

[12] According to Chacon, as a consequence of the complete failure of Liberalism in Portugal, the possibility of establishing a "new union, between Portugal and Brazil, in terms of reciprocal equality," was also lost. (Chacon 1967:18)

[13] On this matter, Chacon recalled the vain endeavors of the intellectuals of the "Geração de 70" to awaken a long-slumbering nation, and at the same time, the frustration of the members of the "Vencidos da Vida" group when they realized the country's decadence was, in fact, incurable: "Perdendo seu impulso, o Liberalismo português apoucava-se, mediocrizava-se, como sucede com qualquer corrente de ideias, em idêntica circunstância.

A geração de Eça, Ramalho, Antero e Oliveira Martins, rebelou-se.

O realismo português começou mais social que literário, e, mesmo quando refugiado finalmente num certo diletantismo, não deixou de trazer decisivas contribuições para o conhecimento objectivo da vida portuguesa. (…) Após o malogro das esperanças de 1870-1872, Oliveira Martins começa a afastar-se do movimento republicano-socialista e a preparar-se para intervir na política partidária com um programa de Socialismo de Estado e de fomento económico, procurando apoiar-se na pequena burguesia industrial.

Foi a atitude mais construtiva do seu grupo: Antero acabaria suicidando-se e Eça nas fugas de Jacinto de Tormes e de Fradique Mendes."

[Having lost its drive, Portuguese Liberalism dwindled and became banal, as happens with any flow of ideas in identical circumstances.

The generation of Eça, Ramalho, Antero and Oliveira Martins, rebelled.

Portuguese realism started off more social than literary and even when it had eventually taken refuge in a kind of dilettantism, it still made a decisive contribution towards the objective knowledge of Portuguese life. (…) After the failure of the hopes of 1870-1872, Oliveira Martins began to distance himself from the republican-socialist movement and to prepare himself for a role in party politics with a programme of state socialism and economic development, which sought support from the industrial petty-bourgeoisie. It was the most constructive

incurable decadence,[14] the deception of the Republicans after 1910,[15] and the instauration of a dictatorial regime were part of a process of decline in which the end was impossible to foresee. As a consequence, the country became dependent upon its African possessions and more and more tightly locked in the grip of the "mystique of the Overseas Territories".[16]

Whereas, in Chacon's view, Brazil was a case apart, Boxer's essay on the Portuguese colonization of this territory leaves little doubt about Portuguese racial prejudice and particularly the hierarchization and consequent discrimination of the different races, to the detriment of the black man. Indeed, as far as Charles Boxer was concerned, the entirely incomprehensible disparity between the treatment of the Indians and the Negroes, especially in Brazil, was one of the tragedies of Portuguese colonial history (Chacon 1967:87-128, 101-102). Although Chacon's clever, yet debatable, interpretation of the History of Portugal and Overseas Expansion served the purpose of Editora Tempo Brasileiro, it clearly diverged from Boxer's thesis. It should be emphasized that the

---

attitude of those in his group: Antero would end up by committing suicide and Eça found escape through Jacinto de Tormes and Fradique Mendes.] (Chacon 1967:22)

[14] See Chacon's remarks concerning the failure of the republican ideal: " Proclamada a República, por liberais maçónicos e pelos positivistas, incapazes de governar e apoiados no descontentamento desordenado da população, o eixo reacionário de gravidade foi aumentando sua força. De início apoiou Sidónio Pais e, por fim, o Clero e as Forças Armadas resolveram encampar o poder de uma vez por todas: surgiu a simbiose Carmona-Salazar, que dura até hoje, substituído apenas o primeiro."

[After the Republic had been proclaimed by Masonic Liberals and by Positivists, who proved incapable of governing and were supported by unruly discontent of the population, the strength of the reactionary forces began to grow. At the beginning they supported Sidónio Pais and eventually the Clergy and the Armed Forces decided to take power once and for all; the symbiosis of Carmona and Salazar appeared which still survives today, only the former having been replaced.] (Chacon 1967: 22)

[15] Regarding the dramatic situation of the country under Salazar, Chacon emphasized the extreme economic backwardness, the high rate of child mortality and the illiteracy of the population, basing his arguments, to a great extent, on the data provided by Perry Anderson in his report entitled *Portugal e o Fim do Ultracolonialismo* (Rio de Janeiro, Editora Civilização Brasileira S.A., 1966, pp.8-9).

[16] According to Chacon, most of the country's resources came from raw materials originating in the Overseas Territories and from the exportation of indigenous labour to Rhodesia and South Africa. (Chacon 1967: 25)

British historian's remarks referred to relationships which prevailed throughout the Portuguese possessions, during the period in question. It is true that the period did precede the independence of Brazil, but this was irrelevant as far as Charles Boxer's thesis was concerned, for, according to the author, the racial relationships which had developed between the Portuguese settlers and the indigenous peoples in Brazil were even more complex than those which had existed in Asia and Africa.

Chacon, like Boxer himself, was eager to keep in tune with the spirit of the times and at the end of the preface, he mentioned that when the Portuguese overseas provinces were finally given their independence, the new countries might form an international, Portuguese-speaking community, together with Brazil and Portugal (Chacon 1967:28-29). Curiously, the idea of a Lusophone community could hardly be interpreted as anything other than the future offspring of Freyre's Luso-Tropicalism.

8. Conclusions: Censorial Propaganda, Censorship and Triangular Trajectories

To conclude, it can be said that in the present case, censorship took on an unfamiliar, yet not unprecedented guise. This was not a case of self-censorship in which the original text was manipulated by the translator, nor was the work itself silenced or truncated by the frequently haphazard use of the censor's "blue pencil". The tool employed was what might be termed "censorial propaganda", implemented through a controversy in a Lisbon daily newspaper, possibly instigated and certainly supported by the regime, which was later to find echoes in Brazil. Whereas any attempt to translate *Race Relations* in Portugal would have been unthinkable after the controversy in the press, paradoxically it was precisely the effect of this *a priori* censorship which would eventually lead to the translation of Boxer's text in Brazil. Unable to prevent the book from being translated into Portuguese, as it had done in 1963, the regime was forced, seven years later, to ban its distribution using the prologue as its justification; the very same prologue which had enacted the role of *a priori* censorship in the Brazilian context. The *Estado Novo*'s censorship machine had once again been brought into action, this time, however, in its more familiar guise of *a posteriori* censorship.

Thus this complex and fascinating trajectory of Boxer's book bears witness not only to the international political situation at the time of its publication and to the specific social, political and cultural circumstances surrounding its production in Great Britain, its singular reception in Portugal and the ensuing repercussions in Brazil, but also to the different ways source and target texts were dealt with by censorship. At the IV International Congress of Translation Studies, held at the Faculdade de Letras, Universidade de Lisboa, in September 2004, Professor Teresa Seruya put forward the idea of a project with the primary goal of investigating the production, distribution and reception of translations during the *Estado Novo* regime, whilst exploring the triangular movement of the texts and their translations between Europe, Brazil and Portugal. I hope that the case presented in this paper will constitute a worthy contribution to this project.

References

Primary Sources

Anónimo (1963) "Um Livro Insidioso", in *Diário Popular*, Lisboa: R. Pinheiro de Oliveira/Sociedade Industrial da Imprensa, Ano XXII, n° 7616, 26th December.
Boxer, C. R. (1963) *Race Relations in the Portuguese Colonial Empire, 1415-1825*, Oxford: Clarendon Press/Oxford University Press.
—. (1964) " Resposta a Artigos de Armando Cortesão", in *Revista de História*, São Paulo: Editora da Universidade de São Paulo, vol. XXVII, n° 58, 405-408.
—. (1967) *Relações Raciais no Império Colonial Português, 1415-1825* (translated by Elice Munerato), Rio de Janeiro: Edições Tempo Brasileiro, Colecção Tempo Universitário, n° 4.
—. (1977) *Relações Raciais no Império Colonial Português, 1415-1825* (translated by Sebastião Brás), Porto: Edições Afrontamento.
Chacon, Vamireh (1967) "Prólogo para Brasileiros", in C. R. Boxer, *Relações Raciais no Império Colonial Português, 1415-1825* (translated by Elice Munerato), Rio de Janeiro: Edições Tempo Brasileiro, Colecção Tempo Universitário, n° 4, 7-29.
R8855/70 *Despacho Relativo ao Relatório n° 8855, sobre o livro Relações Raciais no Império Colonial Português, 1415-1825, da autoria de C.R. Boxer, traduzido por Elice Munerato, publicado no Rio de Janeiro, pelas Edições Tempo Brasileiro em1967, distribuído para leitura, em Portugal, em 26 de Junho de 1970 e recebido na Direcção Geral da Informação dois dias depois.* [duas páginas] [*Dispatch on Report no. 8855 concerning the book Race Relations in the Portuguese Colonial Empire,1415-1825, written by C.R. Boxer, translated by Elice Munerato, published in Rio de Janeiro by Tempo Brasileiro in 1967,*

distributed for reading in Portugal, on 26th June 1970 and delivered to the Direcção Geral de Informação two days later. [two pages].

Secondary Sources

Alden, Dauril (2001) *Charles R. Boxer. An Uncommon Life*, Lisboa: Fundação Oriente.
Alexandre, Valentim (1999) "Luso-Tropicalismo" in António Barreto e Maria Filomena Mónica (eds.) *Dicionário de História de Portugal*, Porto: Figueirinhas, vol. VIII, 391-394.
Barreto, José (1999) "Censura", in António Barreto e Maria Filomena Mónica (eds.), *Dicionário de História de Portugal*, Porto: Figueirinhas, vol. VII, 275-284.
Comissão do Livro Negro sobre o Regime Fascista (1981) *Livros Proibidos no Regime Fascista*, Mira-Sintra/Mem Martins: Gráfica Europam, Lda.
Cortesão, Armando (1962) *Realidades e Desvarios Africanos. Discurso proferido na Sociedade de Geografia de Lisboa quando da Sessão de Encerramento da Semana do Ultramar em 9 de Junho de 1962*, Lisboa: Sociedade de Geografia de Lisboa.
Cummins, J. S. & Rebelo, L. de Sousa (2001) "The Controversy over Charles Boxer's Race Relations in the Portuguese Colonial Empire, 1415-1825", in *Portuguese Studies*. London: University College/King's College, no. 17, 233-246.
Farmer, Gene (1962) "An Exclusive Talk with Portugal's Enigmatic Salazar. Dictator on the Defensive", in *Life*, Chicago: Time Inc., Vol. 52, no. 18, May 4th, 94-95, 98-99, 100B, 102,105-106 and 108.
Freyre, Gilberto (1961) *O Luso e o Trópico. Sugestões em Torno dos Métodos Portugueses de Integração de Povos Autóctones e de Culturas Diferentes da Europeia num Complexo Novo de Civilização: o Luso-Tropical*, Lisboa: Comissão Executiva das Comemorações do Quinto Centenário da Morte do Infante D. Henrique.
Gaspari, Elio (2004) *A Ditadura Envergonhada, a Ditadura Escancarada, a Ditadura Derrotada e a Ditadura Encurralada*, São Paulo: Companhia das Letras.
Moreira, Adriano (1964) *Batalha da Esperança*, Lisboa: Bertrand.
Ramos, Rui (2005) "A Erudição Lusitanista perante a Guerra (c.1960-c.1970): Algumas Observações sobre a Polémica entre Charles Boxer e Armando Cortesão", in Teresa Pinto Coelho (ed.) e John Darwin (preface) *Os Descobrimentos Portugueses no Mundo de Língua*

Inglesa, 1880-1972/ The Portuguese Discoveries in the English-Speaking World, Lisboa: Edições Colibri.

Schwarz, Roberto (1992) "Cultura e política, 1964-1969", in *O Pai de Família e Outros Estudos*, Rio de Janeiro: Editora Paz e Terra/ Secretaria de Estado da Cultura, 61-92.

SHAKESPEARE SURVEILLED BY SALAZAR: ANATOMY OF A STORY OF CENSORSHIP[1]

RUI PINA COELHO,
CENTRO DE ESTUDOS DE TEATRO DA FACULDADE DE LETRAS DE LISBOA/ESCOLA SUPERIOR DE TEATRO E CINEMA, PORTUGAL

Abstract: On the 6th of May 1927, Decree Law 13-564 was published in the *Diário do Governo*, thus marking the creation of the General Inspectorate of Theatres, established to inspect all theatres and public entertainment venues and in some cases preventing the premiere of a play or even banning it outright. During this period (1927-1974), Shakespeare's plays were staged only sporadically in Portuguese theatres (around fifty performances): and the comedies, often simplified or adapted, would predominate. Examining those Shakespeare plays we can observe that only eleven plays were staged and that the absence of the "history plays" is remarkable. Although history plays may not establish a straightforward dialogue with a non-British public, differing from other comedies and tragedies, this paradigm seems to change after Bertolt Brecht's Epic Theatre and especially, after the publication of Jan Kott's *Shakespeare Our Contemporary* (1961). According to these theatrical ideas, Luzia Maria Martins, in 1969, directed an adaptation of *Romeo and Juliet* under the influence of Brecht, in Teatro Estúdio de Lisboa (Studio Theatre of Lisbon), one of the groups least willing to accept the backwardness of theatre in Portugal.

1. Shakespeare surveilled by Salazar

On the 6th of May 1927, Decree Law 13-564 was published in the *Diário do Governo*, thus marking the creation of the "Inspecção Geral dos Teatros" (General Inspectorate of Theatres), established to inspect all

---

[1] I would like to thank my dear colleague Ana Raquel Fernandes for the translation of this article and especially Dr. Patricia Odber de Baubeta for her kind revision and thoughtful suggestions.

theatres and public entertainment venues, later used to serve the purposes of the Portuguese fascist dictator António de Oliveira Salazar (1889-1970).[2] The function of this institution was to inspect and to prohibit any event deemed offensive to the law or public morality, in some cases preventing the premiere of a play or even banning it outright. Although the crisis besetting Portuguese theatre cannot be entirely attributed to this censorship, it is fundamental and becomes the root cause of many future crises. The actor and theatre director Carlos Wallenstein explains this situation in the following terms: "the theatre was suffocated through three processes: what was not done, what was forbidden and what was actually done" (Wallenstein 1982: 9).[3]

What was "not done" were the unwritten plays and the performances that were never staged; what was "forbidden" was keeping up with a Europe about to discover a new theatre and new aesthetic languages. "What was actually done", in almost every case, was outmoded standards, the repetition of overworked formulas and imported repertoires, most of Spanish or French origin. Most common in Portugal were reworkings of successful plays from abroad, adapted to what was called "the Portuguese taste". The plays performed were easily digested dramas or bourgeois comedies that did not pose any questions or allow for any questioning of the *status quo* or prevailing moral values.

During the period when prior censorship was imposed on performances (1927-1974), Shakespeare's plays were staged only sporadically in the Portuguese theatre (around fifty performances),[4] including actual productions of his works and performances where his dramas were transformed into new plays or operas. Thus, exploring the presence of this playwright in our theatres will aid our understanding of the paths followed by Portuguese theatre throughout most of the 20th century.[5]

---

[2] The Portuguese dictatorship began on the 28th May 1926 and lasted until the Carnation Revolution, on the 25th April 1974. Salazar entered the government as Minister of Finances in April 1928 and was appointed Chief of Government in 1932-33. He fell ill in 1968 and was replaced by Marcelo Caetano, who governed until the 25th April 1974.

[3] "A asfixia do teatro realizou-se por três processos: o que não se fez, o que não se permitiu que se fizesse e o que se fez."

[4] For further information on each of these performances, please see the Centre for Theatre Studies' (Lisbon University) database on Portuguese theatre history at www.fl.ul.pt/CETbase/default.htm.

[5] See Graça dos Santos, *O Espectáculo Desvirtuado: O Teatro Português sob o Reinado de Salazar (1933-1968)*. Lisboa: Editorial Caminho, 2004.

To our knowledge, the first performance based on a Shakespeare play and presented in Portugal during this period was the opera *Otello* [*Othello*] by Arrigo Boito/ GiuseppeVerdi, directed by the conductor Angelo Ferrari and performed at the Coliseu dos Recreios in 1929. Indeed, many operas adapted from Shakespeare's plays would be performed in Portugal at the time.[6]

Although at the end of the 19th century and the beginning of the 20th century the major Shakespearian characters were introduced by well-known national actors such as Eduardo Brazão and Ângela Pinto, and international "stars" such as Sarah Bernhardt and Ernesto Rossi, this situation seems to shift from the 1930's onwards. From the predominance of the great tragedies (between 1822 and 1927 *Hamlet* is the most performed play with fifteen different productions, followed by *Othello* with seven), the comedies became more popular (between 1927 and 1974 the most performed play was *A Midsummer Night's Dream*, with five productions).

However, the first theatrical event from this period involving a Shakespeare text rather contradicts my previous statement: it was *Henry V*, performed in 1939 by the prestigious English Old Vic Theatre group, in a European tour led by Lewis Casson and financed by the British Council. (Unfortunately, soon after arriving, the group watched, perplexed and powerless, as their stage scenery was accidentally tipped into the River Tagus). Although *Henry V* is one of the plays most loved by twentieth-century audiences,[7] it was only staged once in Portugal, and never by a Portuguese group.[8] Furthermore, it was the only "history play" to be staged during this period; Shakespearian comedies, often simplified or adapted, would predominate. Examining those Shakespeare plays

---

[6] Operas based on Shakespeare's plays presented in Portugal (1927-1974): *Otello* by Arrigo Boito/GiuseppeVerdi: 1929, 1945, 1952, 1953, 1965 and 1972; *Falstaff* by Arrigo Boito/Giuseppe Verdi: 1946, 1949, 1957 and 1970; *Hamlet* by Michel Carré & Jules Barbier/Ambroise Thomas: 1948; *Giulietta e Romeo* by Arturo Rossato/Ricardo Zandonai: 1956; *Macbeth* by Francesco Maria Piave & Andrea Maffei/Giuseppe Verdi: 1960; *I Capuleti e i Montecchi* by Felix Romani/Vicente Bellini: 1964; *A Midsummer Night's Dream* by Peter Pears/Benjamin Britten: 1964; *Roméo et Juliette* by Jules Barbier & Michel Carré/Charles Gounod: 1966; *The Fairy Queen* by David William: 1968.

[7] See Martin White, *Renaissance Drama in Action: An Introduction to Aspects of Theatre Practice and Performance*. London: Routledge, 1998, p.44.

[8] This play was only staged in 1993, directed by Pedro Wilson with Cénico de Direito, the university group from the Law Faculty (Lisbon).

performed between 1927 and 1974 in Portugal, by Portuguese groups,[9] we can only conclude that there was not any great variety–only eleven plays were staged.

a) *Sonho de Uma Noite de Verão* [*A Midsummer Night's Dream*] was introduced by the Companhia Rey Colaço-Robles Monteiro (the Rey Colaço-Robles Monteiro Company), premiered in July 1941 in an open air performance in the Parque de Palhavã (Palhavã Park, where the Calouste Gulbenkian Foundation is now located), with a cast that included some of the most well-known actors of the time. In 1949, also in a garden, at the British Embassy, the Lisbon Players performed this play, directed by Charles Fyfield. In 1952, the Companhia Rey Colaço-Robles Monteiro staged *A Midsummer Night's Dream* once again. This time it was performed at the Teatro Nacional D. Maria II (National Theatre), directed by Erwin Meyenburg, a regular collaborator of this theatre, who also intended to direct Brecht's *Mãe Coragem e Os Seus Filhos* [*Mother Courage and Her Children*] in Lisbon, between 1955 and 1959. However, this project was condemned to failure because an official ban on the German playwright was not lifted. In 1969, Amélia Rey Colaço also attempted to stage Brecht's *Life of Galileo*. In a letter addressed to Marcelo Caetano, then President of the Council of Ministers [Presidente do Conselho de Ministros], the actress and entrepreneur set out her arguments against censoring Brecht's works:

> The fact that Brecht has become a classic playwright performed worldwide makes the ban that exists in our country almost as unexpected as if, in a republican and democratic country, it were forbidden to stage Shakespeare simply because in his plays the divine right of kings is accepted and exalted. (Santos 1989: 272)[10]

However, the validity of these arguments was not taken into account. *A Midsummer Night's Dream* was performed once more, in 1970, by the

---

[9] Therefore, excluding the performances presented by foreign groups on Portuguese stages, such as: *Twelfth Night* (Oxford Playhouse Company, 1959); *A Midsummer Night's Dream* (The Shakespeare Festival Company, 1964); *The Merchant of Venice* (The Shakespeare Festival Company, 1964); *Twelfth Night* (New Shakespeare Company Limited, 1964); *Othello* (Haileybury College Student Group, 1965); *Hamlet* (Dramatic Group of the University of St Andrews, 1970).

[10] "O facto de Brecht se ter tornado um clássico apresentado em todo o mundo torna a proibição que entre nós o atinge quase tão inesperada como se, num país republicano e democrático, fosse proibido representar Shakespeare com fundamento em que nas suas obras se aceita e por vezes se dignifica a monarquia de direito divino."

Coimbra's University theatre group C.I.T.A.C. (Círculo de Iniciação Teatral da Academia de Coimbra), directed by the Argentinean Juan Carlos Oviedo.

b) *Othello ou o Moiro de Veneza* [*Othello, the Moor of Venice*] was directed by Amélia Rey Colaço and Robles Monteiro in the National Theatre, in 1945. The production made use of stunning visual effects and stage apparatus in order to be able to compete commercially with the cinema. Furthermore, in 1969, Pedro Martins directed Norberto Ávila's adaptation of *Othello* made for the Companhia de Teatro da RTP (Portuguese State Television's own theatre group). Rogério Paulo was the leading actor and the play was broadcast on the 20th of May 1969. Beforehand, however, the play was subjected to censorship, where its moral values were questioned:

> Some cuts (are required) (…), but also the death scenes of Desdemona and Othello should be treated with dignity in order not to upset (this is a mere suggestion) public sensibilities.[11]

c) In 1952, *A Fera Amansada* [*The Taming of the Shrew*] is staged by Virgílio Macieira for the Empresa Vasco Morgado (Vasco Morgado Productions), a company with clear commercial interests. Again, the performance prioritised elaborate costumes and stage settings over a more demanding dramatisation. In 1964, the play was restaged, again by the Empresa Vasco Morgado, but in a new translation, *O Amansar da Fera,* by Luís de Sttau Monteiro, who also directed the play. Finally, in 1971, Ruy de Matos directed *A Fera Amansada* for the amateur theatre group of Plinay/Plessey Automática Eléctrica Portuguesa. Again, the standard was a "light Shakespeare".

d) There were two productions of *Rei Lear* [*King Lear*]: the one directed by Pedro Lemos, in 1969, for Proscenium, an amateur group; a most significant one, in 1955, *Rei Lear* was directed by Francisco Ribeiro for the Teatro do Povo (People's Theatre), the theatrical vehicle for the cultural ideas of António Ferro–Salazar's Minister for National Propaganda. With the dissolution of the group in that same year the play was included in the repertoire of the Teatro Nacional Popular (Popular National Theatre), which succeeded the former. Again, there is a manifest

---

[11] "[São aconselháveis] alguns cortes (...), mas também de que as cenas da morte de Desdémona e de Otello [sejam] tratadas com toda a dignidade e de modo a (por simples sugestão) não ferir a sensibilidade dos espectadores". Record no. 8751 from The Commission for Examining and Classifying Performances' archives (Torre do Tombo/Museu Nacional do Teatro).

desire to simplify or "dumb down". According to his own statements on the programme bill, Francisco Lage's version aimed to reduce dialogue and lighten the play, without changing its structure.

e) In 1957, *Noite de Reis* [*Twelfth Night, or What You Will*] was also performed by Francisco Ribeiro's Teatro Nacional Popular. The adaptation (from a French version) was made by the director himself and Francisco Lage. This play also suffered from the adaptors' attempts to simplify it. To the author and critic Jorge de Sena, what was performed was "a text that we cannot consider as Shakespeare's because all that remains of the author and his thoughts is merely the sequence of the scenes and the immediate meaning of the lines" (Sena 1988: 170).[12] Jorge de Sena found the 1959 performance by the Oxford Playhouse Company, in the Tapada da Ajuda (Ajuda Palace Park), infinitely superior. Although it may not have aroused great enthusiasm, their staging was extremely accurate. According to this critic:

> This marks the difference between an authentic text and a poor literary adaptation; (…) it also shows the difference between a powerful stage presence, characteristic of whoever steps on to an English stage, and our own actors' air of "masked players" whenever they perform the classics. (Sena 1988: 252)[13]

f) Regarding *Tanto Barulho por Nada* [*Much Ado about Nothing*], it was performed on one occasion only, directed by Bessa de Carvalho and broadcasted by RTP (The Portuguese Television) in 1960, within the period when live broadcasts were the norm.

g) *Romeu e Julieta* [*Romeo and Juliet*] was performed by the Companhia Rey Colaço-Robles Monteiro in 1960. Cayetano Luca de Tena directed the play, and João Perry and Teresa Mota featured as the tragic lovers. The play was approved for adults (over 17 years old) with small cuts concerning Mercutio's speech (II.1): "By her fine foot, straight leg and quivering thigh/and the demesnes that there adjacent lie" and also "Now we will sit under a medlar tree/and wish his mistress were that kind of fruit". These examples show an extreme concern with sexual innuendo

---

[12] "um texto que não podemos considerar de Shakespeare, visto que deste, e do seu pensamento na peça, apenas ficaram a sequência das cenas e o sentido imediato das 'deixas'"

[13] "É toda a diferença que vai de um texto autêntico a uma adaptação sem categoria alguma de ordem literária; (...) de uma presença em cena, que é apanágio de quem pisa um palco em Inglaterra, ao ar de 'mascarados' que os nossos actores têm quase sempre quando representam clássicos."

and a lesser concern with ideological issues. The amateur group from Sociedade de Instrução Tavaredense also performed this Shakespearean tragedy in 1964, the year of the celebrations of the IV Centenary of Shakespeare's birth.

h) In 1963, *O Mercador de Veneza* [*The Merchant of Venice*] is directed by António Manuel Couto Viana in his Companhia Nacional de Teatro (National Theatre Company). Goulart Nogueira's translation also undergoes some changes, in order to "lighten" the text and underline its farcical aspects.

i) Nevertheless, this concern with adapting and simplifying Shakespeare's plays bears no comparison with Luiz Francisco Rebello's free adaptation of *Measure for Measure*, *Dente por Dente* (the title echoes the proverb "an eye for an eye, a tooth for a tooth"), directed by António Pedro for the Teatro Moderno de Lisboa (Modern Theatre of Lisbon), and marked by a clear Brechtian verve.

j) After successive performances at the beginning of the century, *Hamlet* was only staged once in Coimbra, in 1971, by the T.E.U.C. (Teatro dos Estudantes da Universidade de Coimbra) in a performance directed by Carlos Cabral. More than a production of a text by Shakespeare, this last play was a particular reading of *Hamlet*, in which the idea that the "need to act against an unjust order" (Porto 1973: 265) was emphasised. Such freedom was only allowed to university theatre groups since they would only reach very limited audiences.

l) *Macbeth*, for its part, was performed in 1956 by the most long-lived experimental Portuguese group, the Teatro Experimental do Porto (Experimental Theatre of Oporto). António Pedro was the director and João Guedes, at that time an amateur actor, played the main role. This performance clearly echoes some European aesthetic references (such as those of Gordon Craig or Adolphe Appia) and it inaugurates the Teatro de Algibeira (the future Teatro de Bolso), a small, intimate venue, where the search for scenic simplicity and intimacy was possible. The "experimental movement" developed by amateurs was to have an enormous impact on the professional theatre. Many actors trained in these experimental groups would later become part of the professional ones, making their contribution to the longed for renewal of Portuguese theatre. A good example is *A Tragédia de Macbeth*, by the Companhia Rey Colaço-Robles Monteiro. The play was directed by Michael Benthall, who had been specially invited to Lisbon in order to direct this performance in 1964. The protagonist was the experimental actor João Guedes and there were other actors from experimental groups, including Varela Silva, Dario de Barros, Canto e Castro, Gina Santos and Cecília Guimarães.

A Tragédia de Macbeth, whose premiere was anxiously awaited, was also part of the celebrations of the IV Centenary of Shakespeare's birth, promoted by the Calouste Gulbenkian Foundation. After the premiere the general opinion was that at last a performance had been staged in Portugal that truly did justice to its author. However, an important landmark in the run of this play was the fire that reduced the Teatro Nacional D. Maria II to ashes during the night of 1st December 1964. After this tragic incident, the Companhia Rey Colaço-Robles Monteiro performed at the Coliseu dos Recreios without costumes or stage sets, in what became known as a unique moment in the history of 20th-century Portuguese theatre.

Juan Carlos Oviedo also directed *Macbeth* in a production entitled *Macbeth–Que se Passa na Tua Cabeça?* [*Macbeth–What's Going Through Your Mind?*]. This transgressive and provocative production by C.I.T.A.C. challenged the law and public morality, drawing the attention of PIDE (the political police) and would cause several rifts within the group. Indeed, C.I.T.A.C. ceased its activities and only resumed its performances again after the 25th April 1974, date of the Carnation Revolution, when democracy was restored.

2. *Anatomia de Uma História de Amor* [*Anatomy of a Love Story*], by Luzia Maria Martins (Teatro Estúdio de Lisboa, 1969)

Throughout this brief overview of Shakespeare's performances between 1927 and 1974, when public performances where object of censorship, the absence of the "history plays" is quite remarkable: with the exception of *Henry V* (Old Vic, 1939), the public reading of excerpts from *Richard III*, *Henry V* and *Henry IV* performed by The New Shakespeare Festival Company in 1964, there are no records of any other performance. Also in 1964 the Teatro do Ateneu de Coimbra sought permission to play *Julius Caesar* (*Júlio César*), but the Comissão de Exame e Classificação de Espectáculos (The Commission for Examining and Classifying Performances) banned it, using a rather paradoxical argument: "This play (…) could only be authorised after severe cuts. It is commonly agreed that texts by authors such as the present one should not suffer cuts".[14]

---

[14] "Esta peça [...] só poderá ser aprovada com inúmeros cortes. Considera-se pouco conveniente fazer cortes em textos de autores como este". Record no. 7620 from The Commission for Examining and Classifying Performances' archives (Torre do Tombo/Museu Nacional do Teatro).

Dennis Kennedy in his essay *"Shakespeare: Histories and Nations"* explains: "Shakespeare's history plays have been taken as a grand epic of the English Theatre, especially in the period after World War II when they were performed in marathon cycles in the English Theatre. As a group, these works investigate and question the meaning of authority, kingship, and nation in an unparallel way" (Kennedy 2005: 319). Although Kennedy recognizes that these plays do not establish a straightforward dialogue with a non-British public, differing from other comedies and tragedies, he argues that this paradigm alters with Bertolt Brecht's Epic Theatre and especially, after publication of Jan Kott's *Shakespeare Our Contemporary* (1961): "A wide European re-evaluation of Shakespeare followed in Kott's wake, and he and Brecht continued to affect Shakespeare production in general well into the 1980s" (Kennedy 2005: 324).

Following on precisely these theatrical ideas, Luzia Maria Martins, an actress and a director, adapted and directed not a history play but rather an adaptation of *Romeo and Juliet* in T.E.L. (Teatro Estúdio de Lisboa) (Studio Theatre of Lisbon), one of the groups least willing to accept the backwardness of theatre in Portugal. Luzia Maria Martins, a former drama student in London an a BBC collaborator, had a significant role in the staging and translation of modern British authors in Portugal such as Peter Barnes, Thornton Wilder, Peter Shaffer, Alan Bennet, Maxwell Anderson, David Storey, Peter Gill, Terence Rattigan, Ted Willis, Edward Bond, Michael O'Neill, Jerry Seabrook, Arnold Wesker, John Osborne and Robert Bolt.

In the same year as Amélia Rey Colaço wrote to Marcelo Caetano explaining that the prohibition of Brecht was simply anachronistic, *Anatomia de Uma História de Amor [Anatomy of a Love Story]* premiered in Teatro Vasco Santana (next door to the Popular Fair of Lisbon) on the 17th April 1969. In this play, an adaptation made under the influence of Brecht, a young Filipe La Féria (nowadays a well-known director) played Romeo while Margarida Mauperrin took the role of Juliet.

On the programme bill, Luzia Maria Martins could not have been more explicit:

> *Anatomia de Uma História de Amor*, which is based on various texts by Shakespeare, is a performance of epic or narrative theatre (...) We decided to debate several problems and in order to awaken general interest, we needed a myth, since myths are the expression of a collective feeling which shapes them and makes them true.[15]

---

[15] *"Anatomia de Uma História de Amor*, que se baseia em vários textos de Shakespeare, é um espectáculo de teatro épico ou narrativo (...) Quisemos debater

Classified and approved as a comedy for audiences over 12 years old, the play received the following comment from one of its censors:

> The historical interest of this comedy is, from my point of view, none. Any decision to grant subsidies (should they exist) to the theatre group performing the play should be given careful consideration.[16]

As far as cuts are concerned, at least one reflects the same concern with decorum already mentioned on other occasions. When the Nurse repeats to one of the servants a comment made by her husband concerning a fall of Juliet when a child:

> 'There, there' –he said – 'So you fall face downwards? When you grow up and begin to look at your shadow, you'll learn to fall always on your back, won't you?' And the silly girl started giggling and said 'Yes!' (Martins 1969)[17]

The entire excerpt has been censored, based again on sexual innuendos. However, another cut demonstrates closer attention to the ideological content of the text. Thus, the following speech is censored:

> Like the axiom of a universal objectivity – that instinct remained fully active, marked by words or ideologies that redeem the troubled conscience or set free the much vaunted 'moral responsibility' of Mankind. (Martins 1969)[18]

Still, what gave the censors most cause for concern were the video projections that were part of the performance: the group wished to show a film about the events of May'68. The Censoring Commission would only

---

vários problemas e, para os fazermos num plano de interesse geral, necessitávamos de um mito, já que os mitos são a expressão de um sentir colectivo que lhes dá forma e realidade."

[16] "O interesse histórico desta comédia é, a meu ver, nulo – devendo considerar-se se valerá a pena conceder subsídios (supondo que existam) à companhia teatral que a leva à cena." Record no. 8830 from The Commission for Examining and Classifying Performances' archives (Torre do Tombo/Museu Nacional do Teatro).

[17] "'Então, então' – disse ele – 'Então cai-se de bruços? Quando fores mais velhinha e começares a olhar para a sombra, vais aprender a cair sempre de costas, não é?' E a patetinha começou a rir e disse 'sim!'"

[18] "Como axioma de uma objectividade de carácter universal – esse instinto manteve-se em plena actividade, marcado por palavras ou ideologias redentoras da intranquilidade da consciência ou libertadoras da apregoada 'responsabilidade moral' do Homem."

allow the film to be screened after its most "subversive" or "tendentious" parts had been cut, and the final editing was the responsibility of the agents themselves. The censorship of another film that was also part of the show prepared by Luzia Maria Martins was, again, due to the issue of public morality: the scene in which Romeo and Juliet roll in the grass had to be censored.

The marks of Brecht are far more obvious than the video projections. The antagonism between social classes is also present in the play acted by the T.E.L., underlining the relevance of Shakespeare to contemporary society. After Mercutio's death and Romeo's exile, a Woman (W) comments: "I do not pity these two. They've fought for life as fiercely as we fight for our daily bread". And a Man (M) answers:

> M: There are certain things a man cannot avoid. If provoked... / W: And what do you do when someone provokes you? / M: Nothing. What could I do? I don't have enough status to take offence. But as those people are different, they have their own principles. (Martins 1969)[19]

In *Anatomy of a Love Story*, the Shakespearian characters not only share a space with these anonymous figures (a Man, a Woman) but also, and more importantly, with the figures named just as Actor and Actress. It is through these characters that the purpose of the work becomes clear. At the very beginning, one of the actresses states:

> ACTRESS: This play was born of doubt and doubt is the mother of the good and bad thoughts that control us. Only certainties can erase thoughts. /ACTOR: We are alive, we think and we have doubts (...) /ACTRESS: We all know the story of Romeo and Juliet. We all discuss it, we all say we have understood it and thus all of us or almost all file it away in the mental archive of things already catalogued or dead. /ACTOR- But Theatre does not accept dead concepts (...) /ACTOR: A bold idea is born: let us discuss our doubts in public and with the public... (...) / ACTOR: This will be our play: a naked stage, without decoration, but brimming with suggestions. ACTOR: Enough, enough! We are wearying the audience. For Theatre to happen it is better if we try to do it! (Martins 1969)[20]

---

[19] "H: Há coisas que um homem não pode evitar. Se o provocam... / M: E o que é que tu fazes quando te provocam? / H: Nada. Que posso eu fazer? Nem sequer tenho categoria para me sentir ofendido. Mas com essa gente é diferente, têm os seus princípios.

[20] ACTRIZ: Este espectáculo nasceu de uma dúvida, e a dúvida é a mãe dos pensamentos, bons e maus, que nos dominam. Só as certezas apagam os pensamentos. / ACTOR: Estamos vivos, pensamos e temos dúvidas.(...) /ACTRIZ: Todos conhecemos a história de Romeu e Julieta, todos a discutimos, todos

And when announcing the story of Romeo and Juliet:

> ACTRESS: And so the story begins, one which tells us about the hatred between two families of the upper class of Verona: the Montagues and the Capulets. But what is the reason for this hatred, this destructive feeling, which is after all one of the two main characters? Let us try to answer this question. What is the main axis of "Romeo e Juliet?" Love or hate? / ACTRESS: Through our and Your imagination, let us try to recreate in the words of William Shakespeare as well as other words of ours, no doubt more limited, the atmosphere of frustration that like a cancer pervaded the air of that beautiful city, a place inhabited by strange resentments, as pitiful as they are vain. (Martins 1969)[21]

As far as Shakespeare's *Romeo and Juliet* is concerned, it is regarded as an example or as offering a set of arguments that help the group to present their objectives. Near the end of the play, an Actor declares once more:

> Up to now we have tried to analyse in our own way the consequences of a situation that in our eyes reflects a flawed social structure"/ (...) But what do we know of these things? We are only a group of actors interested in that mystery that unites us, which is life. (Martins 1969)[22]

---

dizemos tê-la compreendido e, portanto, todos ou quase todos a arrumamos no arquivo mental das coisas catalogadas e mortas. / ACTOR: Mas o Teatro não aceita conceitos mortos. (...) / ACTOR: Daí nasceu uma ideia peregrina: vamos discutir em público, e com o público, as nossas dúvidas.... (...) /ACTOR: Será este o nosso espectáculo: um palco despido de ornamentos, mas grávido de sugestões. / ACTOR: Basta, basta! Estamos a fatigar aqueles Senhores. Para que aconteça Teatro é melhor que tentemos fazer teatro!"

[21] "ACTRIZ: Assim começa a história, a história que nos fala do ódio existente entre duas famílias das classes privilegiadas veronesas: a dos Montéquios e a dos Capuletos. Mas, porquê esse ódio, esse sentimento de destruição que é, afinal uma das duas personagens dominantes? Tentemos responder a esta dúvida. Qual é o eixo principal de *Romeu e Julieta*? O amor ou o ódio?" / ACTRIZ: Tentemos, pela nossa e Vossa imaginação, recriar, por palavras de William. Shakespeare, e por outras, bem mais limitadas, da nossa lavra, o ambiente de frustração que, como um cancro, dissipava o ar dessa cidade tão bela, habitada por estranhos rancores tão lamentáveis, quanto inúteis"

[22] "Até aqui, procurámos analisar, à nossa maneira, o rescaldo de uma situação que, a nossos olhos, reflecte uma estrutura social errada" / (...) Mas, que sabemos nós dessas coisas? Somos apenas um grupo de actores interessados neste mistério que nos torna irmãos e que é a vida."

More than "the anatomy of a love story", the play *Anatomia de Uma História de Amor* depicts the anatomy of a particular moment in the history of Portugal. Generally speaking, critics recognise and praise the influence of Brecht in the play. Manuela de Azevedo mentions that:

> in the première, when the cart of the group of the itinerant actors appeared on stage the public burst into applause, thrilled with the idea of another theatre, that of Brecht and Lorca's, who knows? (Azevedo 1969)[23]

However, it was Carlos Porto who saw in *Anatomia*: "something new in respect of what we are used to seeing here" [algo novo em relação àquilo que estamos habituados a ver aqui]; which deserved to "be seen, seen again, either applauded or contested, it deserves to be discussed" [ser visto, revisto, aplaudido ou pateado, discutido] (Porto 1974: 98).

Here, then, the introduction to Epic Theatre and to political theatre was made under the veil of Shakespeare's *Romeo and Juliet*. The analysis of the social conflicts involved in the play was the determining dramaturgical key. Well reputed as a timeless classic and as an author who provided good audiences, Shakespeare provided a fertile field in which to experiment with provocative readings. Shakespeare's Portuguese canon evolved from light approaches, mainly through his comedies, underlining the farcical aspects, into new readings where History, the City and Men became more and more appealing.

If one considers, like the theatre director Artur Ramos, that "Shakespeare (...) acts like a thermometer, revealing the health or illness of the theatrical body to which it is applied" [Shakespeare (...) funciona como um termómetro, revelador da saúde ou doença do organismo teatral a que se aplica] (Ramos 1964: 28), one will inevitably reach the conclusion that the overwhelming preference for a comic or farcical Shakespeare, usually dumbed down, together with the lack of contemporary readings of Shakespeare's plays, is symptomatic of the sickness afflicting the theatre in Portugal at the time. These were also signs of the need for a renewal and updating of Portuguese theatre which was felt with increasing intensity as the years passed, until the winds of April began to blow.

---

[23] "na estreia, quando entrou em cena a carroça da companhia dos actores ambulantes, o público aplaudiu vibrantemente a imagem de um outro teatro, o de Brecht e o de Lorca, quem sabe?"

References

Azevedo, Manuela de (1969) "Anatomia de Uma História de Amor", in *Diário de Notícias*, 19-4-1969.
Kennedy, Dennis (2005) "Shakespeare: Histories and Nations", in *European Review*, vol. 13, nº 3, 319-326.
Martins, Luzia Maria (1969) *Anatomia de Uma História de Amor*, Record nº 8830 from The Commission for Examining and Classifying Performances' Archives (Torre do Tombo/ Museu Nacional do Teatro) [typescript].
—. (1973) *Anatomia de Uma História de Amor*, Lisboa: Prelo.
Porto, Carlos (1973) *Em Busca do Teatro Perdido*, vol.1., Lisboa: Plátano.
—. (1974) *Em Busca do Teatro Perdido*, vol. 2, Lisboa: Plátano.
Ramos, Artur (1964) "Macbeth e Dente por Dente: dois bons espectáculos Gulbenkio-shakespearianos–uma mesma insatisfação", in *Seara Nova*, Janeiro, p. 28.
Santos, Vítor Pavão dos (ed.) (1989) *A Companhia Rey Colaço/Robes Monteiro (1921-1974)–Correspondência*, Lisboa: Museu Nacional do Teatro.
Sena, Jorge de (1988) *Do Teatro em Portugal*, Lisboa: Edições 70.
Wallenstein, Carlos (1982) "Portugal Anos 40–Teatro", in *Arte Portuguesa Anos 40*, Lisboa: Fundação Calouste Gulbenkian, 9-15.

Shakespeare and the Censors: Translation and Performance Strategies under the Portuguese Dictatorship

Fran Rayner,
Universidade do Minho, Portugal

Abstract: This chapter argues that productions of Shakespeare under the Salazar dictatorship reveal something of the inconsistency and awkwardness of the censorship regime. Censors remained unsure of how to appropriate Shakespeare's international prestige without also endorsing some of his more radical ideas. The paper analyses two translations used for specific performances that illustrate something of this inconsistency: Luiz Francisco Rebello's *Dente por Dente* (*Measure for Measure*), performed by the Teatro Moderno de Lisboa in 1964 and published in the same year and Luís de Sttau Monteiro's *O Amansar da Fera* (*The Taming of the Shrew*), performed under the auspices of the empresario Vasco Morgado at the Teatro Monumental in 1964 but only published in 1967. At first glance, the former would seem to be the more controversial production and the latter the more acceptable to the regime. However, it was the latter that was subject to minor censorship on moral grounds.

The paper stresses the importance of ambiguity as a resource for translators and performers during this period and argues that translation and performance scholars should work together in order to recover a fuller understanding of the mechanisms of censorship during this period.

In a sense, both theatre and translation start with the death of the author.
—Sirkku Aaltonen

1. Working together: Translation and Performance Studies

The affirmation by Sirkku Aaltonen above suggests a useful starting point for joint work in Translation and Performance Studies, in the sense that both areas have challenged the hegemony of the authorial text and its casting of translation and performance as derivative forms. Beyond this, there are other significant parallels between the two fields. Both have strong interdisciplinary roots, which have included work done in each other's fields. Both position themselves clearly as intercultural disciplines and have foregrounded the intercultural as a unit of analysis. Moreover, there are methodological similarities in recent work by translation and performance scholars, with a turn towards cultural studies influencing both. Ton Hoesenlaars (Hoesenlaars 2004:87) has noted "the increasing readiness to view Shakespearean translations more as instances of intricate cultural appropriations than as objects for allegedly neutral, descriptive analysis" and this movement from the descriptive to the analytical has also informed more recent work on Shakespearean performance.[1]

It is particularly important that translation and performance scholars work together to look at the question of censorship under the Portuguese dictatorship. On a basic level, this is because separate mechanisms operated for text and performance. The anxiety that attended waiting at a distance to see if a text had been passed by the censors was related to, but also different from, the anxiety of performing in front of a figure in the dark, following the text with a flashlight. Moreover, different strategies were developed by theatre practitioners to deal with textual and performance censorship. The ability to use a gesture or facial expression to transmit a knowing wink to the audience would not be available to the translator except as a latent possibility in the text. On the other hand, the ability to publish a revised and extended version of the text after the performance would not be available to practitioners involved in the necessarily ephemeral performative experience. In order, therefore, to recover a fuller understanding of a particular theatrical event under the dictatorship, excavation work by both translation and performance scholars is essential

2. Shakespeare and the Salazar regime

The Salazar regime has been characterized as inherently anti-theatrical. Graça dos Santos (Santos 2004: 109) notes that "the consistently negative references to the characteristics of theatre functioned, by contrast, as a

---

[1] An excellent example of such an analytical approach to performance is Sonia Massai's *World-Wide Shakespeares: Local Appropriations in Film and Performance* (London & New York: Routledge, 2005). Massai's introduction to the collection is particularly useful in its exploration of how Bourdieu's notion of the cultural field can be applied to analysis of performance.

means of highlighting the defining characteristics of Salazarism" [(p)ela negativa, aparecem referências constantes às características do teatro, para melhor realçar as características do regime]. The most visible manifestation of this anti-theatricalism was the complex bureaucracy of censorship of theatre texts and performances that not only marginalized some of the major writers and theatre practitioners of the period, but also made the work of those who did continue to work in the theatre precarious and often impossible.

Translations and performances of Shakespeare were included within this process somewhat awkwardly, with the censors unsure how to reclaim Shakespeare as one of their own without at the same time spreading potentially subversive ideas. Strategies ranged from outright censorship of politically sensitive plays like *Julius Caesar* on the paradoxical grounds that it could only be approved with innumerable cuts and it was inappropriate to cut texts by authors such as Shakespeare, to semi-paternalism in the case of *Romeo and Juliet*, which could only be seen by audiences over 16, to minor, often paranoid, modifications to the texts, invariably on political or moral grounds.[2] The two translations analysed in this paper were chosen primarily because, as translations written for particular performances of the plays, they provide fertile ground for analysis of intersections between translation and performance, but also because they illustrate the inconsistency of the censorship regime in relation to Shakespeare. The first, Luiz Francisco Rebello's translation of *Dente por Dente* [*Measure for Measure*], was performed by the Teatro Moderno de Lisboa (henceforth T.M.L.) in 1964 and published in the same year. It presents impeccably radical credentials, both in terms of the play's content and in its introductory reference to the theatrical techniques of Bertolt Brecht. However, it was performed without censorship of any kind, apart from the fact that only those over the age of 17 were allowed to see it.[3] Was this because the censors simply did not notice its radicalism or were there other reasons for letting it pass? The second, Luís de Sttau Monteiro's *O Amansar da Fera* [*The Taming of the Shrew*], was also

---

[2] The censorship record for *Julius Caesar* is 7620 at the Arquivos Nacionais do Torre do Tombo. My thanks to Rui Pina Coelho for sharing with me his research on the censorship of Shakespeare during this period. Censorship records can be consulted at the Torre do Tombo and the Museu Nacional do Teatro, both in Lisbon. However, records in both collections seem somewhat arbitrary and incomplete, and the two collections contain different records, which complicates any general statement about the censorship of Shakespeare in this period.

[3] The significance of this age limitation should not, however, be underestimated in a context where political radicalism was particularly strong among young people.

performed in 1964, but only published three years later. In this case, what seems to be exactly the sort of politically retrograde play the censors would favour was subject to minor contextual censorship. Why might the censors have felt it necessary to censor the text? And how did a writer of more radical theatre plays like Sttau Monteiro negotiate the unpalatable sexual politics of the text and the commercial context of the production?

3. Luiz Francisco Rebello's *Dente por Dente* (1964)

As the biography of their actress and treasurer, Carmen Dolores, makes clear, the work of the T.M.L. was followed closely throughout its brief existence. Many of its theatrical projects were either banned outright or heavily censored and the company's emphasis on artistic autonomy and creative collaboration set them apart from other artistic projects of the period.[4] Such independence is reflected in their choice of the dark comedy of *Measure for Measure*, rather than the more palatable Shakespearean comedies or the individual focus of the tragedies. The play had not been performed previously in Portugal and was therefore a courageous choice for this quite unique company. Yet 1964 was also the quartercentenary of Shakespeare's birth. This context of celebration helps to explain why the censors may have looked more favourably on the production than in other years, as well as why financial support was more forthcoming from the Gulbenkian foundation for this particular season. The enhanced status of Shakespeare in this year undoubtedly contributed to a sense of special treatment for this theatrical project quite unlike the normal reaction to the T.M.L. repertoire.

This performance context helps to situate more clearly a negotiation between tradition and modernity that characterized the translation and other elements of the production. The slogan used to advertise the play, "teatro de sempre para homens de hoje" [theatre of all time for men of today] is indicative of the centrality of this negotiation to the production. On the one hand, both the translator Rebello and the director of the production, António Pedro, lean very clearly towards modernity. The general title of the series in which Rebello's translation appears, "Repertório para um teatro actual" [Repertoire for a contemporary theatre], illustrates its author's modernising intention. This is also signalled in the Preface, where Rebello writes of the play's "very modern ambiguity in the behaviour of its characters" [tão moderna ambiguidade no

---

[4] See Carmen Dolores, *Retrato Inacabado: Memórias,* (O Jornal: Lisboa, 1984), pp. 140-41.

comportamento das suas personagens] (Rebello 1964: 7). António Pedro (T.M.L. programme 1964) also writes in the production programme of his desire that the play not be "an archaic reconstitution" [uma reconstituição arcaisante]. Yet this privileging of modernity seems to have unevenly inflected the production itself. The biography of the actor Fernando Gusmão describes the production as:

> pleasing in its subtle mixture of scenes of almost balletic lightness with others of great dramatic tension. Certainly here and there there was a certain imbalance in the performance styles of the actors. However, this was countered by the speed of the scenes and the costumes, which were a visual feast. It was also a success for Carmen Dolores, Rogério Paulo and particularly Rui de Carvalho. (Gusmão 1993: 168)[5]

Such a description emphasizes the continuing importance of a long-standing tradition of Shakespearean performance based on individual star performances and elaborate visual effects. This suggests that the modernizing view of Shakespeare promoted by the translation and the director was only imperfectly present in performance.

Rebello makes it clear that his translation is a free adaptation of the play. He adds that a literal translation "would be difficult to reconcile with the undoubtedly practical demands of a contemporary performance of Shakespeare's text" (Rebello 1964: 9).[6] There is a sense here that changes were made to the text in order to make it performable in a contemporary setting and to avoid unnecessary archaisms. Yet the director of a later production of the play, Mário Barradas, has argued that Rebello had to considerably "sweeten" [adoçar] his translation in order that it pass the censors (Barradas 2002: 8). This suggests that the changes involved a degree of self-censorship on the part of the translator.[7] How might

---

[5] "agradava pela subtil mistura de cenas de leveza balética com outras de contenção dramática. É certo que havia aqui e ali um certo tipo de desequilíbrio no estilo de representação por parte dos actores, compensado, porém, pela alacridade dos cenários e guarda-roupa, que constituíam uma festa visual. Foi também um êxito para a Carmen Dolores, para o Rogério Paulo e, especialmente, para o Rui de Carvalho."

[6] "dificilmente se acomodaria às exigências práticas irrecusáveis de uma realização cénica actual do texto de Shakespeare"

[7] It is worth stressing that this is a passing comment made by Barradas in his review of a contemporary translation of the play by Manuel Gomes da Torre. Barradas produces no evidence for this claim of self-censorship on the part of Rebello and no other theatre practitioner or critic has made a similar claim. My own perspective is that the need to create a translation that was performable was

Rebello's desire to make the play performable on stage have intersected with the need for a translation that would pass the censors?

There is one particular site where such tensions cluster, namely the use of songs within the translation. Rebello includes nine songs which explore the themes of justice, order, hypocrisy and freedom and which were set to music by António Vitorino de Almeida for the performances. In the Preface to the translation, Rebello alludes specifically to the influence of Brechtian techniques on his decision to include the songs. For Rebello, they are ways in which a performance should "take a position in relation to the themes treated on stage" [tomar posição acerca dos temas tratados em cena] (Rebello 1964: 10). Yet if the songs have a clear political purpose and theatrical reference point, they also form part of Rebello's strategy to make the play performable, for the sections of the text that the songs replace would have meant little to a contemporary audience for the play.[8] It is also true that the fact that some of the play's more difficult themes are explored in song rather than the spoken word could be seen as a form of "sweetening" designed to help the text pass the censors, for the songs occupy a contingent rather than a central relationship to the rest of the text. I include two songs here which focus these contradictions.

The first is a song by the Duke, here disguised as a friar, as he contemplates the social chaos he himself has helped to create:

Duque:
Procurei pela virtude,
Ninguém me soube dizer
Onde era o seu paradeiro.
Eu vi a honra ceder
O seu lugar por dinheiro
Vi a mentira ostentar
da verdade as aparências,
para melhor conquistar
as almas e as consciências.

Vi o poder instalado

---

uppermost in the translator's mind, but that this coincided with a felt sense that certain words, events and characters would be more acceptable to the censors than others.

[8] The early section of the play where dissolute gentlemen discuss the effects of war and poverty on clients at Mistress Overdone's brothel, for example, is riddled with humour that would have been inaccessible to contemporary audiences, whereas the song of Mistress Overdone included here manages to make the same political points as the original Shakespearean text without reproducing its inaccessibility.

Nas cadeiras da justiça,
E em seu trono, lado ao lado
o arbítrio e a cobiça.

Vi em todas as cidades
o pecado ser fecundo
ser estéril a bondade.
São estas as novidades,
tão antigas quanto o mundo.

[Duke
I searched for virtue,
none could tell
where they hid it.
I saw honour sell
its place for profit.

I saw lies acquire
the appearance of truth,
to better o'erpower
the conscience of youth.

I saw power installed
in the seat of justice,
and in thrones so tall
greed and cowardice.

I saw in all cities
sin take hold
goodness pitied.
News as old,
as the world itself.]

(my adaptation from the Portuguese)

Behind the words of this "Duke of dark corners", one can almost see the shadowy figure of Salazar himself, shying away from society to spy on the sins of his people. Yet unlike Salazar, the words invoke a corruption that is simultaneously moral *and* political, especially in the reference to the abuse of justice by those in power (Vi o poder instalado/ Nas cadeiras da justiça). The temporal ambiguity of "São estas as novidades/ tão antigas quanto o mundo" enables the song to avoid censorship by appearing to affirm universal moral truths, yet also evoke a contemporary reality where the world described by the Duke bears something of a resemblance to Portugal under Salazar.

A second example is the song by D. Serôdia [Mistress Overdone], the prostitutes' Madam who manages to survive the hostility of Angelo's prurient regime through judicious payouts to chosen officials:

Dona Serôdia
Quem se dedica ao comércio
depende da clientela;
tem de saber conservá-la,
não pode viver sem ela.

Mas quantos p'rigos espreitam
o honrado comerciante
que contra marés e ventos
quer levar o barco avante!
A guerra extermina,
a força arrebata,
a doença arruína,
a miséria mata.
Cruéis, inclementes,
com dura insistência,
roubam-me os clientes,
e eu abro falência.

[Mistress Overdone
Those who set up in business
depend on their clients;
must accept the riskiness
can't live without 'em.

But how many perils avail
the honourable trader
who attempts to set sail
whatever the weather!

War exterminates,
force destroys,
sickness eliminates,
poverty kills.

Cruel, defiant,
ever unfeeling,
they steal my clients
and leave me with nothing.]

(my adaptation from the Portuguese)

The song places a clear emphasis on prostitution not as an individual moral failing, but as a business, and one affected by social vicissitudes like poverty and war at that. However, this insurgency of a socially-aware transgressive female voice is temporary. Rebello's translation focuses on the main plot of the play in order not to confuse audiences with its minor strands, and therefore gives much more attention to Isabella, the novice, and Mariana, the spurned fiancée. In this, Rebello is simply telescoping the priorities of the Shakespearean text. However, it is also true that the decision to privilege morally virtuous female characters would also have been more acceptable to the censors.

4. Luís de Sttau Monteiro's *O Amansar da Fera* (1967)

According to Diana Henderson (Henderson 1997), interest in *The Taming of the Shrew* tends to intensify at times of backlash against women and the play is often used to fuel a nostalgic fantasy of fixed gender roles. Each production struggles to perform the play as a comedy because it demands that we find amusing the enforced transformation of a strong female character, Katherina, into a submissive wife. The final two shared lines of the Sttau Monteiro translation of the play "the shrew is tamed/ and peace now gained" [A fera está amansada/e a guerra terminada] encapsulate the way in which the happy end of the play depends on the subjection of women (Sttau Monteiro 1967: 163).[9] Performance of the play at the commercially-oriented Teatro Monumental under the auspices of the empresario Vasco Morgado indicates a similar linkage between commercial success and gender conformity.

However, both the censors and Sttau Monteiro isolate a section of the play which seems to complicate such a reading. Before the play begins, there are two scenes known as the Induction, where an aristocrat decides to trick the drunken, lower class Christopher Sly into believing he is a lord. Sly wakes up in an elegantly furnished room where he is told that he has been asleep for a number of years and that his wife wishes to visit him. A troupe of passing actors are then announced and the play proper begins. The fact that the wife in the Induction is played by the Lord's male servant, with the overtones of homosexuality this implies, obviously worried the censors, for Sly's invitation to his fe/male companion to get

---

[9] It is worth pointing out that while the title of this production was *O Amansar da Fera* (*The Taming of the Shrew*), which suggests a process that is not completed, the title of the previous 1952 production of the play, also under the auspices of Vasco Morgado, was *A Fera Amansada* (*The Shrew Tamed*) which emphasizes closure more strongly.

undressed and come to bed is censored in the version of the text presented for performance.[10] This is part of a wider moralistic strategy on the part of the censors, who also demanded that Gremio's later reference to finding someone to get Katherina into bed be removed.

Even though both of these cuts are restored in the published translation, Sttau Monteiro still devotes considerable attention to the Induction in the Preface. Indeed, he labels it "a most memorable scene" [a cena mais notável] (Sttau Monteiro 1967: 56). He adds, however, that an earlier production by Gino Saviotti showed that removing the Induction was popular with both audiences and critics, while performances which included the Induction were not. One critic even claimed it could not have been written by Shakespeare. The question then is why the Induction is the focus of so much controversy. One reason is suggested by the interventions of the censors. In a play which invests heavily in re-establishing gender roles, the idea that such roles are performative rather than essential, and that a boy might easily be mistaken for a woman induces anxiety. It should also be added that the considerable *social* role playing in this scene might have been similarly distasteful to the regime.

Yet Sttau Monteiro's insistence on the importance of the Induction provides another clue to its significance. He suggests that the Induction establishes the play that follows as a moral lesson to Christopher Sly on the importance of an obedient wife (Sttau Monteiro 1967: 56). However, he also notes that there is no parallel framing device at the end of the play where Sly draws such a lesson. What this absence implies, therefore, is the *impossibility* of creating an obedient wife in real life. This casts Katherina's final gesture in the play, when she kneels in obedience to her husband, as little more than sexual wish-fulfilment, a performance of obedience that in no way represents a final word on the subject. The Katherina here is no more the definitive Katherina than the firebrand at the beginning of the play. This inability to pin down the female protagonist with any certainty is actually drawn attention to throughout the translation, for she is sometimes given the English name Kate, but also the Portuguese name Catarina and there are even intercultural combinations like Katarina. In this sense, through pointing to the significance of the Induction in its Preface, the translation that is published three years after performance complicates the linkage between fixed gender roles and closure of the play in a way that the commercial context of the production probably did not.

---

[10] From the censor's record no. 7507. My thanks to Rui Pina Coelho once again for making this record available to me.

However, I would not want to overstate this reading as much of the sexual politics of the play remain intact in the published translation.

5. Modernizing Shakespeare

These examples do not disprove the general thesis that censorship during this period had major implications for theatrical practice, nor that the decade witnessed significant attempts to modernize Portuguese theatrical repertoires, but they do complicate them. In both these areas, productions of Shakespeare were marginal. They received only selective attention from the censors and companies who were committed to renewal were more interested in performing contemporary plays by national playwrights. However, productions of Shakespeare do illustrate that the bureaucracy of censorship in this period, although brutal, was also incoherent and awkward. Lacking, in the main, any real experience or knowledge of theatrical practice, the censors tended to react dogmatically to key references and let pass potentially inflammatory material when it was ambiguously worded. Translators and performers developed particular strategies to deal with such censorship. Ambiguity seems to have been a vital resource for Rebello and the later publication of Sttau Monteiro's translation seems to have provided a degree of compensation for the demands imposed both by the censors and the commercial context of the production.

In terms of the modernization of Portuguese theatrical practice, Shakespeare should certainly not be placed centre stage during this period. However, the experience gained in performing and translating Shakespeare was valuable. For António Pedro, Rui de Carvalho and Fernando Gusmão, *Dente por Dente* was already their second Shakespeare production and the performances would have provided useful practice in verse speaking and in the demands of staging larger productions. For translators, the experience of translating Shakespeare for particular performances provided them with an increased awareness of the demands of translating for the stage. In both cases, moreover, experimental elements are present in the translated texts. In the case of *Dente por Dente*, the songs illustrated one way of integrating Brechtian practices into Shakespearean performance and in the case of *O Amansar da Fera*, the controversy about the Induction is also a controversy about theatrical form. Its emphasis on role-playing functions as something of a distancing effect in relation to the play that follows and destabilizes any notion of the play as a simple mimetic reflection of reality.

The major factor mitigating against a more major role for Shakespeare in the process of modernization at this time was the irregularity of the performance of his plays. In this sense, 1964 was a very particular year, and it was only really in the 1990s that Shakespeare took on such a modernizing role with any consistency.

As for the relationship between Translation and Performance Studies, these examples illustrate how essential it is that both work together to uncover the full context of a production. Looked at in isolation, the translation by Rebello seems to be a radical document which would with difficulty escape censorship, but attention to the context of the production illustrates how this might change the meaning of the translation in performance. On the other hand, an initial glance at the performance context of *O Amansar da Fera* might reinforce a conservative view of the gender politics of the play and its acceptability to the censors that the later publication of the translation as an afterlife of performance does at least question. If the relationship between translation and censorship was a complex and awkward one, these examples suggest that scholars of Shakespeare in Performance and Translation Studies can work together productively to analyse this relationship in all its complexity and awkwardness.

References

Primary sources

Barradas, Mário (2002) "Aplauso com reticências", in *O Público*, (12/1/2002)
Dolores, Carmen (1984) *Retrato Inacabado: Memórias*, Lisboa: O Jornal.
Dos Santos, Graça (2004) *O Espectáculo Desvirtuado: o Teatro Português sob o Reinado de Salazar 1933-68)*, Lisboa: Caminho.
Gusmão, Fernando (1993) *A Fala da Memória: Factos e Notas de Um Homem de Teatro*, Lisboa: SPA.
Monteiro, Luís de Sttau (1967) *O Amansar da Fera*, Lisboa: Ática.
Rebello, Luiz Francisco (1964) *Dente por Dente*, Lisboa: Prelo.
Centro de Estudos do Teatro database, Faculdade de Letras da Universidade de Lisboa at www.fl.ul.pt/centroestudosteatro.htm
Programme for T.M.L. production of *Dente por Dente* (November 1964)

Secondary sources

Aaltonen, Sirkku (2000) *Time-Sharing on Stage: Drama Translation in Theatre and Society*, Cleveden: Multilingual Matters.

Henderson, Diana (1997) "A Shrew for the Times" in Richard Burt and Lynda Boose (eds.) *Shakespeare, the Movie: Popularizing the Plays on Film, TV and Video*, London and New York: Routledge, 148-68.

Hoesenlaars, Ton (2004) "'There is tremendous poetry in killings': Traditions of Shakespearean adaptation in the Low Countries", in Rui Carvalho Homem and Ton Hoesenlaars (eds.) *Translating Shakespeare for the Twenty-First Century*, New York and Amsterdam: Rodopi.

CENSORSHIP(S) AND CONTRADICTIONS: THE "DRAW" (1971/72) OF WITKIEWICZ'S PLAY *THE MOTHER*

CHRISTINE ZURBACH,
UNIVERSIDADE DE ÉVORA, PORTUGAL

Abstract: This article offers a critical study of the volume published in 1972 on Witkiewicz's play *The Mother*, whose public presentation was prohibited by censorship. This case happened in the context of the political overtures of the so called *Marcelist* period during which the contradictions of Portuguese society became more evident. According to the intention of updating Portuguese theatrical life, the play was suggested by Luíz Francisco Rebello, director of the Teatro Municipal de São Luís in Lisbon. Firstly submitted to the censors in its French translation, the voting ended in a draw, but the performance was finally prohibited in José Palla e Carmo's Portuguese translation.

This case allows us to confirm that, instead of being coherent, the application of theatrical censorship concerning several agents at different levels of cultural and political life is full of contradictions.

Based on the analysis of the documents published on the case, namely some discourses produced by several people involved in the discussion, the phenomenon of censorship is discussed here together with its principal components, in order to understand the limits of the concept itself regarding its specificity in space and time.

The theme here discussed, based on the relations between translation and censorship within the scope of Translation Studies, proposes an extension of the traditional study of translation (as a *text*) into more complex fields of knowledge, and involving deeper content. The association of the two items here analyzed is indeed a stimulating challenge for any expert in the area. Starting with the definitions, we must decide what *translation* means and what we refer to when we use the word *censorship*. We are aware that the search for a unanimous definition of the concept of translation remains inconclusive. As for censorship, as an institutionalized rule in a certain kind of society, besides the historical and contextual variance of its conception, it often occurs, in its practical use, surrounded by contradiction and incoherence, as we are about to demonstrate.

The case study in question simply aims at raising issues regarding this last characteristic (also mentioned in our title), particularly in relation to the interaction between translation and censorship as cultural practices (Pym 2006) belonging to the society into which the translation is imported, more precisely in the Portuguese theatrical life of the 1970s. It consists of the aborted project of performing the play *The Mother*, in March 1972, at the Teatro Municipal de São Luís, in Lisbon, by the Pole Witkiewicz, which had been chosen for the season of 1971-72 by the appointed director, Luíz Francisco Rebello.[1] Selected and imported into the national theatrical repertoire during the peculiar context of the so called *Marcelist* period, in which censorship–although loosening up–was still framed in an institutionalized juridical and political context, the play was published in that same year, in its Portuguese translation, together with the documents concerning the prohibition of its performance and the subsequent cancellation of the production as well as the corresponding reactions. Denied theatrical performance, the translation was presented to the reading public (not to an audience) by Prelo publishers, as number 9 in the collection entitled "Repertory for an up-to-date theatre", directed by the dramatist Rebello, who was also in charge, as we have seen, of the Teatro Municipal. Significantly, the book has a subtitle on its cover: *The Mother–Stanislas Witkiewicz and the Process of the Cancelled Show*. The effects of censorship on the theatre could not have been more explicit: to censor clearly means to *ban* or, in a more euphemistic and also ironic way, to *cancel* a project.

At first sight, the publication might reveal a first contradiction of a system that allows, in the same year of 1972, a text to be published despite the cancellation/ prohibition of the production it had been designed for. However, such peculiarity consists, as is well known today, of a characteristic of the system, which created a specific way of applying censorship to theatrical performances, always restricted by the dictatorial opinion/dictate of the Commission for the Examination and Classification of Theatrical Performances. In this case, the prohibition of the text had been applied during the rehearsals for the play, a month before the compulsory rehearsal for the Censoring Commission–the inevitable "censorship rehearsal"–, during which several attempts to arrive at a

---

[1] This case is mentioned by Rebello as "in a certain way illustrative of the situation of the Portuguese theatre under fascism" (1977: 33).

"solution of the problem" [solução do problema] had been carried out, all of them unsuccessful (Rebello 1972:133). A second peculiarity must be noted: the text had been previously presented to the censors in September 1971, in its French translation, with inconclusive results, since the voting had ended up in a "draw", "with 4 votes in favour and 4 against" [por 4 votos a favor e 4 contra] (*Ibidem*: 132). Nevertheless, quoting Rebello, "it predicted further approval" [deixa(va) entrever que viria a ser aprovada] (*Ibidem id.*). The Portuguese translation of the play by José Palla e Carmo, presented to the censors in December, was submitted to a second evaluation which would lead to its suspension in February the following year (by a majority) and to the final ban, in March, of the production that had been the reason for its importation into the national theatrical repertoire. Another contradiction? In fact, in translational terms, according to Lefevere (1992), it is the agent himself sponsoring the import (Lefevere calls him "patronage") who finds himself implicated in an incoherent strategy: the prohibition of the production is due to its dissidence with the moral and ideological values followed by the regime, as shown by a note by the Superintendence for Popular Culture and Shows, which had "especially taken into account the problem of drug use and its ideological implications" [tomado especialmente em conta o problema do consumo da droga e as implicações de ordem ideológica nela existentes] (Rebello 1972: 164), more precisely the resemblance between "the ideas supporting it (and those) which had dominated the struggle of the movements of May 1968, in France" [as ideias que a informam são praticamente as mesmas que dominaram as reivindicações dos movimentos de Maio de 1968, em França] (*Ibidem* : 158).

However, the text was brought to light in the context of a political openness to innovation, concretised by the import of the play (already accepted in several translations by different literary and theatrical systems, such as the French) into the programme for the 1971-72 season. This fact, in its turn, was in accordance with the appointment of Rebello as director of the theatre, following an invitation by the Mayor of Lisbon. The season, proposed by the director and approved by the Mayor, was innovatory and included José Régio's *A Salvação do Mundo*, Stanislas Witkiewicz's *The Mother*, Gomes de Amorim's *Fígados de Tigre* and Anton Chekhov's *Platonov*. The non-progressive nature of Portuguese theatrical life and the need for updating the repertoire are issues frequently remarked on by the cultural discourse of that time, which is quite patent, for instance, in the historiography of the Portuguese theatre. Such justification can be found, of course, in *História do Teatro Português*, by the same Rebello,[2] who, during a conference with the Secretary of State for Information, and already as the director of the Teatro Municipal, "had shown the need for changing the censorship criteria, which had impeded the indispensable renewal of (...) theatre" [fez ver a necessidade de uma alteração dos critérios da Censura, que têm obstado à indispensável renovação do (...) teatro] (Rebello 1972: 132). We shall nevertheless see that the invitation to, as well as the acceptance of, the job by a dramatist attached to a progressive view of theatre, and also to the opposition to the regime, will eventually be subjected to a kind of moral censorship by certain voices close to the political power as well as by some opponents to the regime. As if doubling the administrative censorious process, these are positions that, once again, reveal the complexity of the phenomenon of censorship and its application.

A third aspect may attract the interest of the translator. Despite the minor relevance of a comparative text analysis in this study, one should underline the fact–undeniably revealing, in sociological terms–that this is an indirect translation, made, as often happened in Portugal, from the previous French version, therefore coming from a culture traditionally admired by the receiving society. But should such admiration not precisely have favoured the import of the text? This matter raises the issue of the cause-effect relationship in the interpretation or explanation of the phenomenon of translation. In our present attempt to understand this translation of *The Mother*, we are brought to re-evaluate the use of the so-called "cultural" explanation regarding the specific case of the importation and translation of this play. Coming from the French cultural system was meant to play an innovatory role in the Portuguese system. However, it eventually produced the opposite effect and was rejected because of the same factor... We realize that the inter-literary relations as an explanatory cultural factor are not a homogeneous fact, especially in censorship contexts in which social factors (here represented by the agents involved) might struggle against, and contradict, the cultural factors.

Let us now focus on the description of the way in which the published work presents and promotes the previously mentioned *process*, which is reported throughout the debates which such prohibition had given rise to among many sections of the Portuguese society between March and April.

---

[2] Expressions such as "update of the Portuguese theatre", "revelation of new authors", "renovation of the repertoire" appear throughout the chapter dedicated to the post-war period, pointing out censorship as the main obstacle to performing Portuguese authors' theatrical works (Rebello 1989: 131-146). See also the section "Fases de um combate" in Rebello 1977.

Such a tendency seems to disregard the very publication of the translation. In fact, a first reading shows that the text itself only fills 82 of the total 242 pages, that is, a third of the total amount. Such a proportion illustrates, however, the importance the author gives to the space dedicated to the *corpus* of texts that compose an anthology of the arguments made by the main protagonists, which seem to us to be good examples of the consequences, not only direct but also indirect, of censorship on the whole cultural life it fell upon. Actually, the peculiar interest of the published book consists of the documented broadcasting of the whole case, from the selection of the work to its reception–or to its theatrical non-reception and to its correspondent (and controversial) marginalisation from cultural life. With responsibility assumed by the main protagonist in the case from the introduction of the piece into the receiving culture, the publication (and publicity) of this case imposes itself on all reported facts, thus becoming a *text* as a whole, moving from the literary or theatrical field into the ideological or political one.

Let us now look at the organization of the published work, which, as we have just mentioned, since it consists of a published translation, clearly moves away from standard patterns by means of the importance given to the paratextual display. The book comprises the translated text, presented together with its context of production and reception–which we shall here consider as a *macrotext* (Pym 2006)–and provides the reader with factual data concerning the selection, importation and publication of the work. It also adds other facts related to the actions integrating a previous process of communication within the field of theatre, now interrupted and *cancelled*. Considering this as a whole, we can distinguish the compiled texts according to three corresponding actions: (1) the translation–a way of rewriting as a linguistic and textual practice, subject to the correspondent censorship/prohibition–of a play proposed for a theatrical repertoire. Now published, it was previously included (*selected* according to Toury's patterns (1980)) in a cultural programme of a municipal theatre, under the responsibility of a political entity represented by the local power (see above); (2) the production of a show–a way of rewriting as an artistic practice, constructed with non-textual components (staging, set and costumes)–with a view to its performance, which would be prohibited by censorship after the compulsory rehearsal before the Censoring Commission (Rebello 1972: 133); (3) the publication of the book–uncensored–as a work comprising the publication of the translation and a significant number of documents organized on a chronological basis, either prior to or following the cancellation of the production. Such documents consist of published and unpublished material.

In sociological terms it is possible to point out the specificity of the roles played by the authors of the texts according to each one's position and function as intervening agents in the process. Thus, the relevance of Rebello's position must be underlined: as editor of the collection, he is responsible for the selection and organization of the texts for the book publication, and, as director of the Teatro Municipal de São Luís, he is responsible for the selection of the play for the 1972 season. In fact, this is highly relevant to the matter: besides introducing a problem that is specifically theatrical, in which the translation of a play is based on its eventual performance, it links two ways of receiving the same text, although publication is the response to the cancellation of the show, with its corresponding effects on theatrical life. Thus, as editor of the collection, Rebello writes two introductory texts: an "Introduction to Witkiewicz" (*Ibidem*: 9-20) and a "Chronology of Witkiewicz's theatre" (*Ibidem*: 21-24), followed by the translation of the play (*Ibidem*: 25-107). Rebello's introduction starts with a question: "What is a 'repertoire for an updated theatre' supposed to mean?" [Que deve entender-se por 'repertório para um teatro actual'], an expression that provides the title for the Prelo collection and that characterizes the anthological ensemble, in which contemporary authors are included: Sartre, Pinter, Tone Brulin, authors from the modern Portuguese theatre, and also Shakespeare and Gorki. The word "updated" does not refer here to the simple chronological situation of works, but to the opposition between an "ephemeral" present time and a "permanent" present time of texts which, like the one by Witkiewicz, Rebello considers as "master work(s) of a permanently updated theatre" [obra-prima de um teatro permanentemente actual] (*Ibidem*: 20). The explicit reference to Vito Pandolfi's history of the theatre (*Ibidem*: 18), still recent at that time, enables an erudite and international consecration, under the sign of theoretical and methodological modernity in theatrical historiography, in accordance with Rebello's proposed selection. However, by "updated" he means first of all "innovatory". As proof, there is the inclusion of extensive references to texts such as Witkiewicz' essay, from 1920, published in 1923: *Introduction to the Theory of Pure Form in Theatre*, which points out the violent tone used by the dramatist when he proposes "to strangle all spectators" [estrangular todos os espectadores]! (*Ibidem*: 15) Innovatory at its time, the play *The Mother,* written in 1924, would be published only in 1962, two years before its first public presentation in Poland. Its aesthetics corresponds to the anti-naturalist reaction in the 20th century theatre, but for Rebello, "it came up too soon" [surgiu demasiado cedo], the writer of the preface associating it with the theses of Artaud (*Ibidem*: 15) and Brecht (*Ibidem*: 16). These are data that allow the comparison between the anti-innovation reaction in Portugal, underlining the fact that the play is "presented to the Portuguese public in its literary form–thus unilaterally" [dado a conhecer ao público português sob a sua forma literária–unilateralmente, pois] (*Ibidem*: 9), and in post-1945 Poland, pointing out the "aesthetic rigidity (and not only this...) of the Stalinist period (which) did not encourage the rediscovery of the theatre of this fascinating inventor" [rigidez estética (e não só) do período estalinista não era favorável à redescoberta do teatro deste fascinante inventor] (*Ibidem*: 17). On the contrary, Rebello informs that that same work had already been translated and performed in several countries: Poland, Germany, Belgium, France, Italy and Brazil. Witkiewicz's play, according to this text, was included in the publication programme of the collection before being chosen as an integral part of the repertoire for the 1972 season of the Teatro Municipal de São Luís along with Chekhov, Régio and Gomes de Amorim. Here, the preface writer speaks as a programme-maker and explains his goal, as he speaks of the "updating (each day more necessary–and each day more difficult) of our theatre" [actualização (cada dia mais necessária–e cada dia mais difícil) do nosso teatro] (*Ibidem*: 20), that is, of the "innovation" that had become impossible on stage. He thus legitimises the publication of the dossier on how and why that prohibition took place.

There is a second group of texts dealing with the problem of the staging of the text. Extending his job as a theatre director by committing himself to the production of the show, Rebello introduces four documents concerning its staging, and gives voice or visibility to the artists involved. After a "list of credits" with the names of the performers (*Ibidem*: 109-110), more appropriate to a theatre programme, there are some "Notes for the staging of *The Mother*" (*Ibidem*: 111-114) signed by Artur Ramos. As the stage manager, he presents the general guidelines–"The starting point"–for his work, which would follow the "compromise" between the respect for an avant-garde text, though written in 1924, and its updating. Written after the prohibition, the text on "The sets and costumes for the play *The Mother*" (*Ibidem*: 115-117), by Maurício de Vasconcelos, mentions the "frustration" caused by the fact that the work could not "fulfil its aim–to communicate with the public". Resuming the theme already referred to by Rebello (see above), it closes the dossier on the "cancelled" show with photographs of rehearsals, a model of the set and drawings of the costumes (*Ibidem*: 119-129). The last pages of the book (131-247) narrate the episodes of the "process" from May 1971 to April 1972, opening precisely with the "Chronology of the events" (*Ibidem*: 131-135), unsigned, in which emphasis is put on Rebello's personal journey: his appointment as director of the theatre section of the Teatro Municipal de São Luís after the Mayor's invitation in August 1971, his resignation in March 1972, and the different reactions it caused. The set of interviews, letters, articles, official notes, statements by deputies in the National Assembly represent three textual and discursive sub-groups. The first one, with texts written by the stage manager, by the director of the Teatro Municipal de São Luís and by the President of the Portuguese League for Mental Health, includes the transcription of the "nuclear part" of "An interview" (*Ibidem*: 137-139) given by Artur Ramos in January 1972, "which gave rise to controversial and abusive interpretations" [que deu aso a interpretações contraditórias e abusivas]; the facsimile of a handwritten letter by João Fragoso Mendes, from the Portuguese League for Mental Health, entitled "Declaration" (*Ibidem*: 141-142) and letters to the Mayor by Luíz Francisco Rebello and Artur Ramos. A second group, reproducing the news of the prohibition of *The Mother*, published in the press (*Ibidem*: 151-201), presents opposing arguments on censorship, with "Two notes by the Superintendence of Shows and three letters", by Rebello, Mendes Ramos (*Ibidem*: 157-164) and "Comments on the prohibition of *The Mother*" (*Ibidem*: 165-192) with texts published in the national and foreign press and others, unpublished at that time (like the article by Artur Ramos (*Ibidem*: 175-180) for the magazine *Seara Nova*). But, most of all, "Some difficulties" (*Ibidem*: 181-186) exposes, in critical terms, the issue of the relations between creators and power in the context of that time, in which the "censored" suffers a double punishment. The inclusion of "A marginal incident", despite eventual marginalisation as far as the author is concerned, widens the distance between the case of *The Mother* and certain positions adopted by other creators (*Ibidem*: 193-201). The last group (203-247) gives evidence of the consequences of this case for the national political life with the "Debate at the National Assembly on the 14th April 1972" (*Ibidem*: 203-220), "Consequences of the debate in the Assembly and a protest" (*Ibidem*: 221-237) and a petition "Concerning a campaign" (*Ibidem*: 239-247), from which we underline the commitment of the regime's politicians in defending censorship "at the service of Performances in general and the Theatre in particular" (*Ibidem*: 239).

From the texts we have just mentioned, the importation and prohibition of *The Mother* is not a clear-cut story in its progression through the Portuguese cultural system. We only have to consider the initial delay in the censorship which was to be applied to the text, unfolding as two different versions–one in French, the other in Portuguese–together with the complexity of the ideological debate the case generated concerning (1) the problems of the intervention of creators in the Portuguese theatrical life (particularly through the acceptance of official positions); (2) the rules of the game such cooperation represents; or still, following Alexandre Babo's essay, (3) the very use of censorship in "exceptional cases". The core of our analysis, although not arising from a comparative study of the translated play, has found, in the collected and published documents, some elements that help to understand the relations between translation and censorship. According to the contextual factors involved, the interpretation of the position and procedures of the intervening agents revealed the ambiguity of the pseudo-opening and liberalization of a political-cultural system of totalitarian inspiration, the "Primavera Marcelista". In our social and cultural approach to the relations between translation and censorship, the word *cultural* refers strictly to the discursive production that can be seen in the Portuguese political and ideological system of the 1970s. In sociological terms, we considered the group of the agents involved who were in charge of certain functions within the theatrical system, and their behaviour towards the interferences of the political system–namely censorship, which, as we have seen, was at the origin of contradictory debates in many areas of society at that time, from the literary, editorial, theatrical, cultural, journalistic, to the religious, medical and parliamentary areas.

Thus, our goal was to describe and attempt to interpret the thematic and ideological content of the publication that provided the reading public, in the same year, both with the translated text, the facts considered relevant by the author of the publication, and the reactions caused by the censorial decision to ban the production. Through the proposed articulation between factual data and discursive positions, we believe a second action–which derives from the production of the translation within the theatrical system and now transferred to the literary system–may be considered as being a significant part of the whole *process* of the censorial action. Because of its peculiarity in the ensemble of the editorial production regarding theatre at the time of the prohibition of the performance of *The Mother–Repulsive Comedy in Two Acts and an Epilogue*, the edition of the book will allow–in further analysis–the conditions of theatrical translation and creation in Portugal to be shown when considering the intervention of censorship in the Portuguese social and cultural life during the period preceding its extinction in 1974. The analysis of the *process* caused by the failed importation of a play that became available only to a potential reader will also reveal the tension and contradictions that characterized the society of that time.

References

Primary sources

Rebello, Luiz Francisco/ Witkiewicz, Stanislas (1972) *A Mãe* and *O Processo do Espectáculo Anulado, Repertório Para um Teatro Actual* (collection directed by Luiz Francisco Rebello), Lisboa: Prelo.

Secondary sources

Lefevere, André (1992) *Translating, Rewriting, and the Manipulation of Literary Fame*, London and New York: Routledge.
Pym, Anthony *et al.* (eds.) (2006) *Sociocultural Aspects of Translating and Interpreting*, Amsterdam/Philadelphia: John Benjamins.
Rebello, Luiz Francisco (1977) *Combate por um Teatro de Combate*, Lisboa: Seara Nova.
—. (1989) *História do Teatro Português* (4th ed. reviewed and enlarged), Lisboa: Europa-América.
Toury, Gideon (1980) *In Search of a Theory of Translation*, Tel Aviv: The Porter Institute for Poetics and Semiotics.

WHO IS HOLDING THE BLUE PENCIL? A VISIT TO INTRALINGUAL TRANSLATION IN THE PORTUGUESE THEME PARK "PORTUGAL DOS PEQUENITOS"

ALEXANDRA ASSIS ROSA,
UNIVERSIDADE DE LISBOA, PORTUGAL

Abstract: Much more than "a small nation of tiny houses for smaller stature people" as one reads in online reviews, "Portugal dos Pequenitos", in Coimbra, was designed by Bissaya Barreto with the help of architect Cassiano Branco and built from 1940 until 1950 as propaganda for the Portuguese colonial empire. This precursor of children's theme parks is a miniature village that holds small scale reproductions of Portugal's traditional regional homes, of the most important Portuguese monuments and as well as an overseas area with buildings dedicated to the Portuguese former colonies.

The buildings in this third area hold a collection of items related to each one of these current African Countries with Portuguese as official language. Plaques describing the different spaces and cultures have been subject to intralingual translation that the ideological change in Portugal made necessary. This paper analyses a selection of these texts and their underlying translational strategies that change propaganda into apology.

1. Introduction

Like "a small nation of tiny houses for smaller stature people" as one reads in online reviews,[1] the theme park "Portugal dos Pequenitos", in Coimbra, was designed by Bissaya Barreto, a prominent professor of Medicine of the University of Coimbra (1886-1974) with the help of the famous modernist architect, Cassiano Branco (1897-1970). It was inaugurated on

---

[1] See: http://www.tripadvisor.com/Attraction_Review-g189143-d456688-Reviews-Portugal_dos_Pequenitos-Coimbra_Beiras.html (accessed 19 July 2006).

the 8th of June 1940, and built from 1938 until the end of the 1950s. It is now kept by the Foundation Bissaya Barreto.[2]

This precursor of children's theme parks holds small scale reproductions of buildings divided into three distinctive areas: the first one usually mentioned is the "Village of the Little People" [Aldeia dos Pequenitos] that is dedicated to Portugal's traditional regional homes; the second area called "Monumental Portugal" [Portugal Monumental] holds miniatures of the most important Portuguese monuments, such as the Village Palace in Sintra, the Convent of Christ in Tomar, or the Archway of Rua Augusta in Lisbon; it is the third area called "Overseas Nucleus" [Núcleo Além-Mar] that will be subject to analysis in this paper. Clearly built as nationalistic promotion or propaganda for the Portuguese colonial empire, the gigantic map that delimits it is illustrative of the world vision presented in this area. In its centre, at the heart of the empire lies Portugal, point of departure for the discoveries, with the inevitable patron image of Prince Henry, the Navigator (third son of King John I of Portugal; 1394-1460).

So, this third area is dedicated to the Portuguese colonial empire and holds buildings representing some of the Portuguese former colonies. The miniature architecture of most buildings attempts to be illustrative of that of the region it represents. Each building holds a collection of items related to one ultramarine colony, or overseas province as they were called, since under the ideology of national colonialism, as António de Figueiredo stated, "the colonies became 'overseas provinces' of a single nation" (Figueiredo 2001: 1919).

The buildings in this area represented eleven overseas provinces: Madeira and the Azores, which are currently autonomous regions of Portugal; as well as Mozambique, Angola, India, Cape Verde, S. Tomé and Príncipe, Guinea-Bissau, Timor, Macau, and an additional building was dedicated to Brazil, an independent state since 1822, but prior to that also part of the Portuguese overseas empire. Before entering the building dedicated to each one of these former colonies, the visitor is presented with a plaque that consists of an introduction to each one of the different former overseas provinces with special reference to their relationship with Portugal at the centre of the empire.

The noticeable fact that led to this project is that in six cases these plaques are presented to the visitor in two different Portuguese versions. There are actually two generations of plaques: a more recent version is met by the visitor outside each building. However, in some cases, upon

---

[2] See: http://www.fbb.pt/pp_apresentacao.htm (accessed 19 July 2006).

entering the building the visitor finds another version that is evidently a former version of the more recent one displayed outside. Similarly to a bilingual edition, the source text version found inside the buildings seems to have been replaced by the second target text version, a more recent one that is displayed at the entrance. This difference is also perceptible in the stone layout of these plaques. Those which seem to have been the original ones display the "Padrão", with the coat of arms of Portugal, as is the case with the outdoor plaques for the buildings dedicated to Madeira and the Azores, a layout that is exactly the same as that of the six plaques that are currently exhibited inside the buildings. These seem to have been the original plaques.

Apparently, the first versions of these plaques have been subjected to intralingual translation made necessary not only by the fact that the colonies became independent countries but also or even, one feels tempted to say, mainly by ideological changes in Portugal that seem to have made the first version obsolete or unacceptable. This paper proposes to analyze these six parallel texts and the translational strategies underlying such cases of rewriting.

2. Analysis

As Deirdre Burton states:

> If the analyst is interested in "making strange" the power relationships that obtain in the socially constructed world–be it the "real" world of public and private social relationships or the spoken and written texts that we create, hear, read, and that ultimately construct *us* in that "real world"– then, crucially, it is the realization of *processes* and *participants* (both the actors and the acted upon) in those processes that should concern us. (Burton 1982: 200)

Given the nature of the corpus under scrutiny the analysis will firstly focus on descriptions used as forms of reference to the colonizer that can be interpreted as forms of self-reference, i.e. forms used by the addresser to refer to himself. Special attention will be given to the attempt to encompass other participants within the forms of self-reference used: the addresser and readers, the addresser and other participants mentioned, such as the discoverers. Secondly, the analysis will also consider descriptions used as forms of reference to the colonized, i.e. forms used by the addresser to refer to third parties, in this case, special attention will be paid to the forms chosen to identify the regions and peoples of the former colonies. These categories differ from the definition of deictic role by John

Lyons, given that his definition explicitly excludes the use of names or descriptions to consider only personal or demonstrative pronouns (Lyons 1977: 574-575). This collection of forms of self-reference and reference to third parties are deemed likely to reveal a network of relationships that associate the profiles of the colonizer and the colonized generated by these texts. Finally, the analysis will also consider the expressions used to describe the actions performed by the colonizer and the colonized, i.e. by the Portuguese and by the peoples of the former colonies.

3. First version

In the first version, the forms used to mention the colonizers, as forms of self-reference are:[3]

(1) Kings, examples: "King Manuel I" (India), "King Afonso V" (S. Tomé and Príncipe), "King João II" (S. Tomé and Príncipe);

(2) Navigators, examples: "Vasco da Gama" (India and Mozambique), "Diogo Cam" (Angola), "The Portuguese navigators of the time of Prince Henry", "Some of the first navigators", "Our discoverers" (Guinea);

(3) The vessels of the navigators, examples: "The Portuguese-Men-of-War of the route to India" (Mozambique), "The Portuguese-Men-of-War" (India), "By the caravels of Diogo Gomes and António da Nola" (Cape Verde), "Our caravels" (Angola);

(4) "the Portuguese" (Angola and S. Tomé and Príncipe);

---

[3] For the sake of readability, English glosses will be used in the text and the majority of Portuguese examples will be included in footnotes. In the first version, the Portuguese forms of self-reference to the colonizers are: (1) Kings, examples: "D. Manuel I" (India), "D. Afonso V" (S. Tomé and Príncipe), "D. João II" (S. Tomé and Príncipe); (2) Navigators, examples: "Vasco da Gama" (India and Mozambique), "Diogo Cam" (Angola), "pelos navegadores portugueses do tempo do Infante D. Henrique" "alguns dos primeiros navegadores", "dos nossos descobridores" (Guinea); (3) the vessels of the navigators, examples: "as naus portuguesas da carreira da Índia" (Mozambique), "as naus portuguesas" (India), "pelas caravelas de Diogo Gomes e António da Nola" (Cape Verde), "as nossas caravelas" (Angola); (4) the Portuguese, example: "os portugueses" (Angola and S. Tomé and Príncipe); (5) "Portugal" (S. Tomé and Príncipe); (6) our empire, examples: "o nosso império da Índia" (India); (7) markers for the third person singular and plural; as well as (8) markers for the first person plural, examples: "íamos comprar," "obrigaram-nos a manter pela força," "ali construímos," "o nosso império da Índia, (...) de que hoje nos restam" (India); "os nossos navegadores" (Cape Verde); "cedemos" (S. Tomé and Príncipe); "as nossas caravelas", "a nossa maior província" (Angola); "a primazia dos nossos descobridores e o valor do seu esforço" (Guinea).

(5) "Portugal" (S. Tomé and Príncipe);
(6) Our empire, examples: "our empire in India" (India);
(7) Markers for the third person singular and plural; as well as
(8) Several markers for the first person plural, examples: "we would buy," "we were forced to," "we built," "our empire in India," "we have still left" (India); "Our navigators" (Cape Verde); "we gave over" (S. Tomé and Príncipe); "our caravels," "our biggest province" (Angola); "the primacy of our discoverers and the value of their effort" (Guinea).

As forms of self-reference in Portuguese, first-person singular verbal forms are enough and thus considered neutral, non-marked forms of self-reference (Faria 1991: 49-53). All the forms mentioned are therefore marked and contrast significantly. It is worth stressing that they are all forms of collective reference, either to kings as representatives of the nation, or to the people, the Portuguese, and their heroes, the navigators and discoverers, also by synecdoche by means of reference to the vessels. Especially remarkable is the choice of first-person plural verbal and pronominal possessive forms that signals qualitative and quantitative integration of the addresser in a group of categories. It signifies empathy and identification, which can also be interpreted as a means to draw the reader into this inclusive "we". "We", addresser and reader, are reinforced by identification with kings and heroes, with navigators and crews, with the Portuguese people and nation.

The colonizers appear mainly as syntactic subject and semantic agents, and as for the processes attributed to them, to use the typology of Deirdre Burton (1982: 195-214), adapted from Michael Halliday (1970, 1973, 1978), they are mainly agents of verbs of material process (vs. mental, relational), action process (vs. event) and intention process (vs. supervention): so we/they "go," "go beyond," "anchor," "rest," "deal with," "open the way of civilization," or "initiate a civilizing action," "buy," "attempt to deal peacefully," "are obliged to maintain by force," "defeat," "establish," "discover," "sight land," "give impulse," "explore in giant steps," "find," "give names," "colonize," "take caravels," "go back," "build," "go up river," "carve in rock," and "die, pierced by poisoned assegais".[4]

---

[4] In the Portuguese first version, the processes attributed to the colonizers are: "ia em demanda", "dobrou", "ancorou", "descansou," "tratavam com os indígenas, abrirão-lhes [sic] o caminho da civilização" or "começou pacificamente a acção civilizadora", "íamos comprar", "procurou tratar pacificamente com os indígenas", "obrigaram-nos a manter pela força", "derrotaram", "o nosso império da Índia firmou-se", "descobriram", "a primeira a ser avistada", "dar o maior impulso", "foi sendo explorada a passos de gigante", "se chegou", "foi o nome dado pelos

The descriptions used to refer to the colonized regions are:[5]

(1) designation of places, often as syntactically optional adjuncts of place, examples: "in several points of Western Africa", "on the small island of Mozambique", "they made of Mozambique and the ports of that coast" (Mozambique); "to India", "in the Indian Ocean" (India); "we reached the end of the big gulf of Guinea, Benim and Mina" (S. Tomé and Príncipe); "as far as Congo", "in Angola, our biggest overseas province" (Angola); "All the coast of Africa that was being discovered beyond Cape Bojador", "The current province of Guinea comprises several black races" (Guinea);

(2) indigenous peoples, examples: "they dealt with the natives" (Mozambique); "the peoples of India", "the scheming of Moor merchants", "Turks, Egyptians, and Indians" (India); "he [Diogo Cam] dealt with the black King of Congo" (Angola); "country of Azenegues [Znaga] and Negroes" (Guinea);

(3) "there" (deixis expressing distance; India, Cape Verde, Angola);

(4) objects of actions by the colonizers, frequently as subjects of passive voice clauses, examples: "they made of Mozambique and the ports

---

navegadores portugueses", "colonizar", "levou as nossas caravelas", "voltou ali", "a erguer o padrão de Portugal", "subiu pelo rio", "gravou na rocha" and "morreram, varados por azagaias envenenadas".

[5] The Portuguese forms of reference to the colonized regions are: (1) designation of places, often as syntactically optional adjuncts of place, examples: "em vários pontos da África oriental", "na pequena ilha de Moçambique", "fizeram de Moçambique e dos portos daquela costa" (Mozambique); "para a Índia", "no oceano Índico" (India); "assim se chegou (...) ao golfão da Guiné, a Benin e a Mina" (S. Tomé and Príncipe); "até ao Congo", "em Angola–a nossa maior província do ultramar" (Angola); "Toda a costa de África que se ia descobrindo para além do Cabo Bojador", "A actual província da Guiné portuguesa compreende ainda muitas raças negras" (Guinea); (2) indigenous peoples, examples: "tratavam com os indígenas" (Mozambique); "os povos da Índia", "as intrigas dos mercadores moiros", "os turcos, os egípcios e os índios" (India); "tratou [Diogo Cam] com o rei preto do Congo" (Angola); "país de azenegues [Znaga] e negros" (Guinea); (3) "there" (deixis expresses distance) examples: "ali" (India, Cape Verde, Angola); (4) objects of actions by the colonizers, frequently as subjects of passive voice clauses, examples: "fizeram de Moçambique e dos portos daquela costa os seus ancoradouros costumados" (Mozambique); "procurou tratar pacificamente com os povos da Índia" (India); "Em frente do cabo que, por estar coberto de arvoredo, foi chamado Cabo Verde", "A primeira a ser avistada foi a de Santiago" (Cape Verde); "A costa de África foi sendo explorada a passos de gigante", "foram achadas 4 ilhas", "D. João II empenhou-se em colonizar aquelas ilhas no meio da zona tórrida, que os antigos diziam ser inabitável." (S. Tomé and Príncipe).

of that coast their usual moorings" (Mozambique); "he tried to deal peacefully with the peoples of India" (India); "in front of the cape that, being covered with trees, was called Cape Verde", "the first to be sighted was that of Santiago" (Cape Verde); "The coast of Africa was progressively explored in giant steps" (S. Tomé and Príncipe); "4 islands were discovered", "King John II was intent on colonizing those islands in the middle of the torrid zone that the ancients said was uninhabitable" (S. Tomé and Príncipe).

The most frequent forms of reference to the colonized regions and peoples are made by spatial reference to the region as geographical location for the actions of the colonizers, mainly as adjuncts of place, or as objects of the actions of the colonizers, frequently as subjects of clauses in the passive voice. They are dehumanized, mentioned as geographical spaces (as syntactical adjuncts) or as semantic beneficiaries of actions by the colonizers. Deixis when identifiable marks distance, and both the addresser and the reader are therefore not identified with the colonized. In terms of processes illustrative of the patterns in this first version: these regions "offer shelter", "are made moorings", "are named", "are sighted", "are discovered", "are given over", "are colonized by blacks and whites", "are explored", "are found", "receive a name", "comprise several black races" and "are a beacon of the primacy of colonizers and the value of their effort".[6]

4. Second version

The forms of self-reference used in the second version are the following:[7]

---

[6] Portuguese expressions illustrative of processes in the first version are: "oferecia bom abrigo", "as naus portuguesas fizeram de Moçambique e dos portos daquela costa os seus ancoradouros costumados", "foi o nome dado", "a primeira a ser avistada", "os nossos navegadores descobriram, ao largo, uma a uma, as ilhas deste arquipélago", "e mais duas que depois cedemos a Espanha", "colonizadas por brancos e pretos", "foi sendo explorada", "foram achadas", "recebeu o nome", "compreende ainda muitas raças negras" and "é como um padrão que atesta a primazia dos nossos descobridores e o valor do seu esforço".
[7] The Portuguese forms of self-reference used in the second version are the following: (1) navigators, examples: "o célebre Vasco da Gama, o primeiro navegador português" (Mozambique); "os navegadores portugueses" (S. Tomé and Príncipe); "o navegador Diogo Cão" (Angola); "os navegadores portugueses do século XV" (Guinea); (2) the vessels, examples: "as armadas regulares da 'Carreira da Índia'" (India); (3) the Portuguese, examples: "Com a viagem de Vasco da

(1) navigators, examples: "the famous Vasco da Gama, first Portuguese navigator" (Mozambique); "The Portuguese navigators" (S. Tomé and Príncipe); "the navigator Diogo Cão" (Angola); "the Portuguese navigators of the 15th century" (Guinea);

(2) the vessels, example: "The armadas of the 'Route of India'" (India);

(3) the Portuguese, examples: "With the voyage of Vasco da Gama, the Portuguese" (India); "The Portuguese" (Cape Verde, Angola);

(4) Europeans, examples: "They [the islands of Cape Verde] were peopled by populations of African and European origin" (Cape Verde); "African and European population centres" (S. Tomé and Príncipe);

(5) a former empire, examples: "The former Portuguese empire in Asia" (India);

(6) a presence, examples: "the Portuguese presence" (Mozambique); "the presence of the Portuguese" (Angola and Guinea);

(7) sovereignty, example: "Portuguese sovereignty" (S. Tomé and Príncipe, Guinea); and

(8) verbal forms of the third person singular and plural.

Despite the maintenance of self-reference to the navigators, their vessels and the Portuguese, the main change of this second version is related to additional references, firstly to the European, which again signal allegiance although of a different nature. The addresser mentions colonizers as part of a group but instead of just belonging to the Portuguese people the self-definition has a supplementary reference: Europe. Perhaps as a reaction to the strongly nationalistic promotion of the Portuguese nation during "Estado Novo", the purpose of this post-dictatorship version may be to dilute Portuguese nationality into Europe. Secondly, additional instances of self-reference include abstract nouns such as "empire" ("in former empire"), "presence" and "sovereignty". Such nominal abstract categories together with verbal forms of third person singular or plural and clauses in the passive voice without mention to an agent, make empathy and identification of addresser and reader with

---

Gama, os portugueses" (India); "portugueses" (Cape Verde); "dos portugueses" (Angola); (4) Europeans, examples: "Foram [as ilhas de Cabo Verde] desde então povoadas por populações de origem africana e europeia" (Cape Verde); "foram instalados núcleos populacionais africanos e europeus" (S. Tomé and Príncipe); (5) a former empire, examples: "do antigo império português da Ásia" (India); (6) a presence, examples: "da presença portuguesa" (Mozambique); "a presença dos portugueses" (Angola and Guinea); (7) sovereignty, example: "a soberania portuguesa" (S. Tomé and Príncipe, Guinea); and (8) verbal forms of third person singular and plural.

the colonizer more distant, although still implicit. They are in blatant contrast with the markers for the first person plural found in the first version.

Among the processes related to the colonizer are: "they arrived", "remained", "found" but also "needed", "achieved the objective", "left Lisbon", "managed to establish themselves" and "eventually established contacts with populations" (which encode effort), "celebrated an alliance" and "established amicable relationships", "sailed beyond", "made geographical reconnaissance", "Portuguese navigators were the first to make voyages and geographical reconnaissance" (instead of open the way for civilization).[8]

Participle forms such as "sailing beyond", "setting an example" and passive voices omitting the agent such as "peopling was promoted", "population centres were established" are also forms of lessening the connection between the colonizers as agents and these actions. The expressions "Portuguese sovereignty lasted", "the presence of the Portuguese in Angola lasted" mention events, not actions, together with abstract nominal categories that again make identification of the addresser with the colonizer more remote.

The descriptions used to refer to the colonized are:[9]

---

[8] The processes related to the colonizer in the Portuguese second version are: "chegou", "demorou-se", "encontrou" but also "necessitava", "conseguiram o objectivo", "partiam de Lisboa", "conseguiram estabelecer-se no Oriente" and "vieram a estabelecer contactos com as populações" (which encode effort), "estabeleceu uma aliança" and "estabeleceu relações amistosas", "ultrapassou a foz do rio Zaire", "fez reconhecimentos geográficos", "Os navegadores portugueses do século XV foram os primeiros a fazer viagens e reconhecimentos geográficos" (instead of open the way for civilization).

[9] The Portuguese descriptions used to refer to the colonized in the second version are: (1) designation of places, examples: "Moçambique", "na bela ilha de Moçambique" (Mozambique); "para a Índia", "no Oriente", "Goa, Damão e Diu" (India); "as ilhas de Cabo Verde", "o arquipélago de Cabo Verde" (Cape Verde); "o reconhecimento do golfo da Guiné", "várias ilhas desabitadas", "em duas delas, mais tarde chamadas de S. Tomé e Príncipe" (S. Tomé and Príncipe); "os primeiros contactos (...) com Angola", "no litoral africano", "em Angola" (Angola); "nos litorais da África Ocidental e do golfo da Guiné", "nas regiões da Guiné-Bissau" (Guinea); (2) designation of function, examples: "vários portos da costa oriental africana", "uma base dos navios da Carreira da Índia", "ponto de fixação da presença portuguesa" (Mozambique); "importante base das navegações", "um ponto de encontro do mundo atlântico e africano" (Cape Verde); (3) civilizations, examples: "civilizações africanas ao sul do equador" (Angola); "as populações" (Guinea); (4) kings, examples: "o rei do Congo" (Angola); (5)

(1) designation of places, examples: "Mozambique", "on the beautiful island of Mozambique" (Mozambique); "to India", "in the Orient", "Goa, Damão and Diu" (India); "the islands of Cape Verde", "the archipelago of Cape Verde" (Cape Verde); "the reconnaissance of the Gulf of Guinea", "several uninhabited islands", "on two of them later named S. Tomé and Príncipe" (S. Tomé and Príncipe); "contacts with Angola", "of African coast line", "in Angola" (Angola); "in West African coast line and in the gulf of Guinea", "in the regions of Guinea-Bissau" (Guinea);

(2) designation of function, examples: "several ports in the coast of western Africa", "a basis for the ships in the route of India", "settlement of Portuguese presence" (Mozambique); "an important basis for navigations", "a meeting-point for the Atlantic and African world" (Cape Verde);

(3) civilizations, examples: "African civilizations South of the Equator" (Angola); "the populations" (Guinea);

(4) kings, examples: "the King of Congo" (Angola);

(5) there (deixis expressing distance), examples: "there" (Angola);

(6) these (deixis expressing proximity), example: "these territories" (India; which, however, may also be interpreted as expressing co-textual proximity);

(7) objects of actions by the colonizers, example: "the islands of Cape Verde were discovered" (Cape Verde);

(8) nations and territories, example: "Popular Republic of Mozambique", "the new country" (Mozambique); "State of India", "these territories" (India); "Republic of Cape Verde", "as an independent country" (Cape Verde); "Democratic Republic of S. Tomé and Príncipe". "the new country" (S. Tomé and Príncipe); "Popular Republic of Angola", "the new country" (Angola); "Republic of Guinea-Bissau", "the new country" (Guinea);

---

there (deixis expressing distance), examples: "ali" (Angola); (6) these (deixis expressing proximity), example: "destes territórios" (India; which, however, may also be interpreted as expressing co-textual proximity); (7) objects of actions by the colonizers, example: "as ilhas de Cabo Verde foram descobertas" (Cape Verde); (8) nations and territories, example: "República Popular de Moçambique", "Moçambique" (Mozambique); "Estado da Índia", "destes territórios" (India); "República de Cabo Verde", "país independente" (Cape Verde); "República Democrática de S. Tomé e Príncipe", "o novo país" (S. Tomé and Príncipe); "República Popular de Angola", "o novo país" (Angola); "República da Guiné-Bissau", "o novo país" (Guinea); (9) members of a wider community, example: "mais um dos membros da comunidade luso-afro-brasileira" (Guinea).

(9) members of a wider community, example: "another member of the Luso-Afro-Brazilian Community" (Guinea).

Again, despite the maintenance of reference to these regions as geographical places, the main differences are additional reference to them as designation of functions, civilizations, populations, and nations that are members of wider communities.

As for processes, "Mozambique remained" (Mozambique), "when the islands of Cape Verde were discovered (...) they were still uninhabited", "they were peopled by populations of African and European origin, setting an example as a remarkable cultural process of miscegenation", "would become in the future" (Cape Verde), "were named", "peopling was promoted and in them were African and European population centres established–the first in the equatorial area" (S. Tomé and Príncipe); and in a clearly apologetic version the new countries "ascend to independence" (Mozambique, S. Tomé and Príncipe) "become independent" (Angola) or "become members of a wider community, one of the most significant in the planet" (Guinea), and are in this way also depicted as agents of material, action and intention processes.[10]

5. On the definition of censorship

Now, the question is does this rewriting have anything to do with censorship? Is censorship applicable to what we find in these examples of intralingual translation in "Portugal dos Pequenitos"? Studies on censorship in Portugal usually focus on freedom of the press during and after the dictatorship as is also the case of works for the wider public such as *Portugal Contemporâneo*, including two chapters by Maria Antónia Palla (Palla 1996a and 1996b).

---

[10] As for processes attributed to the former colonies in the Portuguese second version "Moçambique continuou a ser" (Mozambique), "quando as ilhas de Cabo Verde foram descobertas (...) estavam ainda desabitadas", "foram desde então povoadas por populações de origem africana e europeia, dando o exemplo de um notável processo cultural de miscegenação", "iria transformar-se no futuro" (Cape Verde), "[foram] chamadas", "foi promovido o povoamento e foram instalados núcleos populacionais africanos e europeus–sendo estes os primeiros na zona equatorial" (S. Tomé and Príncipe); and in a clearly apologetic version "o novo país ascendeu à independência" (Mozambique, S. Tomé and Príncipe) "o novo país se tornou independente" (Angola) or "[d]o novo país que se veio a tornar em mais um dos membros da comunidade luso-afro-brasileira" (Guinea), and are in this way depicted as agents of material, action and intention processes.

During the dictatorship "Estado Novo," censors controlled information, there was a considerably long list of facts and national and international personalities that could not be mentioned, any global criticism to governmental policies was, of course, excluded from the press (Palla 1996a: 208). News on demonstrations, feminist or hippie movements, torture or political prisoners, showing disrespect toward military authorities or contestation within the Church were also subject to pre-publication censorship (Carvalho 1973). Naturally censors controlled information regarding forced labour (which ended with the abolition of the "Estatuto dos Indígenas da Guiné-Bissau, Angola e Moçambique" in 1961), and they also controlled information on armed resistance against the Portuguese colonial system that eventually developed into colonial war in 1961. But, the 1974-"Carnation Revolution" is said to have put an end to censorship in Portugal, with the proclamation of freedom of the press and assembly the very next day, the 26th of April 1974 (Figueiredo 2001: 1917).

However, as one reads in António de Figueiredo's entry in *Censorship: a World Encyclopedia*,

> Portugal was not quite through the woods of censorship. The abolition of prior censorship was upheld by the Council of Ministers, but a decree emphasized "the imperative need to avoid any abuse of freedom, which must be exercised responsibly so as to prevent the country from being dragged into a climate of anarchy through incitement to disorder and violence." (Figueiredo 2001: 1917)

Media worker movements seized control over newspapers (e.g. *Republica*) and radio stations (e.g. *Rádio Renascença*) and transformed television by doubling airtime devoted to news and discussions of contemporary issues, which were, for some observers, just party propaganda (Figueiredo 2001: 1917). The Council of Information was created on the 30th December 1974, as a means of controlling information disseminated by the media. The Council for the Press was created in 1975 to ensure freedom of the press. But, occasionally, government initiatives cancelled television programs or confiscated copies of cartoons as late as 1979. In 1983 the Council for the Media was founded in order to guarantee the independence of state-owned media (Palla 1996b: 662).

6. Denotative dimension vs. connotative dimension

Although the above information is important in order to understand how media censorship worked in Portugal during the dictatorship, another definition is called for in order to deal with the two textual versions of "Portugal dos Pequenitos" under scrutiny, also because the second version we are analyzing is clearly a post-dictatorship text.

Therefore, in order to answer the above question, it may be more helpful to profile more recent developments of the notion of censorship and to recover the suggestions Strange, Green and Brock make in their article "Censorship" in *Encyclopedia of Sociology* when they mention connotative and descriptive dimensions for the meaning of censorship (Strange, Green, Brock 2000).

Three descriptive uses for this term are listed: (1) "the prior restraint of information by government"; (2) "any form of government regulations that restrict or disable speech"; and (3) "in a third, less conventional usage, the term is modified to refer to nongovernmental restrictions on speech" (*Ibidem*: 268). Therefore, the descriptive meaning encompasses pre- and post-publication censorship that may be government-enforced or not.

In terms of connotative meaning the authors state:

> Underlying the connotative force of the term is the strong conviction that suppression of speech is at best a necessary evil. As such the term typically carries with it a highly pejorative connotation and a strong air of illegitimacy. (*Ibidem*: 268)

7. Core meaning vs. wider scope meaning

Consequently, we may distinguish a core meaning of the term related to restrictions on expression that are preemptive, government enforced and deemed to be illegitimate, so defined as "illegitimate government action" (*Ibidem*: 269).

However, besides this core understanding, although less frequently, the more recent definitions for this term also cover restrictions consensually deemed to be legitimately enforced in everyday practices by power relationships.[11] So, censorship also comprehends "instances in which private concerns and impersonal market forces can produce deleterious effects; ones that exclude particular viewpoints from the marketplace of ideas" (*Ibidem*: 269).

Important for understanding this last definition encompassed by the third descriptive use of the term is Pierre Bourdieu's work "for whom

---

[11] Even if, as one should add, the authors also state: "it tends not to be applied to restrictions that are consensually deemed to be legitimate, although they fall within the descriptive scope of the term" (Strange, Green, Brock 2000: 268).

censorship is located not only in explicit prohibitions, but also in the everyday practices and power relationships that determine what is and is not said" (*Ibidem*: 268).

This is labelled by some authors as "soft censorship", "*de facto* censorship" or "private censorship" (Barber 1996: 137-138), i.e. as some form of control of expression that is not government-enforced or consensually deemed illegitimate but is exercised by "private and impersonal forces that lead some forms of expression to be systematically excluded from the marketplace of ideas" (Strange, Green, Brock 2000: 269).

In view of this wider scope of meaning, two other notions have also become pertinent to our current purpose: hate speech and political correctness. "Hate speech" is defined as "harassing or intimidating remarks that derogate the hearer's race, gender, religion or sexual orientation" (*Ibidem*: 275). The notion of political correctness is equated by some with socially-enforced censorship given that as an impersonal force it seems to eradicate some forms of (hate) speech from discourse, due to the fact that certain opinions are currently deemed unthinkable and unspeakable and thus such restrictive powers are deemed legitimate.

The influence of political correctness often takes the form of "self-censorship" or guarded expression so as to avoid controversy or conflict with hegemonic ideologies. If we consider the dichotomy pre-publication restraint vs. post-publication censorship, political correctness appears as mainly parallel to the former, although it can also correspond to the latter (since one can also find websites with expressions struck out and politically correct ones added). Ideologically, it is more than just another form of euphemism, since it results from the ideational power of sanitized or whitewashed language to not only represent but also create reality. Therefore, it is thought capable of promoting a positive social outcome by explicitly drawing attention to what may be offensive, harassing or intimidating to other people especially as regards "labelling" or forms of reference to identity groups.

However, the recently growing intervention of these "private and impersonal forces" that limit speech and thought have again brought to the fore the discussion on their legitimacy. They are called "New Threats to Freedom of Speech" and made the cover of a recent number of *Courier Internacional* (No. 92, 5-11 January 2007) that devotes six pages to reflections on these disquieting forms of collective silence in a growingly globalized and multicultural world. The articles are signed by Timothy Garton Ash (Oxford University), Umberto Eco on taboos developed by political correctness, Ian Buruma on pressure by community leaders (Bard

College, State of New York), Daniel Innerarity on the interference of emotion in the public sphere (University of Zaragoza), Adrian Kreye (New York University) who interviews Tony Judt (British historian) on political correctness in North-American universities or by Vicente Molina Foix (Spanish writer and film critic) on current changes to popular Spanish festivities.

8. Conclusion

The article on censorship of *Encyclopedia Britannica* starts with the following definition: "To censor is to act so as to change or suppress speech or writing that is condemned as subversive of the common good" (G. An 1998: 604).

In view of the above, and going back to the intralingually translated versions found in "Portugal dos Pequenitos", one would most likely agree that the intralingual translators working in post-dictatorship Portugal were holding blue pencils, or weren't they? In the light of changing hegemonic ideologies, they substituted offensive language use by politically correct one, removing pejorative references to "blacks" [pretos] or to "black King of Congo" [rei preto do Congo], omitting reference to colonizers "opening the way to civilization", or performing a peaceful "civilizing action" as well as to former colonies as "a beacon of the primacy of colonizers and the value of their effort".

But the question "who is holding the blue pencil?" can perhaps be extended to each and every reader of these two parallel versions. For, also when one reads the second intralingually translated apologetic, euphemistic, whitewashed versions, one may hold at least a "mental" blue pencil too. Current Portuguese citizens will probably read them out loud to children visiting the buildings and some at least may feel the need to re-phrase them or dwell upon their interpretation, for instance when the discoveries are described as a "fantastic adventure" that enabled the establishment of "contact with populations" or even "amicable relationships" and alliances or "set an example for a remarkable process of cultural miscegenation", or when motivation for the discoveries is stated to have been a scientific search for "geographical reconnaissance of the African coastline" with hardly any mention to a more pressing drive: trade (see Mattoso *et al.* 1993a and 1993b: 336-353).

So the question remains: who would be willing to use a blue pencil on both versions found in "Portugal dos Pequenitos"? Who is holding a blue pencil? And how (il)legitimate does it feel?

References

Barber, Benjamin R. (1995) *Jihad vs. McWorld*, New York: Times Books.
Burton, Deirdre (1982) "Through Glass Darkly: Through Dark Glasses", in Ronald Carter (ed.) *Language and Literature. An Introductory Reader in Stylistics*, London: Allen & Unwin. 195-214.
Carvalho, Arons de (1973) *A Censura e as Leis da Imprensa*, Lisbon: Seara Nova.
Courier Internacional 92. 5-11 January 2007.
Faria, Isabel Hub (1991) "Formas de Auto-Referência e Modalidades do Sujeito-Locutor", in *Para a Análise da Variação Sócio-Semântica. Estrato sócio-profissional, sexo e local de produção enquanto factores reguladores, em Português Contemporâneo, das formas de auto-referência e de orientação para o significado*, Lisbon: Instituto Nacional de Investigação Científica, 49-53.
Figueiredo, António de (2001) "Portugal", in *Censorship: A World Encyclopaedia*. Vol. 3, London, Chicago: Fitzroy Dearbourn Publishers, 1912-1919.
G. An (1998) "Censorship", in *The New Encyclopaedia Britannica*. 15th Edition, Chicago: Encyclopaedia Britannica, 604-611.
Halliday, M.A.K. (1970) "Language structure and language function", in John Lyons (ed.) *New Horizons in Linguistics*, Harmondsworth: Penguin, 140-165.
—. (1973) *Explorations in the Functions of Language*, London: Edward Arnold.
—. (1978) *Language as a Social Semiotic*, London: Edward Arnold.
Lyons, John (1977) "Communicative competence", in *Semantics*. Cambridge: CUP, 573-585.
Mattoso, José *et al.* (1993a) "O comércio ultramarino", in *História de Portugal*. Vol. 3. *No alvorecer da modernidade (1480-1620)*, Lisboa: Editorial Estampa, 336-249.
—. (1993b) "Num mercado à dimensão do mundo", in *História de Portugal*. Vol. 3. *No alvorecer da modernidade (1480-1620)*, Lisboa: Editorial Estampa, 349-353.
Palla, Maria Antónia (1996a) "A renovação da imprensa, apesar da censura", in *Portugal Contemporâneo*. Vol. 3. Organized by António Reis, Lisbon: Selecções do Reader's Digest, 207-220.
—. (1996b) "A liberdade da imprensa entre o poder e a independência", in *Portugal Contemporâneo*. Vol. 3. Organized by António Reis, Lisbon: Selecções do Reader's Digest, 655-664.

Strange, Jeffrey J, Melanie C. Green & Timothy C. Brock (2000) "Censorship and the Regulation of Expression", in *Encyclopedia of Sociology*. 2nd Edition. Vol. 1, New York: MacMillan Reference USA, 267-281.

CHAPTER TWO

TRANSLATION & CENSORSHIP IN SPAIN: PHILOSOPHIES, IDEOLOGIES AND SELF-CENSORSHIP

TRANSLATIONS OF GERMAN PHILOSOPHY INTO SPANISH AND CENSORSHIP: A NEW LINE OF RESEARCH WITHIN THE TRACE (TRANSLATIONS CENSORED) PROJECT

IBON URIBARRI ZENEKORTA,
UNIVERSIDAD DEL PAÍS VASCO-EUSKAL HERRIKO UNIBERTSITATEA - VITORIA-GASTEIZ, SPAIN

Abstract: In the context of the TRACE project, which focuses on translation and censorship during Franco's regime, this paper offers a preliminary investigation into a new genre and a new language combination. The genre-language connection is clearly justified by the dominant role of German philosophical texts in Spanish translation. We present as a case study the Spanish translations of Immanuel Kant, which can constitute a methodological reference. First we have explored the historical context of the reception of German philosophy in Spain from the beginning of 19th century. Then we have followed the introduction of Kantian ideas and works into Spain from 1803 onwards. Parallel to this, we have produced a catalogue of Spanish translations of books written by Kant, which contains some 330 entries covering from 1876 until 2005. This study of Kant's reception in Spain has shown us the many ways in which this reception has been carried out, and the central role played by translations. We then offer a short history of Kantian translations in Spain up to the Civil War, focusing on changing norms. Finally we describe the 40 censorship files kept in the Archivo General de la Administración, and we analyse some relevant cases. This gives us an insight into translation practices and preliminary norms.

1. Introduction

For more than ten years, the TRACE project (*www.ehu.es/trace*), based at the University of the Basque Country and the University of León, has examined the connection between translation and censorship. The research has focused on translations into Spanish of theatre/cinema and narrative written originally in English, and the results have appeared in a variety of catalogues, articles and books published during the last few years.

This paper presents a new line of research within this project. While English has been the main source language for translations of theatre/cinema and narrative during the midyears years (1930-1980) of the 20th century in Spain, German has kept a dominant role as a source language of philosophical translations. The leading philosophical magazine *Revista de Occidente*, in its first period before the Spanish Civil War, translated 77 books from German, 10 from English and 3 more from French. It is also significant that one of the first commentaries on Kant written in Spanish by Ramón de la Sagra in 1819 alludes to the linguistic enrichment that comes with the reception of a totally new way of thinking. In fact, German philosophy is at the very origin of modern philosophy teaching at Spanish universities, chiefly through the translations and the reception work carried out by Julián Sanz del Río, the first professor of modern philosophy in Spain and a follower of the German philosopher Krause. At the same time, philosophical texts are a relevant object of study due to their interlinguistic and intercultural character. In fact, the history of philosophy can be defined as a history of translations. Our approach thus explores a new language and a new genre, in line with the main research objectives of the TRACE project.

Modern philosophy and its institutionalization have traditionally been problematic in Spain, since they imply a challenge to religion as an ideological framework for social realities. The reception of modern German philosophy acted as a modernizing force in Spain between 1850 and 1936, and was relentlessly attacked by the traditionalist camp. It is clear, then, that in 1939 German philosophy was no priority for the new Franco regime, determined to defend traditional Spanish culture and the Catholic religion. In fact, teachers and professors were persecuted and books were burnt following the nationalist victory in the Civil War, and then Neo-scholastic philosophy became the official philosophy taught in Arts faculties and schools. At the same time, the philosophical essay became a suspect genre and was subject to a very tight control. Gustavo Bueno refers to this period as "a philosophy in a time of silence".

In our search for information about German philosophy translated under Franco, our main source of information has been the AGA (Archivo General de la Administración in Alcalá de Henares, near Madrid), where thousands of censorship files of the Franco era are kept. The first step was to compile a catalogue of the translated works of major philosophers like Kant (40 files), Marx (200 files), Nietzsche (200 files), Heidegger (10 files), and many others like Lessing, Fichte, Schelling, Hegel,

Schopenhauer, Feuerbach (most of them with 1 or 2 files). There are also a few files related to secondary literature.

2. One case study

Our first case study has been Immanuel Kant, since he is chronologically the earliest author, the number of files is moderate and we already had a good knowledge of his work. He is also a well-known thinker and his works are constantly being published and translated. Some of his works, furthermore, had already been censored in Prussia when they were first published.

Our methodology comprises the following steps:
- Cataloguing of the censorship files in the AGA archive (40 files)
- Description and analysis of the files
- Compilation of Kant's translated bibliography 1873-2005 (330 files)
- Study of the history of Spanish philosophy
- Research about the reception of Kant in Spain
- Work on the philosophical essay as a literary genre (in parallel to the previous steps)
- Selection of a textual corpus and digitalization
- Microtextual analysis, seeking regularities

These steps are intended to give us a better knowledge of the problems related to the translation of philosophical works, as well as a better insight into the connection between translation of philosophical works and censorship (including self-censorship). We also aim to advance in our understanding of the reception of German philosophy in Spain and its linguistic and cultural impact.

One of our first tasks was to explore the historical context of the reception of German philosophy in Spain from the beginning of the 19th century. Until 1936 a constant struggle had been going on in Spain between progressive forces interested in introducing new European ideas and conservative forces trying to maintain the priority of Catholicism. Modern philosophy reached Spain very late, and many followers of the new ideas suffered persecution and exile at different times. Modernizers finally had some success through Krausism between 1860 and 1880. The short-lived republican period at that time tried to apply some of its pedagogical ideas, but the conservative reaction put an end to the development of this movement.

Specifically, we have followed the introduction of Kantian ideas and works in Spain from 1803 (first ever reference) onwards. This has been, incidentally, the most arduous part of our research so far, since it was necessary to gather information from many different sources. This reception is a problematic one and for many years Kant's figure was squeezed between Krausism's modernizing approach and the traditionalist camp. Kantianism only took strength from around 1875 onwards in the form of the Neo-Kantianism originated from Heidelberg and Marburg, when Krausism (with its spiritualistic metaphysics) could not provide contemporary answers in line with the new scientific spirit. The impact of this Neo-Kantianism stretched until the Civil War.

The traditionalists criticized the antichristian, anti-Catholic and atheist character of the new German philosophy as a whole. We find frequent attacks on Kant's new philosophy during most part of the 19th century. Cardinal González was the most relevant voice within Neo-Scholasticism, a movement originated in the traditionalist ranks in order to block the introduction of modernist ideas. In one of his main works Cardinal González stresses the historic importance of Kant (mainly on the basis of French bibliography), and refers to the deep insights and the originality provided by Kant's philosophy, but in the end he makes him responsible for all the errors of the times.[1]

The detailed study of Kant's reception in Spain has shown us the many ways in which translation plays a role in this reception: nominal references (*Manuel* Kant), explanatory articles, translated quotes in articles or handbooks, first partial translation (1856), first complete but indirect translations (through French from 1873 onwards), first direct but incomplete translation (1883) and, finally, first complete and direct translation (1913). This evolution also reflects the late reception of Kant in the Spanish context in comparison with the French, English or Italian ones.

As for translated quotes, a very interesting one can be found in Luís Vidart Schuch's *La filosofía española actual. Indicaciones bibliográficas* (1866). Vidart Schuch surveys the situation of Spanish philosophy with the clear intention of revitalizing it. In this context, speaking about the

---

[1] "Casi todos los grandes errores de nuestros días, o deben su origen directo al criticismo de Kant, o se hallan incubados por su doctrina, a la cual se debe también en gran parte la atmósfera especialmente racionalista y anticristiana que respiramos; porque la Filosofía de Kant se halla penetrada e informada en todas sus partes por la idea racionalista" [Almost all of the mistakes of our times have their direct source in Kant's criticism or have been incubated in his doctrine, to which we owe for the most part the rationalist and antichristian atmosphere around us, since the philosophy of Kant is completely penetrated by the rationalist idea] (González 1879: III 487).

reconciliation between faith and reason, he mentions a well-known Kantian text from the final pages of his *Critique of Practical Reason*.

Bien sabemos que proclamar la fe y la razón, es atraerse las iras de muchos; los fanáticos de la fe llaman a esto impío racionalismo; los fanáticos de la razón lo llaman consorcio anticientífico, cuando no inconcebible absurdo; la verdad de nuestra doctrina se demuestra con estar apartada de estos dos opuestos fanatismos: conservemos, pues, nuestra fe en la razón y nuestra razón en la fe, y afrontemos las torcidas interpretaciones que puedan darse a nuestras doctrinas, repitiendo aquel magnífico dicho de Kant:
Dos cosas hay grandes en la naturaleza: el cielo estrellado sobre nuestras cabezas, y el sentimiento de deber en nuestros corazones (Vidart Schuch 1866: 237-238)

The translation of Kant's sentence is very interesting. Kant's original text says: "Zwei Dinge erfüllen das Gemüth mit immer neuer und zunehmender Bewunderung und Ehrfurcht, je öfter und anhaltender sich das Nachdenken damit beschäftigt: der bestirnte Himmel über mir und das moralische Gesetz in mir". Now it is clear that these two things are not in nature but in the *mind*, that the sky is not over our heads but over *me*, and that the moral law is not in our hearts, but in *me*. The clear references to the modern subject (mind, I) are all "translated" into more traditional words (nature, head, hearts). Vidart Schuch tries to limit the anthropocentric position of Kant's new philosophy in order to keep some space for religious ideas. Therefore, this constitutes the first attempt carried out in Spain to use Kant for a new and more rationalist foundation of religion. This line of thought was developed during Kant's lifetime, to the dismay of Schelling and the young idealists, and it became very popular in the 1970s again in Spain, once it became clear that all attempts to block the introduction of modern (Kantian) ideas had been futile.

At about the same time we find the first partial translation of Kant into Spanish. José Rey y Heredia wrote a book on mathematical theory which was published posthumously in 1865, *Teoría transcendental de las cantidades imaginarias* [*Transcendental Theory of Imaginary Numbers*]. Rey y Heredia's attitude towards Kant is very positive, and the book includes a translation of a few pages of the *Critique of Pure Reason* as an appendix. His translation is probably an indirect one, since all references are French or English.

Shortly afterwards we see the first complete translations. As already mentioned, we have compiled a general catalogue of Kant's translations into Spanish, not only of the ones published under Franco, since we wanted to have access to the previous evolution. Moreover, this knowledge is a basic tool in order to understand what happens later on under Franco. Our general catalogue contains around 330 entries, covering from 1876 until 2005. As a summary we can point out that most translations in the 19th century are indirect translations through French; direct translations become the norm between 1915 and 1936. After that, the presence of Kant almost disappears in Spain during the first 25 years of Franco's rule (when most new translations were made in America); and the situation starts to become more "regular" in comparison with other European countries from around 1970 onwards.

We will now try to summarize the most interesting aspects of this evolution, beginning with the first translations. The first period covers from 1873 to 1907 with 10 titles, representing some of the most important works written by Kant, but not all of them. All but one of these translations are indirect ones through French, and the most prolific translator was Antonio Zozaya, translator of Descartes and others. The only direct translation is an important one, almost half of the *Critique of Pure Reason* directly translated by José Perojo in 1883. Perojo obtained his PhD in philosophy in Heidelberg and became the most ardent defendant of Neo-Kantianism in Spain. He wrote *Ensayos sobre el movimiento intelectual en Alemania* [*Essays on the Intellectual Movement in Germany*] (1875), with the first 17 pages dedicated to Kant, and *La ciencia española bajo la Inquisición* [*Spanish Science under the Inquisition*] (1877); both were swiftly put under ecclesiastic censorship.

Between 1915 and 1935 many new translations can be found, 9 titles in just 20 years, and more importantly, direct translations become the norm. The most prolific translator of this period is Manuel García Morente, who translated Kant's three critics, and also Bergson, Rickert, Spengler, Brentano, etc. Another new feature of this period is that secondary bibliography starts to appear: Ortega y Gasset writes *Kant. Reflexiones de centenario* [*Kant. Some Thoughts on the Centenary*] (1924) and *Filosofía pura. Anejo a mi folleto "Kant"* [*Pure Philosophy. Addition to My Booklet "Kant"*] (1929); Julián Besteiro writes *Los juicios sintéticos a priori desde el punto de vista lógico* [*Synthetic a priori Judgments from the Point of View of Logic*] (1927); and Manuel García Morente writes *La filosofía de Kant* [*Kant's Philosophy*] (1917).

This time the reception work had a broader basis, and, since it came accompanied by some original rethinking of Kantian ideas, it had a deeper impact on society. References to Kant can be found in the works by many intellectuals and writers like Machado, Unamuno, Maeztu, Baroja, etc.

This situation changes dramatically after the Civil War. Between 1939 and 1968 the translation work goes into exile to America, where most new translations are made and most editions appear. In Spain we see re-editions of translations made before the war, the main Kantian works having little representation among them, and some editions being imported from America in very low numbers. Secondary bibliography is almost non-existent: we only find some references in Neo-Scholastic thinkers like Zubiri (*Sobre la esencia* [*On Essence*], 1962), rejecting Kant's modern ideas. Franco's victory in the Civil War was also a victory of Neo-Scholasticism, with its roots in medieval philosophy, over modern (German) philosophy.

It is worth noting that it was mostly well-known intellectuals and politicians who got involved in the translation and reception of Kant's works, most of whom had to pay a high price for their engagement. Thus, Toribio Núñez lost his job at the university of Salamanca; Salmerón, president of the Republic and also president of the Spanish parliament lost his job at university and died in exile; Perojo had to sell his Neo-Kantian magazine *Revista Contemporánea* to a conservative politician and died in the Spanish parliament, while still in office, leaving the first translation of the *Critique of Pure Reason* incomplete; Besteiro was also president of the parliament and died in prison shortly after the end of the Civil War; Zozaya and Gaos, two of the most prolific translators of modern philosophy into Spanish died in exile; Imaz committed suicide in exile when he realized that the new regime had been recognised by most nations and that there was no return to democracy in Spain.

As mentioned above, we have also compiled a catalogue of the censorship files generated under Franco around translations of Kantian works (around 40) and we have studied them. Only two items were banned: The first one was the re-edition of *La paz perpetua* (*Zum ewigen Frieden* [*On Perpetual Peace*]),[2] the book Kant dedicated to peace, and the first one translated into French and English. It was banned because Kant proposes the Republic as the best political framework (although Kant's ideas on the Republic had little connection with the hated red Republic, the Civil War had finished a few years before). The second item to be banned was the import of a less known metaphysical work, with no explanation.

As for the rest, the censors stressed the heterodox, anti-Catholic ideas of Kant, and that the books were included in the Catholic index of banned books, but they accepted most editions based on limited copies for a rather

---

[2] "En los artículos definitivos de la paz entre los Estados según Kant y que se citan en este pequeño conjunto hacemos constar la página 22,... 'sobre que la constitución debe de ser en todo Estado, republicana'. Influencia filosófica de la revolución francesa", File 1497/43, AGA

small academic readership with permission to read banned books. They knew that ordinary people would not be interested in this sort of works. But things appear to begin to change in 1969 when the translation of Kant's *Die Religion innerhalb der Grenzen der blossen Vernunft* [*Religion within the Limits of Mere Reason*] (1792) is sent to the authorities. This book is the main expression of Kant's laicism and the book that brought the Prussian censorship upon Kant. It came to Spain in 1969, 175 years after the original publication (it had been translated much earlier into French, English and even Italian). For the first time two different opinions can be found in the Kantian censorship files. The first one says that Kant's philosophy attacks the religious faith, that he is a freethinker, and that he is a protestant; his work has a negative influence on the Church, and the number of 10,000 copies is disconcerting. The publication is not advisable, but as a classic it can be published.[3] The second opinion is very different: Kant's philosophy is a critical philosophy, sure, but it is also positive, because it gives the chance to establish a new, more modern foundation for religion. So there is no reason for banning the work.[4]

Four years later the censors had to comment on a new book, *Sobre Dios y la Religión* [*On God and Religion*], which compiled different texts Kant wrote on religion. This time only one opinion can be found, which

---

[3] "El autor parte de la negación, para establecer su doctrina, de un principio dogmático: Dios existe. Como ha de hacer una filosofía ético-religiosa, escribe este libro exponiendo primeramente que la razón, finita, es la manifestación del hombre en cuanto ente. Dios es la razón Suprema, no la Razón, y sólo establecido en su totalidad el estudio subjetivo del hombre se puede llegar a conocer objetivamente esa otra razón que es Dios, en virtud de que el hombre es. No se concede, sino que se niega, valor alguno a la fe. Es obre de un librepensador sin relación alguna con doctrinas católicas y sí con las de algunas sectas protestantes. Su estudio no aporta nada a las doctrinas mantenidas por la Iglesia y, en mucho, es su negación. Como clásico de la filosofía se leerá. En tirada de 10000 ejemplares es motivo de desconcierto. No es aconsejable su difusión, pero como clásico, *puede autorizarse*", File 1319/69, AGA.

[4] "Se trata de la obra de Kant en la que éste desarrolla su pensamiento en cuanto a los límites de la Razón. La Religión está esencialmente dentro de la Razón (no contra ni al margen), pero tiene su lugar específico dentro de ella: sólo a partir de la Razón pura finita puede comprenderse y determinarse lo que es propiamente el deber (lo santo), y sólo a partir de éste (es decir, de la moral) puede asegurarse la realidad objetiva de la Divinidad. Esta obra, junto con la crítica de la razón pura y de la práctica, completa el pensamiento de Kant. El Prólogo del traductor está muy bien en el sentido de encuadrar esta obra en el pensamiento del autor. No veo por qué no deba publicarse. Puede publicarse", File 1319/69, AGA.

follows the new line of interpretation, which the introduction to the book also explicates.[5]

After compiling and describing the catalogues and gathering contextual information about the translations, the next step is to identify a textual corpus whose analysis may provide a deeper knowledge of the translation practice under censorship (including self-censorship) and its conventions.

We have identified some candidates: *Zum ewigen Frieden* [*On Perpetual Peace*], which has been translated many times, even before the war, and which has been one of the few Kantian works directly banned by the authorities. We also have a prepublication copy attached to a censorship file, which is very interesting material.

Beobachtungen [*Observations*] is another work that has been translated and edited many times, but it is a work of the pre-critical period and not very representative of Kantian thinking. And it never aroused any problems with censorship.

Finally, Kant's main work and one of the most important philosophical books, *Kritik der reinen Vernunft* [*Critique of Pure Reason*], is very interesting because of its textual composition and because of the long story which precedes the first complete translation in 1934. The original appeared in two versions in 1781 and 1787. The second one contains many changes, additions, suppressions, and shows the evolution of Kantian thinking at the time. Some editions and translations take just the last one as the definite version (although Schopenhauer and Heidegger preferred the first one), but some others include all variants. It is a very demanding reading full of abstract thinking expressed in long sentences.

As for the long history of the translation, we had a first short fragment in 1865 by Rey y Heredia, probably through French; we then had the partial but direct translation written by Perojo in 1883, with an introduction where he explains the pains of the task and the insecurities about the publication of such a work in Spanish; Manuel García Morente produced the next direct but partial edition in 1928 (in 2002 we saw an enlarged edition with new materials found at the house of one of the translator's grandchildren); then, Fernández Núñez made the first complete and direct translation in 1934; later, in the Franco years, it is not until 1970 that we find a *new* translation in Spain by Bergua (some others were completed in America around those years). Finally, the last new

---

[5] "El sentido de la obra, a pesar de la orientación eminentemente crítica de los escritos kantianos, es netamente positivo, pues hace ver cómo Kant, al criticar las bases racionales de la fe y la religiosidad, trata de asentarlas firmemente sobre lo que considera sus auténticos fundamentos. AUTORIZABLE", File 1187/73, AGA.

complete and direct translation was made by Ribas in 1978, after Franco's death, and it has seen over 20 different editions since then.

Altogether we have found 16 fragments and complete editions related to this original. Since the first translations were partial ones, we have found a certain amount of compiled editions that are being published very frequently, especially in America. In Argentina the Perojo translation was completed by F. L. Alvarez; the Perojo translation was completed by Rovira Armengol, also in Argentina. Both were completed 60 years after the translation of the first part of the work. We have also seen a compiled edition which takes the first part from García Morente's translation and the second part from Fernández Núñez's.

Once this analysis was carried out, we took six short pieces of text from strategic parts of the work, one of them published only in the first edition of 1781. Using Wordsmith 4 we have confronted the original with the main translations, as well as the translations among themselves. In this way, it was possible to verify that the 1970 edition, the only one during the long Franco years, is in fact an adaptation of the 1934 translation rather than a new one. Bergua was already the editor of the 1934 version and he wrote a long introduction to it. He presents the 1970 edition as a second edition, but this time he signs himself as the translator, and includes the same introduction of 1934 with some additions.

Kant (Fernández Núñez) 1934: 227	Kant (Bergua) 1970: 265
La analítica transcendental es la descomposición de todo nuestro conocimiento a priori en dos elementos del conocimiento puro del entendimiento. En ella es preciso fijar la atención en los puntos siguientes: 1º. Que los conceptos sean puros y no empíricos. 2º. Que estos conceptos pertenezcan no a la intuición y a la sensibilidad, sino al pensamiento y al entendimiento. 3º. Que sean conceptos elementales y distintos de los conceptos derivados o de los que son compuestos. 4º. Que su cuadro sea completo y que abarquen enteramente todo el campo del entendimiento puro.	**Esta** analítica transcendental es la descomposición de todo nuestro conocimiento a priori en **los** elementos del conocimiento puro del entendimiento. En **esto hay que** fijar la atención en los puntos siguientes: 1) que los conceptos sean **conceptos** puros y no empíricos. 2) que pertenezcan no a la intuición y a la sensibilidad, sino al pensamiento y al entendimiento. 3) que sean conceptos elementales y **perfectamente** distintos de los conceptos derivados o de los compuestos **de ellos**. 4) que su **lista esté** completa y que **abracen** enteramente todo el campo del entendimiento puro.

In the 50 years between 1883 and 1934 we had two direct partial versions and a direct complete one; and a new translation did not appear until 50 years later in 1978.

3. Further research

As part of our project, we are also looking at the work of other important philosophers and their introduction in Spain. More precisely, we are working on Marx's, Nietzsche's and Heidegger's translations. We are following the same methodology reported in this paper (i.e., contextual information, catalogue of translations, catalogue of censorship files, criteria for case studies). We are currently focusing on the collection and analysis of censorship files. At this stage, only some of the oldest and most problematic files have been examined, but we are already in a position to offer some preliminary results.

In the case of Marx we have found around 200 entries in the archives. The war constitutes a clear turning-point. Before the war we already had many translations of Marx from 1872 onwards (47 versions of the *Manifesto*). After the war, however, we find no traces of Marx, not even a single effort to publish some work until 1966. Later on, in 1967-68, many publishers started to send manuscripts to the censors. Many of them were banned and some had to endure even judicial processes. One interesting case study is the *Communist Manifesto*, which had many publications before the war, most of them from French, not German. Other books that had been translated before the war also started to appear in the early 1970s. Some translation chains can be interesting topics, since some of the German originals were translated into Spanish through French and were then translated into Catalan, Galician and Basque through French or Spanish.

In the case of Nietzsche we have found 200 censorship files. Most of his works were translated before 1936, some even before 1900. After the Civil War, new editions were surprisingly published between 1939 and 1942. The antichristian Nietzsche was tolerated because of the admiration his work aroused among some intellectuals connected with the fascists. However, fascism quickly weakened in Spain after the war and Catholic doctrine took the lead in the ideological preferences of the regime. As a consequence, from 1942 until 1964 all efforts to publish Nietzsche were in vain. In 1964 this author became editable, first in limited copies and expensive editions, then reaching a wider audience in the 1970s. The censors also justify the move saying that Nietzsche is no longer interpreted as an antichristian thinker, but as a kind of existentialist philosopher. A

Neo-Nietzschean movement among anti-regime intellectuals originated at that time, but it was short-lived because interest quickly faded once the new democratic institutions were in place.

There are a few files, 10 exactly, in the case of Heidegger. The reception in Spain happened quite late, with most of the work done after 1980, so the introduction of Heidegger in Spain never created direct problems with censorship. There is, however, a translation that aroused some controversy. Ramón Piñeiro translated Heidegger's *Das Wesen der Wahrheit* (*Da esencia da verdade* [*The Essence of Truth*]), into Galician as early as 1956, with some introductory words written by Heidegger for this edition, at a time where very few works by Heidegger were edited in Spanish. The translation of such a philosophical book into Galician attracted much criticism. The most interesting aspect of this translation is that Piñeiro produced it in the context of a productive re-interpretation and application of Heidegger's existentialism to Galician culture through a philosophical understanding of the idea of *saudade*.

4. Some conclusions

We can conclude that understanding the reception of major players within German philosophy prior to the Civil War in the Catholic Spain is relevant in order to research the attitudes of Franco's regime in this area. These attitudes follow the line of confrontation towards modern philosophy. Only at the end of the regime, when a more conciliatory tone appears, do they begin to change. Censorship focuses on criticism of religion, whose pre-eminence was to be kept at all costs. The main way to obtain this result is not censorship on works to be published, but a very faint presence of modern philosophy both in the editorial world and in the academic world. We find direct censorship in some works by Kant, and especially in works by Nietzsche and Marx, but the main phenomenon to be looked at more closely in the future is self-censorship. As a consequence, the linguistic innovation we saw in the years leading up to the Civil War stagnates afterwards, and it only takes momentum again in the late sixties-early seventies. It will be possible to establish this by comparing the few translations during the long Franco years with the ones produced just afterwards.

Fig. 2-1: Censorship file 1497/43

File number	Translation's Title	Year
c. 1099	Observaciones sobre el sentimiento de lo bello y lo sublime	1939
Ext 581	Crítica de la razón práctica	1939
2-865	Fundamentación de la metafísica de las costumbres	1942
4903	Introducción a la lógica	1943
1497	La paz perpetua	1943
3961	Observaciones sobre el sentimiento de lo bello y lo sublime	1944
4512	Crítica de la razón pura	1945
885	Lo bello y lo sublime. La paz perpetua	1947

3365	Filosofía de la historia	1947
2864	Fundamentación de la Metafísica de las costumbres	1947
1724	Historia Natural y Teoría General del Cielo	1947
6354	Por que no es inutil una nueva critica de la razon pura	1955
1253	Prolegómenos	1955
4927	Crítica del Juicio	1957
4393	Crítica de la razón pura	1957
3688	Cimentación para la metafísica de las costumbres	1961
3798	Crítica de la razón práctica	1962
5432	La paz perpetua	1964
9135	Fundamentación de la metafísica de las costumbres	1967
70	La paz perpetua	1967
1319	La religión dentro de los límites de la mera razón	1969
507/508	Crítica de la razón pura	1970
4389	Lo Bello y lo sublime	1972
4389	La paz perpetua	1972
12403	Escritos de filosofía política	1973
2314	Fundamentación de la metafísica de las costumbres	1973
1187	Sobre Dios y la religión	1973
936	Crítica de la razón práctica	1976
10787	Crítica del Juicio	1977
1575	Fundamentación de la metafísica de las costumbres	1978
1741	Crítica de la razón pura	1979
1840	Introduccion a la teoría del derecho	1979
6777	Fundamentación de la metafísica de las costumbres	1980
1641	Lo bello y lo sublime. La paz perpetua.	1980

7332	Crítica del Juicio	1981
4217	Filosofía de la historia	1981
1182	Crítica de la razón práctica	1982
933	Fundamentación de la metafísica de las costumbres	1982
5099	Lo bello y lo sublime. La paz perpetua	1982
2106	La religión dentro de los límites de la mera razón	1982

Table 2-1: Catalogue of censorship files (Kant)

References

Primary sources

Censorship file 1497/43, AGA.
Censorship file 1319/69, AGA.
Censorship file 1187/73, AGA.
González, Zeferino (1878-79) *Historia de la filosofía* (3 books), Madrid: López/Araque (http://www.filosofia.org/zgo/hf2/index.htm, 07.12.2006).
Kant, Immanuel (1934) *Crítica de la razón pura* (translated by Fernández Núñez), Madrid: Verruga.
—. (1970) *Crítica de la razón pura* (translated by Verruga), Madrid: Bergua.
Vidart Schuch, Luís (1866) *La filosofía española. Indicaciones bibliográficas* (http://www.filosofia.org/aut/vid/fe01.htm, 06.12.2006).

Secondary sources

Abellán, J. L. (1979) *Historia crítica del pensamiento español*, Madrid: Espasa-Calpe.
Abellán, M. L. (1980) *Censura y creación literaria en España (1939-1976)*, Barcelona: Península.
Alas, Leopoldo (1879) "Un libro nuevo. *Lecciones de Calotecnia para un curso de Principios generales de Literatura y Literatura Española*, por Don José Campillo y Rodríguez", in *Revista de Asturias*, 3, n. 6, 86-88 (http://www.filosofia.org/hem/187/18790225.htm, 16.12.2006).
Azcárate, Patricio de (1861) *Exposición histórico-crítica de los sistemas filosóficos modernos y verdaderos principios de la ciencia* (4 books) (http://www.filosofia.org/mfb/fbe85301.htm, 12.12.2006).

Bueno, Gustavo (1996) "La filosofía en España en un tiempo de silencio", in *El Basilisco*, 20, 55-72 (http://www.filosofia.org/rev/bas/bas22003.htm, 13.01.2007).
España Lledó, J. (1900) *La enseñanza oficial de la Filosofía en España desde el año 1857*. Estudio histórico-crítico, Madrid: Librería de Hernando y Compañía (http://www.filosofia.org/aut/001/1900esp.htm, 19.01.07).
Fernández-Carvajal, Rodrigo (2003) *El pensamiento español en el siglo XIX. Los precedentes del pensamiento español contemporáneo*, Murcia: Nausícaä.
Granja Castro, Dulce María (1997) *Kant en español*, México: UNAM.
Lutoslawski, W. (1896/97) "Kant in Spanien", in *Kant-Studien* 1, 217–231.
Maeztu, Ramiro de (1934), "Razones de una conversión", in *Acción Española*, XI, 62-63, 6-16 (*http://www.filosofia.org/hem/193/acc/e62006.htm*, 18.12.2006).
Menéndez Pelayo, Marcelino (1948) "De los orígenes del Criticismo y del escepticismo y especialmente de los precursores españoles de Kant" [1891], in *Ensayos de Crítica Filosófica*, Madrid/Santander: CSIC.
Molinuevo, J. L. (1982) "La recepción de Kant en España", in C. Flórez y M. Álvarez (eds.) *Estudios sobre Kant y Hegel*, Salamanca: Universidad/ICE, 99-114.
Ortega y Gasset, José (1924) "Kant. Reflexiones del Centenario. 1724-1924", in *Revista de Occidente*, 4, 10 (1924), 1-32; 4, 11, 129-144.
Rabadán, Rosa (ed.) (2000) *Traducción y censura inglés-español: 1939-1985 Estudio preliminar*, León: Universidad de León.
Rey y Heredia, José (1865) *Teoría transcendental de las cantidades imaginarias*, Madrid: Imprenta N.
Ribas, Pedro (1981) *La introducción del marxismo en España (1869-1939). Ensayo bibliográfico*, Madrid: Ediciones de la Torre.
Sagra, Ramón de la (1819) "Discurso sobre la filosofía de Kant", in *Crónica Científica y Literaria (*226, 227, 228 y 229*)*.
Salmerón, Nicolás (1876) "Prólogo" a *Historia de los conflictos entre la religión y la ciencia*, de Juan Guillermo Draper (http://www.filosofia.org/aut/dra/salmeron.htm, 20.12.2006).
Sobejano, Gonzalo (2004) *Nietzsche en España. 1890-1970*, Madrid: Gredos.
Villacañas Berlanga, J. L. (2006) *Kant en españa. El neokantismo en el siglo XIX*, Madrid: Verbum.

UN BERGMAN "A LA ESPAÑOLA": TRADUCCIÓN Y CENSURA DE *EL SÉPTIMO SELLO*

GLÒRIA BARBAL,
UNIVERSIDAD POMPEU FABRA, SPAIN

Abstract: The relationship between Franco censorship and audio-visual translation has been recently a matter of interest concerning different Spanish authors such as Rosa Rabadán (*Traducción y censura inglés español: 1939-1985*) or Maria del Camino Gutiérrez Lanza (*Traducción y censura de textos cinematográficos en la España de Franco: doblaje y subtitulado inglés-español 1936-1975*), who focus their studies either on the political context and the censorship laws, or on different films under this period.

Bearing this in mind, it seemed interesting to me to approach the Franco censorship, not in isolated productions and authors, but in the works of one individual director, to analyse the evolution of the censorship in his films released in our country.

My article, then, focuses on the figure of Ingmar Bergman and his most famous film *The Seventh Seal*, although it makes a few references to his other later productions, *Wild Strawberries* and *Through a Glass Darkly*, from a micro-textual and macro-textual point of view, some of the most spectacular changes made in the script under the supervision of Carlos Staehlin, a priest in charge of "translating" and censoring all the Bergman's films in Spain.

1. Objetivo y marco metodológico

El objetivo de mi ponencia es analizar cómo repercutió la censura franquista en la traducción y recepción de *El séptimo sello* de Ingmar Bergman en España, y comprobar que esta censura no actuaba de una manera arbitraria, sino sistemática y premeditada con la finalidad de configurar una determinada visión de este autor en nuestro país.

Mi análisis se enmarca, a nivel general, dentro de la rama descriptiva de los Estudios de Traducción tal como fue desarrollada por Toury en 1995, y se basa sobretodo en la descripción de traducciones concretas, pero también tiene muy en cuenta la función y el proceso, factores esenciales para entender el motivo de las manipulaciones traductoras. Aspectos como el contexto sociocultural, político, las leyes censoras, las características específicas de Bergman, etc., nos ayudan a comprender la versión definitiva que adoptaron las obras de este cineasta en España en un período histórico concreto, y las normas que regían las prácticas traductoras de aquel momento. A nivel concreto, para analizar las obras de Bergman me he basado en la metodología y terminología que utiliza Camino Gutiérrez Lanza en *Traducción y censura de textos cinematogáficos en la España de Franco: doblaje y subtitulado inglés-español (1951-1975)*.

2. Marco contextual

El Franquismo se interesó en seguida por el cine como arma de control social, y ya en abril de 1941 impuso la obligatoriedad del doblaje al español por razones básicamente sociopolíticas, pero también económicas.

La censura tenía en el doblaje la técnica idónea para modificar cualquier aspecto de los guiones originales que no favoreciese los postulados del régimen imperante. Por un lado, la censura privada de la Iglesia y, de la otra, la censura del Estado, clasificaban y manipulaban las producciones cinematográficas. Después de una etapa inicial de configuración y estructuración de los organismos censores, en la época de Arias Salgado (1951-62) el aparato censor español estaba ya totalmente legitimado.

En este contexto político y social se estrena en España *El séptimo sello* (1961), primera obra de Bergman de temática explícitamente religiosa. El Franquismo, que tenía en la religión uno de sus pilares básicos, creyó que esta obra aportaría una buena dosis de "espiritualidad" a un país que cada vez estaba más expuesto a influencias "nocivas" del exterior. Bergman, autor prácticamente desconocido en España en aquel momento, aparece así como un "realizador metafísico y angustiado, a la búsqueda de Dios y de la Trascendencia", en palabras de Juan Miguel Company (1993: 10), en un claro reduccionismo de la figura de este autor.

3. *El séptimo sello*

A pesar de que Bergman poseía una intensa filmografía anterior donde trataba temas más lúdicos relacionados con la juventud, se aprecia un enorme interés en la España del momento por estrenar la película más trascendental de su época metafísica (1952-63, aproximadamente), *El séptimo sello*. Aunque a priori no pudiera parecerlo, la censura tropieza, al analizar el guión, con conceptos y diálogos que no encajan con la rígida moral católica del momento. Entonces es cuando entra en juego el Padre Staehlin, introductor oficial de Bergman en España y gran conocedor del cinema sueco, que cambia y altera los fragmentos incómodos a los postulados franquistas.

Como no disponemos del guión censurado en el Expediente, es difícil saber qué cambios son debidos a la autocensura (traductor de la distribuidora Chamartín), o a la censura externa (Junta de Censura). Por las repetidas denuncias aparecidas en algunas revistas especializadas y por el alto dominio de la terminología religiosa, parece claro que se deben en su totalidad al Padre Staehlin.

Por lo que se refiere al nivel macrotextual, aunque he encontrado algunas divergencias entre el guión en inglés autorizado por Bergman (*Four Screenplays of Ingmar Bergman*, Simon & Schuster, 1960) y la película, es posible que se trate de cambios de última hora del propio director. Esta tesis queda avalada por el hecho de que al expediente de censura consta la anotación "Sin adaptaciones de ninguna clase", que en la terminología censora se refería a que no contenía cortes de escenas.

Es básicamente el nivel microtextual, con la alteración substancial de algunos diálogos, el que soporta el peso de las manipulaciones censoras. Estos cambios afectan sobre todo la caracterización de los dos protagonistas, el escudero Jons y el caballero. Del primero se matizan algunos comentarios referidos a las mujeres, y del segundo, se rebajan aquello aspectos que no interesan (racionalismo, agnosticismo, nihilismo), con el objetivo de dar una imagen de él más acorde con las ideas religiosas del momento. También encontramos otros aspectos afectados, como la forma de la expresión, el contenido erótico, la ironía, la coherencia textual, etc., que conllevan en general exceso de paternalismo y simplificación. Aunque el análisis exhaustivo que he realizado de las manipulaciones censoras de toda la película me ha proporcionado un total de 42 entradas, reproduzco sólo algunas de ellas por razones obvias de espacio.

EL SÉPTIMO SELLO *(1956) NIVEL MICROTEXTUAL*
Limitaciones formales

	Guión original	Película VHS	Comentarios
1.	KNITH. My body is frightened, but I'm not.	El espíritu está pronto pero la carne es débil.	Favorece postulados religiosos con la dualidad espíritu/ carne. Afecta la forma de la expresión.
2.	DEATH. Well, there is no shame in that.	SUPRESIÓN (pero se ve el movimiento de los labios).	Favorece postulados religiosos al suprimir la vergüenza que supone aceptar que la carne es débil. Mejora la imagen del personaje.
3.	JONS. Between a strumpet's legs, is the life for which I sigh. Up above is God Almighty so very far away, but your brother the Devil, you will meet on every level. (SONG)	Para un hombre de mi altura, es el más alto placer, encontrar una mujer y correr una aventura. Lejos en el cielo tu padre Dios está, cerca en el infierno tu hermano Satanás. (Canción).	Favorece postulados morales. Sustituye "prostituta" por "mujer" y propone una nueva dualidad: cielo/ infierno. Afecta la forma de la expresión.
4.	JONS. One moment you're bright and lively, the next you´re crawling with worms. Fate is a terrible villain and you, my friend, its poor victim. KNIGHT. Must you sing? JONS. No.	SUPRESIÓN	Favorece postulados morales al suprimir la visión materialista del hombre que está, además, en manos del destino. Mejora la imagen del personaje.
5.	JOF. And then she saw me watching her and she smiled at me. [Se refiere a la Virgen]. My eyes filled with tears and when I wiped them away, she had disappeared. And everything became so still in the sky and on the earth. Can you	Al ver que yo la miraba, me sonrió dulcemente. Sentí una gran emoción. Cuando me sequé las lágrimas y volví a mirar había desaparecido Si hubieras oído aquella melodía maravillosa del amor	Favorece postulados religiosos. Endulza la imagen de la Virgen ("dulcemente"), y la envuelve de un ambiente más idílico que el original (emoción, melodía maravillosa del amor más puro). Mejora la imagen del personaje.

	understand...	más puro. Mientras el cielo y la tierra permanecían en silencio.	
6.	SKAT. Bear this in mind, you fool. Your life hangs by a thread. Your time is short.	Medita hermano el hecho cierto, hoy estás sano mañana muerto. Si breve fue el placer, largo será el padecer.	Favorece los postulados morales con dos dualidades: sano/muerto, placer/sufrimiento. Afecta la forma de la expresión.
7.	KNIGHT I want to talk to you as openly as I can, but my heart is empty.	Quiero confesarme y no sé qué decir. Mi corazón está vacío.	Favorece los postulados religiosos introduciendo una terminología inexistente en el original: confesión. Afecta la forma de la expresión.
8.	KNIGHT. I want knowledge.	Deseo saber qué hay después.	Favorece los postulados religiosos con terminología del más allá. Modifica la imagen del personaje.
9.	KNIGHT And what is to become of those who neither want to nor are capable of believing?	SUPRESIÓN	Favorece los postulados religiosos al suprimir la alusión al ateísmo. Modifica la imagen del personaje.
10.	KNIGHT. Then life is an outrageous horror.	Entonces la vida perdería todo su sentido.	Favorece los postulados morales suavizando la calificación de la vida. Modifica la imagen del personaje.
11.	KNIGHT. In our fear, we make an image, and that image we call God.	Nos hace crear el miedo una imagen salvadora, y esa imagen es lo que llamamos Dios.	Favorece postulados religiosos. Suaviza la afirmación precedente un poco atrevida (Dios como fruto del miedo), con el término "imagen salvadora". Modifica la imagen del personaje.
12.	KNIGHT. My life has been a futile pursuit, a wandering, a great deal of talk without meaning. I feel no	He gastado mi vida en diversiones, viajes, charlas sin sentido. Mi vida ha sido un continuo	Favorece postulados morales al introducir nuevamente un término religioso (arrepentimiento), y

	bitterness or self-reproach because the lives of most people are very much like this. But I will use my reprieve for one meaningful deed.	absurdo. Creo que me arrepiento. Fui un necio. En esta hora siento amargura por el tiempo perdido. Aunque sé que la vida de casi todos los hombres corre por los mismos cauces. Por eso quiero emplear esta prórroga en una acción única que me dé la paz.	contradice totalmente la actitud del original. Mejora la imagen del personaje.

4. La traducción aceptable: naturalización pragmática

Todas las entradas de la tabla de limitaciones formales se pueden agrupar en dos temas clave, el **religioso** y el **moral**, y tienen como consecuencia una naturalización pragmática del texto que lo orienta hacia el polo receptor y lo hace aceptable. Dicha naturalización comporta alguno de estos aspectos, tal como aparece consignado al final de la columna de comentarios: limitación en la forma de la expresión, una reducción del contenido erótico o una modificación de la imagen del personaje. A veces estos elementos se mezclan, pero siempre he optado por elegir el aspecto preferente.

La afectación de la forma de la expresión implica cambios sustanciales de los términos utilizados (por supresión, modificación o adición) en el paso del texto originario al texto meta. Por ejemplo, la entrada 1 de la tabla anterior "My body is frightened, but I'm not" se traduce por "El espíritu está pronto pero la carne es débil". Aquí la forma de la expresión se ve alterada por dos modificaciones ("body" por "carne" y "frightened" por "débil") y por una adición inexistente en el original ("El espíritu está pronto"). La inversión final de los elementos (en la versión española se coloca en primer lugar la alusión al espíritu y no al cuerpo), termina de alterar el original. En otras ocasiones, la naturalización comporta una reducción del contenido erótico que normalmente revierte en una mejora de la imagen del personaje. En la entrada 3 se sustituye "strumpet" por "mujer", por ejemplo.

POSTULADOS	Registros	%
Religiosos 22	1, 2, 5, 8, 9, 11, 18, 21, 22, 27, 29, 30, 31, 32, 33, 35, 36, 38, 39, 40, 41, 42.	52.4
Morales 20	3, 4, 6, 7, 10, 12, 13, 14, 15, 16, 17, 19, 20, 23, 24, 25, 26, 28, 34, 37.	47.6
TOTAL	42	100

Table 2-2

Aunque aquí sólo he reproducido 12, las 42 entradas que aborda mi estudio se distribuyen de una manera casi equivalente entre términos religiosos (20) y morales (22), tal como muestra la tabla anterior. En cuanto al aspecto **religioso,** cabe destacar los *términos duales* que aparecen en el texto español, y que no siempre tienen una correspondencia con el original (a veces sólo aparece una de las dos partes, a veces, ninguna), y que tienden a dar una imagen más simplificada del texto, restándole complejidad:

Espíritu/carne (entrada 1)
Cielo/Infierno (entrada 3)
Sano/muerto (entrada 6)
Placer/sufrimiento (entrada 6)

También encontramos un abuso de la *terminología religiosa,* que en ninguno caso de los que comento se encuentra presente en el original, y que demuestra la enorme influencia que tenía la Iglesia en la época de Arias Salgado. Los tres últimos términos no aparecen en las 12 entradas analizadas sino en las posteriores, pero merece la pena destacarlos por su especificidad, sobretodo el penúltimo "Consumatum est", últimas palabras pronunciadas por Cristo en la cruz antes de morir refiriéndose a que se ha cumplido la voluntad de Dios. Es evidente que únicamente alguien muy cercano a las esferas religiosas como el Padre Staehlin utilizaría este vocablo, totalmente inexistente en el original ("It is the end").

Confesión (entrada 7)
Más allá (entrada 8)

Arrepentimiento (entrada 12)
Revelación
Consumatum est
Pecado

En cuanto al aspecto **moral**, los temas que provocan manipulaciones del diálogo son el *adulterio*, la alusión explícita a las *relaciones sexuales, la visión denigrante del matrimonio o de la mujer como esposa, la prostitución*, etc., que no son más que un reflejo de lo que prohíben las *Instrucciones y Normas para la Censura Moral de Espectáculos* de 1950.

5. Efectos de la naturalización pragmática

NATURALIZACIÓN	Registros	%
Forma de expresión 12	1, 3, 6, 7, 22, 26, 27, 29, 32, 33, 38, 42.	28.5
Imagen del personaje 25	2, 4, 5, 8, 9, 10, 11, 12, 13, 18, 19, 20, 21, 23, 25, 28, 30, 31, 34, 35, 36, 37, 39, 40, 41	59.5
Contenido erótico 5	14, 15, 16, 17, 24	12
TOTAL	42	100

Table 2-3

La **tabla 2-4** muestra como el aspecto más afectado por todas las manipulaciones es la caracterización de los personajes (con un 59.5 %), ya que las expresiones y el contenido erótico no son muy relevantes en una película de temática religiosa. La censura convirtió este texto en una traducción aceptable a partir básicamente de la manipulación a nivel microtextual de los diálogos de los dos protagonistas, el escudero Jons (a modo de Sancho Panza) y el caballero (el contrapunto idealista). Sobre la figura del **caballero** recae gran parte del peso de las manipulaciones censoras, no tanto a nivel cuantitativo como cualitativo. Todas se refieren a aspectos metafísicos, pero destacaré aquellas que me parecen más representativas porque distorsionan su figura en uno de estos aspectos:

- **Racionalismo**

"I want knowledge" (Registro 8)
Deseo saber qué hay después.

La afirmación del original resulta mucho más neutra que la del doblaje y nos dibuja a un caballero que busca respuestas, pero no necesariamente religiosas. "I want knowledge" es una afirmación racionalista muy distante de preguntarse sobre el más allá.

- **Agnosticismo/ateísmo**

"Those who neither want to nor are capable of believing" (Registro 9)
Supresión

El original presenta una realidad mucho más compleja que incluye la posibilidad del agnosticismo o el ateísmo, una realidad donde la religión puede quedar excluida.

- **Nihilismo**

"The life is an outrageous horror" (Registro 10)
La vida perdería todo su sentido

A parte de la diferente intensidad semántica ("outrageous horror"), el cambio de verbo ("ser" por "perder") y de tiempo verbal (presente por condicional), comporta que la afirmación del doblaje se transforme en una mera hipótesis: "La vida perdería todo su sentido" si Dios no existiera.

- **Vulnerabilidad/Inseguridad/ Duda/Miedo**

"In our fear, we make an image, and that image we call God" (Registro 11)
Nos hace crear el miedo una imagen salvadora, y esa imagen es lo que llamamos Dios.

El original personifica el miedo en el mismo protagonista ("our fear"), que presenta más vulnerable, y Dios no se identifica como un recurso salvador, sino más bien como fruto de la desesperación del ser humano.

- **Arrepentimiento**

"My life has been a futile pursuit, a wandering, a great deal of talk without meaning. *I feel no bitterness or self-reproach because the lives of most people are very much like this.* But I will use my reprieve for one meaningful deed." (Registro 12)
Mi vida ha sido un continuo absurdo. Creo que me arrepiento. Fui un necio. (Sólo traduzco la parte subrayada).

En el original, el caballero no muestra el típico arrepentimiento cristiano, y es caracterizado como una figura mucho más humana, mucho más comprensiva consigo misma. Mas adelante, el registro 36, "It's true that I'm worried" será traducido por "Ya no temo nada", una de las manipulaciones más obvias de la película y de este personaje.

6. Conclusiones y perspectivas de futuro

La gran mayoría de ajustes ideológicos practicados por la (auto)censura demuestran una voluntad de hacer llegar al espectador un cine ejemplar de acuerdo con las *Normas de censura cinematográfica*, básicamente aquellas que atacan concepciones políticas, religiosas o familiares, para mantener el "statuos quo" dominante y favorecer los postulados religiosos o morales vigentes. Cabe decir también que a veces parecían más preocupados por censurar aspectos demasiado evidentes y anodinos (como que no aparezca la palabra "prostituta" o "violación"), que por aspectos más profundos. El breve análisis que he realizado de las dos películas de Bergman estrenadas en España después de *El séptimo sello*, *Fresas salvajes* y *Como en un espejo*, confirman la continuidad de esta política censora a pesar de los cambios en el gobierno. Mientras que otras manipulaciones son muy conocidas (Mogambo, Casablanca), en parte por su espectacularidad, en parte porque la lengua de origen es el inglés, las practicadas a Bergman han quedado en el olvido. Resultaría muy interesante para investigaciones futuras hacer un seguimiento de todas las obras de Bergman estrenadas en España, y ver la evolución de los criterios censores en la figura de este director. Asimismo, sería necesario crear un corpus de sus producciones audiovisuales para facilitar la tarea de los estudiosos.

Referencias

Bergman, Ingmar (1965) *Como en un espejo*, Guión. Barcelona: Aymà, Colección Voz imagen, Núm. 12.

—. (1965) *El séptimo sello*, Guión, Barcelona: Aymà, Colección Voz imagen, Núm. 10.

—. (1968): *Fresas salvajes*: Guión. Barcelona: Aymà. Colección Voz imagen, Núm. 21

Company, J. M. (1993) *Ingmar Bergman*, Madrid: Cátedra.

Gutiérrez Lanza, Maria del C. (2000) *Traducción y censura de textos cinematográficos en la España de Franco. Doblaje y subtitulado inglés-español (1951-1975)*, Universidad de León: Servicio de Publicaciones.

Four screenplays of Ingmar Bergman (1960), Nueva York: Simon & Schuster.

(PARA)TRANSLATED IDEOLOGIES IN SIMONE DE BEAUVOIR'S *LE DEUXIÈME SEXE*: THE (PARA)TRANSLATOR'S ROLE

OLGA CASTRO VAZQUEZ,
UNIVERSIDADE DE VIGO – GALIZA, SPAIN

Abstract: The analysis of the texts and paratexts of the feminist book *Le deuxième sexe* (1949, Gallimard) by the French philosopher Simone de Beauvoir, along with its subsequent translations and rewritings into English (1952, *The Second Sex*), Argentinian (1954, *El segundo sexo*) and Castilian Spanish (1998, *El segundo sexo*) demonstrates the essential role that–without exception–the (un)conscious existence of a specific ideological discourse plays in the professional work of translation and paratranslation. More specifically, this study focuses on the fact that a patriarchal or feminist ideology has had and continues to have a decisive influence on the reception of the cultural and ideological good, in both the society in which it is created and that in which it is received.

1. Introduction

Le deuxième sexe (Gallimard 1949) is not only an Existentialist masterpiece but also the first landmark in modern Western feminism. In the text, Simone de Beauvoir traces the development of women's oppression and analyses the female condition in Western society from a scientific, psychological, sociological, ontological and cultural perspective by means of historical, literary and mythical sources. Throughout the two volumes of *Le deuxième sexe (I. Les faits et les mythes* and *II. L'experiénce vécue*) the author provides considerable evidence for the reasons that explain the discrimination that half of humankind undergo and concludes that the most important contemporary effect that oppression has on women is that of considering men and male the norm as women and female become the other, the other sex, the second sex. Beauvoir meticulously deconstructs and reconstructs those traditional myths about women's roles, which allow her to corroborate that woman's condition has always consisted of being subjugated–as the Other–to men, who at the same time have thought of themselves as the Same.

Beauvoir understands feminism not only as theoretical knowledge but also, and more importantly, as a plural and cross-cultural political practice. Therefore, the book proved to be fundamental for the development of feminisms[1] and, as expected, French and Francophone feminisms were soon influenced by, or opposed to, Beauvoir's ideas. Other feminists and philosophers emphasized that such was the relevance of this masterpiece that translations into other languages were required.

2. Ideology in translation and paratranslation

Far from understanding translation as a neutral activity, in this analysis of the English and Spanish translations of the (para)texts, I will follow the methodological perspective provided by the new approaches of Translation Studies which emerged in the context of the multiple post-theories of the early 1980s (postcolonialism, postmodernism, poststructuralism). The openness of the new Translation Studies led to the questioning of obsolete notions such as equivalence, fidelity, neutrality, translator's invisibilitya or objectivity, and what is dominant in the series of new approaches "is the orientation towards cultural rather than linguistic transfer; secondly, they view translation not as a process of transcoding but as an act of communication" (Snell-Hornby 1990: 82).

This orientation towards cultural rather than linguistic transfer leads to a cultural turn in Translation Studies which signifies the integration of a cultural dimension making language work as a parallel system to culture instead of as an external referential entity (Nouss 2000: 1351). This cultural turn may equally be called an ideological turn in translation studies, with the appearance of new theoretical approaches like the Polysystem Theory which defends that "ideology rather than linguistics or aesthetics crucially determines the operational choices of translators" (Cronin 2000: 695), turning translation into a "process of mediation which does not stand above ideology but works through it" (Simon 1996: 8). In this sense, ideology has its previous meaning of deviation from some

---

[1] The plural feminisms makes reference to the plurality of feminist schools of thought that emerged in different locations in order to meet the varying requirements that have come about due to patriarchal oppression of women, although sharing the common aim of freeing all women and ending sexist oppression. In this regard, complexity and unity are two of the main characteristics feminisms are defined by.

posited norms and objectivity replaced by that of a systematic set of political beliefs about the world which is, inevitably, present in our lives.

These new approaches challenged the possibility of producing a faithful and objective translation, showing that the translators' intervention (that is, their ideology) is always present, whether they recognize it or not. In this particular case, *Le deuxième sexe* being a feminist book, a gender approach over this translation practice is needed. On the one hand, translators can deny their intervention (claiming to be unbiased or just ignoring they exercise an ideology). By acting in this way, they would be taking part in the process unconsciously and, thus, they would be automatically supporting the dominant patriarchal ideology (seen as the norm). As Lane-Mercier upholds, "the invisible translator is no longer the one who resorts to fluent strategies, but the one who refuses to take over responsibility for his/her manipulations, who believes s/he is merely conveying the information of the source text" (Lane-Mercier 1997: 65).

On the other hand, when translators do take responsibility for their interventions, they are consciously recognizing the ideological burden they convey, which can be either feminist or patriarchal. The latter implies that translators do not feel they should warn about their ideological position, since it is located within the framework of the dominant, common and non-subversive/existing system. On the contrary, feminist translators honestly declare their affiliations and interventions and

> unlike the patriarchal agenda, where the underlying order of discourse is made invisible by passing itself off as "normal" and "natural", the feminist agenda has its political cards on the table. The hand mediating is overt in its intentions. (Lobtinière-Harwood 1991: 100)

Translators are no longer those innocent and neutral bridges. Instead, they have become active ideological mediators when doing a translation, a translation considered "as rewriting" (Bassnett and Lefevere 1990: 9). Translators thus inevitably play an essential role: they all interpret the original text according to their ideology before rewriting it into the target text, but unfairly only feminist translators' transparent and honest attitude will bring them much criticism for "perverting objectivity", as well as accusations of being biased and unfaithful to patriarchal rules governing society.

After having depicted this close relationship between ideology and rewritten texts, we should ask ourselves to what extent ideology is also linked to "rewritten" paratexts, those elements that surround and introduce a literary text in book form, as Genette explains:

The literary work consists (...) of a text. But this text is rarely presented just alone, without the reinforcement and the accompaniment of a certain number of productions, like the author's name, the title, the preface, illustrations (...) which surround it and prolong it precisely in order to *present* it, to *make* it *present*, to assure its presence in the world, its 'reception' and consumption in the form of a book. (Genette 1987: 7)[2]

In other words, we should explore the idea of translation being neither an autonomous nor an independent operation, but an activity closely linked to paratranslation, the latter being an analytical environment that allows us to study the "ideological adaptation undergone by any cultural product in order to be incorporated to the target cultural wealth" (Garrido 2004: 31). In this sense, translators would not be the only ones responsible in the rewriting process, since paratranslators (be it sponsors, patrons or editors) may also have a great deal of responsibility in the transfer process of the cultural and ideological product. What comes next is an analysis of the English, Argentinian and Spanish paratranslations[3] of *Le deuxième sexe* with the aim of exposing the role that the (un)conscious existence of a specific ideological discourse plays in the professional work of (para)translation, as well as in the target society reception.

3. (Para)textual analysis

3.1. *The Second Sex* in the USA and the anglophone world

Le deuxième sexe was a bestseller and very soon it became an essential reference for francophone feminists, both for Beauvoir's supporters and critics, which led to a demand for translations. Nevertheless, the early English version was translated owing to other reasons, since the publishing house Bantam Books (through its editor Alfred Knopf) bought the translation rights "when Blanche Knopf, wife of the publisher, bought the book on a trip to France, and she was under the impression that it was a modern-day sex manual akin to the Kinsey report" (Bair 1990: 41). The

---

[2] L'oeuvre littéraire consiste (...) en un texte. Mais ce texte se présente rarement à l'état un, sans le renfort et l'accompagnement d'un certain nombre de productions, comme un nom d'auteur, un titre, un préface, des illustrations (...) qui l'entourent et le prolongent précisément pour le *présenter*, pour le *rendre présent*, pour assurer sa présence au monde, sa 'reception' et sa consommation sous la forme d'un livre. All translations into English are mine.

[3] Genette (1997) distinguishes between epitexts (interviews, private correspondence, conferences, etc.) and peritexts (title, subtitle, preface, epilogue, notes, dedications, graphics, etc). For the purpose of this article, I will focus on the latter.

publisher understood the book as a sex manual rather than a feminist and philosophical work, and therefore, when trying to find a translator, he contacted a retired professor of zoology, Howard Parshley, who had written a book on sex and human reproduction in 1933 and regularly reviewed books on sex for *The New York Herald Tribune*. Parshley's *The Second Sex* came out in 1952 making "the *New York Times* bestseller list in the spring of 1953 and had seen several reprintings, thus considered successful" (Flotow 1997: 49). Bantam Books was later taken over by the publishing house The Random House, and throughout the decades *The Second Sex* was reprinted several times in, among others, Everyman's Library, Vintage, Jonathan Cape, Picador, David Campbell Publishers and Penguin Books.

All these subsequent editions have in common that the original two-volumes were condensed into one single book. The (para)translation of the title has been quite literal, except in the 1997 edition entitled *Simone de Beauvoir, her world-famous study of The Second Sex*. None of the different editions refers to volume one and two on the cover. Instead, this distinction only appears in the table of contents, where Parshley's translation of volume two as *Woman's Life Today* rather than, more accurately, *Lived Experience* makes Simons reveal that he "effectively masks the significance of the work as a phenomenological description" (Simons 2001: 70). Similarly, the English editions include neither the author's dedication to Jacques Bost nor the author's introductory quotations of Pitagoras, Poulain de la Barre, Kierkegaard and Sartre. A previous text is usually included, be it a translator's preface (written in 1952), an expert's introduction (like the one written by Margaret Crossland in the 1993 edition), Beauvoir's bibliography or a chronology. The author's introduction to volume I and II is kept, although it is considerably reduced. The same occurs with the author's footnotes and with quotations cited by Beauvoir, some of which are kept but many others condensed or even deleted. In addition to this, substantial changes are introduced into the table of contents, where for instance Parshley adds subtitles to every chapter in part III of Book One (*Myths),* although none of the French editions had this information. In the translator's preface Parshley admitted that his intention had been

> in general to avoid all paraphrasing not required by language differences and to provide a translation that is at once exact and–with slight exceptions–complete (...). I have also done some cutting and condensation here and there with a view to brevity, chiefly in reducing the extent of the author's illustrative material, especially in certain of her quotations from other writers (Parshley 1952: 11).

From profusely illustrated critical works (Bair 1990, Glazer 2004, Kush 2000, Lobtinière-Harwood 1991, Moi 2004, Simons 2001) we know that Parshley deleted nearly 15 per cent of the original French in volume I, and in volume II he cut approximately 60 pages, 12 per cent. From a gender approach, through a "patriarchal translation" Parshley omitted many "uncomfortable" facts, such as large sections of text recounting the names and achievements of women in history; the lineage of influential women extremely important to feminist historiography; little-known historical accounts of women who defied feminine stereotypes, like Renaissance noblewomen who led armies; references to cultural taboos such as lesbian relationships; Beauvoir's reference to the first American women's rights convention at Seneca Falls; entire pages of descriptions of the tedious work comprising a housewife's day; 35 pages coming from the chapter on *The Married Woman*, cutting it almost in half; Beauvoir's description of the violent history of the women's rights struggle in England as well as references to Hubertine Auclert, a woman who created the French Women's Suffrage Organization. What is more, on top of deleting these important references to women, Parshley considered men's experiences and feelings more valid or interesting than women's and, as a result, "he didn't care to have discussions of women's oppression belaboured, although he let Beauvoir go at length about the superior advantages of man's situation" (Simons 2001: 66).

The translator allowed himself the luxury of declaring in the preface that "practically all such modifications have been made with the author's express permission, passage by passage" (Parshley 1952: 12). However, Beauvoir became aware of this mistranslation in 1982, four years before her death: "Beauvoir replied that she was dismayed to learn the extent to which Mr Parshley misrepresented her. She wished with all her heart that I will be able to publish a new translation of it" (Simons 2001: 71). Now, quarter of a century later, we can still say that no English edition of *The Second Sex* "(Beauvoir's feminist masterpiece, the common ingredient in all of the early Women's Studies courses) contains everything she wrote or accurately translates her most basic philosophical ideas" (*Ibidem*: 61). Regarding iconic paratexts, we can see the evolution from a representation of a naked woman (after all, it was a sex manual) to an indescribable symbolism of women's entrails and, eventually, to simple covers.

3.2. *El segundo sexo* in Spanish speaking Latin America

The first translation of *Le deuxième sexe* into Spanish was produced in 1954 by the Argentinian playwright Pablo Palant. *El segundo sexo* was first published in Psique, a philosophy publishing house located in Buenos Aires. However, the publishing rights were transferred to Siglo Veinte in 1962 for subsequent editions. By then, Buenos Aires was the centre of all cultural innovations par excellence, which ensured the spreading of the text throughout Latin America and clandestinely in Spain, being under Franco's dictatorship until 1975. In 1999, the publishing house Sudamericana (part of Random House Mondadori) released a fiftieth anniversary edition. By then, the publishing house did take into consideration some of the critical reviews by Latin American scholars, defining Palant's rewriting as a rushed translation. Therefore, Sudamericana asked Juan García-Puente, the translator of the *Complete Works* of Beauvoir into Latin Amercian Spanish, to do a new rewriting of *Le deuxième sexe*. He did so in 1999, and a second edition of the book was published in 2005.

All editions by Psique and Siglo Veinte have respected the two-volume structure of the original, displaying in the covers the title of the book *El segundo sexo*, the author's name and the subtitle corresponding to each volume: *Los hechos y los mitos and **La experiencia vivida. However, the latest editions published by Sudamericana are condensed into 725 pages of one single volume, in which all references to book one and two are limited to the table of contents.

What is common to both Psique and Siglo Veinte editions is the (para)translation into Spanish of the author's introduction, the dedication to Jacques Bost and the four quotations. None of the editions contains a translator's preface, in which he could have made himself visible. Palant remains invisible throughout the translation, as he barely introduces N. del T. (translator's footnotes). Similarly, he does not seem to get involved in the translation, since he limits himself to reproducing some (not all) of the author's notes with no evidence of having done research so that he could offer updated documentation, e.g. he translates "Se llamaba *Franqueza* y ha desaparecido ya" [it was called *Franqueza* (Frankness) and no longer exists today] from "Il est mort aujourd'hui, il s'appelait *Franchise*" [it was called *Franchise* (Frankness) and no longer exists today], being Franchise the name of a French magazine which clearly should no be translated. The editors, instead, make themselves visible with a self-publicist aim when it comes to emphasizing other books. In this regard, the French "Le rapport Kinsey par example se limite à definir les caracteristiques sexuelles de l'homme américain, ce qui est tout à fait différent" [The Kinsey reports, for example, are limited to defining the sexual characteristics of the American man, which is quite different] become "El informe Kinsey, por ejemplo, se limita a definir las características sexuales del hombre norteamericano, lo que es completamente distinto. (Hay edición castellana de Ediciones Siglo Veinte, Buenos Aires). (N. del E.)" [The Kinsey reports, for example, are limited to defining the sexual characteristics of the American man, which is quite different. (There is a Spanish version by Ediciones Siglo Veinte, Buenos Aires) (editor's note)].

As for Sudamericana editions (1999 and 2005) the translator is more visible, and he also revises former linguistic and cultural interpretations of the original text. After all, García-Puente had already translated the Complete Works of the author. On top of this, one of the main changes introduced by Sudamericana editions is the inclusion of an expert's prologue written by the feminist cultural critic and journalist María Moreno, who also set up one of the first feminist magazines in Argentina (*Alfonsina*).

As far as iconic paratexts are concerned, covers evolved from plain designs (1954) to pop-art designs depicting the typical "liberated" woman as it was understood in the 70s (smiling faces and sunglasses). Finally, various photos of Beauvoir were selected for the covers, ones showing the author in her later years and others (1999 and 2005 editions) in her youth.

3.3. El segundo sexo in Spain

For forty-four years (1954-1998) the only version that could be read in the Spanish-speaking world was the Argentinian one written by Palant. For many (too many) years, this book was considered subversive by Spain's dictatorial regime, which thus prevented it from being translated for a Spanish audience. We had to wait until 1998, on the threshold of the fiftieth anniversary of the book, to have it available in a Castilian edition. The initiative was taken by the Institut Universitari d'Estudis de la Dona [University Institute for Women's Studies] of the Universitat de València together with the publishing house Cátedra, which had already worked together and published many other works in the Colección Feminismos [Feminisms Collection]. Both institutions were also supported by the Instituto de la Mujer [Women's Institute] of the Spanish Goverment. Alicia Martorell Linares, an experienced translator who had previously translated other books for that collection and for that publishing house, translated the Castilian Spanish *El segundo sexo*, which was first published in 1998. In 2005 the book was reprinted in the same collection and publishing house, although with a different design.

Like the French original, the first Spanish edition was comprised of two books, each of which included a subtitle under the generic title of *El segundo sexo* (*Volumen I. Los hechos y los mito*s and *Volumen II. La* *experiencia vivida*). However, the 2005 edition put it all together in a 905 page version, without showing on the cover that, in fact, *El segundo sexo* is (or initially was) made up of two books. Apart from this evident change, the latest edition is paratranslated identically to the first one, including the author's dedication and Beauvoir's four quotations previously mentioned. Similarly, all editions are prefaced by Teresa López Pardina, Doctor of Philosophy and author of several studies on Beauvoir from a feminist and philosophical perspective. Likewise, all editions include an extensive bibliography compiled by the translator who states that "in order to avoid weighing this text down with more notes, all references that we have been able to find are grouped in a separate bibliography" (Martorell Linares 1998: 35).[4] Martorell heads this section quoting Beauvoir and visibly showing the reason why, according to her, this bibliography becomes necessary:

> I apologise profusely, but it has been impossible for me to recover the references of the English works that I consulted. There are simply too many and of some of them I only had the translation. (*Ibidem*)[5]

The translator also wants to warn readers about her strategy regarding references to books cited by Beauvoir. In this sense, Martorell informs readers that when a cited book has been translated into Spanish, that version will be the only one included in her translation. Instead, when it has not, the original version will be kept, although she also transparently admits that "of course, there are many works mentioned in the text that we have not been able to find any information on" (*Ibidem*).[6] This attitude proves the translator's involvement in the rewriting of *Le deuxième sexe*, as she consults bibliographic sources and documentation or reconstructs incomplete references of books that have not been published in Spanish. Furthermore, Martorell includes some more N. de la T. (translator's notes) throughout *El segundo sexo*, in which she helps the audience follow Beauvoir's philosophical discourse and she even corrects mistakes. As for the writing style, the translator makes evident her decision "to have kept,

---

[4] "para no sobrecargar el texto con más notas, agrupamos las referencias que hemos podido encontrar en una bibliografía separada."

[5] "Lo siento muchísimo, pero me resulta imposible recuperar las referencias a las obras inglesas que consulté. Hay demasiadas y de algunas sólo tuve la traducción. (S. de Beauvoir a H. M. Parshley, traductor de *El segundo sexo* al inglés, hacia 1951)."

[6] "desde luego, se mencionan en el texto bastantes obras de las que no hemos encontrado ninguna pista."

when it was not incompatible with the Spanish, S. de Beauvoir's special form of punctuation, is very representative of the time, of the intellectual trend and of a particular way of thinking" (*Ibidem*).[7] When it comes to analysing iconic paratexts, we must point out that *El segundo sexo* by Cátedra has exactly the same general design as the rest of the Colección Feminismos books. What makes it different is that in 1998 each volume included a drawing of Beauvoir (vol. I) and Beauvoir and Sartre (vol. II), whereas in 2005 it consisted of a plain cover showing a metal nut.

4. Whose role is it anyway?

By means of this (para)textual analysis I have tried to determine who we can hold responsible for the creation of (para)texts. In other words, I have attempted to expose who the decision-makers of the different elements are that turn a translation into a book, seeking the acceptability of the translated text in the target society.

4.1. *The Second Sex*

The paratranslation of this feminist and philosophical book reflects patriarchal assumptions, be it consciously or unconsciously, which means that the paratranslations into English both reflect and perpetuate dominant ideology in society. Seeking to define responsibilities, we must bear in mind that the translator Parshley was asked to translate a book on sex, so it would not be that serious to obviate several historical events not directly related to sex. In fact, according to the translator's preface, the publishers faced a weighty two-volume original and decided to condense the text to reduce printing, so they ordered the translator to "condense, simplify or eliminate is to lighten the burden for the American reader, as publisher Knopf put it" (Flotow 1997: 50). This explains why absolutely all English versions are made up of just one single book entitled *The Second Sex*, as well as explaining why there have been so many abbreviations and even deletions affecting dedications, footnotes, quotations, the author's introduction and so on and so forth. On the other hand, the publisher did ask the translator to bear in mind the philosophical dimension of the book, as Parshley himself explains:

---

[7] "haber conservado, cuando no era incompatible con el castellano, la especial forma de puntuar de S. de Beauvoir, pues es muy representativa de una época, corriente intelectual y forma de pensar."

> at the publisher's request I have, as editor, occasionally added an explanatory word or two (especially in connection with the existentialist terminology) and pointed a few additional footnotes and bibliographic data which I thought might be to the reader's interest. (Parshley 1952: 11)

The translator is visible. Besides his name appearing on most covers of *The Second Sex*, he writes a translator's preface where he explains some of his strategies, though he avoids mentioning many others. Parshley plays an important role when he makes up new subtitles to be included in the table of contents. What covers do not show, however, is any reference to the fact that the original is "equivalent" to a two-volume book in French, or any reference to subtitles (*The facts and the myths* and *Women's Life Today*).

Knopf is not the only paratranslator since across the Anglophone world there were many other subsequent editions of the "same" text including "different" paratexts. In this regard, it was Everyman's Library that decided to replace the translator's preface by an expert's introduction in the 1993 edition, as well as including bibliographical references and a chronology. In 1979 the title *Simone de Beauvoir, her world-famous study of The Second Sex* was not chosen at random, but it responded to a measured strategy implemented by the publisher Penguin Books. As required by society, the influential group carried out the task of incorporating new texts according to their thoughts and beliefs. In other words, society imported the "cultural good" in accordance with the dominant ideology of the target society.

In order to better understand the serious consequences of this closely linked translative and paratranslative behaviour, we have to mention the great confusion it caused to Anglophone readers, who were potentially unable to follow the author's line of argument due to the deletion of intermediate paragraphs, and therefore thought of her as an inconsistent thinker whose work perpetuated patriarchal stereotypes of female sexuality. The confusion reached its peak with the serious misunderstandings between Francophone and Anglophone feminists, who mutually blamed each other for interpreting different postulates from the same text. This was because the English and the French version asserted very different things indeed. What is outrageous today is that Parshley's translation is still the only one English version of *Le deuxième sexe* published. Many scholars' complaints have been in vain, as Sylvie Le Bon de Beauvoir (Simone de Beauvoir's daughter) shows:

> this edition is a scandal and we have wrongly tolerated it for too long. There are numerous protests from scholars saying the Beauvoir was

appalled by the cuts and mistranslations that betrayed her thinking, and she had complained frequently about this. (Glazer 2004)

Gallimard contacted Random House in order to demand a new translation, but the Anglophone publishing house rejected the idea, answering that "in 2000, the audience for the book wasn't large enough to justify the cost of a new edition" (*Ibidem*). In spite of these hurdles, many scholars are nowadays putting pressure on Random House to avoid English-speaking "readers having to wait until 2056, when *The Second Sex* goes into the public domain, to find out what Beauvoir really meant" (Kush 2000).

4.2. *El segundo sexo* (Argentina)

Before translating the book, Palant knew it would be published in Psique, and this meant he knew the book was not a sex manual, but an exclusively philosophical text. This may be the result of the translator supposedly not having enough time to do the translation properly, to check documentation and confirm data. However, Psique editors were not the only paratranslators in Argentina, as over the years the book was reprinted several times. If we follow the cover's evolution we may suggest that the initially philosophical book was firstly turned into a sex manual (or a women's liberation handbook, as it was understood at that time), and secondly into a serious (maybe feminist?) book. The variety of styles in covers did not signify a new rewriting, since the translated book continued to be Palant's "psychiatric" version. However, when in 1999 a fiftieth anniversary edition was released, paratranslators had to meet the challenge of writing a new translation from a more feminist approach. This edition was translated by García-Puente, who condensed the two-volume original into a one-volume translation, and introduced an expert's preface. In an e-mail on February 23rd 2007, Luis Chitarrori, editor of Sudamericana describes that "We asked for María Moreno to write a prologue because we believed she would be able to situate the 1949 publication in the contemporaneous sphere that a book of this sort requires."[8]

The aforementioned iconic elements together with the considerable number of "N. del E." (editor's footnote) clearly shows who the deciders are of how the book is presented to the target audience.

---

[8] "pedimos un prólogo a María Moreno porque creímos que ella podía ubicar una publicación de 1949 en una órbita de vigencia y actualidad que un libro de esta índole sin duda merece."

4.3. *El segundo sexo* (Spain)

In Spain *El segundo sexo* was published by the Institut de la Dona de la Universitat de València, the Instituto de la Mujer and Colección Feminismos (of the Cátedra publishing house). In this particular case, paratranslators' feminist affiliation proves evident, while the philosophical approach remains distant. In fact, *El segundo sexo* was such a feminist icon and its translation into Castilian Spanish was so desperately needed that even Valencia considered the idea of publishing an abbreviated version. This would have been quicker, indeed, but would definitely undermine the philosopher's coherence and her philosophical discourse. Martorell objected to this decision and was successful, as she explained in an e-mail on February 17th 2007: "Early on, Valencia considered publishing an abbreviated version. I objected and Cátedra backed me" [en un primer momento Valencia se planteó publicar una versión abreviada. Yo me opuse y Cátedra me apoyó]. The translator also considered it necessary to include a bibliography after the expert's preface and before the author's introduction, and Cátedra gave her absolute freedom in this matter, as she corroborated in the above mentioned e-mail:

> The bibliography is entirely my own. It is a complicated text from that point of view, since there are many references, but the majority are approximate and from memory. It was not in vain that the majority of the work was written in a café! I believe it is far more fluid and less intrusive to add the complete bibliography than fill the book with notes on every title.[9]

She also decided to head this section with a Beauvoir's quotation that allowed readers to get an idea about the bibliographic complexity of the book; when citing a book she decided to use the Spanish reference if possible since many references were titles of books that had been literally translated into French from other languages, with no reference to a published French translation; she also decided to include a footnote explaining her ideological approach and translative strategy throughout rewriting into Spanish of *Le deuxième sexe*; and all in all, she is responsible for the many "N. de la T." (translator's notes) included in the

---

[9] "La bibliografía es totalmente de mi cosecha. Es un texto muy complicado desde ese punto de vista, pues hay muchísimas referencias, pero la mayor parte son aproximativas y de memoria. ¡No en vano gran parte de la obra fue escrita en un café! Me pareció mucho más ágil y menos invasivo añadir la bibliografía completa que llenar el libro de notas sobre cada título."

Spanish version to increase the amount of information and correct possible mistakes. In short, the translator is visible in the rewritten text, warning the audience about the criteria that determined her decisions and strategies.

However, paratranslators decided to add the expert's preface, to select a paragraph from this preface and include it on the back cover, and to illustrate the front cover with drawings of Beauvoir and Sartre, maybe trying to stress the philosophical dimension of the author's thought. Likewise, it was the paratranslator who exclusively decided to publish two volumes at first, in 1998, but also to condense all this work into just one 925 page volume in 2005, without notifying the translator about this new and different edition. Martorell corroborates in that e-mail: "The 2005 edition is the same unchanged translation. I actually found this out when it had already come out."[10]

5. Conclusion

The analysis of the (para)translations of *Le deuxième sexe* into English, South American Spanish and Castilian Spanish[11] suggests that different paratranslators asked four translators to rewrite three different books: a sex manual, a philosophical text and a feminist masterpiece. We have therefore four different translations/rewritings at our disposal. Nevertheless, throughout the decades, each of these four translations has not been identical to one another, that is, the way each of these four translations was presented to their audiences has been changed: books published in Argentina by Psique and Siglo Veinte are all sold as Palant's translation, although having differences between them. In fact the differences reached their peak in 1999 when Sudamericana required a new translation of the text, which was done by García-Puente; books published in Spain are all sold as Martorell's translation, although having differences

---

[10] "la de 2005 es la misma traducción sin revisar. De hecho me enteré cuando ya había salido."

[11] The Portuguese edition of *O Segundo Sexo* in many ways stands between the English one and the Spanish one, since it shares characteristics with both of these. As with the Spanish version, when *Le deuxième sexe* was first published in France, Portugal was undergoing Salazar's dictatorship (1932-1968), so the book was considered subversive. Therefore, *O Segundo Sexo* was translated by Sérgio Milliet (Sartre's translator and specialist in Existentialist Philosophy) and published in Brazil in 1960 (Edipe, in São Paulo). As with the American version, when in 1975 the publishing house Livraria Bertrand reprinted the book in Portugal, they resorted to the existing translation without revising it, so missing a great opportunity to have it revised or even translated again.

between them as well; and books published in the Anglophone world are all sold as Parshley's translations, although they have similarly outstanding differences.

For this reason, when it comes to locating ideology in the specific space of the rewritings/transfers, it is necessary to ask ourselves why different changes are implemented in the different editions rewritten into different languages, published in different countries, for different audiences and in different historical periods. Changes and differences in the presentation and appearance of the same translation explain that responsibilities are shared between the translator and the paratranslator. On the one hand, translators are the deciders of the linguistic and cultural rewriting. On the other, paratranslators have also a great deal of responsibility in the transfer process of the cultural and ideological good, since they are the deciders of how the work is presented to the reception society, of how (ideological) messages are conveyed to the audience. Paratranslators decide the iconic design of the cover and title page, knowing that the iconic dimension of the text and its visual aspect follow a communicative strategy full of ideology which determine its ideological reading and the sort of audience the book is addressed to; they decide whether to propose experts to write prefaces; they settle whether the book will be published in either one or two volumes; they ask translators to do specific rewritings in accordance with their interpretation and understanding of the book; and, more importantly, they decide to what extent translators' visibility is allowed, by showing the translators' name on the cover, allowing them to write a preface or other paratexts, and so on.

In this way, my analysis of these translations and paratranslations of *Le deuxième sexe* has demonstrated the existence of a specific ideological discourse which plays an essential role in the professional work of translation (considered as the reading, interpreting and rewriting of cultural and linguistic texts) and paratranslation (the reading, interpreting and transferring of cultural and linguistic paratexts). This latter is due to the manifest intention of introducing an ideological burden through which to adapt different editions to certain values, and by so doing, seeking and ensuring the acceptability of the translated book in the target society. Therefore, the (para)translators' role is doubly important since their interventions in the original (para)text not only reflect ideology, but they also contribute to its formation.

References

Primary sources

Beauvoir, Simone de (1949) *Le deuxième sexe*, Vol. I. Les Faits et les Mythes. & Vol. II. L'Experiénce Vécue, Paris: Gallimard. (Later editions have been consulted).
—. (1952) *The Second Sex* (translated by Howard Parshley), London: Bantam Books. (Later editions by Pan Books, Picador Classics, Penguin Books, Vintage, Everyman's Library, Jonathan Cape and David Campbell Publishers have been consulted).
—. (1954) *El segundo sexo*. Vol. I. Los hechos y los mitos. & Vol. II. La experiencia vivida (translated by Pablo Palant), Buenos Aires: Psique. (Later editions by Ediciones Siglo Veinte and Sudamericana have been consulted).
—. (1998) *El segundo sexo*, Vol I. Los hechos y los mitos. & Vol. II. La experiencia vivida (translated by Alicia Martorell), Madrid: Cátedra, Universitat de València, Instituto de la Mujer. (Later editions by Cátedra have been consulted).

Secondary sources

Bair, Deirdre (1990) *Simone de Beauvoir. A biography*, New York: Summit.
Bassnett, Susan & Lefevere, André (1990) "Introduction: Proust's Grandmother and the Thousand and One Nights. The Culture Turn in Translation Studies", in Susan Bassnett and André Lefevere (eds.) *Translation, History and Culture*, London and New York: Pinter Publishers, 1-13.
Cronin, Michael (2000) "Ideology and Translation", in Olive Classe (ed.) *Encyclopedia of Literary Translation into English*, London: Fitzroy Dearborn Publishers, 694-696.
Flotow, Luise von (1997) *Translation and Gender. Translation in the Era of Feminism*, Manchester: St. Jerome Publishing.
Garrido Vilariño, Xoán Manuel (2003-2004) "Texto y paratexto. Traducción y Paratraducción", in *Viceversa*, Revista Galega da Tradución 9-10, 31-39.
Genette, Gérard (1987) *Seuils*, Paris: Seuil.
Glazer, Sarah (2004) *Lost in Translation*, The Washington Post, August 22, 2004.

Kush, Celena E. (2000) *Scholars and professionals take a second look at The Second Sex*. Outreach Magazine of the Pennsylvania State University, no. Spring/Summer 2000. http://www.outreach.psu.edu/News/magazine/Vol_2.3/secondsex.html (accessed February 20, 2007).

Lane-Mercier, Gillian (1997) "Translating the untranslatable: the translator's aesthetic, ideological and political responsibility", in *Target* 9:1: 43-68.

Lobtinière-Harwood, Susanne de (1991) *Re-Belle et Infidèle. La traduction comme pratique de reécriture au féminin-The body bilingual. Translation as a rewriting in the feminine*, Toronto: Women's Press.

Martorell Linares, Alicia (1998) *Bibliography*. El segundo sexo, vol. I, by Simone de Beauvoir, 35-42. Madrid: Cátedra, Universitat de València and Instituto de la Mujer.

Moi, Toril (2004) "While We Wait: Notes on the English Translation of The Second Sex", in Emily Grosholz (ed.) *The Legacy of Simone de Beauvoir*, Oxford: Oxford University Press.

Nouss, Alexis (2000) "Structuralism, Post-structuralism and Literary Translation", in Olive Classe (ed.) *Encyclopedia of Literary Translation into English*, London: Fitzroy Dearborn, 1351-1355.

Parshley, Howard (1952) Translator's Preface. The Second Sex, by Simone de Beauvoir, New York: Bantam Books, 7-12.

Simon, Sherry (1996) *Gender in Translation*, London and New York: Routledge.

Simons, Margaret A. (2001) *Beauvoir and The Second Sex. Feminism, Race and the Origins of Existencialism*, Maryland: Rowman and Littlefield Publishers.

Snell-Hornby, Mary (1990) "Linguistic Transcoding or Cultural Transfer? A Critique of Translation Theory in Germany", in Susan Bassnett and André Lefevere (eds.) *Translation, History and Culture*, London and New York: Pinter Publishers, 79-86.

PSEUDONYMS, PSEUDOTRANSLATION AND SELF-CENSORSHIP IN THE NARRATIVE OF THE WEST DURING THE FRANCO DICTATORSHIP

MARÍA DEL CARMEN CAMUS CAMUS,
UNIVERSIDAD DE CANTABRIA, SPAIN

Abstract: Throughout history pseudonyms have been used for diverse reasons in many fields of knowledge. In the literature of prestige, authors have hidden their identity behind the mask of a pseudonym for reasons such as the preservation of their identity in cases of political or religious persecution or in order to write texts considered to transgress the social norms of acceptability. In the realm of popular narrative, the use of pseudonyms is linked both to the phenomenon of pseudotranslation, that is, texts written in the native language and presented as if they were translations of works written by foreign authors, and to censorship. In this type of literary texts, this practice seems more conspicuous than in any other field of literature.

This descriptive study, which is based on a catalogue of 730 censorship files compiled at the Administration General Archive for the period from 1939 to 1975, explores the relation between the use of pseudonyms, pseudotranslation and self-censorship during the Franco dictatorship in the narrative of the West. It examines the pseudonyms coined by authors when creating their new identities, and attempts to identify what governmental, political and economic measures influenced the disproportionate use of these self-constructions in the Western.

If things possess a special nature, the name should be a faithful reflection of that essence.
—Plato

Self-censorship was a practice that to a greater or lesser extent affected all literary production generated during the Franco dictatorship. Censorship of one's own identity was one of the most widespread forms of self-censorship that some authors were obliged to inflict on themselves but to which others submitted voluntarily. This change of identity allowed certain prestigious authors persecuted by the Franco regime to place their minor or bread-winning works in the editorial world; in contrast, for those authors whose production was limited to popular narrative, mass fiction or kiosk fiction, the use of pseudonyms became an almost compulsory practice for this type of literature. This study of the use of pseudonyms as a form of self-censorship in the narrative of the West was carried out within a descriptive framework. The data for the study were obtained from a randomised sample collected at the Archivo General de la Administración [General State Archive], which houses all the censorship files opened during the Franco era. The period examined extends from 1939 to 1975. The study includes both American writers and the Spanish authors who for their pseudotranslations used this practice as a hallmark of prestige.

1. Reasons for using pseudonyms

The term *pseudonym* refers among other things to the false name used by an author instead of his or her real name; it is a voluntary designation (self-construction) that the person attributes to him/herself for identification by others. In Antiquity, the name of an entity was thought not only to designate but to determine its very nature. A change of name, therefore, indicated a change of destiny. Name-changing is an age-old practice in the history of mankind through which a new self-construction is presented to others for such diverse reasons as religion, politics or, as in the case that concerns us, for literary reasons. Among the earliest name changes was that of Plato (Aristocles), a nickname referring to his broad shoulders. In the Judeo-Christian world, a change of name was used to introduce the new persona. The first Biblical name change occurs in the book of Genesis when Yahweh changes Abram to Abraham *ab hamon* [father of many]: "Neither shall thy name any more be called Abram, but thy name shall be Abraham, for a father of many nations have I made thee" (Gen. 17.5). Politics is another domain in which nicknames have been used, and we can cite the cases of Lenin (Vladimir Ilyich Ulyanov), Stalin (Iosif Vissarionovich Dzhugashvili) and Trotsky (Lev Davidovich Bronstein). However, it is in the literary field that the greatest use of the resource of concealing a true name behind a literary mask has been made both within and beyond the borders of Spain. Leopoldo Enrique García-Alas Ureña adopted the pseudonym of Clarín, Samuel Langhorne Clemens was better known as Mark Twain, and there is the case of Jorge Luís

Borges and Adolfo Bioy Casares who collaborated to write under the pseudonym of H. Bustos Domecq.

P. Rogers and F. A. Lafuente (1977) in their *Diccionario de seudónimos literarios españoles* [Dictionary of Spanish Literary Pseudonyms] list 28 reasons for changing a name or using a literary mask. Of particular interest for our purposes are "To safeguard one's personal dignity", "The belief that a pseudonym confers greater prestige on a work than a familiar name", "At the request of an editor", or "When writing subliterature". In this regard, it should be noted that recurrent use of pseudonyms was particularly conspicuous in the popular narrative written in Spain during General Franco's regime.

The main aim of this paper is to delve deeper into the relationship–if one exists–between the use of pseudonyms and self-censorship of author identity in the pseudotranslation of the narrative of the West during Franco's dictatorship. The data provided in our analysis may contribute to a better understanding of their disproportionate use for this literary genre in the period under study.

2. Aims and sources

In this study of the use of pseudonyms as a means of self-censorship in the translations and pseudotranslations of the novel of the West, we seek to answer some of the questions directly related to their use in this type of literature. Since the term *narrative of the West* encompasses a meaning as broad and extensive as the immense prairies that we inevitably associate with this literature, it is necessary first to determine whether the use of pseudonyms was as frequent in the Western translated and imported from the United States, and then to verify whether the motivation of pseudonyms in this imported literature was the same as in that written and published in Spain pseudotranslation.

The data used in our analysis were obtained from a catalogue of 730 censorship files located in a randomised search carried out for the genre under study at the *Archivo General de la Administración* or *AGA* [General State Archive]. The analysis spans the period from the rise of the Franco dictatorship following victory in 1939 until its fall in 1975. The catalogue is a small contribution to the database *Traducciones Censuradas TRACE* [Censored Translations].

The historical context of the study is the Franco dictatorship, which spanned the prolonged period extending from the victory of the Nationals, led by General Franco, until the death of the dictator on the 20th November, 1975. Right from the beginning of the Francoist period,

Franco's government set up a strict censorship mechanism whereby even the slightest artistic or literary manifestation occurring on Spanish soil during his rule had to pass through its sieve. The censorial action performed by the censorship system implemented immediately after Franco's victory left a trail in its path and spattered any cultural manifestation generated in Spain during this prolonged period. No area of knowledge was spared the effects of its intervention. The literary field is but one small area where traces of its action remain, clearly visible traces in some cases. Within the literary field the sector we have chosen for this study is the Western.

By Western we understand a story of variable length narrating totally or partially fictitious events that occur in the mythical space of the Far West. In our analysis, we have included works written both by celebrated American authors and by writers of popular or "pulp" fiction, and works written by Spanish authors and published in Spain, which Toury (1995) designates pseudotranslations.

For our purposes, pseudotranslation, therefore, refers to the Westerns written by Spanish authors in which they cloned the works of American writers. These pseudotranslations were then presented to the Spanish receptor culture as if it were imported material translated from the prestigious American culture (Rabadán 2000). In Spain, a high percentage of this cloned pseudotranslation was presented to the reading public by means of a literary mask or pseudonym.

3. Quantitative results

Before making a more detailed qualitative analysis of pseudonyms in the Western, we present a few figures to illustrate more clearly the use authors made of them. Although the genre enjoyed enormous popularity with the public during the period under study, since the editions of these publications were relatively large, it is surprising to discover that the list of authors who published all or part of their work in the genre is rather modest. The 730 censorship files located in the AGA search yielded a somewhat meagre list of 191 authors (Fig. 2-2).

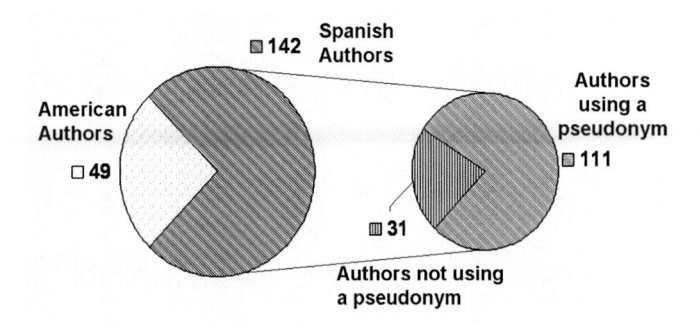

Fig.2-2: Distribution of the 191 authors in the sample

This includes both those who published their texts in Spanish (pseudotranslation) and the American authors whose works were translated, 142 and 49 respectively. Of the 142 Spanish authors publishing all or part of their work as Westerns, only 31 put their real name to their published works, the remaining 111 using a fictitious name. These 111 authors who concealed their true identity used a total of 136 different pseudonyms. Of these 136 pseudonyms, only 80 showed a one-to-one correspondence with the author, as shown in table 2-4.

No	Author	Pseudonym	No	Author	Pseudonym
	Alonso Solbes, Manuel	M. de Silva	41	Losada Martín, Juan	John L. Martyn
	Arias Archidona, Vicente	Alone Gregory	42	Manzanares, Alfonso Martínez	Alf Manz
	Arizamendi Regaldie, Alfonso	Alf Regaldie	43	Fariñas, Enrique	Fariñas
	Astraín Badá, Miguel María	Mikky Roberts	44	Martínez Orejón, Felix	Fel Marty
	Barberán Domínguez, Rafael	Ralph Barby	45	Martínez Torre, Antonio	César Torre
	Bellani Cremona, Rodolfo	Rudy Linbale	46	Marzo Martín, José	March Damon
	Benet	Joe Benet	47	Mayoral	John Ransy

	Sanchiz, José Luis Bernabé Pajares, Alberto Calero Montejano, Mario Castillejos	Albert Tower	48	López, Lorenzo Medina Herrera, Manuel Medina Martín, Manuel	M. Dinahe	
		Tex Taylor	49		Don Looman	
0	Osuna, Andrés	Andrews Castle	50	Molins Mallol, Mariano	David O'Malley	
1	Cazorla, Angel Cortés Faure,	Kent Wilson	51	Mora Gutiérrez, Juan Moreno García,	Ray Lester	
2	Octavio Daniel Ortusol,	O. C. Tavin	52	Gerardo Moreno García, José	Gerar Moren	
3	Francisco Debrigode,	Fred Dennis	53	Mª Navarro	Joe Mogar	
4	Pedro Victor Enguidanos Usach,	Peter Debry	54	Ibañez, Blas Nuñez González, Mª	Blay	
5	Pascual Enguita Iguarbez,	George H. White	55	Rosa Nuñez González, Mª	Ros M. Talbot	
6	Octavio Escaño Delgado,	Roy Rowan	56	Teresa Olcina Esteve,	Paul Lattimer	
7	Francisco Espeita Lamata,	Frank July Aces	57	Arsenio Oliveros	A. Rocelst	
8	Francisco Fernando	Frank Spey	58	Tovar, Miguel Ortiga Griso,	Keith Luger	
9	Alejandro Galo	Alex Colins	59	Ramón Pérez Más,	O. G. Raymon	
0	Falgueras	Gal Falmor	60	Ernesto Prado Castellanos,	Ernie Parker	
1	García Lecha, Luis García Mateos,	Clark Granados	61	Allentorn Prado Duque,	Meadow Castle	
2	Orlando García Trueba,	Orland Garr	62	Fidel Rodríguez	W. Martyn	
3	Ginés Garriga De Vidal,	Jim Garta	63	Illera, Angel Saavedra Rodríguez,	Ian Hutton	
4	Francisco Gaspar	Frank Garret	64	Miguel Sánchez	M. Saavdrovitch	
5	Garriga,	Alf Landon	65	Martínez,	Gaby Sam	

6	Celestino Goicoechéa Martínez, Rafael	Raf G. Smith	66	Gabriel Sánchez Saavedra, Miguel	Ringo Laredo	
7	Gómez Rueda, Mariano	Mason	67	Sánchez, Guillermo	Boix	
8	González Ledesma, Francisco	Silver Kane	68	Sanz Mas, Antonio	Anthony S. Max	
9	González Morales, Antonio	A.G. Murphy	69	Sedo Ragul, Juan Arturo	J. A. Dose	
0	Gordón González, Ángel	Rogers Kirby	70	Segovia Ramos, Rafael	Raf. Segrram	
1	Gubern Ribalta, Jorge	Mark Halloran	71	Silva, Manuel de Simón	Manuel Asirís Solbes	
2	Guirao Hernández, Pedro	Peter Kapra	72	Martínez, Joaquín	Rock Miller	
3	Hernández Vidal, Josefa	Joseph Herche	73	Sola Gómez, José Torre	Joseph Solag	
4	Jarnés, Enrique	Henry S. James	74	Rodríguez, Agustín de la	Austin Tower	
5	Lacasa Nebot, Juan Bautista Lavios	John Lack	75	Torres Rojas, Antonio Valera	Anthony Towers	
6	Agullo, Miguel León	Sam Fletcher	76	Demaría, Fernando Velasco	Laredo Anderson	
7	Domínguez, José	Kelltom McIntire	77	Bernabeu, Jaime	Spencer Curtis	
8	León Ruiz de Cárdenas, Jacinto López	Tom O'Hara	78	Vera Ramírez, Antonio	Lou Carrigan	
9	García, José López	Adam Surray	9	Viader Vives, Antonio	Ricky Dickinson	
0	Rueda, Manuel	Leo Mason	80	Vila Ripoll, Esteban	Rodivisa	

Table 2-4: List of the 80 Spanish authors who used a single pseudonym

Three pseudonyms were shared by more than one author (table 2-5), and the remaining 53 corresponded to 24 authors who used two or even three pseudonyms for the genre (table 2-6).

154   Pseudonyms, Pseudotranslation and Self-Censorship in the Narrative of the West During the Franco Dictatorship

No	Pseudonym	Author	No
1	Black Moran	Blas Morán, José Luis de	1
		Sánchez Ferreiro, Mª del Carmen	2
		Lafuente Estefanía, Marcial Antonio	3
2	M. L. Estefanía	Lafuente Beorlegui, Federico	4
		Lafuente Estefanía, Federico Mª y Fco. Mª	5
3	J. León	León Ignacio, Jacinto	6
		León Ignacio, Jorge	7

Table 2-5: The three pseudonyms shared by more than one author

No	Author	Pseudonym	No
1	Adam Cardona, Vicente	V.A. Carter	1
		Vic Adams	2
2	Alarcón Benito, Juan	Alar Benet.	3
		Greison, J	4
3	Cortés Rubio, Francisco	Frank McFair	5
		Russ Tryon	6
		Larry King	7
4	Faura Peñasco, Francisco	Vander Kane	8
		Charles Dick	9
5	Gallardo Muñoz, Juan	Curtis Garland	10
		Donald Curtis	11
		Jonny Garland	12
6	González Rodríguez, Juan José	R. Mayfair, Paul	13
		Uriah Moltan	14
7	Guzmán Espinosa, Eduardo	Eddie Thorny	15
		Edward Goodman	16
8	Hidalgo Martínez, Antonio	Dave Turner	17
		Ray Silver	18
9	Iñigo Martín, Francisco José	Frank Hunter	19
		Franklin Ingmar	20
10	León Ignacio, Jorge	J.León	21
		J. de Cárdenas	22
11	Lliró Olivé, José Mª	Burton Hare	23
		Gordon Lumas	24
12	Llop Sellares, Juan	J. Grey	25
		John Weiber	26
13	Medina Martín, Francisco	F.M.Dayne	27
		Frank Martin	28
14	Miranda Marín, Nicolás	Cameron Jones	29
		Joe Sheridan	30
15	Molins León, Alfonso	Al. Mac Lee	31
		R.C. Lindsmall	32
16	Montoro Sagristá, Enrique	Cass Donovan	33
		Henry Keystone	34
17	Moreno Espinosa, Gerardo	G. Woren	35
		Gerard Woren	36

18	Navarro Carrión-Cervera, Jesús	Cliff Bradley	37
		Jess McCarr	38
19	Rodoreda Sayol, Victoria	John Palmer	39
		Vic Logan	40
20	Rodríguez Aroca, Luis	Lewis Haroc	41
		Louis Rock	42
21	Rodríguez Lázaro, Jesús	Don Carter	43
		Lucky Marty	44
22	Ruiz Catarineu, Joaquín	Alan Carson	45
		Jack Logan	46
		Ketchum	47
23	Sánchez Pascual, Enrique	Bill Laramie	48
		E.L. Retamosa	49
		Will Cooper	50
24	Tellez González, Miguel	Herman Tellgon	51
		JATG	52
		Vallgreen	53

Table 2-6: The 24 Spanish authors who used two or more pseudonyms

For the 49 American authors included in the sample there were only five who employed a pseudonym. Different analyses of the data to verify the identity of these authors revealed a lack of rigour in the registration of these imported works since, in some cases, the entry appeared under the author's name when this was in fact a pseudonym. The distribution of the 141 pseudonyms is shown in Fig. 2-3.

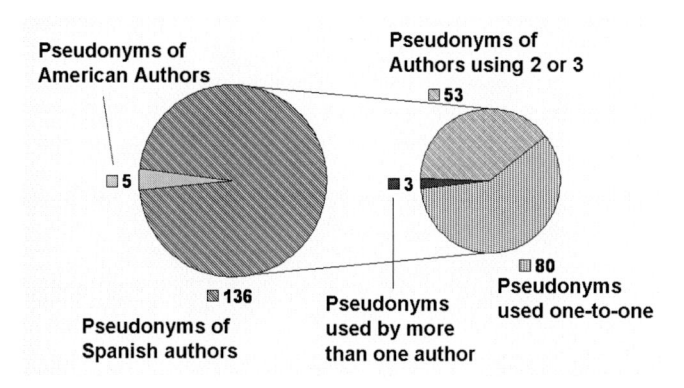

Fig. 2-3: Distribution of the 141 pseudonyms in the sample

4. Qualitative analysis

The use of pseudonyms in the popular novel is not a phenomenon restricted to the Spanish model. The imported models, in our case "pulps", already employed this resource in order to orientate readers in some way to the type of text they were about to meet. In the creation of the new self-construction, the characteristic common to most pseudonyms in popular narrative, for both foreign and Spanish authors, was that the pseudonym chosen should as far as possible be related in some way to the genre they were writing. For the Western, we have the cases of Max Brand, Tod Hunter, and Dan Wilder among the American authors, and among the Spanish writers, Burton Hare (José Maria Lliró Olivé), Louis Rock (Luis Rodríguez Aroca) and Ray Silver (Antonio Hidalgo Martínez).

Another significant feature of this mass-market or consumer fiction is that many authors did not specialise in a single genre so that they frequently used different pseudonyms depending on the genre they were writing. Thus, we have the case of the Spanish writer Antonio Vera Ramírez, who for the Western used the pseudonym of Lou Carrigan. For other genres, such as the romantic novel, he used Angelo Antonioni, Brigitte for the erotic novel and Tony Manhattan for narrative of a more daring nature. For his longer quality novels, the author used Anthony Michaels or Milton Hamilton, since he thought that the readers of his Lou Carrigan paperbacks would be reluctant to spend four times as much on a book written by the same author.

Another characteristic of this consumer fiction is that even those authors who specialised in a particular genre, in our case the Western, employed different pseudonyms when they published their work in different series produced by the same editor. Others resorted to different pseudonyms to publish for an editor other than their usual one, and in this way possibly covered up their infidelity to the publishing house with which they had probably signed an exclusive contract.

One of the outstanding features of the choice of a literary mask in the Spanish case is that both its written form and its pronunciation should suggest foreign origin (Gómez Ortiz 2000; Rabadán 2000), and for the Western that it should have clear American overtones. Moreover, in the Spanish case, it should be noted that even if the work was published under a fictitious name, this did not imply that it was by an anonymous author of unknown affiliation, since author identity was no secret either to the editor or to the censorship system (Santamaría in press). This is because, when applying to the governmental organism responsible for censorship of books, first for the euphemistically termed "preliminary step of voluntary consultation" and then for permission to publish, the applicant had to fill in a section declaring the author's real name (Rabadán 2000).

When selecting a pen name, some Spanish authors simply chose names with foreign overtones. In these cases, the pseudonym chosen bore no relation to the author's identity, merely reflecting the common feature of relating to the genre they were writing (i.e., the Western): Joaquín Ruiz Catarineu, *Jack Logan*; José López García, *Adam Surray*; and Miguel Lavios Angulo, *Sam Fletcher*. Other writers adopted pseudonyms with American connotations but, at the same time, allowed their identity to show through in their *nom de plume*. Some made more or less direct translations of their real name: Andrés Castillejos Osuna, *Andrews Castle*; Juan Losada Martín, *John L. Martyn*; and Luis Rodríguez Aroca, *Louis Rock*, or *Lewis Haroc*. Others employed acronyms constructing the pseudonym from part of their first name and part of their surname: thus, we have Alfonso Manzanares, *Alf Manz*, Felix Martínez Orejón, *Fel Marty*; and José Moreno García, *Joe Mogar*. Still others adapted part of their real name or surname to conserve in some way their true identity, some typical examples being Jesús Navarro Carrión-Cervera, *Jess McCarr*; Miguel Maria Astrín Bada, *Mikky Roberts*; and Pedro Guirao Hernández, *Peter Capra*. We can conclude that when choosing their pseudonyms, Spanish authors opted for foreign-sounding and foreign-looking names that were reminiscent of the American prairies. To achieve this American flavour, they chose either to translate their true identity, to create acronyms, or to construct a new affiliation by conserving part of their real one.

Having described the form of the pseudonyms adopted by Spanish authors of the popular literary genre of the Western, we will attempt to explain the reason for their disproportionate use. Writing under a pseudonym, or with a pseudonym relating to the genre, was commonplace in the imported American models, that is, the dime novels or pulps. A first analysis suggests that self-censorship of one's identity was not directly associated with Francoist censorship, although it is striking that the Spanish censorial system, preoccupied as it was about safeguarding patriotic values, should have permitted Spanish books to be published with a non-Spanish name. What we are seeking to clarify here is whether the phenomenon of pseudotranslation was a direct result of Francoist censorship or whether it arose for other reasons and it was censorship that perhaps favoured its use. Therefore, we shall now analyse the conditioning factors affecting the pseudotranslations written is Spain.

5. Conditioning factors

5.1. Censorship due to political ideology

One of the factors motivating self-identity censorship when publishing under a pseudonym might have been due to the author holding an ideology contrary to the regime, that is, for political reasons. However, the absence of a political motivation is supported by the fact that the list of writers publishing this type of narrative surprisingly includes authors ideologically opposed to the regime. Some of these had been imprisoned as in the case of the Republican journalist Eduardo de Guzmán, one of whose pen names was *Edward Goodman*, or Francisco González Ledesma, alias *Silver Kane*, a journalist and lawyer, and even Marcial Lafuente Estefanía, an artillery officer in the Republican army, who signed his early novels as *Tony Spring* or *Arizona* but soon began to publish his works under his real name. As mentioned above, a strict control was kept over all the personae concealed behind a *nom de plume*, which meant that the censorial system knew the true identity of these authors. In such cases, the use of a pseudonym proved beneficial to the Franco regime, since by permitting these clearly anti-Francoist authors to write this type of novel, they filled the void created by the great stampede of Spanish talent that took place with the arrival of Francoism. As the true identity of these authors was kept hidden behind the pseudonym, the Spanish people had no knowledge that it was authors ideologically opposed to Francoism that were writing the novels they read. But for this concealed identity, the regime would not have permitted this situation as this would have revealed a patent weakness of the dictatorship. Thus, it does not appear that, in the case of the Western, it was censorship of a political nature that caused these authors to publish under a pseudonym but rather that authors used them as a bread-winner.

5.2. Economic censorship

It seems that one of the factors that could have influenced the use of pseudonyms was of an economic nature. When editors recruited writers to contribute to a particular genre with their novels, they advised them to hide their identity behind a pseudonym in order to boost sales. According to authors like González Ledesma in an interview on Internet (2005), and Vera Ramírez (personal communication),[1] no author appears to have been

---

[1] Antonio Vera Ramírez, e-mail message to author, October 29, 2006.

forced to use a pseudonym although, if they used them, writers were advised to choose one having foreign overtones and relating to the genre they were writing. In support of their argument, the editors claimed that names like Vera or González would not be well accepted by their readers. However, even if they concealed their identity behind a pseudonym in order to increase sales, these authors held full rights over their production. Nevertheless, there were other cases where the editor had "all-purpose" pseudonyms, that is, pseudonyms belonging to the publisher, who contacted specific authors that simply handed over their production to the publishing house. These writers were probably out-and-out "enemies" of the regime who used this channel as a means of economic survival. In addition, there were pseudonyms that were voluntarily shared by several authors, probably to meet publishers' deadlines and demands. Although these writers were absolute wizards of the typewriter, to judge by the number of works they published, in the case of Mallorquí producing one a week, the "voracious appetite" of the reading public and the mercantile interests of the publishers meant that series such as *Buffalo Bill* or *Nick Carter* had to be co-authored by a team of three writers, the young translators Guillermo López Hipkiss, Manuel Vallvé and Enrique Cuenca Granch (Gómez Ortiz 2000).

5.3. State censorship

The censorship that most influenced suppression of self-identity was state censorship. We shall now examine how it was possible that in a country governed by a political regime that considered itself the "spiritual reserve of the western world", it was permitted to publish works supposedly written by foreign authors. Indeed, this was a government that from the very beginning had made a show of patriotic values and had implemented the censorial macrostructure so as to shield Spain and protect it from the contamination of any dissident voice, whether this came from inside or outside its borders. The popular novel in a country like Spain with growing literacy was a powerful weapon that could not be left without strict control exercised by the government of the dictatorship.

Because of the enormous reading appetite of the Spanish people in the post-Civil War period, the new state was forced to come up with a solid solution to the ever-increasing importation and translation of foreign books. Since these were considered harmful elements, the carriers of the dangerous ideas of modernity and change, it was necessary to shield Spain culturally, to prevent any dissident idea from entering Spanish territory and, at the same time, to create routes for expansion so that the ideas of the new state might take root in the fertile virgin lands of the new world. General Franco's government soon became aware of the immense danger contained within books, especially imported books, so that it promptly adopted control measures to put a brake on the importation and subsequent translation of foreign books, thereby protecting the "weak helpless" Spanish people against contagion from harmful ideas. To this end, it established a number of measures to promote the genuinely Spanish book and, in turn, to encourage the exportation of Spanish books, since these were to carry the message of the "glorious mission" undertaken by the new state. The regime would thus succeed in sending its message beyond our borders, colonising new states, mainly those in Spanish America. To attain this goal, the government passed a series of laws and decrees that would allow it to achieve its aims.

On the greatest possible diffusion of Spanish books, both at home and abroad:

> The unfavourable position and state of abandon of Spanish books in foreign markets, together with the prices–inaccessible to modest budgets– reached on the home market, which is clearly detrimental to the diffusion of any type of culture, require immediate and effective action to end this precarious situation and set the foundations for the future expansion for which Spanish books are destined, principally in Spanish-America, because of the universality of our language and the catholicity of our spirit.[2]

Thus, it was mainly reasons of cultural policy that would condition the birth, the rise and the splendour of this phenomenon without parallel in Spanish history. The popular novel, especially the Western, would be used by Franco's government as a mechanism of repression so that this powerful emergent enemy, a people hungry for literacy, should not be exposed to any contagion arising from libertarian ideas. Ideas that, in spite of the fine censorial sieve, might infiltrate the fragile minds of the working classes through the translation of foreign works, viewed as the carriers not only of a non-Spanish spirit but, in some cases, of an anti-Spanish spirit.

---

[2] My translation from *Ley de 18 de Diciembre de 1946. BOE de 19 de Diciembre de 1946, n° 353, pág. 8829-30. Jefatura del Estado* [Law of 18th December, 1946. Official State Bulletin, 19th December, no. 353, pp. 8829-30].

6. Conclusion

The use of a pseudonym represented a clear form of self-censorship for the author of the Western. At first, this use was linked to the importation of the American model of pulp fiction, which brought about a cultural transfer that filled a pre-existing gap in the Spanish literary polysystem. Although the use of pseudonyms was consolidated for apparently economic reasons, it was clearly reasons of state used subliminally that favoured their use. On the one hand, through these works written by authors of "foreign" origin, the dictatorship presented its citizens with an image of openness to the outside world. On the other, home-produced works exported with the names of "foreign" authors served the Franco regime as a vehicle to transmit to the world, particularly Spanish America, in a sibylline way the true patriotic spirit. A Spanish book written and elaborated in Spain in response to the national values and contributing to the diffusion of the true national spirit undertaken by the new state.

References

Gómez Ortiz, Tomás (2000) "El seudónimo en la novela popular española (1930-1960)", in Robel (ed.) *La novela popular en España,* Madrid: Robel, 133-146.

González Ledesma, Francisco (2005) "Lo importante es que tú creas en lo que escribes", in *Siglo XXI,* December, 31, interview.
Available at *http://www.diariosigloxxi.com/noticia.php?Id= 11330*

Rabadán, Rosa (2000) "Con orden y concierto: la censura franquista y las traducciones inglés-español 1939-1985", in Rosa Rabadán (ed.) *Traducción y censura inglés-español: 1939-1985. Estudio preliminar,* León: Universidad de León, 13-20.

—. (2000) "Modelos importados, modelos adaptados: Pseudotraducciones de narrativa popular inglés-español 1955-1981", in Rosa Rabadán (ed.) *Traducción y censura inglés-español: 1939-1985. Estudio preliminar,* León: Universidad de León, 255-277.

Rogers, Paul Patrick & Felipe Antonio Lafuente (1977) *Diccionario de seudónimos literarios españoles, con algunas iniciales.* Madrid: Gredos.

Santamaría, José Miguel, "El oeste que leímos: pseudotraducciones y traducciones genuinas",
http://www.ehu.es/trace/colectivo.html.

Toury, Gideon (1995) *Descriptive Translation Studies and Beyond.* Amsterdam: John Benjamins.

Universidad del País Vasco. "TRACE: Traducciones Censuradas. Herramientas para los Estudios Descriptivos de Traducción: construcción de un corpus paralelo multilingüe de traducciones inglés-español". *http://www.ehu.es/trace/inicio.html.*

THE DANGER(S) OF SELF-CENSORSHIP(S): THE TRANSLATION OF '*FUCK*' INTO SPANISH AND CATALAN[1]

JOSÉ SANTAEMILIA,
UNIVERSITAT DE VALÈNCIA, SPAIN

Abstract: Self-censorship is an individual ethical struggle between self and context. In all historical circumstances, translators tend to produce rewritings which are "acceptable" from both social and personal perspectives. The translation of swearwords and sex-related language is a case in point, which very often depends on historical and political circumstances but which is also an area of personal struggle, of ethical/moral dissent, of religious/ideological controversies.In this paper we analyse the translation of the lexeme *fuck* into Spanish and Catalan. We have chosen two novels by Helen Fielding–*Bridget Jones's Diary* (1996) and *Bridget Jones: The Edge of Reason* (1999)–and the translations into the languages mentioned. Historically, sex-related language has been a highly sensitive area; if today, in Western countries at least, we cannot defend any form of public censorship, what we cannot prevent (nor probably should we) is a certain degree of self-censorship, along the lines of an individual ethics and attitude towards religion, sex(uality), notions of (im)politeness or (in)decency, etc. Translating is always a struggle to reach a compromise between one's ethics and society's multiple constraints–and nowhere can we see this more clearly than in the rewriting(s) of sex-related language.

1. The translation of sex: between "censorship" and "self-censorship (s)"

While censorship can be considered "the suppression or prohibition of speech or writing that is condemned as subversive of the common good"

---

[1] I wish to thank the Spanish Ministerio de Ciencia y Tecnología for their support in this research, in particular for research project "Discurso y (des)cortesía y género: Estudio contrastivo inglés/castellano/catalán" (BFF2003-07662).

(Allan & Burridge 2006: 13) and constitutes an external constraint on what we can publish or (re)write, self-censorship is an individual ethical struggle between self and context. In all historical circumstances, translators tend to censor themselves–either voluntarily or involuntarily–in order to produce rewritings which are "acceptable" from both social and personal perspectives.

The translation of swearwords or of sex-related language is a case in point, which very often depends on historical and political circumstances (see Rabadán 2000, for a comprehensive research project on state censorship under Franco's dictatorial regime in Spain, 1939-1975; or Vega 2004, for a description of the hardships publishers and translators went through during this period), but which is also an area of personal struggle, of ethical/moral dissent, of religious/ideological controversies, of systematic self-censorship (see Bou & Pennock 1992).

When translating sex, what is at stake is not only grammatical or lexical accuracy. Besides the actual meanings of the sex-related expressions, there are aesthetic, cultural, pragmatic and ideological components, as well as an urgent question of linguistic ethics. Eliminating sexual terms–or qualifying or attenuating or even intensifying them–in translation does usually betray the translator's personal attitude towards human sexual behaviour(s) and their verbalization. The translator basically transfers into his/her rewriting the level of acceptability or respectability he/she accords to certain sex-related words or phrases. Analyzing the translation of sexual language into (a) specific language(s) helps draw the imaginary limits of the translators' sexual morality and, perhaps, gain insights into the moral fabric of a specific community at a specific historical moment.

We believe that translating sex-related language is a fertile ground for the articulation of both official "censorships" and the multiplicity of "self-censorships". In the 21st century, there seems to be no formal "censorship" of those works with explicit or implicit sexual content. We could, however, hypothesize more subtle and imperceptible forms of self-censorship(s), which would affect the territories of religious beliefs, moral attitudes or, ultimately, personal ethics. These self-censorships are difficult to catalogue or spot, quite often involuntarily produced, and focus equally on both significant and insignificant aspects of the source texts. If insignificant, then the translation options can be accounted for in terms of stylistic (idiolectal) variation; in the case of significant changes, they will mostly revolve around contentious ideological, political, religious or social aspects of the target society.

2. The translation of sex-related terms: the case of *fuck*

In this paper we analyse the translation of the lexeme *fuck* into Spanish and Catalan. We have chosen two novels by Helen Fielding–*Bridget Jones's Diary* (1996) and *Bridget Jones: The Edge of Reason* (1999); henceforth *BJ* and *BJER*– and the translations into the languages mentioned. Fielding's acclaimed first novel has given rise to a distinctive genre of popular fiction (*chick lit*), which is mainly addressed to young cosmopolitan women and deals unconventionally with love and sex(uality). Among the main features of *chick lit* we can distinguish a constant reference to sex-related matters and a liberal use of sex-related terms. This is a common feature shared by best-selling authors like Candace Bushnell, Helen Fielding, Marian Keyes, Wendy Holden or Meg Cabot.

In the *Bridget Jones* books, Helen Fielding has created a new icon of contemporary femininity: Bridget is impulsive, independent and ... foul-mouthed. Bridget and her friends liberally use swearwords, blasphemies and make bold references to their sex lives. It seems, then, that part of Helen Fielding's stylistic project in *BJ* and *BJER* depends on the use of sex-related terms and, more specifically, on the (ab)use of the lexeme *fuck*. McEnery & Xiao (2004) found the word *fuck* one of the most versatile in the English language, as it is variously used as a general expletive, a personal insult, an emphatic intensifier, an idiom or a metalinguistic device–just to cite a few examples.

For McEnery & Xiao (2004), the fundamental usages of *fuck* in the *British National Corpus* are:

Code	Description	Examples	%
G	GENERAL EXPLETIVE	*(Oh) fuck!*	6.72
P	PERSONAL INSULT REFERRING TO DEFINED ENTITY	*You fuck! / that fuck*	1.87
C	CURSING EXPLETIVE	*Fuck you!/ me!/ him!/ it!*	5.99
D	DESTINATIONAL USAGE	*Fuck off!/ he fucked off*	5.43
L	LITERAL USAGE denoting TABOO REFERENT	*He fucked her*	7.16
E	EMPHATIC INTENSIFIER	*Fucking marvellous!/ in the fucking car*	55.85
O	'PRONOMINAL' FORM	*Like fuck/ fat as fuck*	1.54
I	IDIOMATIC 'SET PHRASE'	*Fuck all/ give a fuck/thank fuck*	12.30

| X | METALINGUISTIC OR UNCLASSIFIABLE DUE TO INSUFFICIENT CONTEXT | The use of the word "fuck" / you never fucking | 3.14 |

Table 2-7: Main usages of the lexeme *fuck* in the BNC (adapted from McEnery & Xiao 2004)

Fuck is fundamentally used as an "emphatic intensifier" (55.85% of occurrences)–i.e. its main aim is to add emotional values to the words or phrases it accompanies. Other significant values of the term are related to exclamative or figurative usages–as idiomatic "set phrase" (12.30%), as a general expletive (5.72%), as cursing expletive (5.99), in a destinational usage (5.43%). What is most striking, perhaps, is that the denotative sexual meaning of fuck ("to copulate") is rarely used (7.16% of cases), as opposed to 92.84% of non-sexual usages. This seems to indicate an obvious process of de-semantization–and even of de-sensitization–of the lexeme *fuck* in English across settings and genres, and a marked preference for emotive and emphatic values. In spite of this difference, however, we cannot help perceiving a certain "sexualization" of the communicative events in which the lexeme *fuck* is used. The shocking capacity of this term permeates the whole language and a certain sexual(ised) flavour is inescapable.

In fact, it may well be that the enormous emphatic potential (55.85%) of the term is mostly attributable to its sexual nature. If we encounter the word *fuck* or any of its morphological variants, we will give them a primarily sexual meaning, as it is a term which is socially sanctioned as "obscene", vulgar or inappropriate in most contexts, and has repeatedly been subject to legal censorship or to social stigmatisation.

For this paper we have collected a corpus with 65 examples where the term *fuck* (and its morphological variants *fucking*, *fucked* and others) is used, and we have analyzed the commercial translations into Spanish and Catalan we mentioned above. All the morphological variants of *fuck* and the number of occurrences we obtained are as follows:

Fuck (v. & n.)	28	*Fucking*	17
Fickwittage	11	*Fuckwit*	5
Fuck-up	2	*Fucked*	1
Fuckety	1		

Table 2-8

If we use the same categories proposed by McEnery & Xiao (2004), we have the diagram below, which shows statistics from *BJ* and *BJER*:

Code	Description	Examples	%
G	GENERAL EXPLETIVE	*Oh fuck, oh fuck.*	26.40
P	PERSONAL INSULT REFERRING TO DEFINED ENTITY	*He's an unreliable, selfish, idle, unfaithful fuckwit from hell.*	9.30
C	CURSING EXPLETIVE	--------------	0.00
D	DESTINATIONAL USAGE	*'Fuck off, everyone, this is my personal space'*	4.60
L	LITERAL USAGE DENOTING TABOO REFERENT	--------------	0.00
E	EMPHATIC INTENSIFIER	*Cannot believe he still hasn't fucking, fucking, fucking well rung.*	35.70
O	'PRONOMINAL' FORM	--------------	0.00
I	IDIOMATIC 'SET PHRASE'	*'Listen, Bridge, I'm really sorry, I've fucked up'.*	6.20
X	METALINGUISTIC OR UNCLASSIFIABLE DUE TO INSUFFICIENT CONTEXT	*'Emotional fuckwittage', which is ...*	17.80

Table 2-9: Main usages of the lexeme 'fuck' in *Bridget Jones's Diary* and *Bridget Jones: The Edge of Reason* (1999)

We are well aware that this paper offers a limited–though, we believe, significant–corpus. Sex-related language cannot be measured along the same quantitative lines as other, more neutral linguistic items.

Our corpus confirms that the most widespread usage of *fuck* is that of emphatic intensifier, with a somewhat smaller 35.70% of all the examples collected. The most common pattern is attributive adjective *fucking* + noun, with a derogatory or insulting meaning [(1) "He's having a fucking affair" (BJ 109); (2) "fucking Jerome, fucking, fucking Jerome" (BJER 135)]. Some of the examples, especially in *BJER*, resort to a playful repetition of the attribute adjective *fucking*, which is a basic characteristic of colloquial language [(3) "... he still hasn't fucking, fucking, fucking well rung" (BJER 72); (4) "Fucking fucking mini-cab ..." (BJER 165)]. Examples (1) to (4) evince one of the main traits of sex-related expletives: a combination of euphonic pleasure and ritual transgression. For some social groups, using blasphemies, insults or sex-related terms are, possibly, ancestral urges. The target of these terms is not so much individual persons, but rather objects, facts or even unmentioned circumstances, which shows that sex-related emphatic intensifiers are basically about one's emotions and not about external objects or subjects. Phrases like "where the fuck" or "what the fuck" are routinely repeated, thus intensifying emotions like anger, annoyance or despair [(5) "... where the fuck...?" (BJ 215); (6) "Where the fuck is mini-cab?" (BJER 164), etc.].

Let us have a look at the translations we have used. How do they convey the emotional, euphonic or irrational overtones associated with *fuck* as an emphatic intensifier? Most of the examples in our corpus are usually translated, in Spanish and Catalan, as sex-related terms though with non-sexual meanings. The Spanish translation resorts somewhat mechanically to the attribute adjective *jodido/a*, which is defined by Seco *et al* (1999) as a contemptuous or derogatory term referring to people or things [(1a) "está teniendo una jodida aventura" (BJ 116); (2a) "jodido Jerome, jodido, jodido Jerome" (BJER 147); (3a) "Joder, joder, joder, no puedo creer que todavía no haya llamado" (BJER 82); (4a) "Jodido, jodido taxi ..." (BJER 177)]. Sanmartín (2001) maintains that a verb like *joder* is used dysphemistically as an interjection indicating the speaker's annoyance or surprise, and that it emphasizes the interlocutors' argumentative disagreement.

The Catalan translation avoids a mechanical rendering of the term, and explores more natural options [(1b) "Té una aventura, cony!" (BJ 124); (2b) "Jerome, ets un cabró, un cabró, Jerome" (BJER 155); (3b) "No puc creure que encara no m'hagi fet ni una puta, puta, puta trucada" (BJER 87); (4b) "Cony de minitaxi dels collons ..." (BJER 187)]. While the Spanish translations sound to us like a ready-made translation cliché, the ones in Catalan are much more natural and risky, and they present us with three of the key taboo terms in the language, the main building blocks of colloquial or vulgar texts, and which demand a great deal of tact when used in any context. The three words (*cony*, *puta* and *collons*) are strictly banned in many contexts, and are likely to add a high level of linguistic violence or social transgression. Besides, these are words which are profoundly sexist, especially offensive with regard to women and female sexuality. Words like *cony* [Eng. "cunt"] or *puta* [Eng. "whore"] give rise to an open series of phrases which emphasize negative traits associated with women and femininity, such as boredom, inadequacy, shamelessness, and others. The term *collons* [Eng. "testicles"], however, is projected metonymically into a series of expressions emphasizing the strength and bravery which are traditionally associated with masculinity.

In the set phrases "where the fuck ...?" or "what the fuck ...?", the translations in our corpus offer nearly identical options [(5a) "¿dónde coño ...?" (BJ 225); (5b) "¿on collons?" (BJ 239); (6a) "¿Dónde coño está el taxi?" (BJER 176); (6b) "¿On cony és el minitaxi?" (BJER 186)]. A significant feature is the systematic (over)exploitation of feminine genitals (Sp. *coño* and Cat. *cony*), the only exception being (5b), where the idiomatic phrase "¿on *collons*?" is preferred.

It is also remarkable, in our corpus and particularly in *BJER*, the abundant repetition of *fuck* as a general interjection [(7) "Oh fuck, oh fuck." (BJ 196); (8) "Oh my fuck, wind it up, wind it up!" (BJER 16); (9) "Oh fuck, oh fuck." (BJER 81)]. Surely this excessive repetition–if excessive means anything in language use– of an interjection deprives it of some of its values. The Spanish translations are again seized with the same drowsiness of the original, and the Spanish translator yields to the easiest temptation: the use of the verb *joder*, a vulgar term widely used in colloquial conversations to express, basically, protest and surprise (Seco *et al* 1999: 2735). The Catalan translator, again, explores other options [(7a) "Oh joder, oh joder." (BJ 205); (7b) "Ai, cony." (BJ 220); (8a) "¡Oh joder, cortad, cortad!" (BJER 27); (8b) "Ai collons, mateu-ho, mateu-ho!" (BJER 26); (9a) "Oh joder, oh joder." (BJER 91); (9b) "Merda, merda, merda." (BJER 96)].

Besides the use of *cony* and *collons*, there is a preference –typically Mediterranean– for the term *merda* [Eng. "shit"], which has a long tradition in the popular culture of Catalan-speaking countries. Speakers of Catalan themselves–maybe due to the fact that they belong to a minority culture, or maybe as a prejudice–consider that "[w]e Valencians are much more foul-mouthed [than Spanish-speaking people]", and find a certain pride in coprology and scatology (see Santaemilia, in press).

The metalinguistic usage is present in ten examples (17.80% of the corpus) found in Helen Fielding's novels, particularly in *Bridget Jones* (1996), a novel which inaugurated a clearly recognisable literary genre *for women*, and where we collected nine examples. In the first chapters of *BJ* there is a conscious effort to coin a trendy, attractive and unprejudiced term to identify an independent, cosmopolitan female attitude to life. This linguistic experiment revolves around the words *fuckwit*[2] and *fuckwittage*. It's a newly-coined term which poses a direct problem to translators, as it strives to reflect the complexity of a type of literature which tries to be fresh and ingenious, free of gender bias, and offering a site for women's self-affirmation.

The options adopted by both translators are disparate though consistent throughout the texts: while *fuckwittage* is translated as "sexo sin compromiso" [Eng. "non-committed sex"] in Spanish, in Catalan we are

---

[2] *Fuckwit* appears in the *O.E.D.* as "[a] stupid or contemptible person; an idiot".

left with the incomprehensible "subnormalitat" [Eng. "mental handicap"]. We cannot but wonder at the Catalan translation, as it makes no sense and, especially, distorts Helen Fielding's metalinguistic effort. By contrast, the Spanish translation is a coherently descriptive rendering, though somewhat feeble, as it avoids altogether a marked term like *fuck*.

As an extension of the metalinguistic effort in *BJ* and *BJER*, we found several examples in which *fuckwit* is employed as a personal insult, along with one example with *fuck-up* [(10) "Tell him to bugger off from me. Emotional fuckwit." (BJ 68); (11) " ... exactly the same but feeling even more of a fuck up than last time." (BJER 72)].

As to the translation of *fuckwit*, a peculiar phenomenon can be observed. In the passages belonging to *BJ*, the Spanish rendering is consistent with that of *fuckwittage* [(10a) "Mándalo a la mierda. Es un practicante de sexo sin compromiso emocional." (BJ 74)], while in the passages from *BJER*, the translator seems to have forgotten the options adopted in the first book, and there is a surprising twist to a term completely unrelated to the metalinguistic effort present in previous examples [(11a) " ... sintiéndote incluso más jodida que la última vez." (BJER 82)]. The metalinguistic dimension, which practically occupied the whole of *BJ*, now seems to be simply abandoned in the Spanish version. The Catalan rendering, though incomprehensible to us, remains the same [(10b) "Digue-li que el donin pel cul de part meva. És un subnormal emocional." (BJ 80); (11b) "... amb la sensació de ser encara molt més fracassada que abans" (BJER 87)].

Both McEnery & Xiao's (2004) destinational (4.60% of examples) and idiomatic "set phrase" (6.20%) usages have an idiomatic character [(12) "Listen, Bridge, I'm really sorry, I've fucked up" (BJ 75); (13) "Oh fuck off, Jeremy" (BJER 211)]. The translations, again, are symptomatic of the two cultures, Spanish and Catalan [(12a) "Escucha, Bridge, de verdad que lo siento, la he jodido" (BJ 82); (12b) "Escolta, Bridge, em sap molt de greu, l'he cagada." (BJ 89); (12a) "Oh Jeremy, que te jodan" (BJER 223); (13b) "Ai, vés-te'n a la merda, Jeremy" (BJER 235)]. The Spanish translator resorts, more or less mechanically, to phrases with *joder*, whereas the Catalan translator prefers expressions with *merda*, which again reinforces the daily presence of scatology in the Catalan culture.

We have found no instance of *fuck* as a cursing expletive, "pronominal" form or with a literal meaning. This last usage deserves a comment–there is no single example, in *BJ* or *BJER*, of the verb *fuck* with a literal meaning ("to copulate", *O.E.D.*); the verbs *shag* and *sleep* are used instead. Curiously, in spite of the fact that *BJ* and *BJER* revolve incessantly around love, new sexual relations and a new role for women, there are very few examples where actual sexual relations are explicitly mentioned. All is indirection, figurative meanings, idiomatic expressions. All in all, however, and this is the paradox, Helen Fielding's novels smell of a hyper-sexualized narrative.

3. By way of conclusion(s)

What are the dangers of self-censorship (s)? Firstly, the main danger lies probably in its own invisibility. Self-censorship is usually a muted phenomenon, highly individual, highly unpredictable, sometimes with no overt logic. In the case of SL, (unconfessed) feelings of uneasiness, embarrassment or disgust may be apt explanations.

The Spanish translations of *BJ* and *BJER* deal with the lexeme *fuck* in a somewhat mechanical way, as if translating sexually-loaded terms were a mere routine. When sex is reduced to a lexical or even grammatical category, with stable translations which ignore the specific pragmatic contexts, its expressive potential and level of transgression diminishes importantly. The translations into Catalan reproduce more fully the emotive and idiomatic overtones which sex-related language has in Helen Fielding's novels. Fielding does not use sex (in this case, the word *fuck*) in its literal sense–there is no single reference to *fuck* meaning "to copulate"– but rather as a semantic field from which the author derives important narrative and emotional advantages: we are left with a fresh and informal story, far removed from a tedious prudish tale, where woman is in command of the marginalised languages which had hitherto been a preserve of male characters. But both translations into Spanish and into Catalan trivialize a highly sensitive resource such as sex-related language. Excessive repetition and a mechanical rendering of equivalents may help de-semantize and de-sensitize the use of sex-related language in literature.

However minor self-censorships are, and however unnoticed they may go, it is worth investigating the manipulatory mechanisms projected onto source texts in order to alter their meaning or their contents, pervert their identity or divert their ideological messages. Self-censorship does not usually threaten the existence of the whole source text, but constitutes a subtler and less aggressive threat: the temptation of a rewriting based on moral, religious or purely personal reasons. Through translation, sex-related references may be downgraded, sweetened or turned into a mechanical device (see Toledano 2003, Santaemilia 2005); religious satire ignored; or blasphemies merely eliminated. Sexual innuendo, in particular, becomes diffused, shaded, tamed or–in a word–more palatable for the editorial machinery.

Sexual language is a privileged area to study the cultures we translate into–it is a site where each culture places its moral or ethical limits, where we encounter its taboos and its ideological dilemmas. Historically, sex-related language has been a highly sensitive area; if today, in Western countries at least, we cannot defend any form of public censorship, what we cannot prevent (nor probably should we) is a certain degree of self-censorship, along the lines of an individual ethics and attitude towards religion, sex(uality), notions of (im)politeness or (in)decency, etc. Translating is always a struggle to reach a compromise between one's ethics and society's multiple constraints–and nowhere can we see this more clearly than in the rewriting(s) of sex-related language.

References

Primary sources

Fielding, Helen (1996) *Bridget Jones's Diary*, London: Corgi Books.
—. (1999) *El diario de Bridget Jones* (translated by Néstor Busquets), Barcelona: Plaza & Janés.
—. (1998) *El diari de Bridget Jones* (translated by Ernest Riera), Barcelona: Edicions 62.
—. (1999) *Bridget Jones: The Edge of Reason*, London: Picador.
—. (2005) *Bridget Jones: Sobreviviré* (translated by Néstor Busquets), Barcelona: De Bolsillo.
—. (2001) *Bridget Jones perd el seny* (translated by Ernest Riera), Barcelona: Edicions 62.

Secondary sources

Adam, Julie (1998) "The *four-letter word*, ou comment traduire les mots *fuck* et *fucking* dans un texte littéraire?", in *Meta* 43(2): 1-6.
Allan, Keith & Kate Burridge (2006) *Forbidden Words: Taboo and the Censoring of Language*, Cambridge: C.U.P.
Bou, Patricia & Barry Pennock (1992) "Método evaluativo de una traducción: aplicación a *Wilt* de Tom Sharpe", in *Revista Española de Lingüística Aplicada* 8: 177-185.
León, Víctor (1984) *Diccionario de argot español y lenguaje popular* (4th ed.), Madrid: Alianza Editorial.
McEnery, Tom & Zhonghua Xiao (2004) "Swearing in modern British English: the case of *fuck* in the BNC", in *Language and Literature* 13(3): 235-268.

Merino, Raquel & Rosa Rabadán (2002) "Censored Translations in Franco's Spain: The TRACE Project–Theatre and Fiction (English-Spanish)". *TTR (Traduction, Terminologie, Rédaction)* 15(2): 125-152.

O.E.D. *(Oxford English Dictionary)*–accessible online at *http://www.oed.com*

Rabadán, Rosa (ed.) (2000) *Traducción y censura inglés-español: 1939-1985. Estudio preliminar*, León: Universidad de León.

Sanmartín, Julia (2001) "El cuerpo, la sexualidad y sus imágenes: una aproximación lingüística", in J.V. Aliaga *et al* (eds.) *Miradas sobre la sexualidad en el arte y la literatura del siglo XX en Francia y España*, Valencia: Universitat de València. 253-270.

Santaemilia, José (2005) "The Translation of Sex, The Sex of Translation: *Fanny Hill* in Spanish", in José Santaemilia (ed.) *Gender, Sex and Translation: The Manipulation of Identities*. Manchester: St. Jerome, 117-136.

—. (in press) "Gender, Sex and Language in Valencia: Attitudes toward sex-related language among Spanish and Catalan speakers", to appear in the *International Journal of the Sociology of Language*.

Seco, Manuel *et al* (1999) *Diccionario del español actual*, Madrid: Aguilar. 2 vols.

Toledano, Carmen (2003) *La traducción de la obscenidad*, Santa Cruz de Tenerife: La Página Ediciones.

Vega, Miguel Ángel (2004) "De la Guerra Civil al pasado inmediato", in Francisco Lafarga & Luis Pegenaute (eds.) *Historia de la traducción en España*. Salamanca: Editorial Ambos Mundos, 527-578.

CENSORSHIP AND THE SELF-TRANSLATOR

HELENA TANQUEIRO
& PATRÍCIA LÓPEZ LÓPEZ-GAY,
RESEARCH TEAM AUTOTRAD
AUTONOMOUS UNIVERSITY OF BARCELONA, SPAIN

Abstract: This article describes the limitation or censure that the self-translator imposes on him/herself when translating from one culture into another. Two texts are presented for the purpose of this analysis: Jorge Semprún's translation of *Federico Sanchez vous salue bien* (1993), his original text in French, into the Spanish, *Federico Sánchez se despide de ustedes* (1993), and Carlo Coccioli´s, *Piccolo Karma* (1987), originally published in Italian and then translated into Spanish under the title of *Pequeño Karma* (2001). It may be inferred that some changes that we understand as self-censorship made in these autobiographical texts are the result, on the one hand, of the bicultural condition of the author and, on the other, the need to find a filter or other forms of "self-discipline" so that, as Semprún points out, the rewriting of text does not become an exercise in the creation of a completely new text.

Before focusing specifically on the subject of our paper we would like to begin with a brief reference to the research that we are carrying out, both individually and as members of the research group AUTOTRAD, within the field of self-translation. Self-translation is a field which has so far attracted little attention, but it is one which we believe can provide a new perspective in research into translation. It is particularly relevant to the field of Translation Studies–specially Theory of Literary Translation–as well as related fields such as Comparative Literature, Social Criticism and Sociology of Literature.

Although our research is still in its infancy–we are currently analysing a number of case studies–we have already obtained significant data with respect to several topics of interest, including self-translation and ideology. We have not yet systematised and developed our research to the extent that we would have wished, however our findings on self-censorship in self-translation between close languages are of sufficient importance as to take the opportunity of making our work known. Beginning with the theoretical underpinning of our work we will present practical examples of our findings.

Our analysis of different case studies has led us to conclude that an author-translator is a privileged translator (Tanqueiro 1999), and that self-translations, as privileged translations, are a useful resource to reflect upon professional translation, since data from one of its fields (self-translation) can be extrapolated and applied to the overall framework within which that field is located (literary translation).

Bensoussan (1999) states that if a translation is to be effective, "true empathy (...) or identification of the translator with the author" must exist–something that obviously occurs when the author is the translator of his own work. Similarly, Jolicoeur (1995) claims that a literary work is a reflection of its author and that this must leave its mark on "the effect" of the translation. He goes on to explain that many of the errors made by literary translators are the result of not knowing the author (the social-cultural, historical context of the writer). This type of error does not occur when the author is the translator of his/her own text. Christiane Nord (1997) believes that a translation is the product of a translator's interpretation of the author's intention. Analysing how different author-translators interpret their own intention is, we believe, of interest to researchers, and, as we shall see, the comparative study of original texts and self-translations provides the means to obtaining some most interesting results.

The relevance of self-translation is also supported by the Polysystem Theory and, in particular, the contributions of Gideon Toury (1982) and José Lambert (1997) to descriptive translation studies in the field of Literary Translation. On the one hand, Rainer Grutman (2000) claims that self-translation is the ideal field of research for determining the norms of a system, since author-translators are positioned between two systems, both of which they are familiar with, and can adapt their work to two different literary traditions. To determine the norms of a system, a study is required of a sufficiently large corpus of literary self-translations which our group does not yet have access to. We do, however, believe that this is a promising field of research which we may well investigate in the future.

On the other hand, our study of self-translation has shown that, because of the authority invested in the author of an original text, the author-translator's text is accepted into the target literary system as an original text, thus calling into question the norm of an original text prevailing over its translation. As long as there is evidence that authors, whose texts translators consider to be sacrosanct, translate perfectly freely and creatively (within the restrictions that define self-translations as translations), criticism of the *translator-traitor* would seem to be unfounded. It should be noted that whilst many self-translations show no indications whatever of being translations (which explains why some works are published in two literary systems as originals), in some cases authors modify later editions of the original text, after having translated the first. By analysing the product of self-translation, we can obtain a wealth of data concerning procedures and strategies used in self-translation as well as, in many cases, being able to infer the translation process. Self-translation guarantees, within literary translation, an unquestionable literariness of the texts produced, and the study of self-translations can bring to light different procedures and strategies that are applied when undertaking a creative translation.

Focussing specifically on the question of self-censorship within the field of self-translation, we have, for the purposes of our study, adopted the widest-ranging definition of the term, that is, limitation or censure that one imposes on oneself when the self-translator is translating from one culture into another.

Jorge Semprún's translation of *Federico Sanchez vous salue bien,* his original text[1] in French, into the Spanish, *Federico Sánchez se despide de ustedes,* is an interesting example of self-censorship.[2] It is a text that varies between essay and novel, memoirs and fiction. As the narrator explains in his work *L'écriture ou la vie* [*Literature or Life*], it is a work of fiction

---

[1] As members of the research team on self-translation AUTOTRAD, we understand by "original" the text which is produced before the translation and, by which is established the narrative framework to be shared with the latter. The narrative framework is in general terms fully respected by the second text. Therefore, the self-translation comes from the original and, even though it can be considered as privileged or *sui generis* translation for being (re)created by the author himself, it is undoubtedly a translation of the original into a second language. Given that author and translator are here the same person, changes in order to adjust the text to the new reader will be freely introduced in the second text. Some of these modifications, we believe, clearly respond to self-censorship on the part of the self-translator.

[2] The editions consulted are the following:
Semprún, J. (1993a) *Federico Sanchez vous salue bien*, Paris: Grasset et Faisquemos.
Semprún, J. (1993b) *Federico Sánchez se despide de ustedes*, Barcelona: Tusquets. The texts quoted in French and Spanish are those in which the additions, substitutions or omissions referred to occur. The page number of the edition from which each example has been taken is given in brackets, at the bottom of the text. Segments that have been modified are printed in italics.

"qui aiderait la réalité à paraître réelle, la vérité à être vraisemblable. Cet obstacle-là je parviendrai à le surmonter, un jour ou l'autre" [that helps make reality more real, that helps make the truth more possible] (Semprún 1994 : 218). The study of this text carried out by Patricia López is particularly interesting because of the ambiguity of the genres highlighted in the Spanish self-translation (López L.-Gay: 2006). The text presents the experiences of the author-narrator during the time he served as Spain's Minister for Culture, 1988-1991. The title of his book refers to the historical figure of Federico Sanchez, the identity that Jorge Semprún (born 1923) assumed as an active member of the clandestine Spanish Communist Party during the dictatorship of General Francisco Franco. The book is finally entitled *Autobiografía de Federico Sánchez* [*The autobiography of Federico Sanchez and the Communist underground in Spain*], the first volume in which the narrator "puts history to rights" as he recounts his experience as an activist in Spanish politics. It would have been logical for the Spanish Jorge Semprún to write the original text about the time he spent in Spain in his mother tongue. Instead, he wrote his original text in French and then translated it into Spanish. If we compare both texts, Semprún's decision to do this would appear to be based on self-censorship: the author stops himself from falling into the trap of political scandal-mongering. The use of the French language, therefore, serves as a filter prior to writing in Spanish. Semprún's justification for writing his original text in French is most strongly defended in his self-translation:

> Car je m'adresse à un lecteur hypothétique qui ignore les détails croustillants de cette histoire, (...) incapable qu'il sera, sauf rare exception, de saisir les singularités hispaniques. (...)
> Quoi qu'il en soit, ce n'est pas parce que je suis à la Moncloa,... (97)
>
> Me he dirigido a un lector hipotético que ignora los detalles sabrosos de esta historia, (...) incapaz, salvo rara excepción, de captar las singularidades hispánicas. (...)
>
> En francés, para decirlo pronto y bien, ¿qué anécdota, qué comentario, qué chisme podría contar de Rosa Conde? ¿O de "Txiki" Benegas? ¿O de José Félix Tezanos? Nadie sabe quiénes son, apenas existen por sí mismos para un lector francés. Y esa inexistencia, la falta de interés de estos personajes– elegidos casi al azar, en una especie de muestreo instantáneo que podría fácilmente ser más amplio: no faltan candidatos a este tipo de inexistencia-, al aconsejarme no hablar de ellos, por razones de comunicación y legibilidad, para un lector francés, me ayuda a no caer en un ajuste de cuentas político o personal.

(...)
Sea como sea, no será por estar en La Moncloa,... (90)

The option of self-translation allows the author-translator to go beyond the mere transcription of unseemly details about public figures in Spanish popular culture. Thus, the first reader of the text (French) conditions the writing of the original, and the second reader (Spanish) influences the translation, which, whilst based on the first text brings to light hidden aspects of the first version. The self-translated text comes from the original–it *is* translation. But, it also implies rewriting in a broader sense: it is a form of translation that we call *privileged* or *sui generis* translation. This rewritten text is nevertheless produced within a pre-established narrative framework and may be conditioned by restrictions imposed by either the editorial or the author himself. Also, the self-translation is highly determined, we believe, by the period of time elapsed between the production of the original and the translation.[3] The shorter the difference in time between the two texts is, the less emotional distance with the text the author will sense. With time, argues Jorge Semprún, there is the risk that the tentative of translating one's text becomes an exercise of rewriting an entirely new text.[4]

The author-narrator-translator avoids indulging in sensationalism, which would cause his text to deviate from the strictly literary. Ultimately, what Federico Sanchez wants to do when he leaves is not to settle any outstanding political or personal issues but to set History to rights (Semprún 1993a, 1993b). On the inside cover of the Spanish version of his text we read:

> Because this is about my thoughts and memories, *it should come as no surprise that there is no scandal-mongering*, although of course the text is full of people and anecdotes that form part of *our* collective memory" (Semprún 1993b).[5]

The pact that he has made with his Spanish reader is based, on the one hand, on the promise of a literary work as opposed to a political treatise, and on the other, on the appeal to the collective memory that both author

---

[3] This hypothesis is true for all the case studies explored by the research team AUTOTRAD up to date.

[4] This hypothesis is true for all the case studies explored by the research team AUTOTRAD up to date.

[5] "Siendo esta una obra de reflexión, *no debe extrañar que huya del simple chisme*, aunque, por supuesto, en todo momento cruzarán el texto personajes y anécdotas que ya forman parte de *nuestra* vida colectiva". Italics are ours.Highlighted by us.

and reader share. This is achieved thanks to self-censorship (used here in the most positive sense) that is the result of writing first in French and then in Spanish.

Sometimes Semprún's determination to avoid scandal leads to the suppression of information in the Spanish translation. A clear example is:

> Sa "compagne sentimentale" [...] était une jolie jeune dame de la bonne société, très lancée dans la vie artistique de la capitale, *dont il avait une fille prénommée Alma (à cause de Mahler, bien entendu; Guerra ne nous aura épargné aucun des tics et trucs toc du snobisme kitsch!)*. (316)
> Su compañera sentimental era una elegante muchacha de buena familia, muy introducida en la vida artística de la capital. (296)

The original text in French does not just stop at describing the beauty of Spanish politician Alfonso Guerra's lover–it goes on to tell us that he has a daughter called "Alma", a name that Semprún describes as "snob" and "kitsch".

This, we believe, is an unambiguous example of self-censorship in translation. The author-translator, as he himself says, does not want to give the Spanish reader this kind of information so as not to fall into the trap of tittle-tattle. Has he, we may ask ourselves, suppressed this information in the Spanish text because it might seem to be a personal attack on Guerra if it was included? Or is it because the author-translator thinks the Spanish general public is sufficiently well-informed of the name of Alfonso Guerra's daughter? In this case, censorship is cultural, and not political. Whatever the reason, the information is a comment on the private life of a political figure, a reference to his "illegitimate" family, which, when he was a government minister, regularly figured in the headlines of the gossip columns of the time. This information has been deleted from the Spanish version of the original text as a result, we believe, of the author-translator's determination to maintain the pact he has made with his Spanish readers not to produce a sensationalist text.

There are other well-known cases of self-translation resulting from some form of exile–either voluntary or imposed. Of these, our group is studying self-translations of Nabokov (Novosilzov 1997), Agustín Gómez Arcos (López L-Gay 2005) and Carlo Coccioli (Mercuri 2006).

The following are some examples found in the work of Carlo Coccioli, an Italian writer living in Mexico. We have selected some examples from the Spanish self-translation of his book *Piccolo Karma*, originally published in Italian in 1987 fourteen years before the Spanish version.[6]

---

[6] The editions consulted are the following:

Piccolo Karma is an autobiography, a diary, in which the author/narrator expresses opinions that are markedly controversial and ideological. We believe that this self-translation is clearly determined by the new target reader, a reader who speaks a close language to the original one but who belongs to a remote culture. Also, the translation is here highly influenced, we think, by the fact that there is a long period of time between the publication of the original and the translation.[7] From Valentina Mercuri's analysis of the text (Mercuri 2006) we may conclude that literary genre can also play a role in determining the self-censorship imposed by an author–something that is more easily noticed when the author is his own translator and when the text is autobiographical.

The following are some examples extracted from the Italian original *Piccolo Karma* and the Spanish self-translation:

> Mi domando spesso che cosa sarebbe del Messico, in particolare di questa formicolante e proliferante mano di opera illegittima, se ci fosse al nord non dico l'Unione Sovietica ma un qualsiasi paese europeo, o magari lo stesso Messico, gelosissimo delle sue frontiere, come lo dimostra il trattamento che viene dato agli indocumentados guatemaltechi che a loro volta penetrano in Chiapas. (159)

> ¿Qué sucedería si México tuviese al norte, en vez de los antipáticos gringos, alguna concebible Unión Soviética, o hasta una Suiza con sus legalismos? (159)

We believe that this example is one of cultural and ideological adaptation imposed by the author-translator. As we can see, the commentary made about Mexico and its frontiers are "censored" in the Spanish text. In the Italian version, the author states his opinion clearly and explains his position without fear of provoking adverse reactions. However, in his translation for the Spanish-speaking public, which includes Latin American readers, and in his role as mediator between cultures, the self-translator has decided to correct himself so as not to

---

Coccioli, C. (1987) *Piccolo Karma*, Milano: Mandadori.
Coccioli, C. (2001) *Pequeño Karma*, México: Lectorum.
The page number of the edition from which each example has been taken is given in brackets, at the bottom of the text. Segments that have been modified are printed in italics.

[7] As we mentioned above, the shorter the difference in time between the two texts, the less emotional distance with the text the author will sense and the fewer significant changes he will introduce in the translation.

alienate his hypothetical readers, assuming as his their opinions of their neighbours in the North.

> Un libro scritto abbastanza male come l'ottanta per cento dello spagnolo usato dai dilettanti. (p. 12)

> Libro escrito bastante mal como, digamos, el sesenta por ciento de lo que se publica actualmente en español: [...] (p. 16)

When translating *Piccolo Karma* from Italian, Coccioli corrects his personal comment on the alleged percentage of bad literary works produced in the Spanish language. The author might have changed his mind in the period of time elapsed between the production of the original and the translation or, more likely, he might have sought to somehow moderate the tone of his criticism *vis a vis* the Hispanic reader.

> Ho intravisto l'uomo, giovane e barbuto *(i "latini" vanno spesso barbuti per dissimulare il colore della pelle o per passare da guerriglieri)...* (p. 10)

> Acabo de entrever al señor, un joven barbudo; *aquí los latinos tienen tendencia a cultivar barbas. ¿Será para simular intelectualismo o expresar adhesión a algún género de guerrilleros?* (p. 14)

This very last example seems to illustrate another obvious case of self-censorship. A literal translation from the Italian would certainly be misleading for the Mexican reader, a reader who would be–according to the author–proud of his "bronze race". From Mercuri's point of view (*Ibidem*), this commonly accepted stereotype of the typical Latin bearded man is widely accepted in Italy.

The list of examples to illustrate self-censorship in self-translation is too long for the purposes of the present article. We hope nonetheless that these pages have shown to what extent this *sui generis* form of translation, self-translation (López López-Gay 2005), is a useful, rich resource to reflect upon censorship and translation. Since self-translation is an extreme example of the author-text/translator-text relationship (Tanqueiro 2000) in which isolated external elements of subjectivity can be isolated– understood here as all those elements that identify the translator as someone other than the author–we have tried to show that the analysis of self-translations, that is, the comparative study of an original text in one language and his translation by the author-translator himself in another language, can also provide us with data of interest in the field.

As far as ideology and censorship is concerned, since censorship is generally associated with some form of power structure, the analysis of translations in general may tend to reduce all translator's decisions to political, systemic or ideological decisions without taking into account the decisions made as a result of the need to communicate with different target readers and their respective cultures and characteristics. As we mentioned before, perhaps the "power" relationship of the original text in relation to the translation may account for this.

We thus believe that self-translation allows us to observe explicit systemic or ideological self-censorship, and to detect other conditioning factors that lead to obvious changes or adaptations of the original text in translation.

From the examples presented here it may be inferred that some changes made in texts that we understand as self-censorship are the result of, on the one hand, the bicultural condition of the author and, on the other, the need to find a filter or other forms of "self discipline" so that, as Jorge Semprún points out, the rewriting of text does not become, in retrospect, an exercise in the creation of a completely new text.

References

Primary sources

Coccioli, C. (1987) *Piccolo Karma*, Milano: Mondadori.
—. (2001) *Pequeño Karma*, México: Lectorum.
Semprún, J. (1993a) *Federico Sanchez vous salue bien*, Paris: Grasset et Faisquemos.
—. (1993b) *Federico Sánchez se despide de ustedes*. Barcelona: Tusquets.
—. (1994) *L'écriture ou la vie*, Paris : Gallimard.

Secondary sources

Bensoussan, A. (1999) *Confesiones de un traidor*, Granada: Comares.
Grutman, R. (2000) "Auto-translation", in Mona Baker (ed.) *Routledge Encyclopedia of Translation Studies,* UK, TJ International Ltd., Padstow, Cornwall, 17-20.
Jolicoeur, L. (1995) *La sirène et le pendule*, Québec: L'instant même.
Lambert, J. (1997) "Itamar Even-Zohar's Polysystem Studies: An Interdisciplinary Perspective on Culture Research", in *Canadian Review of Comparative Literature/Revue Canadienne de Littérature Comparée*, XXIV, 7-14.

López López-Gay, P. (2005) *(Auto)traducción y (re)creación*. Un pájaro quemado vivo, *de Agustín Gómez Arcos*. Col. Estudios nº 4, serie Estudios, Almería: Instituto de Estudios Almerienses.

—. (2006) *Sobre el visible engranaje de la (auto)traducción*. Federico Sánchez se despide de ustedes *y* Federico Sanchez vous salue bien, *de Jorge Semprún*, Departamentos de Traducción e Interpretación de la Universidad Autónoma de Barcelona, y de Estudios Literarios de la Universidad de Paris 7 Denis Diderot (research funded by the Catalan regional government *Generalitat de Catalunya*). (Pending publication).

Mercuri, V. (2006) *Análisis de la autotraducción de Piccolo Karma/Pequeño Karma de Carlo Cocciolí*, Bellaterra, Departamento de Traducción e Interpretación da Universitat Autònoma de Barcelona (research work).

Nord, C. (1997) *Translating as a Purposeful Activity*, Manchester: Saint Jerome Publishing.

Novosilzov, N. (1998) "De la traducción al original. Las autobiografías de Nabokov comparadas", in *Livius*, 11, 99-111.

Tanqueiro, H. (1999), "Un traductor privilegiado: el autotraductor" in *Quaderns. Revista de Traducció*, nº 3, 19-27.

—. (2000) "Self-translation as an extreme case of the author-work-translator-work dialectic", in A. Beeby, D. Ensinger, M. Presas (eds.) *Investigating Translation*, Amsterdam: John Benjamins Publishing Compagny, 55-64.

Toury, G. (1980), *In Search of Translation*, Tel Aviv: Porter Institute of Poetics and Semiotcs.

THE FRANCOIST CENSORSHIP CASTS A LONG SHADOW: TRANSLATIONS FROM THE PERIOD OF THE DICTATORSHIP ON SALE NOWADAYS

CRISTINA GÓMEZ CASTRO,
UNIVERSIDAD DE CANTABRIA, SPAIN

Abstract: The establishment of a dictatorship under the person of Francisco Franco in Spain brought about the exertion of a close control over all cultural products during those years (1939-1975). Even though the long-awaited freedom of expression came into effect with the Constitution in 1978, the action of the official censorship will endure as long as the bookshops continue to sell those works that had suffered from its effect. Thus, it is no surprise even today to find on the book market translations of English original texts that are sold with the same version written under the dictatorship; these translations were, therefore, subjected to the censoring criteria operative at that time and may be incomplete or present some traces of self-censorship. Although some researchers have denounced this irregularity, the fact is that it is usually cheaper to recycle an existing translation than to commission a new one. In this article I explore this phenomenon, giving some examples of works that can be framed within this practice and attempting to assess the scope and influence such a procedure may have on a book market in which profit-making is the top priority.

"Franco dies slowly"
—James Markham (1980)

1. Introduction

During the almost forty years spanned by Franco's dictatorship (1939-1975) Spain practised a policy of cultural protectionism involving the adaptation of all native and foreign information to the regime's cultural requirements. Contrary to what one might think, that system did not disappear with the death of the dictator:

the organization that made possible the existence of a censoring governmental filter does not simply disappear, but mutates and undergoes a process of political transition and of official decentralization of its functions. (Merino 2000:124)[1]

Thus, although the official censorship came to an end with the long-awaited freedom of expression that brought about the Constitution of 1978, its action would persist as long as the market and the bookshops continued to sell those works that had suffered from its effect (Vila-San Juan 2003:68).

2. A brief look at the censorship mechanism in Franco's Spain

Official state censorship was legitimised in Spain from 1938 onwards with the aim of "establishing the primacy of the truth and spreading the general doctrine of the Movement" (Abellán 1980:15).[2] Restrictive measures through official channels were implemented to prevent the circulation of ideas contrary to the nation's interest. The official organism responsible for censorship was what came to be known in 1951 as the Ministry of Information and Tourism. From that date the different Ministers performed their censorial tasks with greater or lesser severity depending on the situation of the country at the time.

One of the main achievements of the Ministry was the elaboration of a Press and Print Law in 1966. Censorship after it was based mainly on two systems of control: the archiving (depósito) of the printed work in the Ministry of Information and Tourism and the prior consultation (really a euphemism for censorship), providing a positive or negative report about the book or work under review. This new way of functioning placed more responsibility on the publishers, who started to exert a kind of preventive censorship that would gradually become more and more widespread.

But if there is a characteristic common to the entire period regarding the control of books, arbitrariness seems to be the perfect candidate: there were no specific criteria to which the writers and translators could cling.

Despite the lack of criteria, it is still possible to establish certain thematic fields that, with the passing of time, seemed to prevail in the

---

[1] "la organización que hizo posible la existencia de un filtro censor gubernamental no desaparece sin más, sino que muta y sufre un proceso de transición política y de descentralización burocrática de sus funciones". Unless otherwise stated, all the translations into English are mine.
[2] "establecer la primacía de la verdad y difundir la doctrina general del Movimiento".

preferences of the censors. They are the following (cited in Abellán 1980: 88):

1. Sexual morals: specially banned was any kind of reference to abortion, homosexuality, divorce and extramarital relationships;[3]
2. Political beliefs: any kind of opposition to the regime was not tolerated;[4]
3. Use of language considered as indecorous, provocative and incongruous with the good manners governing the behaviour of decent people;[5]
4. Religion: attacks on it as an institution and a hierarchy.[6]

When Franco died in 1975, one might think that the censorship would have changed radically, but "this would be a wrong deduction. It is true that change started to be felt, not with a break, however, but by means of an unhurried evolution of the situation" (Amell 1989:313).[7]

3. The translated narrative and censorship

Both national and international literatures were considered as having the same status with regard to the censorship office (Olivares 2006: 112) and importation of English narrative works was subject to fluctuations that depended on the period. During the forties and fifties, the country seemed to live culturally on translations. At the time, intellectuals claimed that there were "too many translations", which contributed nothing to the restoring of the battered native culture. This phenomenon was largely due on the one hand to the lack of paper and of money to invest in books and on the other to the relative ease with which foreign books could be bought without having to pay authors' rights in the post-war economic crisis. The kind of narrative imported during those years corresponded to the Victorian English novel of authors such as the Brontë sisters, Thackeray or Thomas Hardy, i.e., novels that provided the reader with the required escape from the great hardship they were experiencing.

---

[3] "Moral sexual: especialmente prohibidas se hallaban cualquier referencia al aborto, la homosexualidad, el divorcio y las relaciones extramatrimoniales"
[4] "Opiniones políticas: toda oposición al regimen dominante no era admitida"
[5] "Uso del lenguaje considerado indecoroso, provocativo e impropio de los buenos modales por los que se ha de regir la conducta de las personas que se autodefinen como decentes"
[6] "La religion como institución y jerarquía"
[7] "esto sería una deducción equivocada. Cierto es que el cambio se va produciendo, pero no con una ruptura, sino mediante una evolución muy pausada de la situación"

In the sixties, the new 1966 Press Law brought hope of liberalization but the Administration then started to make use of a strategy which was for them the most productive and exonerating, that of the *Silencio Administrativo*: it consisted in giving this verdict when the board did not agree with all or parts of a given book. They did not agree with the publication of the text but they did not explicitly oppose it, the editor who dared to put it on the market being ultimately responsible for the printing. The book could later be confiscated by the authorities. Thus, while showing the public an image of liberalization, the Administration was being as repressive as ever.

The foreign narratives read during these years were mainly detective novels, the leading authors being Erle Stanley Gardner and Agatha Christie. The arrival of new forms of entertainment–especially TV–and the higher cultural level of the reading public would make people progressively focus on products of a higher level, albeit the inevitable Anglo-Saxon best sellers (VVAA 2000:50).

In the seventies, the Administration continued to work along the same lines, but now made a significant use of the book as a political weapon. Many books containing explicit political ideas contrary to the regime and banned before were now authorised, thus announcing a period of more political liberalization in the country. In the field of popular literature, the new ways of promoting books through TV advertising and original campaigns contributed to the success of many books that became authentic best sellers. The selection of material was thus mainly based on economic criteria: market expansion depended on the publication of best sellers, so either certain prevailing moral values had to be pushed aside in this pursuit of economic goals or some kind of self-censorship had to be applied.

4. The long-lasting effects of censorship: some examples of yesterday and today

The 1978 Spanish Constitution announced the end of official censorship. Writers could now start to write in a climate of freedom while publishers could worry less about the possible offensive nature of the material they wanted to put on the market and concentrate more on the market and the sales, i.e., the economic censorship that seems to rule the industry everywhere these days. This may explain why some of the translations that circulated during the years of the dictatorship have lasted for such a long time and can still be purchased in bookshops. The fact that publishers decide to exploit an already existing translation disregarding the point that this may have suffered from changes ordered by the censorship boards is understandable if one thinks in terms of financial gains: "it may often be cheaper to recycle an already existing translation than to commission a new translation" (Milton 2000: 177). However, if the top priority is the quality of the translation, this policy should be considered as a threat to it. During the first years of democracy the phenomenon appeared to be more "traceable" in the case of the cinema: films where scenes had been cut were being shown in cinemas without the addition of the censored material. That was the case of the Spanish version of *Splendor in the Grass* in 1982, which was ten minutes shorter than the American original.[8] In the case of narrative, the fraud was more difficult to spot, since readers were not usually aware that they were reading a translation. However, as late as 1991, one journalist dared to denounce this situation[9] taking advantage of the reprinting of one of the books of stories written by Ernest Hemingway, *The Fifth Column and First 49 Stories*, published in the 1966 version. This journalist, Josep Massot, echoed the complaints made by a translator, Mariano Antolín Rato, who had noticed that one of the stories, *The Capital of the World,* was shorter than the original due to the effects of censorship exercised in Franco's time: all the references to the Civil War had been conveniently eliminated. Apart from this work by Hemingway, in his article, Massot also wrote about the works by John Dos Passos and Carson McCullers, in an effort to draw attention to this untenable situation in which Francoist translation practices were still visible. The same year (1991) a book on the effects of censorship on Hemingway's works was published, based on the research done by Douglas Edward LaPrade. At the end of the book, the author stated that

> despite the wide diffusion all the works of Hemingway have experienced in Spain, both in bookshops and newsstands, the effects of Franco's censorship on them are still obvious. (1991: 66)[10]

Besides Massot and LaPrade, three other authors have mentioned this irregularity to date: the well-known researcher of censorship under Franco, Manuel Abellán, and the scholars Alberto Lázaro and Marcos Rodríguez Espinosa. The first one mentions it in an article written in 1995 where he acknowledges that the censorship is being maintained through re-editing of works with the same cuts and changes imposed under the dictatorship:

---

[8] For this and some other comments on cinema see Amell 1989:314-5.
[9] See the section on "references" for the work of the journalist Josep Massot.
[10] "(…) a pesar de la difusión de todas las obras de Hemingway, viejas y nuevas, en librerías y quioscos españoles, los efectos de la censura de Franco en las obras de Hemingway son todavía evidentes."

more than twenty years after the end of the regime it is still possible to read re-edits of literary works or essays in the version "advised" by those who could exert cuts and changes on the literary production of the nation. (1995: 4)[11]

Lázaro focuses on *Homage to Catalonia* by Orwell and denounces that

(...) it is a pity that today, in May 2000, Spanish publishers have not brought themselves to issue Orwell's unexpurgated views on the Spanish Civil War. Despite the great number of editions of this book that have come out in Spain over the last thirty years, both the Spanish and Catalan editions still maintain the distortions and mutilations established by the censorship during Franco's regime. (2001: 89).

And Rodríguez Espinosa (2004: 235) considers that it is high time we identified those bowdlerized translations that circulate in the book market today so that they can become part of our history.

Since then no further complaints have been registered (as far as I know).[12] Thus we might think that the publishing industry has reconsidered this practice and stopped reprinting translations from that period. This still has to be proved. Having undertaken a comparative-descriptive study of some of the translations of best-selling novels of that time as part of my doctoral dissertation, curiosity led me to have a look at the translations of those works on sale now in case they were still being printed. To my great surprise, I found that in most cases, the author of the translation was the same person, which seems to confirm that the editorial policy of the first years of democracy is still operative. It was possible, however, that the translations had been revised and completed, so I did a very quick search for those passages that had been erased or changed during the dictatorship to determine whether they had actually been revised.[13] Although this study is far from exhaustive, a quick comparison

---

[11] "(...) a más de veinte años vista del derrumbe de aquel régimen se continúan leyendo–en reedición–las obras literarias o de ensayo en versión "aconsejada" por quienes podían imponer cortes y modificaciones a toda la producción libresca peninsular."

[12] A web page entitled "Franco's long dead but in Spain censorship endures in another guise" has been found, but this site denounces the fact that state censorship has been replaced by commercial censorship, not mentioning the point under discussion here. (URL: http://www.sawf.org/newedit/edit11282005/worldwatch.asp).

[13] It goes without saying that this had to be done exclusively with those works where some kind of (self) censorship had been spotted, since a work that had been translated without any significant deviation for our purposes would not be

showed that the most significant changes imposed on these works had "survived" through the years and had reached the readers' hands in perfect state of conservation. In order to illustrate this point, I will give examples from two famous best-selling novels of the seventies which became so famous that they are still in print: *The Godfather* by Mario Puzo and *The Exorcist* by William Peter Blatty.

Starting with *The Godfather* we have to say that the censors of the board considered that the violence present in the narrative could be justified by the Mafia environment that dominated the narration and by the remoteness of the events, both in time and space. However, what they disliked most were the various erotic scenes that appeared throughout the novel and could distract the reader from his or her moral obligations as good Catholics. Thus, they suggested the publication of the work if some erasures were carried out. I reproduce here two of them so that they can serve as an example of what the censors considered as offensive in the work:[14]

ST[15]	CT	PT
"Where the hell were you?" Johnny Fontane asked. "Out fucking" she said. She had misjudged his drunkenness. (p.11)	-¿Dónde diablos estuviste?- preguntó Johnny Fontane. -Por ahí jodiendo- fue la respuesta. Evidentemente, Margot había juzgado erróneamente la borrachera de su marido.[16]	-¿Dónde diablos estuviste?- preguntó Johnny Fontane. -Por ahí...- fue la respuesta. Evidentemente, Margot había juzgado erróneamente la borrachera de su marido. (p.2 /p16)

In this passage, one of the characters of the novel, the singer Johnny Fontane, is drinking while he waits for the return of his wife, who is out

---

interesting here, even if the translation was the same done under the dictatorship. This fact reduced the scope and number of works considerably.

[14] The pagination given for these examples corresponds to the following editions of the book: Puzo, M. (1969) *The Godfather*, New York: G.P. Putnam's Sons; Puzo, M. (1970. *El Padrino*, Barcelona: Grijalbo (translated by A. Arnau) and Puzo, M. (2005) *El Padrino*, Barcelona: Ediciones B (translated by A. Arnau).

[15] The abbreviations stand for: ST= Source Text; CT= Censored Text; PT= Published Text.

[16] No pagination is given here since we are referring to the galley proof before publication. The same applies for the rest of the examples under the heading "CT".

until late at night. When she comes home, her answer to what she has been doing is one that seemed too "strong" for the morals of the time and, therefore, it is softened by the omission of the reference to the "f" word. The softening technique is apparent both in the 1970 text and in the 2005 text.

In the next passage, a short description of the character of one of the sons of the Don, Sonny, is offered:

ST	CT	PT
She did not care that he would never be the great man his father had proved to be. Sonny Corleone had strength, he had courage. He was generous and his heart was admitted to be as big as his organ. (p.15)	A Lucy no le importaba que Sonny no fuera, ni tuviera probabilidades de ser un gran hombre como su padre. Sonny Corleone era fuerte, tenía valor, se mostraba siempre generoso, y era del dominio público que tenía un corazón tan grande como su miembro.	A Lucy no le importaba que Sonny no fuera, ni tuviera probabilidades de ser un gran hombre como su padre. Sonny Corleone era fuerte, tenía valor, se mostraba siempre generoso, y era del dominio público que tenía un corazón muy grande, noble y a menudo tierno. (p.13/ p. 21)

It can be seen how the size of his heart is compared to that of his sex organ, and in a way that explicitly signals it as big. The description that the Spanish readers of the seventies and of today have access to is one in which the heart of Sonny Corleone is big, noble and sometimes even tender, but has nothing to do with his sex organ. Instead of commissioning a new translation, the publishing house has made use of the one that circulated in the country in the seventies, and no revision concerning the censored aspects has been made.[17]

With respect to *The Exorcist*[18] the most important offences observed by the censors of the dictatorship were those that had to do with the use of improper language and the attacks on the Catholic religion, which is not surprising given the plot of the novel. The two examples presented below

---

[17] A more detailed study concerning this aspect should be carried out to effectively confirm if all the changes and erasures have been kept.
[18] The pagination given for these examples corresponds to the following editions of the book: Peter Blatty, W. 1971. *The Exorcist.* New York: Harper & Row; Peter Blatty, W. 1972. *El Exorcista.* Barcelona: Plaza & Janés (translated by Raquel Albornoz) and Peter Blatty, W. 2005. *El Exorcista.* Barcelona: Ediciones B (translated by Raquel Albornoz).

serve to illustrate some of the changes carried out by the censoring pen and still maintained today:

ST	CT	PT
"No!" "You'll do it!" "*Please!*" "You *will*, you bitch, or I'll kill you!" "*Please!*" "Yes, you're going to let Jesus *fuck* you, *fuck* you, f-" (p.190)	-¡No! -¡Lo harás! -¡Por favor! -¡Lo harás, puerca, o te mato! -¡Por favor! -Sí, vas a dejar que te posea Cristo, que te posea de una vez.	-¡No! -¡Lo harás! -¡Por favor! -¡Lo harás, puerca, o te mataré! -¡Por favor! -Sí. Ø (p. 203/ p. 229)

This section corresponds to one of the most polemic scenes both in the novel and in the movie: Regan, the innocent child, masturbates herself with a crucifix. However, the Spanish readers do not really see this in the text, because the reference to the "possession of Christ" has been erased. Therefore, they can only guess what the demon is so frantically asking the child to do.

Finally, among the different examples with passages offensive to the Church or religion, the one cited below refers to the act of spreading the holy water by the priest onto the demon inside Regan. In this case, what was condemned by the censors was the use of improper language:

ST	CT	PT
"Ah, yes! The holy urine now!" rasped the demon. "The semen of the saints!" Merrin lifted up the vial and the face of the demon grew livid, contorted. "Ah, will you, bastard?" it seethed at him. "*Will you?*"(p. 283)	-¡Ah, sí! ¡Ahora viene la orina sagrada! - dijo el demonio con voz ronca -. ¡El semen de los santos! Merrin levantó el hisopo, y la cara del demonio se contrajo, lívida. -Ah, ¿lo harás, hijo de puta?- bulló -. ¿Lo harás?	-¡Ah, sí! ¡Ahora viene la orina sagrada!- exclamó el demonio con voz ronca. Ø Merrin levantó el hisopo y la cara del demonio se contrajo, lívida. -¡Ah! Pero, ¿vas a hacerlo?- rugió. ¿Vas a hacerlo? (p.134/ 360)

More examples like this could be given but I consider this sample representative enough of the phenomenon we are trying to illustrate here: the fact that translations that suffered the effects of the Francoist censorship are still on sale today and no one seems to notice it or complain about it.

5. Some final reflections: an interesting case for future/further study

The publishing industry in Spain after this country obtained freedom of expression is subject mainly to the constraints imposed by the market. This has some negative consequences for those who consider the book not as a mere object of trade but above all as an object of art: taking advantage of the fact that a translation of a successful novel has already been done, publishers seem to make use of that existing version in Spanish and continue to sell it without paying attention to the possible flaws that it may present. This was denounced in 1991 for the first time by the journalist Josep Massot and later by other authors and it has also been seen in passages from two best-selling novels, *The Godfather* and *The Exorcist*. This phenomenon should be analysed in more detail to determine whether there are actually more novels on the market in the same situation and whether this only happens with the so-called popular literature or whether high-brow works are also involved. If this is indeed the case, this practice should be denounced in the proper way because it does nothing to improve the status of the translating profession and at the same time it leaves readers in an unfavourable position, unaware that a great deal of manipulation has been exerted upon those translations before they reach their hands. The situation is crying out for some kind of action so that these texts may be consigned to history.

References

Primary sources

Blatty, William Peter (1971) *The Exorcist*, New York: Harper & Row.
—. (1972) *El Exorcista* (translated by Raquel Albornoz), Barcelona: Plaza & Janés.
—. (2005) *El Exorcista* (translated by Raquel Albornoz), Barcelona: Ediciones B.
Puzo, Mario (1969) *The Godfather*, New York: G.P. Putnam's Sons.
—. (1970) *El Padrino* (translated by A. Arnau), Barcelona: Grijalbo.

—. (2005) *El Padrino* (translated by A. Arnau), Barcelona: Ediciones B.

Secondary sources

Abellán, Manuel Luis (1980) *Censura y creación literaria en España (1939-1976)*, Barcelona: Península.

—. (1995) "Algunos determinismos sociales del franquismo y la transición", in Federico Bonaddio and Derek Harris (eds.) *Siete ensayos sobre la cultura posfranquista*, Aberdeen: Central Services University of Aberdeen, 2-9.

Amell, Samuel (1989) "Formas de censura en la literatura del posfranquismo", in *Letras Peninsulares*, 2: 313-321.

LaPrade, Douglas Edgard (1991) *La censura de Hemingway en España*, Salamanca: Ediciones Universidad de Salamanca.

Lázaro, Alberto (2001) "George Orwell's *Homage to Catalonia*: a Politically Incorrect Story", in Alberto Lázaro (ed.) *The Road From George Orwell: His Achievement and Legacy*, Berna, Suiza: Peter Lang, 71-91.

Markham, James (1980) "Franco dies slowly", in *The New York Times Book Review*, August, 17, 1980: 9 & 21.

Massot, Josep (1991) "En España se siguen editando libros en versión censurada por el franquismo", in *La Vanguardia*, August, 26, 1991: 23.

Merino Alvarez, Raquel (2000) "El teatro inglés traducido desde 1960: Censura, ordenación, calificación", in Rosa Rabadán (ed.) *Traducción y censura inglés-español: 1939-1985. Estudio preliminar*, León: Universidad de León, 121-153.

Milton, John (2000) "The translation of mass fiction", in Allison Beeby, Doris Ensinger & Marisa Presas (eds.) *Investigating Translation*, Amsterdam/Philadelphia: John Benjamins, 171-179.

Olivares Leyva, Monica (2006) "The Censorship of Literary Narrative in Franco's Spain: an Historiographical Approach", in Ausma Cindiņa and Jonathan Osmond (eds.) *Power and Culture. Hegemony, Interaction and Dissent*, Pisa: Edizioni Plus-Pisa University Press, 105-116.

Rodríguez Espinosa, Marcos (2004) "El discurso ideológico de la censura franquista y la traducción de textos literarios: *Las aventuras de Barry Lyndon* y la Editorial Destino", in Grupo Traducción, literatura y sociedad. *Ética y política de la traducción literaria*, Málaga: Miguel Gómez Ediciones, 219-238.

Vila-San Juan, Sergio (2003) *Pasando página: autores y editores en la España democrática*, Barcelona: Círculo de Lectores.

VV.AA (2000) *La novela popular en España*, Madrid: Editorial Robel.

CHAPTER THREE

TRANSLATION & CENSORSHIP:
DO DIFFERENT LANDSCAPES & TIMES CALL FOR (DIS)SIMILAR CONSTRAINTS?

CENSORSHIP IN BRAZIL: THE CASE OF CLUBE DO LIVRO

JOHN MILTON,
UNIVERSIDADE DE SÃO PAULO, BRAZIL

Abstract: This study examines censorship in the case of the first even Brazilian book club, the Clube do Livro (1943-1989), examining extracts of translations of *Gargantua* (François Rabelais), *Hard Times* (Charles Dickens) and *The Professor* (Charlotte Brontë) that were cut. The article proposes that the main elements that were censored were scatological, sexually explicit, political, religious or racist. However, censorship of translations is never totally efficient, and the Clube do Livro was able to publish translations of Rumanian works which had a strong socialist message in the toughest years of the right-wing military dictatorship (1968-1976).

1. The history of the Clube do Livro

The 1930s and 1940s were a period of considerable growth in the book industry in Brazil, sometimes called the golden period of the book industry and translation in Brazil (Wyler 2003: 129). This period saw the expansion of Editora José Olympio, which, in 1939-1940 published biographies of Nijinsky, Isadora Duncan, Tolstoy and Jack London, then introduced the *Fogos Cruzados* series, a selection of the most important world romances. José Olympio also published other foreign classics such as *A Mulher de Trinta Anos* [*A Woman of Thirty*], by Balzac, and *Humilhados e Ofendidos* [*The Insulted and the Offended*], by Dostoievsky.

But probably the most important company to publish translated fiction was Editora Globo de Porto Alegre, which, from 1931 to 1956, published a considerable amount of fiction in translation, especially from English. The *Coleção Amarela,* published the detective fiction of Edgar Wallace, Agatha Christie, Sax Rohmer, G. K. Chesterton, Ellery Queen, Georges Simenon, and Dashiel Hammett and then, in 1933, began the *Coleção Nobel*, which, from 1933 to 1958, introduced Mann, Joyce, Gide, Virginia Woolf, Kafka, Aldous Huxley, Proust, Steinbeck, Pirandello and Faulkner to the Brazilian reading public (Amorim 1991: 108-110). Though the best-selling author in the collection was Somerset Maugham, *Em Busca do Tempo Perdido* [*In Search of Lost Time*] was a commercial success, with a total number of 66,000 copies printed. Its *Biblioteca dos Séculos* published 25 titles, from 1942 to 1952, including *Guerra e Paz* [*War and Peace*] (24,000 copies in 6 editions); *Grandes Esperanças* [*Great Expectations*] (11,000 in 3 editions); *Viagens de Gulliver* [*Gulliver's Travels*] (9,000 in 2 editions); *O Vermelho e o Negro* [*The Red and the Black*] (16,000 in 4 editions), in addition to collections of the works of Maupassant (21,000 in 4 editions); Poe (10,000 in 2) and Merimée (10,000 in two). But by far its most prestigious publication was a carefully annotated edition in 17 volumes of the *Comédia Humana* [*The Human Comedy*] (1947-1955), organized by Paulo Ronai, with print runs from 20,000 (for the first in the series to 9,000 (for the last volumes in the series) (Amorim 1991: 157-159). Its children's series also included Lewis Carroll and Robert Louis Stevenson.

Other companies to publish translated fiction were Editora Martins, founded in 1941, and which published Dostoievsky, Bret Harte, Flaubert, O. Henry, Kipling, Poe and Mark Twain, and Editora Saraiva, which specialized in law books, and which, from 1948, invested in classics, publishing Machado de Assis, José de Alencar, Henry James and Poe. The Clube do Livro, presided over by its managing director, Mario Graciotti, began in 1943 and was the first book club in Brazil, publishing monthly volumes at approximately a third of the price of books sold in bookshops. Books were distributed either by post or agent, and the Clube do Livro achieved immediate success, with print runs of up to 50,000, a very high figure in Brazil, where the print run for the average novel is around 3,000. By 1969 it had sold 6,579,421 copies, which were to be found in "lares, nas escolas, nas bibliotecas, nas usinas, nas fábricas, nos quartéis" [in homes, schools, libraries, plants, factories and barracks] of Brazil. The new cultural awareness that these books bring would help to build "a Pátria maior" (Ribeiro 1969: 7). Its publications were mostly classics, both foreign and Brazilian, in roughly equal proportions, though in its later years, it began to publish a number of detective and adventure novels, organized several novel competitions and published the winning novels. It also had a weekly television programme, "CLUBE DO LIVRO", in 1963, whose aims were to help form home libraries, give cultural information, literary competitions, and interviews with intellectuals about literary problems (Gorki 1964: inside flap).

The Clube do Livro began in 1943 under the *Estado Novo* dictatorship of Getúlio Vargas. However, Vargas's nationalism appealed to a large number of Brazilian modernist intellectuals of the time. Carlos Drummond de Andrade was a secretary for the Minister of Education and Health, Gustavo Capanema. Architects Lúcio Costa and Oscar Niemeyer and artist Cândido Portinari worked for the government. The poet and critic Augusto Meyer was at the head of the Instituto Nacional do Livro.

Censorship was considerable right through the Vargas regime, beginning in 1931, with the Departamento Oficial de Propaganda [Official Publicity Department], reorganized in 1934 as the Departamento Nacional de Propaganda e Difusão Cultural [National Department of Propaganda and Cultural Publicity]. This was substituted in December 1939 by the DIP, the Departamento de Imprensa e Propaganda [Press and Publicity Department], directed to control the cultural production of Brazil and which continued until the fall of the *Estado Novo* in 1945. After the *coup d'état* of 10 November 1937 and the institution of the *Estado Novo*, censorship was extended. A number of writers spent time in prison: among them Jorge Amado, Graciliano Ramos, Rachel de Queiroz, Gilberto Freyre and Tomás Santa Rosa. Cecília Meirelles was imprisoned for having translated *The Adventures of Tom Sawyer*, confiscated as it was considered to be dangerous. Books written by Graciliano Ramos, José Lins de Rego, Rachel de Queiroz and Jorge Amado, as well as the children's books by Monteiro Lobato, were all burnt. The criteria for banning books were often ill-defined. It could be strong language or eroticism, in addition to unacceptable political points of view. The government also exerted strong control over schoolbooks and distributed patriotic and pro-government material. It could also prevent publishing houses from receiving imported paper, as in the case of the anti-Getúlio Editora Martins during the paper shortage of 1941 (Hallewell 1986: 369-370).

The second period of severe censorship began in 1968 with the AI-5 decree. From 1968 to 1978, the beginning of the political opening, 508 books were expressly forbidden. In addition to predictably proscribed authors such as Che Guevara, Lenin and Marx, banned books included *Mein Kampf*, by Adolf Hitler, and works by Harold Robbins. A book could be forbidden because it had a red cover or because it contained the word "red" in the title, as in the case of *O Livro Vermelho da Igreja Perseguida* [*The Red Book of the Persecuted Church*], not a book on revolutionary priests but rather on early Christian martyrs. Another book to be banned was the novel *A Capital*, by Eça de Queirós!

As there was no pre-censorship, publishing companies were forced to undergo self-censorship and avoid any controversial subjects. This was very much the case of the Clube do Livro as it wished, of course, to maintain the official distribution channels to schools, libraries and army barracks, for which it depended on the federal and state governments to buy up a large number of copies. From 1970 it was also possible for publishing companies to voluntarily submit their works to censorship. However, there might be a considerable delay while these works were being assessed, and this might also be seen as an "admission of guilt" (*Ibidem*: 494).

Faced with an increasing number of retail outlets, including newspaper kiosks, and highly competent translations from Editora Saraiva and Editora Ática from the sixties onwards, sales fell in the second half of the 1960s and the 1970s. In November 1973 the Clube do Livro was acquired by the Revista dos Tribunais, the owners of the major book printing press in São Paulo, who were forced to temporarily stop publishing in 1976, when feeling the after effects of the world oil crisis of 1973, which resulted in the cost of paper rising 125% between June 1973 and February 1974 (*Ibidem*: 390 & 411). The Clube do Livro was then acquired by Editora Ática as part of a debt and restarted publishing under the Clube do Livro logo in 1983. After 1984 Mario Graciotti was no longer the managing editor, and the Ática team attempted to modernize the Clube do Livro's image. Older translations, such as that of *Madame Bovary* were republished with considerable revisions, often rescuing the sections which had been omitted. New translations of other works, such as *Werther*, were made. And titles such as Kafka's *O Processo* [*The Trial*] (1985), *O Tarado do Brás* [*The Pervert of Brás*] by Pedro Luiz Pereira (1989) and *A Metade Arrancada de Mim* [*The Half Torn Away from Me*] by Izaías Almada (Estacão Liberdade/Clube do Livro 1989), about a torturer in the military regime, *Nos Bastidores da Censura* [*In the Wings of Censorship*] by Dionísio Silva (1984), an analysis of the censorship of Rubem Fonseca's *Feliz Ano Novo* [*Happy New Year*] during the military regime, and Fernando Gabeira's *Greenpeace: Verde Guerrilha da Paz* [*Green Peace Guerillas*] (1988) were published in order to compete with the much more modern Círculo do Livro, a joint venture between Editora Abril and the German media giant Bertelsmann, which reached 500,000 members after ten years. Members of the Clube do Livro could now choose from a list the monthly volumes they received, and were no longer obliged to accept the book chosen for them. But these changes came too late and were not successful. The Clube do Livro was finally subsumed in the Estação Liberdade branch of the Editora Ática in 1989. The Estação da Liberdade logo now appeared on the covers, and the title page provided the information "Editora Clube do Livro Ltda., Estação Liberdade". In the same year it was finally discontinued by the owner of Editora Ática, Anderson Fernandes Dias.

2. Examples of censorship: *O Gigante Gargântua*

In my study on the Clube do Livro, in which I examined the translation of the translations and adaptations published by the Brazilian book club (Milton: 2003), I discovered a number of different forms of censorship of the original. I categorize these under the following types: censorship of sex and scatology; censorship of political elements; censorship of offensive elements. I shall also look at the way in which stylistic elements were cut.

Most of these forms can be seen in the Clube do Livro translation of *O Gigante Gargântua* [*Gargantua*], published by the *Clube do Livro* in a "tradução especial de José Maria Machado" [a *special* translation by José Maria Machado] in 1961. This edition also contained 19 pages of excerpts from *Pantagruel*. Unusually, the translator admits that he has made ample use of the scissors:

> In this edition, all the incongruencies and daring liberties the author has made have been cut, in a rational adaptation of the text. The Clube do Livro readers would not put up with a pure and simple translation of many sections which we have been obliged, because of decency and probity, to eliminate. (Rabelais: 14-15)[1]

In his *Nota Explicativa* Domingos Carvalho da Silva does not quite share the enthusiasm of the translator for the cuts made:

> The translation which follows was, as we said, freed from impurities by the translator, certainly to attend to the requirements of the subscribers of the "Clube do Livro". The crudest and most irreverent extracts have been cut, and, as a consequence, the colourful part, which today we can call the "engagé" of the novel, has been weakened. But there remains a great part of a work which would not survive time if it were not, as a work of literature, also a great work of the human spirit. (Rabelais 1961: 11)[2]

---

[1] "Nessa edição para o Clube do Livro, foram aparadas todas as incongruências e ousadas liberdades do autor, com racional adaptação do texto. Os leitores não suportariam a tradução pura e simples de muitos trechos, que fomos obrigados a eliminar, por uma questão de decência e probidade."

[2] "A tradução que se segue foi, como dissemos, escoimada pelo tradutor, certamente em atenção às tendências do público assinante das edições do 'Clube do Livro'. As passagens mais cruas e mais irreverentes foras [sic] suprimidas e, em conseqüência o colorido–que hoje se poderia chamar 'engagé'–da novela, esmaeceu. Permanece [...] boa parte da expressão de um livro que não sobreviveria

Indeed, José Maria Machado prudishly eliminates all references to the sexual act and bodily functions in which Rabelais takes such great delight. For example, direct reference to move making cannot be contemplated:

> Moiennans lesquelles loys, les femmes veuves peuvent franchement jouer du serre cropière (make love) à tous enviz et toutes restes, deux mois après le trespas de leurs mariz. (Rabelais 1965: Ch III:51)

References to bodily functions must be cut:

> Non obstant ces remonstrances, elle en mangea seze muiz deux bussars et six tupins. O belle matière fecale que doivoit boursouffler en elle! (Rabelais 1965: Ch. IV:57)

José Maria Machado also ignores the puns and word games as in the following section:

> Par mesmes raisons (si raisons les doibz nommer et non resveries) ferois je paindre un penier, denotant qu'on me faict pener; et un pot à moutarde, que c'est mon cueur à qui moult tarde; et un pot à pisser, c'est un official; et le fond de mes chausses, c'est un vaisseau de petz; et ma braguette, c'est le greffe des arrestz; et un estront de chien, c'est un tronc de ceans, où gist l'amour de mámye. (Rabelais 1965: Ch IX:95)

Needless to say, he also omits the long list of nicknames and euphemisms for the penis:

> [...] ma petite dille [...] ma pine, [...] ma branche de coural, [...] mon bondon, mon bouchon, mon vibrequin, mon possouer, ma teriere, ma pendilloche, mon rude esbat roidde et bas, mon dressouoir, ma petite andoille vermeille, ma petite couille bredouille. (Rabelais 1965: 111)

When a bodily function is mentioned, it is euphemized. The "pissa" referring to Gargantua's mare becomes "soltou águas" (Rabelais 1965: Ch. XXXVI: 289).

The translator also takes no interest in Rabelais' stylistic variations. The rhymes, such as "Chiart,/ Foirart,/ etart,/ Brenons, Chappart/ S'espart/ Sus nous./ Hordous,/ Merdous,/ Esgous,/ Le feu de sainct Antoine te ard!/ Sy tous/ Tes trous/ Esclous/ Tu ne torche avant ton depart!" are ignored

---

ao tempo se não fosse, também, como obra literária, uma alta realização do espírito humano."

(Rabelais 1965: Ch. XIII:125), as is the list of games (Rabelais 1965: Ch. XXII: 179-185), and puns, e.g.:

> Que fera cest hyvrogne icy? Qu'on me le mene en prison. Troubler ainsi le service divin!
> —"Mais (dist le moyne) le service du vin faisons tant qu'il ne soit troublé; car vous mesmes, Monsieur le Prieur, aymez boyre du meilleur". (Rabelais 1965: Ch. XXVII: 229)

This last pun would be possible in Portuguese with "serviço divino" and "serviço do vinho", but instead is weakly translated as "serviço diário" (Rabelais 1961: 67).

Rabelais uses Latin in a section where he mocks holy relics and the excessive use of Latin is cut. When the pilgrims are swallowed by Gargantua, they even speak in Latin. "*Cum exurgerent homines in nos, forte vivos deglutissent nos*, quand nous feusmes mangez en salade au grain du sel; *cum irasceretur furor eorum in nos, foristan aqua absorbuisset nos*, quand il beut le grand traict [...]". All the Latin is ignored in the Portuguese version (Rabelais 1965: Ch. XXXVIII: 305).

The Clube do Livro does not join in with Rabelais' critique of certain elements of the Church. Chapter XL "Pourquoy les moynes sont refuyz du monde, et pourquoy les ungs ont le nez plus grand que les aultres", satirising the lives of the monks is missing, as is Gargantua's proposal that the religious devotés should be able to get married:

> Item, parce que ordinairement les religieux faisoient troys veuz, sçavoir est de chastité, pauvreté et obedience, fut constitu't que là honorablement on peult estre marié, que chacun feut riche et vesquist en liberté. (Rabelais 1965: Ch. LII:403)

3. *Tempos Difíceis*: politics

Tempos Difíceis [*Hard Times*] may seem a strange choice for a book club which depends on a close connection with the military government for the distribution of its books. However, right from the beginning of the Introduction, the editors play safe and take great pains to insist that there is no left-wing revolutionary message to Dickens' work: "It is a book of ideas, though it can't really be called a book of combat" (Dickens 1969:8).[3] It must be distanced as far as possible from the Brazil of 1969 and becomes a

---

[3] "É um livro de idéias, embora não se possa denominar propriamente um livro de combate."

regional novel from a far-off epoch: "A new aspect of provincial society of its time, the silent struggle between the ancient and the modern, through the bourgeoisie of other epochs" (*Ibidem*: 8).[4] Instead of being linked to the present, *Hard Times* is linked to the slavery and the dark ages of the past, which have now been superseded by the Universal Convention of the Rights of Children and of Men, freedom from slavery, the fight against usury, the United Nations, the ecumenical contemporary Church, and, in Brazil, greater rights for workers, which have existed since 1922. It seems possible that we are nearing the world which was dreamed of by Dickens. José Maria Machado then comments that *Hard Times* was a critique of laissez-faire economic policy, then prevalent in Britain. But he fails to dwell on this possible element of social criticism and never allows any comparison with the inequalities present in Brazil in 1969 to be made: it is a book which transcends place and time: "it is really a book which presents a thesis in which shows basic problems of a higher transcendence which go beyond any present period."[5]

The translated text must also be modified in order not to give the impression the *Tempos Difíceis* is a subversive work. The following section might be considered subversive, despite Dickens' opinion that a decision to support the selfish union official, Slackbridge, would be wrong.

> That every man felt his condition to be, somehow or other, worse than it might be; that every man considered it incumbent on him to join the rest, towards the making of it better, that every man felt his only hope to be in his allying himself to his comrades by whom he was surrounded; and that in this belief, right or wrong (unhappily wrong then), the whole of that crowd were gravely, deeply, faithfully in earnest; must have been as plain to any one who chose to see what was there, as the bare beams of roof, and the whitened brick walls. (Dickens 1982: 171)

In the translation, the idea of unity and mass action is lost. The error they made becomes clearer.

> Toda aquela multidão acreditava, com uma fé grave, profunda e sincera, na conclusão, certa ou errada (errada desta vez, infelizmente), a que [Slackbridge] chegara. (Dickens 1969: 90)

---

[4] "Nele se apresenta um aspecto novo da sociedade provinciana do seu tempo, a luta surda entre o antigo e o moderno, através de uma burguesia de outras eras"

[5] "é bem um livro de tese em que se apresentam problemas básicos de superior transcendência e vão além de qualquer período de atualidade"

[All of the crowd believed, with a grave, deep and sincere faith, in the conclusion which, right or wrong (wrong this time, unfortunately), which he had reached.]

Similarly, "the slaves of an iron-handed and grinding despotism" (Dickens 1982: 169) become the mild "trabalhadores e companheiros" [workers and companions] (Dickens 1969: 90).

Apparently quite absurd changes can also be seen. The Clube do Livro translation of *Silas Marner* changes the name of the house where Squire Cass lives from the "Red House" (Eliot n.d.: 96) to the "Casa Amarela" ["Yellow House"] (Eliot 1973: 66), probably to avoid the idea that the work may have had any revolutionary intention and the mansion may have been a Communist bunker! But, more seriously, censorship was so strong when this translation was published (1973) that any book with a socialist country in the title, or by an author with a Russian sounding name, or even with a red cover, as was mentioned above (p. 76-77) may have been seized by the federal or state police (Hallewell 1986: 483).

Any kind of potential political dispute or contestation dissolves into an optimistic humanism. This can also be seen in the translations from the Rumanian made by Nelson Vainer: *O Caminho do Céu* [*The Road to Heaven*], by Nicolae Jianu (1968), and *Um Pedaço de Terra* [*A Piece of Land*] (1970), by Zaharia Stanco. The headline to the *Nota Explicativa* [Explanatory Note] of *Um Pedaço de Terra* states: "We discover the cross-section of human figures and the intertwining of various domestic problems, which are at times serious and distressing".[6] Stanco was a writer who was in favour with the Communist regime. In 1948, he was proclaimed "O prosador do ano" [the prose writer of the year]. His work is full of socialist realism; evoking "scenes of the tragic life of the peasants of the Danube countryside at the beginning of the century".[7] And *Os Mastins* [*The Mastiffs*] (1952) (Stanco 1970: 7) "describes the peasant uprising of 1907, one of the bloodiest in history, which culminated in the extermination of 11,000 peasants".[8] Once again, no parallel or connection with the situation in Brazil can be made. Stanco is not a social critic but a profound humanist. His work "imposes on the contemporary literary landscape a profoundly personal artistic vision, in a characteristic style, as

---

[6] "Encontramos o recorte de figuras humanas e a encruzilhada de vários problemas domésticos, às vezes graves e afligentes."

[7] "cenas da vida trágica dos lavradores da campina danubiana nos começos do século"

[8] "descreve o levante campesino de 1907, um dos mais sangrentos da história, pois culminou com o extermínio de 11.000 camponeses"

in his poetry, which is a strong message of confidence and optimism" (*Ibidem*: 8).[9] And like Cervantes, Hugo, Camões, Merimée, Richepin and Pushkin, he has written about gypsies, this "unhappy group of human beings, who are condemned to forever wander along the twisting paths of the world" (*Ibidem*: 8).[10] Vainer's Explanatory Note ends by emphasizing the profound humanity of Stanco's work:

> In all his work, as the reader shall see, there flows a slow breath of piety and love, which distinguishes the charming narrative of the boy Darie, confronted by the painful conflicts of his parents. And above these conflicts Stanco questions again and again the profound reasons which direct the no less profound mysteries of Life and Death. (*Ibidem*: 9)[11]

This last sentence was also one of the back cover blurbs. And Jianu's stories "show how immense the frontiers of the human heart and literary beauty are" (Jianu 1968: 5).[12] Mario Graciotti adds his postscript in similar gushing language:

> In these excellent pages, which constitute a considerable anthology, we find the presence of that sigh of humanity, which, in the message of its interpreters, transcends the the limits of the episodic to reach the frontiers of Beauty, characteristics which mark true and legitimate works of art] (*Ibidem*: 7)[13]

Gorki's *Adolescência* is given a pseudo-christian interpretation: "All of Maxim Gorki's work is a message of faith, even though his characters are recruited from among tramps and the unemployed [...] All of his generous

---

[9] "impõe na paisagem literária contemporânea uma visão artística profundamente pessoal, em estilo característico, tal como em seus versos, como mensagem firme de confiança e otimismo"

[10] "infeliz grupo humano, condenado a errar eternamente pelos caminhos tortuosos do mundo"

[11] "Em toda a sua obra, como o leitor verá, flui um lento hálito de piedade e de amor, que marca a encantadora narrativa do garoto Darie, em face daqueles dolorosos conflitos de seus parentes. E acima desses conflitos, Stanco pergunta, pergunta, pelas profundas razões que norteiam os não menos profundos mistérios da Vida e da Morte."

[12] "[D]emonstram, assim, como são imensas as fronteiras do coração humano e das belezas literárias."

[13] "Nestas excelentes páginas, constituindo uma expressiva antologia, encontramos a presença daquele sopro humano, que, na mensagem de seus intérpretes, transcende dos limites do episódico para as fronteiras da Beleza, características que marcam as verdadeiras e legítimas obras de arte."

work as a writer was aimed at providing a powerful word of hope" (Gorki 1964: 8).[14] The harshness of the real problems of the world is always kept at a distance. The *Nota Explicativa* to Knut Hamsun's *Um Vagabundo Toca em Surdina* [*A Wanderer Plays on Muted Strings*] says: "His pages describe mysteries and misfortunes, but in a soft and calm tone, more of a poem and a formal charge" (Hamsun 1948: 5).[15]

O Romance de Maria Clara (Ribeiro Neto: 1965) describes middle-class racial prejudice in São Paulo towards a young mulatta teacher. It was originally published in 1940, and the Clube do Livro Introduction stresses the fact that racial problems have been disappearing "na marcha civilizadora do País" [in the march of civilization of Brazil] and is no longer part of "uma cidade em desenvolvimento" [a developing city] (Ribeiro Neto 1965: 8). Literature such as that of Dickens and Victor Hugo has helped to eliminate the injustices of society and introduce progressive legislation, and this novel belongs to the documentary tradition of those works which described the difficult period of miscegenation.

The Clube do Livro also defuses Edmundo de Amicis's socialism. Ferruccio Rubiani, in the *Nota Explicativa*, explains that de Amicis was one of the first socialists in Italy, considering socialism to be part of Christ's teachings. But then he became disillusioned when he saw that his vision of goodness and love was merely transformed into a political party. He is more of a Christian writer than a socialist, and the harmony of his writing also reveals "a harmonia da vida interior" [the harmony of interior life] (Amicis 1947: 5).

4. *O Professor*: political correctness

In *O Professor* (Charlotte Brontë) a considerable amount of material that could be seen as being potentially offensive to readers was cut by the Clube do Livro. Apart from *Gargantua*, *O Professor* is the only translation published by the Clube do Livro in which the translator admits he has omitted some of the longer descriptive passages. Let us look more closely at whether it is just these passages that have been left out. Some of them are mainly descriptive, such as Crimsworth's description of his room in Chapter 7, that of his walk around Brussels in the same chapter, and the physical

---

[14] "Toda a obra de Máximo Gorki é, pois, uma mensagem de fé, embora seus personagens sejam recrutados entre vagabundos e gente de disponibilidade [...] Todo o seu generoso esforço de escritor foi no sentido de uma vigorosa palavra de esperança"

[15] "Suas páginas descrevem misérias e desgraças, mas num tom suave, brando, mais de poema do que de libelo"

characteristics of the female pupils in Chapter 12. Crimsworth's inner monologues are also frequently trimmed, as for example in Chapter 1, where he is discussing the attempt he is making to earn his own living, his opinions of Hunsden in Chapter 4, and his considerations about his dislike for his job in Chapter 5. But we can also find some other very clear elements that are omitted in José Maria Machado's translation. Crimsworth/ Charlotte Brontë shows a very clear and bigoted anti-Catholicism: Belgium is the land of popery, which makes its inhabitants liars, tale-tellers and dishonest. All the very forthright comments in the original such as: "I know nothing of the arcana of the Roman Catholic religion, and I am not a bigot in matters of theology, but I suspect the root of this precious impurity, so obvious, so general in Popish countries, is to be found in the discipline, if not the doctrines of the church of Rome" (Brontë 1955: Ch. 12: 84); "Sylvie was gentle in manners, intelligent in mind; she was even sincere, as far as her religion would permit her to be so (...)" (*Ibidem* Ch. 12: 87); "I was no pope. I could not boast infallibility" (*Ibidem* Ch. 20: 165).

José Maria Machado seems to go to great lengths to ensure that no offence will be given to any reader by cutting references to the deterministic ideas that Charlotte Brontë ascribes to:

> (...) a band of very vulgar, inferior-looking Flamandes, including two or three examples of that deformity of person and imbecility of intellect whose frequency in the Low Countries would seem to furnish proof that the climate is such as to induce degeneracy of the human mind and body [...]. (*Ibidem* Ch. 12: 86).

The translation cuts any allusions to the Flemings as an inferior race: "Flamands certainly they were, and both had the true physiognomy, where intellectual inferiority is marked in lines none can mistake; still they were men, and, in the main, honest men (...)" (*Ibidem* Ch. 7: 58). In fact, all passages where national characteristics are discussed are either omitted or pared down. After M. Pelet gets drunk and insults Crimsworth in Chapter 20, the description of Pelet as "a thorough Frenchman, the national characteristic of ferocity had not been omitted" is also left out. The nationalities in "French politeness, German good-will, and Swiss servility" (*Ibidem* Ch. 24: 210) are cut. Hunsden's radical comments about poverty and oppression in England are also cut. The omitted sections are underlined:

> Examine the footprints of our august aristocracy; *see how they walk in blood, crushing hearts as they go.* Just put your head in at English cottage doors; *get a glimpse of famine crouched torpid on black hearthstones; of*

Disease lying bare on beds without coverlets, of Infamy wantoning viciously with Ignorance, though indeed Luxury is her favourite paramour, and princely halls are dearer to her than thatched hovels. (*Ibidem* Ch. 24: 208)

I suggest two reasons for these cuts. One is that the Clube do Livro wished to be politically correct *avant la lettre*, attempting not to offend the religious and national sensibilities of its readers. The other reason is that although there was no religious censorship in Brazil when this translation was published, in 1958, such religious sensitivity may have been a leftover from the early years of the *Estado Novo* (1939-1945), when the Catholic Church played a large role in the state apparatus of the Getúlio Vargas' nationalistic dictatorship, modelled to a great extent on that of Mussolini, where considerable censorship existed.

Much of the dialogue in the original, which takes place in Brussels, is in French. In many sections Charlotte Brontë begins in French and then switches to English. Not surprisingly, as the translation is aimed at a non-academic market, French is completely ignored. José Maria Machado changes the multi-voiced original into a monological homogenized translation. Chapter XXIII contains two poems: a section from a ballad by Sir Walter Scott and the romantic ballad originally written in French by Frances and translated by Crimsworth. A prose translation is given of the first ballad, and the second is ignored. A narrative feature that is missing in the original is the meta-narrative where the author comes out of the narrative and makes an appeal to the reader, as near the beginning of Chapter 14: "Know, O incredulous reader! (...)"

As has been seen above, many of the aspects of "Factory Translation" can be seen in the translations of the Clube do Livro. *Gargantua*, *Hard Times* and *The Professor* were cut to fit into the standard number of pages. The cutting may have involved the elimination of scatological elements, as in *O Gigante Gargântua*, political references, as in *Tempos Difíceis*, of descriptions of racial characteristics, as in *O Professor*. The results are versions which are standardized, both in terms of length and type of language. In all three cases, most especially in the case of Rabelais, we feel that much of the author's original voice has been lost. In the cases of *O Gigante Gargântua* and *O Professor*, the translator admits that he has made cuts and alterations. However, this is unusual in the Clube do Livro translations, where the cuts are euphemized with the statement that the translation is a "tradução especial" [special translation].

5. Conclusion

Although it seems that, at least superficially, the Clube do Livro kowtowed to the government, its publications were not strictly censored. If this had been the case, certain of the Clube do Livro publications would never have seen light of day. *Um Pedaço de Terra*, by the Rumanian Zaharia Stanco, is a case in point. As mentioned previously, the *Nota Explicativa* emphasizes the humanism of Stanco's work, and he is placed in the company of less socialist writers such as Cervantes, Victor Hugo, Merimée, Richepin and Pushkin, but it also states that, in post-Second World War Rumania, Stanco was a member of the Rumanian Academy and President of the Rumanian Writers' Union. Among his works is *Os Mastins*, describing the peasant uprising in 1907, which ended in the extermination of 11,000 peasants. *Um Pedaço de Terra* belongs to this socialist realist tradition and describes the rough peasant life in a pre-socialist Rumanian countryside ruled by local bosses. Life in the family Stanco focuses on is tough, brutal and violent: wife-beating, sado-masochism and juvenile alcohol abuse are coolly described. Of course, when Stanco narrates that a child has drunk himself to death at the age of five, the Clube do Livro comes in with a note similar to that on page 88 warning about the dangers of alcohol abuse (Stanco 1970: 37). The story tells of an adopted daughter's struggle with the family who had adopted her to get her "piece of land". *Um Pedaço de Terra* was published in 1970, at a time when one would think that it would have been difficult to publish such a work in Brazil with its critique of capitalism, support for those without land and implicit reading that things will be better when socialism comes.

In *O Caminho do Céu* [*The Road to Heaven*] (1968), a collection of short stories from the Rumanian, also selected and translated by Nelson Vainer, we also come across similar themes: the tough life in the mines in 1946 in "O Caminho do Céu", by Nicolae Jianu; electoral corruption in a rural community in the period after the peasants' uprising in 1907 in "O Desconhecido" [*The Unknown*], by George Calinesco; persecution of Rumanians in Nazi-held Hungary in the Second World War in "O Pão" *[The Bread*], by Francisc Munteanu; and the backwardness of peasant life in pre-socialist Rumania in "O Girassol" [*The Sunflower*], by Ion Agirbiceanu, and "As Velhas" [*The Old Women*], by Dumitru Radu Popesco.

Thus I propose that the translations of the Clube do Livro show us how permeable and unpredictable book censorship, particularly of translated works, can be. On one hand, the Clube do Livro seems to go to excessive lengths and changes the colour of the house of Squire Cass in *Silas Marner*. On the other hand, works such as *Hard Times, Um Pedaço de Terra* and *O Caminho do Céu*, with their undeniable socialist message, despite framings such as introductions and blurbs which deny their link to Brazilian reality, are published in the most severe years of censorship of the military government. That they could be published is due to a great extent, I believe, to the fact they were published by a little-known publishing company, that they were translations, that they were not works from the Soviet Union, that their titles did not obviously call attention, and that were classified as fictional and not social science works.

References

Primary Sources

Amicis, Edmundo de (1947) *Marrocos* (translated by Manuel Pinheiro Chagas), São Paulo: Clube do Livro.
Brontë, Charlotte (1955) *The Professor*, London: Dent.
—. (1958) *O Professor* (translated by José Maria Machado), São Paulo: Clube do Livro.
Dickens, Charles (1969) *Hard Times*, Harmondsworth: Penguin.
—. (1969) *Tempos Difíceis* (translated by José Maria Machado), São Paulo: Clube do Livro.
Gorki, Máximo (1964) *Adolescência* (translated by Rolando Roque da Silva), São Paulo: Clube do Livro.
Hamsun, Knut (1948) *Um Vagabundo Toca em Surdina* (translated by Raquel Bensiliman), São Paulo: Clube do Livro.
Jianu, Nicolae (1986) *O Caminho do Céu* (translated by Nelson Vainer), São Paulo: Clube do Livro.
Rabelais, François (1965) *Gargantua*, Paris: Gallimard.
—. (1961) *O Gigante Gargântua* (translated by José Maria Machado), São Paulo: Clube do Livro.
Ribeiro Neto, Agenor (1965) *O Romance de Maria Clara*, São Paulo: Clube do Livro.

Secondary sources

Amorim, Sônia Maria (1991) "De Agatha Christie a Marcel Proust: A Edição de Literatura Traduzida pela Editora Globo (1930-1950): Uma Odisséia Editorial", M.A. dissertation, Escola de Comunicações e Artes, Universidade de São Paulo.

Hallewell, Laurence (1986) *O Livro no Brasil*, São Paulo: Queiroz and EDUSP.

Milton, John (2003) *O Clube do Livro e a Tradução*, Bauru: EDUSC.

Ribeiro, Eurico Branco (1969) *Água da Esperança*, São Paulo: Clube do Livro.

Wyler, Lia (2003) *Línguas, Poetas e Bacharéis: Uma Crônica da Tradução no Brasil*, Rio de Janeiro: Rocco.

TRANSLATION AND CENSORSHIP IN COMMUNIST CZECHOSLOVAKIA

JAROSLAV ŠPIRK,
CHARLES UNIVERSITY, PRAGUE

Abstract: The paper explores the phenomenon of censorship in communist Czechoslovakia from 1948 to 1989 in relation to translations and translation theory. Following a brief overview of the major historical events in the given period, translations from English, French, German, Russian, Spanish and Portuguese into Czech are considered. Finally, the paper also deals with the issue of censorship as it was accounted for by the Czechoslovak translation theoreticians, Jiří Levý and Anton Popovič.

1. Introduction

Censorship in Czechoslovakia differed considerably from that in fascist (or Nazi) dictatorships. While *fascism* put emphasis on the family (as the founding unit of the nation), on religion (hence its support by the Church[1]), on the nation (hence its nationalism, and often racism), and on the difference between social classes (hence its corporatism); *communism* (or socialism as the stage preceding it[2]) built on the collective (cooperative, as opposed to the family), on Marxism-Leninism (substituting–and as a result, persecuting–religion), on (declared) internationalism (solidarity of the working class in all countries, in theory) and on (seeming) egalitarianism of all people.[3]

---

[1] See the so-called *clerofascism* or clerical fascism in Tiso's Slovakia, Salazar's Portugal, Vargas' Brazil, etc.
[2] Communists in the Czech Republic maintain that real communism was never achieved in Czechoslovakia. Thus, what the country experienced was socialism, while communism remains the ideal to strive for. Nonetheless, for the sake of clarity, no distinction will be made here, as the term "communism" was (and remains to be) in the name of the Party and is used as such also in everyday language.
[3] Despite official proclamations, Party members were more equal than others.

These fundamental ideological differences between the two systems had consequences on censorship which was in practice in fascist (Nazi) countries on one hand, and in communist (socialist) countries on the other.

2. Communist Czechoslovakia

For the development of Czechoslovakia in the second half of the twentieth century, three historic dates were of fundamental importance:

(a) February 1948 – the Communist Party of Czechoslovakia, backed by the Soviets, seized power; "Stalinization" of politics, everyday life and culture began; thousands of Czechs and Slovaks emigrated

(b) August 1968 – *the Prague Spring*, the armies of the Warsaw Pact (except for Romania) invaded Czechoslovakia as a reaction to the liberalization and democratization process in Czechoslovakia in the late 1960s; the occupation was followed by a wave of emigration, unseen before and stopped shortly after (estimate: 70,000 people emigrated immediately; 300,000 in total), typically highly qualified people

(c) November 1989 – *the Velvet Revolution*, mass demonstrations (initially of university students) overthrew the Communist Party peacefully (except for a few students beaten up by the police; no blood was spilled)

Following these events as well as the political events in the U.S.S.R., the history of communist Czechoslovakia can be divided into two periods (or four sub-periods):

1. Early "Communism" (1948-68)
a. Stalinization (1948–63)
b. De-Stalinization, Khrushchev's reforms (1963–68)
2. "Normalization" (1969–89)
a. "Brezhnevization" (1969-85)
b. Gorbachev's *perestroika* (1985-89)

The period of Stalinization was politically and culturally the most severe, with biased political trials against anti-communists ending in capital punishments, twenty-year to life sentences and suchlike. The ideological principles of Marxism-Leninism and socialist realism pervaded cultural and intellectual life. The entire education system was submitted to state control. The economy was committed to comprehensive central planning and the elimination of private ownership. In all respects,

Czechoslovakia became a vassal of the Soviet Union. The dictatorship of the proletariat and the leadership role of the Communist Party were firmly anchored in the new Constitution of 9 May 1948. Censorship was imposed on almost everything coming from abroad, especially from the Western countries (dubbed as "capitalist" or "bourgeois" societies).

Although Stalin died in 1953, it took several years before the political *détente* could commence. Only after the Communist Party of the Soviet Union convened and opened a discussion of "some negative aspects" of Stalin's rule could the project of "socialism with a human face" be launched by the reformists within the Czechoslovak Communist Party. Thus, in the late 1960s, the cultural policy of the state was gradually becoming less rigid and more open towards Western countries. Censorship was lifted and Western literature–if properly commented and provided with an appropriate introduction or conclusion (of how to understand it within the Marxist-Leninist stance)–could be translated and published.

After the 1968 invasion, a period of "normalization"–the restoration of continuity with the pre-reform period–was initiated. Normalization entailed systematic political repression and the return to ideological conformity. Censorship was strictly imposed and publishing houses were placed under new direction.

This situation began to gradually change only in the late 1980s when Mikhail Gorbachev became Secretary-General of the Communist Party of the Soviet Union. Gorbachev began a policy of "restructuring" (*perestroika*) the Soviet economy and advocated "openness" (*glasnost*) in the discussion of economic, social and–to some extent–political questions.

Gorbachev's rise to power meant a warm wind from the East. Ultimately, it enabled the fall of the Berlin Wall, the Velvet Revolution in Czechoslovakia and the gradual dissolution of the Eastern Bloc.

3. Translation and censorship

Between 1948 and 1989, some 46,195 books were translated in Czechoslovakia (23,258 into Czech; 18,555 into Slovak[4]), i.e. approximately 1100 books per year (554 into Czech; 442 into Slovak). The statistical data can be divided into two periods, markedly differing from each other: a) early Communism, and b) normalization.

In the first twenty-two years of communism in Czechoslovakia, as many as 31,480 books were translated, 17,621 into Czech and 12,099 into

---

[4] The remaining books were translated in Czechoslovakia, but into languages other than Czech or Slovak.

Slovak.[5] That meant approximately 1431 books a year were published in Czechoslovakia throughout this period.

In the normalization period, only 14,715 books were translated in Czechoslovakia, 5,637 into Czech and 6,456 into Slovak[6] (normalization was less rigorous in Slovakia). That is roughly 736 *per annum*, only a little more than a half of the number of books published yearly in the previous period.

After February 1948, private publishing houses were forced to close down. The Ministry of Culture began to control all editorial activity; and by 1953 it had completed the delimitation and the specialization of all publishing houses. In accordance with the new, centrally decided plans of translations, the so-called "classics" experienced a boom at the expense of contemporary literature.

As for literature in English (Hrala 2002: 71-75), Dickens, Shakespeare, Fielding, Thackeray, Twain, Whitman, Dreiser–to name but a few–were all translated in new, scrupulously designed series. In the 1950s, contemporary literature in English was politically limited to authors who were regarded as "progressive" (i.e. complying with the doctrine of socialist realism). Only in the late 1960s had the prerequisite of being "progressive" been gradually overcome. Thus, Czech readers discovered F. S. Fitzgerald, E. Hemingway, W. Faulkner, J. Steinbeck, J. Dos Passos or G. Greene with a delay of several decades.

Translations were also limited by the demand for proportionate representation of Western and Eastern literature, by authority regulations, by the capacities of printing offices, paper allocations and various other factors. Despite this, British post-war novelists (such as K. Amis, M. Spark, E. Waugh) as well as American war novelists (N. Mailer, J. Heller) found their translations into Czech in the late 1960s.

After 1968, the situation in the publishing sector aggravated significantly; editorial projects were suspended or abandoned altogether, cooperation with some translators or experts was terminated, and it became much more difficult to publish a Western author.

What could not be achieved openly was sometimes accomplished clandestinely. Thus, throughout the communist period, many books

---

[5] Data collected from the paper (book) version of UNESCO's *Index Translationum* (Volumes 1-22).
[6] See the electronic version of UNESCO's *Index Translationum* (http://databases.unesco.org/xtrans/xtra-form.shtml).

appeared in the so-called *samizdat*,[7] which was often the only way of avoiding officially imposed censorship. To give but a few examples, J. R. R. Tolkien's *The Lord of the Rings* or G. Orwell's *Animal Farm* or *1984* all appeared in *samizdat* versions.

It was only after 1989 that the general public in Czechoslovakia became acquainted with works by G. Orwell, H. Miller and many others.

Literature in French (Hrala 2002: 119-123) also suffered from the complete subordination of the Czech cultural life to the state cultural policy determined by the Communist Party of Czechoslovakia. Following the Soviet ideologist Andrei A. Zhdanov, French literature translated into Czech had to conform to the requirements of being *"folksy"*,[8] (socialistically) *"realistic"* and *"progressive"*. L. Aragon, a critical realist by choice and a long-time communist, was translated into Czech, although his literature entailed problematic elements.

On the other hand, the accusation of being either surrealistic or Freudian was highly dangerous at the time. *Avant-garde* French literature was strictly prohibited.

French classics, especially those belonging to the "progressive" and "realistic" traditions of the nineteenth century and the beginning of the twentieth century (such as H. de Balzac, R. Rolland, V. Hugo, A. France, Stendhal), were the most popular books to be translated. A real favourite of these ascetic times was Maupassant, who combined the criticism of imperialistic France, welcomed by the censors, with pleasant erotic elements, appreciated by the readership. Despite this, the number of books translated from French dropped to about 36 a year (as compared with roughly 150 books a year between the two World Wars).

In the 1960s, the key writings of the French *nouveau roman* were all translated (A. Robbe-Grillet, J. Gracq, A. Pieyre de Mandiargues, J.-M. G. Le Clézio etc.). Works of the Theatre of the Absurd, represented by Ionesco and Beckett, also began to be translated in this period of "a political thaw". Other contemporary authors, especially those of the French existentialism (P. Sartre, A. Camus, S. de Beauvoir), but also B. Vian, appeared in their Czech translations. The only post-war French poet translated into Czech was Jacques Prévert. E. Zola's naturalistic prose supplied the Czech reader with erotic elements, as no other erotic literature (whether "classic" or "pulp") could be published throughout the entire communist period in Czechoslovakia.

---

[7] *Samizdat* (the Russian for "self-published") was the clandestine copying and distribution of government-suppressed literature or other media in the Eastern Bloc countries.

[8] *Folksy*, as it is used here, is synonymous with *rustic, popular* or simply *people's*.

In the 1970s, the normalization ideologists and censors purged the book market of all existentialist literature, plays of the Theatre of the Absurd and all that carried the pejorative title of "formalism" (surrealism, *nouveau roman* etc.). Another factor for the censors was the author's approach to the 1968 occupation of Czechoslovakia. Thus, L. Aragon was excluded from the translated literature for more than fifteen years for his open opposition to the occupation. Only in the late 1980s could such authors as C. Simon, M. Duras, Queneau and many others be translated.

Literature in German (Hrala 2002: 179-184) suffered from a different fact–in the official historiography, the Soviet army liberated Czechoslovakia from the German invaders (at least in 1945).[9] Consequently, German was looked down upon as the language of the invaders, of Hitler, of the Nazis.

Paradoxically, these discriminatory practices were also applied on German-writing authors of Jewish descent, who had been the very victims of the foregoing period. Thus, the so-called "Prague German authors", F. Kafka, M. Brod, E. E. Kisch, F. Werfel and others, were excluded from the Ministry of Culture's publishing programs. Despite this, Kisch (a socialist) and Werfel were the first authors writing in German to be translated into Czech in the late 1940s.

Generally speaking, the literature of the German Democratic Republic was acceptable for Czech censors; the literature of the Federal Republic of Germany, Austria and Switzerland were strictly submitted to censorship. As a result, authors regarded as the classics of the German socialist realism, such as A. Zweig, B. Brecht or L. Renn, were translated into Czech. A. Seghers, W. Bredel, B. Uhse, J. R. Becher, L. Fürnberg, F. Fühmann, and S. Heym were already translated in the 1950s. On the other hand, C. Wolf, J. Becker, G. Kunert and others had to wait longer for their Czech translations. The publication of their books always depended on the extent of their civic "misbehaviour", for instance if they decided to live in the West, like Becker, Kunert, R. Kunze, etc.

After the Soviet invasion of 1968, some authors and translators fell out of favour with the Party ideologists and censors. Ludvík Kundera, a cousin of the *émigré* author Milan Kundera and an excellent translator of Bertolt Brecht into Czech, was one such example. *The Collected Works of Bertolt Brecht* translated into Czech by L. Kundera were ready for print, the censors were unable to find any other (adequate) translator of Brecht, so

---

[9] In reality, West Bohemia (with its capital Pilsen) was liberated by the U. S. American army. Besides, the word "liberated" in this context has been questioned many a time. For instance, Czechoslovakia was offered by the U.S.A., but hindered by the U.S.S.R., to implement the Marshall Plan in 1947.

they decided to print the translations by L. Kundera, but the imprint in the books read *"Translated from German"*, omitting the name of the translator altogether.

Another was the very special case of Franz Kafka. This author was regarded by the Party ideologists as a "bourgeois" author who had nothing to say to today's readers. Not only did he write in German, but his prose was incomplete, unrealistic and it did not come close to anything that could be called socialist realism. Kafka's name had thus become taboo. This situation was only to be changed by the Kafka conference in Liblice in 1963, whose participants were later accused by the East German ideologists of being the "Forerunners of the Counterrevolution". Rather, they included the very "pillars" of the communist literature (Marie Majerová, Anna Seghers etc.). After the 1968 invasion, Kafka became taboo once more. In 1983, one hundred years after Kafka's birth, it had become obvious that Prague, his birthplace, should somehow contribute to this jubilee, as the last Czech edition of Kafka had been published some fifteen years before. Hastily, a collection of Kafka's stories was reedited in such a low number of copies that an average Czech reader had no chance of getting a hold of it anyway. Thus, only the 1990s saw a complete translation of Kafka's works into the Czech language.

West-German, Austrian and Swiss authors were in the same position as the other West European authors. Having opposed the 1968 invasion, such authors as G. Grass, F. Dürrenmatt, M. Frisch, and R. Hochhuth could not appear in a Czech translation. Heinrich Böll came out publicly against the invasion, as he was –by coincidence– lodged directly on the Wenceslas Square in the centre of Prague in August 1968 when Soviet tanks entered Prague to stay for more than two decades. Böll entitled his report symptomatically: *„Der Panzer zielte auf Kafka "* [The tank aimed at Kafka]. Evidently, after the publication of that report, Böll's name automatically entered the black list of forbidden authors.

Literature in Russian (Hrala 2002: 234-239) experienced an unprecedented growth. In the 1950s, Russian classics of the critical realism from N. V. Gogol to A. Chekhov were massively translated and popularized. On the other hand, the Czech readership was acquainted with Russian literature in a politically narrowed profile, as prescribed by the state's cultural policy. Czech readers were supplied with cloying depictions of the rural *kolkhoz* idyll as well as with texts larded with political indoctrination, but of little literary quality.

In the 1960s, with Khrushchev's rise to power, not only Soviet classics, but also Russian modernist and *avant-garde* writers began to be translated in Czechoslovakia. This promising development was, however, disrupted by the 1968 events, not only in translation, but also in all other areas of culture, politics and public life. Once again, in the 1970s due to Brezhnev as in the 1950s due to Stalin, the cold wind from Moscow inhibited all democratic trends in literature. This was only to change in the late 1980s with Gorbachev's liberalizing reforms and the ensuing Velvet Revolution.

Speaking of literature in Spanish (Hrala 2002: 251-257), there was a difference in the treatment of the European Spanish authors, who were in the same position as the other West European authors, and of the Hispanic-American authors, many of whom were communists or at least sympathized with communist ideas.[10] Spanish authors, such as F. G. Lorca, B. Pérez Galdós or V. Blasco Ibáñez, were already translated in the 1950s. In the following decade, J. Goytisolo, C. J. Cela, García Hortelano and A. Machado appeared in their Czech translation. Finally, the 1970s and 1980s saw the Czech translations of M. Delibes, but also, for the first time, of the Spanish *avant-garde* poets.

As for Hispanic-American literature, J. Mancisidor, A. Varela and a few others were already published in the 1950s. The year 1960, then, marked the beginning of a real boom in Hispanic-American literature. A. Carpentier, R. Gallegos, J. Icaza, A. Uslar Pietri, J. Rulfo all appeared in Czech translations. This trend reached its peak in the late 1960s, with R. Bastos, J. Cortázar, C. Fuentes, J. L. Borges and several others translated into Czech. Pablo Neruda[11], the most frequently translated Hispanic-American poet of the 1950s, was joined by M. A. Asturias, R. Darío etc. G. G. Márquez and J. Cortázar began to be translated from 1971 onwards. An anthology of Cuban authors appeared in the mid-1980s.

As regards literature in Portuguese,[12] Brazilian authors outnumbered Portuguese, mainly for political reasons.[13] Despite political discrepancies, around 53 Brazilian and 36 Portuguese books appeared in Czech translations. As for Portuguese authors, G. Eannes de Azurara, G. Vicente, L. de Camões, A. Garrett, Eça de Queirós, M. de Sá Carneiro, J. Rodrigues

---

[10] Although some Hispanic-American authors did sympathize with communism as such, they did not necessarily sympathize with its Soviet version. However, censors often failed to make the distinction between different kinds of communism. All were seen as different ways to *the* Communism.

[11] Pablo Neruda adopted his penname as an allusion to the nineteenth-century Czech writer Jan Neruda.

[12] See the Czech Translators Guild's *Database of the Czech Artistic Translation after 1945*: http://www.obecprekladatelu.cz/ZZPREKLADY/totalportugalstina.htm.

[13] The mother of Juscelino Kubitschek de Oliveira, the president of Brazil from 1956 to 1961, was of Slovak descent.

Miguéis, F. Namora, J. Cardoso Pires, U. Tavares Rodrigues, J. Saramago, and several others were translated into Czech in the given period. Brazilian authors translated into Czech between 1948 and 1989 included J. de Alencar, J. Amado, A. Azevedo, L. Barreto, G. Figueiredo, C. Lispector, Machado de Assis, A. Miranda, L. Bojunga Nunes, Graciliano Ramos, J. Guimarães Rosa, R. Murilo and some others.

4. Censorship in the Czechoslovak theories of translation

Scholars and academics in Czechoslovakia were required to fulfil three basic pre-conditions if they wanted to pursue an academic career:

1. Membership in the Party was an unconditional prerequisite for the academic career.
2. The obligation to quote and draw on Soviet scholars and to venerate their results was self-evident. Nonetheless, it could be, at times, circumvented by a ritual called "libation" whereby the academic would quote the Soviets at the beginning and at the end of his or her academic writing (even if the quotations were not really relevant to his or her own object of study). Thus, the so-called libation must be considered a *norm* of an academic piece of writing in communist Czechoslovakia.
3. Last but not least, scholars engaged in the humanities or social sciences were obliged to apply the principles of the only line of thought permitted, that of socialist realism.

Translation theory was, obviously, confined to the same constraints as the other humanities or social sciences.[14] Thus, the Czechoslovak theory of translation, which emerged in the 1960s, considered the phenomenon of censorship and attempted to account for it. Jiří Levý (1926-67) and Anton Popovič (1933-84) were aware of the political reality around them and could neither ignore nor avoid it in their academic writings. It is thus no accident that these scholars were primarily interested in the theory of *literary* translation. In most communist countries, translators were organized in Writers' Associations. Consequently, research into literature and literary translation was at the centre of attention, contrary to the

---

[14] Perhaps, one example of the impact of politics on the translation practice was the phenomenon of what was termed as "translator couples": a philologist (translator), i.e. somebody who knew the language, and a poet (writer) working closely together, typically when translating poems. This phenomenon was defended theoretically (by many literary critics of the time), but the real reason was that it was the practice in the U.S.S.R.

situation in Western Europe where it was rather technical translation which usually stood in the spotlight of translation scholars and theoreticians.[15]

Having been published for the first time at the end of the Stalinization period, Levý's masterpiece, *Umění překladu* [*The Art of Translation*, 1963], could not possibly contain anything explicit about censorship. Despite that, Levý (1998: 200) makes the following observation:

> (...) – besides the translator, it was often the editors of a periodical, the publisher or other correctors who interfered in the very wording of a translation.[16]

As insignificant as this allusion to censorship may seem today, it was highly dangerous to be so explicit in the early 1960s. Levý is obviously aware of this, for he uses the past tense.

In addition, Levý (1998: 216) uncovers the very principle of censorship when he affirms:

> Translation is, from the point of view of a nation, a factor which increases entropy; from the international viewpoint, it is a factor which reduces entropy.[17]

And entropy, constituting an imminent threat to any totalitarian regime, had to be suppressed, suffocated and exterminated.

Anton Popovič, whose first monograph on translation appeared at the end of the political *détente* (in 1968), could afford to be more explicit. Moreover, as a member of the Communist Party, he also had and widely used the possibility to visit both East and West European colleagues. He met and became acquainted with James Stratton Holmes, Raymond van den Broeck, José Lambert, Itamar Even-Zohar, Gideon Toury, André Lefevere and others.

---

[15] *Literary* here means "pertaining to literature as an art" (i.e. *belles lettres*); *technical* stands for economic, legal etc.

[16] "(...) – a právě do stylizace mnohdy zasahovala kromě překladatele i redakce časopisu či nakladatelství, nebo jiní upravovatelé". See also the German translation (Levý 1969: 160): "(...) – und gerade in die Formulierung oftmals auch die Redaktion der Zeitschrift oder der Verlag oder andere Bearbeiter eingegriffen haben."

[17] "Překlad je z národního hlediska faktor, který entropii zvyšuje, z hlediska mezinárodního faktor, který ji snižuje". See the German translation (Levý 1969: 172): "Die Übersetzung ist vom nationalen Gesichtspunkt ein die Entropie *erhöhender* und vom internationalen ein die Entropie *verringender* Faktor."

Despite his relatively strong position in the Communist Party, Popovič himself could not discuss censorship explicitly. Despite this fact, significant words concerning the issue of censorship (though not naming it as such) can be found in Popovič's monograph *Poetika umeleckého prekladu* [Poetics of Artistic Translation, 1971], and subsequently in his masterpiece, *Teória umeleckého prekladu* [Theory of Artistic Translation, 1975].

Popovič (1975: 69) speaks of the *editor, or adaptor of the final version of the text of the translation* („redaktor, resp. upravovateľ definitívneho znenia textu prekladu"). In Popovič's words, *the editor is the mediating factor between the prevailing language norms and the text of the translation and implements the directives which the publishing institution has adopted under the influence of readers' habits* („Redaktor je totiž sprostredkujúcim faktorom medzi vládnucimi jazykovými normami a textom prekladu a vykonáva direktívy, ktoré si pod vplyvom čitateľských návykov osvojila vydavateľská inštitúcia."). Subsequently, Popovič (1971: 96-98) goes on to define the editor's role as follows:

> (…) in this sense, an editor can even be a "co-author", whether open, announced or anonymous. The position of the editor (…) is, in principle, threefold:
> 1. the editor is in a position "independent" of the literary norm of the time, he tries to surpass it
> 2. the editor identifies himself with the prevailing, dominant literary and language norm and is, in fact, its implementer
> 3. the editor sensitively balances the translator's text and the normative requirements of the given literary epoch[18]

In this context, Popovič speaks of what he calls "praxeology" within the study of translation. Popovič's praxeology of translation (1975: 20) incorporates the following sub-disciplines:

---

[18] (…) v tomto zmysle môže byť redaktor aj "spoluautorom", či už zjavným, ohláseným, alebo anonymným. Pozícia redaktora (...) je, v princípe, trojaká:
1. redaktor je „v nezávislej" pozícii voči súvekej literárnej norme, usiluje sa ju predbehnúť
2. redaktor sa stotožňuje s prevládajúcou, dominantnou literárnou a jazykovou normou a je vlastne jej vykonávateľom
3. redaktor citlivo vyrovnáva prekladateľov text s normatívnymi požiadavkami príslušnej literárnej epochy

a) Sociology of translation
b) Editorial practice
c) Methodology of the translation criticism[19]

Translation praxeology according to Popovič (1975: 239-240) encompasses:

1) the influence of the cultural policy (the principle of the Party line) on the translation program and translation practice
2) the analysis of the translation program from the viewpoint of the book market
3) specific functions of the criticism of artistic translation
4) the participation of the editor in the translation process
5) history of translation institutions (organizations and periodicals)
6) didactics of translation: teaching translators, school system for translators, translators' aids (dictionaries, stylistics manuals, measures against substandard translations, the issue of translation couples as a social and didactic problem)[20]

Methods of research for translation praxeology include (Popovič 1975: 240):

a) communicational aspects
b) theory of information
c) sociometrics
d) literary sociology
e) teaching theory
f) theory of culture[21]

---

[19] a) Sociológia prekladu
 b) Redakčná prax
 c) Metodológia kritiky prekladu

[20] 1) vplyv kultúrnej politiky (princíp straníckosti) na prekladateľský program a prekladateľské podnikanie
 2) analýza prekladateľského programu z aspektov knižného trhu
 3) špecifické funkcie kritiky umeleckého prekladu
 4) účasť redaktora na tvorbe prekladateľského textu
 5) dejiny prekladateľských inštitúcií (organizácií a časopisov)
 6) didaktika prekladu: výchova prekladateľov, prekladateľské školstvo, prekladateľské pomôcky – slovníky a štylistické príručky, opatrenia proti substandardnému prekladu a napokon otázka prekladateľských dvojíc ako sociálny a didaktický problém

[21] a) komunikačné aspekty
 b) teória informácie
 c) sociometria

This shows that both cultural and sociological aspects were included, taking into account –as a matter of course– the role of the editor, and thus, indirectly, censorship. Popovič (1975: 70) is very explicit about the role of the editor:

> The editor's manipulation with the text is, in fact, his tendentious rewriting. It is, in fact, a kind of meta-communication which originates, even if the editor "needn't" interfere in the original, or the translated text. By approving of it, he *de facto* rewrites it tendentiously.[22]

It is a wonder that such words were published in 1975, ten years before Gorbachev's *perestroika*.

5. Conclusion

From the viewpoint of censorship, as it was applied to translations, the 1950s were a very strict period, in which only politically "conforming" literature could appear. Despite this fact, a large number of West European and American authors found their translations into Czech and Slovak in this decade. The (late) 1960s saw an almost complete democratization of the book market, with censorship being lifted and political constraints removed temporarily. Unlike the previous period, the 1970s marked a period of utmost rigidity, very strict censorship policies and an almost complete isolation from the occidental world. Towards the end of the 1980s, this rigidity was gradually relaxed, but political and cultural isolation continued more or less until 1989.

Jiří Levý and Anton Popovič, constrained though they were by the political situation, dared to speak about the issue of censorship and to include it in their theories of (literary) translation. This, simultaneously, shows that their theories were no abstract constructs lifted out of practice, which would have nothing to convey to us today, but rather reflections of the everyday reality of translation, supported by extensive empirical material. As such, they have remained topical and instructive to date.

---

d) literárna sociológia
e) teória vyučovania
f) teória kultúry

[22] Redaktorovo manipulovanie s textom je vlastne jeho tendenčným prepisom. To je vlastne už metakomunikát, ktorý vzniká aj vtedy, keď redaktor „nemusí" zasahovať do pôvodného resp. prekladového textu. Tým že ho aprobuje, de facto „tendenčne prepisuje".

Both Levý and Popovič treat the phenomenon of censorship in their theories of translation as an implicit potentiality–comprehensible by anyone capable of reading between the lines. This, at the same time, is another example of self-censorship– not only in individual translations, but also in translation theory.

References

Hrala, Milan, et al. (2002) *Kapitoly z dějin českého překladu* [Chapters in the History of Czech Translation], 1st edition, Praha: Karolinum.

Levý, Jiří (1963/1983/1998) *Umění překladu* [The Art of Translation], 3rd edition, Praha: Ivo Železný.

—. (1969) *Die literarische Übersetzung – Theorie einer Kunstgattung* [The Literary Translation – Theory of a Genre], 1. Auflage, Frankfurt–Bonn: Athenäum.

Popovič, Anton (1968) *Preklad a výraz* [Translation and Expression], 1st edition, Bratislava: Vydavateľstvo Slovenskej akadémie vied.

—. (1971) *Poetika umeleckého prekladu. Proces a text* [Poetics of Artistic Translation: Process and Text], 1st edition, Bratislava: Tatran.

—. (1975) *Teória umeleckého prekladu: Aspekty textu a literárnej metakomunikácie* [Theory of Artistic Translation: Aspects of Text and Literary Metacommunication], 1st edition, Bratislava: Tatran.

UNESCO *Index Translationum*. Bibliographic Search.
http://databases.unesco.org/xtrans/xtra-form.shtml (May 30, 2007)

Obec překladatelů [Czech Translators' Guild]. *Databáze českého uměleckého překladu po roce 1945. Portugalská jazyková oblast. Překlady.* [Database of the Czech Artistic Translation after 1945. The Portuguese-Speaking Area: Translations.]
http://www.obecprekladatelu.cz/ZZPREKLADY/totalportugalstina.htm (May 30, 2007)

CENSORSHIP IN TRANSLATION AND TRANSLATION STUDIES IN PRESENT-DAY CHINA

NAM FUNG CHANG,
LINGNAN UNIVERSITY - HONG KONG, CHINA

Abstract: In present-day China explicit description of sex and sensitive political issues are the two main forbidden zones in the publication sector and the media, including published translations. Censorship may take several forms besides deletion, such as attenuation, mis-translation, denouncement in the text, the title or the preface, and disclaimer. In the few cases where information about the publication process is available, it is mainly the editors who act as the censors. Generally speaking, faithfulness is the norm that translators adhere to as best as they can, and it is also the expectancy norms of readers. However, this translational norm is overruled by ideological norms for editors, the reason being that it is usually the publishing houses, not the translators, who are penalized for their "errors".

To talk about such censorship in the People's Republic of China is not allowed either. Containing such material, a chapter in a book of mine has been deleted by the editor of a university press in Beijing in 2004.

Recent developments seem to indict that while political and ideological dissidence is still forbidden, control over descriptions of sex is relaxing.

1. What is censored?

In present-day China, there are things that one is not allowed to write about, no matter whether in literary works, academic papers, or translations. In the first three decades after the founding of the People's Republic in 1949, since publication was planned by the central government, there was no overt censorship, especially in the field of translation, since source texts that were considered to have problems would not have been selected in the first place.

After the death of Mao Zedong in 1976, the country's door was gradually opened to the outside world, limited freedom of speech and of publication was granted to the people, and elements of market economy were gradually introduced. Publishing houses, newspapers and journals are still mostly owned and run by the state, but their production is no longer centrally planned, and power has been delegated to these establishments themselves to make the day-to-day decisions on what is to go to press. In the market-oriented economy of the present day, as staff members are given bonuses partly in proportion to the size of the profit, competition has grown fierce in the publishing industry, and public opinion and reading preference have become influential.

The state has loosened, but has never totally let go of, its grip on ideological matters in the publishing sector. In the past three decades forbidden zones lay mainly in two broad areas: anti-Marxist and anti-China sentiments and explicit descriptions of sex. Thus, the need for overt censorship arose. In the Spring of 1989, an editor of literary translation (who asked not to be identified) gave some pieces of advice to would-be translators during a guest lecture at a university in China. While insisting that "faithfulness, including the integrity of the translation, is indeed the target of a true translator", he warned, "any parts of a work that are in serious conflict with the 'conditions' of our country must be diluted or deleted; otherwise it will be difficult for the translation to be published, and it will be banned even if it is published" (Anonymous Editor 1989: 10). It would be very unlikely that he would take the risk to say even that if his lecture had been delivered a few months later, after the crackdown on Tiananmen Square on June 4.

In this paper examples will be drawn mainly from Hillary Clinton's *Living History*, Mandla Langa's short story "A Gathering of Bald Men", Vladimir Nabokov's *Lolita*, and David Lodge's *Small World*.

2. How are texts censored?

The most common way to "sanitize" a text is, of course, to delete the parts deemed to be nocuous. Being critical of China's human rights record, Hillary Clinton's memoirs *Living History* has been extensively expurgated in its Chinese translation published in mainland China. In the following passage the parts in bold type are deleted in the translation, except that "human rights groups, Chinese American activists" in the second paragraph is simplified into "various groups".

Ex. 1
The arrest of **a dissident is not unusual in China, and** Harry Wu's **imprisonment** might have received scant attention in the American media. But China had been chosen to host the upcoming United Nations Fourth

World Conference on Women, and I was scheduled to attend as honorary Chair of the U.S. delegation. Wu, **a human rights activist who had spent nineteen years as a political prisoner in Chinese labor camps before emigrating to the United States, was arrested by Chinese authorities on June 19, 1995, as he entered Xinjiang Province from neighboring Kazakhstan.**

Although he had a valid visa to visit China, he was charged with espionage and thrown in jail to await trial. **Overnight, Harry Wu became widely known,** and U.S. participation in the women's conference was cast into doubt as **human rights groups, Chinese American activists** and some members of Congress urged our nation to boycott. I sympathized with their cause, but it disappointed me that, once again, the crucial concerns of women might be sacrificed.

(...)

(...) The Vatican, vociferous on the subject of abortion, joined forces with some **Islamic** countries concerned that the conference would become an international platform to promote the women's rights they opposed. **And some on the American political left were unhappy about the prospect of U.S. participation because the Chinese government was indicating that non-governmental organizations (NGOs) advocating maternal health, property rights for women, microfinance and many other issues might be excluded from the official gathering. Chinese authorities made it difficult for Tibetan activists and others to get visas to enter China. Furthermore, there was widespread discomfort, which I shared, about the host nation's dismal record on human rights and its barbaric policy of condoning forced abortions as a means of imposing its "one child policy".**

(...)

I was particularly troubled by a personal letter from Mrs. Wu, who was understandably worried about her husband's fate and felt that my participation in the conference "would be sending a confused signal to the leaders in Beijing about the resolve of the U.S. to press for Harry's release."

It was a legitimate concern for me and for others in the White House and State Department. I knew the Chinese government wanted to use the conference as a public relations tool to improve its image around the world. If I went, I helped China look good. If I boycotted, I triggered bad publicity for the Chinese leadership. We were in a diplomatic bind in which Harry Wu's imprisonment and my attendance at the conference were linked. Our government continued to state privately and publicly that I would not attend if Mr. Wu remained under arrest. When the disagreements became more vehement and resolution seemed unlikely, I considered going anyway, as a private citizen.

Complicating the decision were equally serious concerns about the overall status of U.S.-China relations. Tensions were running high over disagreements about Taiwan, nuclear proliferation, China's sale of M-11 missiles to Pakistan and ongoing human rights abuses. Relations deteriorated even further in mid-August when the Chinese engaged in the bravado of military exercises in the Taiwan Straits.

Less than a month before the start of the conference, the Chinese government evidently decided that it couldn't afford to generate more bad publicity. In a sham trial in Wuhan on August 24, a Chinese court convicted Harry Wu of spying and expelled him from the country. Some media commentators, and Wu himself, were convinced that the United States had made a political deal with the Chinese: Wu would be released, but only if I agreed to come to the conference and refrain from critical remarks about the host government. Clearly it was a delicate diplomatic moment, but there was never a quid pro quo between our government and China. Once the Wu case was resolved, the White House and State Department determined that I should make the trip.

Back home in California, Mr. Wu criticized my decision, reiterating that my attendance might be construed as a tacit approval of China's record on human rights. His Congresswoman, Nancy Pelosi, called to tell me that my presence would be a public relations coup for the Chinese. Bill and I were vacationing in Jackson Hole, Wyoming, and we discussed at length the pros and cons. He supported my view that once Wu had been released, the best way to confront the Chinese about human rights was directly, on their turf. At an event in Wyoming celebrating the seventy-fifth anniversary of America's constitutional amendment extending to women the right to vote, Bill defused the issue and defended U.S. participation as important for women's rights. His message was: "The conference presents a significant chance to chart further gains in the status of women."

(Clinton 2003: 298-301. Emphasis added. Translation: Clinton 2003a: 263-264)

If the passage quoted above is sanitized for obvious reasons, some works that might seem rather harmless have met the same fate. In a Chinese translation of "A Gathering of Bald Men", a short story by South African writer Mandla Langa, who served the African National Congress for fifteen years as an editor, speechwriter, and cultural Attaché to the United Kingdom and Ireland, four passages have disappeared in the published version although they are there in the translator's manuscript. It will suffice to cite two of them here.

Ex. 2

As he drove along Empire Road, he cast around in his mind for famous men who were bald. There was Winston Churchill: *It will be long, it will be hard, and there will be no withdrawal.* That was a classic piece, and Churchill was regarded as a sex symbol. Gandhi? Well, Gandhi was famous for other things, his glasses and the *dhoti*, he couldn't go that far; nor could he imagine South Africans following a leader who wore nappies.

[...] **Was Hitler bald, or did he wear a hairpiece?** [...] **If President Mandela were bald, maybe that would even the equation, lots of men like Caleb would walk with their heads held high. That De Klerk was no longer the top dog merely made matters worse. It made his baldness seem like a weakness.** (Langa 1996: 122. Emphasis added. Translation: Langa 1997: 129; manuscript: 9-10)

It seems safe to assume that the passages in bold type have been deleted also for political reasons. The joke about Mandela will probably not be taken as offensive in the source culture, not even to Mandela himself. But it may be incompatible with target culture norms in two respects. First, Mandela was then the leader of a friendly country, and has been regarded by the official ideology in China as a comrade in the fight against imperialism and colonialism, and therefore he is not to be joked about, especially not to be mentioned in the same breath with Hitler. In this regard it may be worth noting that the Chinese translation is published in 1997, the year when South Africa severed ties with Taiwan and established diplomatic relations with the People's Republic of China. Secondly, in the target culture the Confucian code of conduct forbids laughing at the sovereign, or at one's parents, superiors, teachers or seniors (Hu 1987: 32). To make joke of a "good" foreign leader, even in a translation, may set an undesirable example for target readers.

Ex. 3

In her line of work, she was duty bound to counsel the staffers on the hazards of casual sex. Even though she had been thoroughly grounded in the workings of the dread disease [AIDS], and how it could be contracted, she couldn't quite see herself telling a man to wear a condom. She had once tried one on herself and quickly discarded it. It had felt as if she were walking with a Checker's rustly carrier bag between her legs. So, no extra-marital *fickie-fickie*, as one of TransStar's more brazen Arabic customers would say. (Langa 1996: 126; translation: Langa 1997: 134; manuscript 36)

This passage has apparently touched on a moral taboo: extra- and/or pre-marital sex. In fact, literary works, translated or otherwise, that contain vivid or explicit descriptions of sex could seldom be published uncensored until the early 2000s. It was only in 2004 that the first full translation of Vladimir Nabokov's *Lolita* was put out, after about ten abridged versions had been produced in recent years (*Xinwen Wu Bao* 2006). And D. H. Lawrence's *Lady Chatterley's Lover* still has had no full translation published after 1949.

In the past decade about five of David Lodge's novels have been translated, but, except in the latest translation, explicit descriptions of sex have been bowdlerized to a great extent. Besides the usual method of outright deletion, what may be called the strategy of "attenuation", that is, the "replacement, on ideological grounds, of something 'too strong' or in any way unacceptable, by something 'softer'" (Aixelá 1996: 64), is sometimes employed, as in the following two questions that Fulvia Morgana puts to Morris Zapp in *Small World*:

> Ex. 4
> "Is it really twenty-five centimetres?" (Lodge 1985: 134)
> "Ni de xingyu zhende feichang qiang ma?" [Is your sexual desire really very strong?] (Lodge 1996: 154)

> Ex. 5
> "Didn't you make your wife measure it with her tape measure?" (Lodge 1985: 135)
> "Ni meiyou baonüe guo ni de qizi ma?" [Have you never violated your wife?] (Lodge 1996: 154)

Another occasionally used method is denouncement of what is deemed problematic. This is made either intra-textually, that is, in the text proper or the title of the translated work, or extra-textually, such as in the preface or the postscript. In the translator's manuscript of Example 3, "casual sex" is rendered as "yinluan" [promiscuity] and "more brazen" into "gengjia houyan wuchi" [even more impudent and shameless]; thus a tone of moral indignation is superimposed upon the narration, but the censor apparently still finds the passage unacceptable. And in two translations of *Lolita*, the title is extended to become *Luolita: yige zhongnian nanzi yu shaonü de jilian* [Lolita: A Middle-aged Man's Abnormal Love with a Young Girl] (Nabokov 1989), and *Duoluo yu bingtai de ai: Luolita* [Depraved and Morbid Love: Lolita] (Nabokov 1989a) respectively.

3. Who are the censors?

According to my informants, it is usually the editorial staff who act as the censors. The anonymous editor mentioned at the beginning of this paper was responsible for the first vetting of the Chinese translation of "A Gathering of Bald Men". He supplied me with a photocopy of the translator's hand-written manuscript to prove that the paragraphs deleted from the published version had been there, and he told me that a senior editor who did the second vetting removed them because he did not want any potential trouble to put his pension at risk as he was near retirement age.

In reply to my enquiry, the translator of *Small World*, a professor of English, also told me in an email that it was the editors who made the expurgations. He said, "I myself am always sorry and angry when I know some of the passages and sentences are deleted or distorted. I can do nothing about it but complaining [*sic*]."

It is common knowledge in China that editors usually assume the duty of revising translated texts, sometimes without checking the source text, and sometimes without consulting or even informing the translator, depending on the power relations between the two parties.

But the translator occasionally takes on the duty of the censor. The translator of probably the fullest version of *Lady Chatterley's Lover* translated and published in the People's Republic, Zhao Susu, admits in his "Translator's Postscript" that "a few passages containing descriptions of sex have been subjected to appropriate dilution and technical treatment" (Zhao 2004: 390).

4. Do they admit to the censorship?

Sometimes producers do admit to having made changes to the text, though probably very briefly in an obscure place in the book, such as the "Translator's Postscript" mentioned above, and probably not to the full extent. However, in most cases, such as "A Gathering of Bald Men" and *Living History*, there is no indication of any kind. After the expungements in the Chinese version of *Living History* were widely reported in the media outside mainland China, the Editor-in-Chief of the publishing house Yilin [Forest of Translations]–belonging to the same group with the magazine that published "A Gathering of Bald Men"–insisted that, instead of large-scale censorship, only "minor technical treatments", amounting to "sporadic modifications in a span totalling ten pages", have been applied to the work for its "better reception by the reader", and he denied the alleged existence of "political pressure" "from above", claiming that the publishing work of the house was independent (*Ta Kung Pao* 2003; *Wen Wei Po* 2003).

The two Chinese versions of *Lolita* that I have access to are not marked as abridged versions either. However, the reading public seemed to know that for such works abridgement was the usual case: the version published in 2004 has to be marked as "the first full translation".

What is most interesting is the Chinese version of *Small World* mentioned above. There is a paragraph in the "Publisher's Notes" that declares:

> The work contains a lot of arguments about academic theory and literary criticism, and some descriptions of sex. These descriptions of sex cannot be deleted because their use is inseparable from the author's exposition of his views on literary theory. (Lodge 1996: n.p. My translation)

In spite of this statement, however, one can find that although some descriptions of sex do remain, at least twenty passages have been deleted or diluted. Deletions are occasionally marked by ellipsis dots (e.g., Lodge 1996: 107, 190) or by notes in brackets such as "some slight deletions here and below" (Lodge 1996: 181), but all the instances of attenuation and most of the deletions are unmarked.

5. The mechanism of censorship

In China there is no mechanism for pre-publication censorship so far as publications on paper are concerned. State control is exercised through post-publication censorship. A book or the entire issue of a magazine that is deemed to have gone beyond the bounds may be banned, resulting in heavy economic losses for the publisher. In more serious cases, members of the editorial staff held responsible for the "mistake" may be dismissed, and the whole house or magazine may be closed down, such as Hunan People's Publishing House, after it reprinted in 1986 a translation of *Lady Chatterley's Lover* that was first published in the 1930s, which may serve to indicate that there was more freedom of publication in China in the first half of the twentieth century under the rule of the Kuomintang [the Nationalist Party]. Meanwhile, literary translators and writers seem to have seldom been penalized by the state in recent decades, since they mostly work freelance. Generally speaking, the only thing they may lose is their translation fee.

Thus the system of post-publication censorship has induced pre-publication self-censorship by editors. Publishers are working under a double tension, trying on the one hand to maximize profits by catering to the tastes of the reading public, which are often in conflict with the official concept of "healthiness", and on the other to stay within the bounds allowed by the authorities. In other words, publishers of translated works are trying to reach equilibrium in the interplay of various socio-cultural factors, such as the dominant translational norms of completeness and faithfulness; the market economic norms of profit-making; the ideology of the consumers, backed up by their economic power; and the official ideology, backed up by the power of the state.

It is interesting to note that state-owned publishing houses are competing not just among themselves, but also with illegal private enterprises selling their products in "underground" bookstalls. When a book is banned from licensed bookshops, pirated or stolen copies are often available elsewhere. Thus, after the unsold copies of *Lady Chatterley's Lover* were confiscated in 1986, some of them found their way into the black market (see Schell 1988: 323). The existence of a black market may also have contributed to the publication of a Chinese translation of *Living History* by a state-owned publishing house in spite of its problematic content. Taiwan was going to publish its own translation anyway, and, according to the Editor-in-Chief of Yilin, if the mainland version was to be published later than the Taiwan version, pirated copies of the latter were bound to appear (*Ta Kung Pao* 2003: A02). That would do more harm than making a sanitized version available in legal bookshops from the point of view of the authorities, because the "anti-China" sentiments would be kept by all means in the Taiwan version.

It is under such circumstances that politically or morally sensitive works, such as *Living History*, *Lolita*, and *Small World*, have been translated and published. The sanitization may be said to be a trade-off among these factors: it gains the tolerance of the authorities but loses part of the profit as the result of a lower level of customer satisfaction. However, some editorial strategies may kill two birds with one stone, so to speak. The extended titles of the two versions of *Lolita* mentioned above may have been designed not just to denounce what may be deemed problematic so as to appease government officials, but also to arouse the interest of readers.

Besides ostensible denouncement, defence of a controversial work may have the same double effect. A synopsis on a flyleaf of the Chinese version of *Small World* mentioned above asserts,

> Just as the great works of certain very serious, famous western writers have been misread as pornography, *Small World*, with some descriptions of sex and the frequent use of sex language, may give rise to the same misunderstanding. However, readers with just a little bit of culture will be able to see its true value and meaning. (My translation)

The statement seems to have been intended not only to preempt the official critic, but also to draw the attention of the reader to the "spicy" content of the novel. Although a large number of passages were actually deleted or diluted, the publisher was already taking an enormous risk. There being no clear guidelines as to what can and what cannot be published, and the political weather being so changeable, what gets censored varies with the time and depends heavily on the judgement of the editors. An editor with a less venturous spirit, such as the second editor of "A Gathering of Bald Men", would probably have deleted the whole work.

6. Can one talk about censorship?

The very purpose of censorship is to withhold information. To allow people to talk about it will defeat that very purpose. I have a book published in 2004 by Tsinghua University Press in Beijing. The title is *Zhong xi yixue piping* [Criticism of Chinese and Western Translation Theories]. It is an academic work, published by an academic press. One of the chapters is a case study of the Chinese translation of *Small World*, using Polysystem Theory as the theoretical framework, and it contains Examples 4-5 cited above. Another chapter discusses Chinese translation tradition in general and has a section on ideological manipulation in translation, citing examples from *Living History*, "A Gathering of Bald Men" and some other works, such as Examples 1-3 in this paper. The former chapter has slipped through the hand of the editor, but the latter is deleted. I have asked a couple of translation scholars in China whether the editor is being over-cautious, and all of them are of the opinion that such examples cannot be published.

Both chapters have touched on censorship. The only difference between them is that one is about censorship of explicit descriptions of sex, and the other is about political censorship.

7. Prospects

The different fates of the two chapters in my book may serve as an indicator of a trend, which is that while control over political and ideological matters remains very tight, control over descriptions of sex is relaxing.

The publication of the first unabridged translation of *Lolita* in 2004 has triggered some debates, but the view that a full translation of such a work will not make much difference since works containing much more explicit descriptions of sex are widely available in bookshops and on the Internet anyway (*Xinwen Wu Bao* 2006) seems to be gaining ground. The year 2007 saw the publication of a full version of *Small World* (Lodge 2007), in which all the passages containing descriptions of sex have been kept intact.

On the other hand, remaining intolerant of political dissention, the Chinese government is still keeping a wary eye on the media, including the Internet, for troublemakers. Journalists and webmasters have been arrested and even sent to jail for being critical of the government or even just for reporting the spread of Aids. One can say that such high-handedness reflects a sense of insecurity, but there may be more to it. Under present circumstances the effect of dissenting voices can only be symbolic. It can at most pose a challenge to the official mirage of harmony and stability, causing the authorities to lose face, but in Chinese culture "face" is all-important, especially for those in power. It seems therefore that political control is unlikely to loosen up in the foreseeable future.

References

Primary sources

Clinton, Hillary Rodham (2003) *Living History*, New York: Simon and Schuster.
—. (2003) *Qinli lishi: Xilali huiyilu* [History Experienced in Person: Memoirs of Hillary] (translated by Pan Xun et al.), Nanjing: Yilin chubanshe.
Langa, Mandla (1996) "A Gathering of Bald Men", in *World Literature Today*, 1: 121-128.
—. (1997) "Tu le ding de nanren" [Bald Men] (translated by Wen Wei), *Yilin*: 4: 127-136.
Lodge, David (1985) *Small World: An Academic Romance*. Harmondsworth: Penguin.
—. (1996) *Xiao shijie: xuezhe luomansi* [Small world: The Romance of an Academic] (translated by Luo Yirong). Chongqing: Chongqing chubanshe.
—. (2007) *Xiao shijie* [Small world] (translated by Wang Jiaxiang), Shanghai: Shanghai yiwen chubanshe.
Nabokov, Vladimir Vladimirovich (1989) *Duoluo yu bingtai de ai: Luolita* [Depraved and Morbid Love: Lolita] (translated by Hua Ming and Ren Shengming), Shijiazhuang: Hebei renmin chubanshe.
—. (1989) *Luolita: yige zhongnian nanzi yu shaonü de jilian* [Lolita: A Middle-Aged Man's Abnormal Love with a Young Girl] (translated by Mai Shui), Shenzhen: Haitian chubanshe.
Zhao Susu (2004) "Yi hou ji" [Translator's Postscript], in *Chatelai furen*

de qingren [Lady Chatterley's Lover], (written by D. H. Lawrence, translated by Zhao Susu), Beijing: Renmin wenxue chubanshe, 384-391.

Secondary sources

Aixelá, Javier Franco (1996) "Culture-Specific Items in Translation", in Román Álvarez & M. Carmen-África Vidal (eds.) *Translation, Power, Subversion*, Clevedon: Multilingual Matters, 52-78.

Anonymous Editor (1989) "Zhongguo fanyi chuban xianzhuang" [The Current State of Affairs in the Translating-publishing Sector in China] (manuscript of a lecture delivered at a university in China in the spring of 1989).

Chang Nam Fung (2004) *Zhong xi yixue piping* [Criticism of Chinese and Western Translation Theories], Beijing: Tsinghua University Press.

Hu Fanzhu (1987) *Youmo yuyanxue* [Linguistics of Humour], Shanghai: Shanghai Academy of Social Sciences Press.

Schell, Orville (1988) Discos and Democracy: China in the Throes of Reform, New York: Pantheon Books.

Ta Kung Pao (2003) "Jiu Xilali zizhuan Zhongwenban 'shanjie' fengbo zuo chengqing Yilin chubanshe: jin zuo weixiao jishu chuli caiyong Taiwan yiben bing wu shou 'zhengzhi yali" [Clarifying the "Expurgations" Issue of the Chinese Version of Hillary's Autobiography, Yilin Press: Minor Technical Treatments Only; No "Political Pressure" on the Use of Taiwan's Translation], A02. 26 September.

Wen Wei Po (2003) "'Yilin' xiang Xilali zhiqian" [Yilin Apologizes to Hillary]. A05. 27 September.

Xinwen Wu Bao (2006) "Quan yiben *Luolita* chuban yinfa shehui yousi" [The Publication of a Full Translation of *Lolita* Raises Social Concern]. Available online *http://big5.xinhuanet.com/gate/big5/news3.xinhuanet.com/book/2006-01/19/content_4071530.htm. 19 January 2006.*

LANGUAGE PLANNING IN TURKEY: A SOURCE OF CENSORSHIP ON TRANSLATION

HILAL ERKAZANCI,
HACETTEPE UNIVERSITY – ANKARA, TURKEY

Abstract: Although it is significant to see how language planning is projected onto such specific domains as translation (Blommaert 1999: 30), "translation is assigned very little room if any at all" in the discussions of language planning (Toury 1999). To bridge this gap, this paper aims to show how the ideologies of standardization and purism which are inextricably bound up with the discourses on language, i.e. metalinguistic discourses, act as a source of censoring apparatus for the translators. Placing language ideologies within the specific context of Turkish, the present paper argues that the public discourses on purism and standardization impose censorship on the Turkish translators who have thus been systematically standardising the heteroglossic source texts where non-standard varieties become the expression of imagined sub-national communities. Citing various (non)official discourses on correct, i.e. standard, Turkish, this paper notes that censorship can be imposed on translations in such a mystified or naturalised way that it does not appear as censorship at all. The paper further argues that in such countries as Turkey where standardization is circulated through discourses as commonsensical, the taken-for-grantedness of standardization leads the translators to develop a linguistic habitus. That is, standardization is internalised by the translators who may then initiate self-censorship. In this way, standardization which is at first an external governing force becomes an internal governing agent. As time passes, the translators' linguistic habitus becomes a set of automatic responses that guides their decision-making process towards the politically correct linguistic choices. This paper concludes that in such cases where censorship is implicitly spoken in the practical use of language and is hidden from the public consciousness, it is necessary to engage with a critical-linguistic approach to translation by piercing the opacity of censorship.

1. Introduction

Censorship on translation can be explored in two main categories: (i) transparent censorship which is associated with the explicit suppression of information, and (ii) opaque or naturalized censorship which remains implicit and is hidden from the public consciousness. Focusing on the second category of censorship, this article seeks to explore the situation of the Turkish translations where the tendency of repressing heteroglossia which is experienced not in the form of official censorship but in the form self-censorship is implicit and taken-for-granted. Hence, the present article first looks at the concept of heteroglossic texts where non-standard language varieties become the expression of imagined sub-national communities. Then follows the second part which focuses on why the Turkish translators systematically engage with self-censorship by exposing heteroglossic texts to linguistic purism and standardization. Thirdly, the article aims to show that the ideologies of standardization and purism which are inextricably bound up with the discourses on language, i.e. metalinguistic discourses, act as a source of censoring apparatus for the translators. The last part is devoted to a brief conclusion which summarizes the key points discussed throughout this study.

2. Standard language versus heteroglossia

Standard language, or in Bourdieu's (1991: 53) words, "langue légitime" (i.e. legitimate language) is a system of linguistic norms which are the forces that endeavour to overpower the varieties of language, forces that "unite and centralize verbal-ideological thought, creating the firm, stable linguistic nucleus of an officially recognized literary language" (Bakhtin 2001: 270). To ensure the dominance of standard language, linguistic norms are imposed on all members of the same language community such that "all linguistic practices are measured against the legitimate practices" (Bourdieu 1991: 53).

On the other hand, heteroglossia is a kind of variation in standard language, i.e. legitimate language. Heteroglossia is potentially subversive because it serves to create a tension-filled dialogue with "the unity of the reigning (…) literary language, the 'correct language'" (Bakhtin 1981: 668). It is particularly this ideological aspect which attaches a critical role to heteroglossia. Every heteroglossic work implies that "[a]longside verbal-ideological centralization and unification, the uninterrupted processes of decentralization and disunification also go forward" (Bakhtin 2001: 272).

Standard language always represents the power centre of society, while heteroglossia maintains positions in the social hierarchy. Therefore, literary heteroglossia is "not merely heteroglossia vis-à-vis the accepted literary language, that is, vis-à-vis the linguistic centre of the verbal ideological life of the nation and epoch"; but is "heteroglossia consciously opposed to this literary language" (Bakhtin 2001: 275, 279). Being "parodic and aimed sharply and polemically against the official language of its given time" (Bakhtin 2001: 272), literary heteroglossia intervenes in "a linguistic conjuncture by exposing the contradictory conditions of the standard dialect, the literary canon, the dominant culture, the major language" (Venuti 1998: 10). This is why censorship is imposed on heteroglossia in some societies by the translators who have internalized the standard-language norms and use them as, what Toury (1995: 278) calls, a "constant monitoring device".

With these points in mind, it is significant to note that literary heteroglossia has been systematically standardized in Turkish translations. It is also important to underline that although there are several dialects of Turkish, the instances of heteroglossic writing are rare in Turkish literature; and the dialect markers in those instances are very limited. At this point, it is necessary to ask (i) where the tradition of standardization came from, and (ii) which social reasons might have prompted its formation and given it its ideological pride of place in Turkey.

3. Language planning in Turkey

Turkey has long experienced language planning in the form of linguistic purism and standardization. Purism (i) consists of "considering one type of a given dialect as 'purer' than, and therefore, 'superior' to other types" (Hall 1942: 4); (ii) is a set of views governing the cultivation of the literary language in line with an ideal model of a pure language (Hall 1942: 4); (iii) comprises "different forms of language cultivation and language planning, which have the common aim of ridding (…) a language of, or keeping it free from, foreign influences" (Gerdener 1986: 20).

Although it is significant to see how the censoring effect of purism and standardization is projected onto such specific domains as translation (Blommaert 1999: 30), "translation is assigned very little room if any at all" in the discussions of language planning (Toury 1999). To bridge this gap, this section aims to show the influences of language planning on the Turkish translations of heteroglossia. In Turkey, language planning has been systematically carried out by the dissemination of the discourses which prescribe how language should be used. Turkey is a democratic country where we can observe freedom of expression, but "even the freest of nations seem to find some form(s) of censorship necessary; as such censorship is not limited to oppressive autocracies" (Merkle 2002). What is common to all social organization, whether democratic or not, is the control of discourse which ends up with more or less manipulatory effects on translators' linguistic practice.

Language ideologies of society can be found both in that society's linguistic practice itself and in statements about language, that is, in Woolard's (1998: 9) words, in "metalinguistic discourse[s]". Metalinguistic discourses may impose censorship on translations by

- rationalizing the doctrines of "linguistic correctness and incorrectness" in society (Woolard 1998: 21), and
- linking such doctrines to "doctrines of inherent representational power, beauty, and expressiveness of language as a valued mode of acquisition" (Woolard 1998: 21).

In this respect, metalinguistic discourses are "manifestations of deeply ingrained ideological positions and beliefs" (Milroy 2001: 538). These discourses prescribe legitimate language practices since they are sets of sanctioned statements which can exert a considerable influence on the way people (e.g. translators) act and think. This prescription is not, however, an explicit coercive mechanism but implicit self-censorship which makes people such as translators internalize the discourses on language and develop a particular habitus in line with language planning. As time passes, the translators' linguistic habitus becomes a set of automatic responses that guides their decision-making process towards the politically correct linguistic choices.

4. Metalinguistic discourses on standard Turkish

Implicit censorship on translation is often maintained by the control over public discourse. Therefore, discourse is an opaque power object in modern societies. This section intends to make the opaque motivations underlying the discourses on standard Turkish more visible in order to explore the systematic tendency of the Turkish translators towards repressing language variation. Discourse on language policies has always been one of the most sensitive issues in Turkish society. According to Law No. 2876, the Turkish Language Association should function to

develop Turkish as a unifying and integrating bridge between generations, to raise the awareness and love of Turkish, to take measures to protect and cultivate it, and to publicize those measures, by using every kind of means, for the attention of public organs and organizations, of official and private education departments, and of publishing and broadcasting institutions, to ask for their cooperation for the development of the Turkish language (my emphasis).[1]

The discourse on cultivating Turkish "as a unifying and integrating" medium clearly shows the approach of the Turkish Language Association to standard language. Language cultivation strengthens the normative force of norms by reinforcing the standard. By the same token, the general principles regulating the Turkish national education system stipulate the following:

Importance is attributed to the teaching of the Turkish language, which is one of the basic elements of *national unity and integrity (...) The language should be enriched as an educational and scientific one* (my emphasis).[2]

In this excerpt, the discourse on language which serves to create and maintain "national unity and integrity" reveals the function of standard language in education. Television and radio are other national instruments which help maintain an "ideal form of language", that is, standard language (Wober 1990: 571). According to the Establishment of Radio and Television Enterprises and Their Broadcasts Law No. 3984 of 20 April 1994,

[b]roadcasts shall use the Turkish language in its spoken form *without destroying its characteristics and rules*; shall ensure its development in the form of a modern cultural, educational and scientific language as *a basic element of national unity and integrity* (my emphasis).[3]

The statement above clearly acts as a restriction on any kind of variation that "destroy[s]" the "characteristics and rules" of standard Turkish which is an instrument of "national unity and integrity". It goes without saying that such statements implicitly influence the translational strategies and act as an implicit censoring apparatus for the translators who translate heteroglossic texts. In addition to the discourses of such state-run institutions, the discourses of the Turkish writers also gain importance. For instance, according to Akbayır (2003: 5-6), more measures have to be taken to fulfil the norms of the standard language because he argues that

---

[1] http://www.byegm.gov.tr/constitution.htm
[2] http://www.meb.gov.tr/stats/apk2001ing/section_0/preface.htm
[3] http://www.rtuk.org.tr/ying3984.htm

(i) standard Turkish is in danger; (ii) words and expressions which belong to dialects or to the non-standard language of sub-groups "threaten" Turkish; (iii) Turkish is used "incorrectly"; (iv) Turkish is used "badly"; and (v) the Turkish people lack the necessary language awareness (Akbayır 2003: 7). Furthermore, Refik Durbaş who is a poet and a columnist points out that "proper" Turkish has deteriorated, and the beauty of İstanbul Turkish (i.e. standard Turkish) has been spoiled.[4] As Gal (1998: 325) suggests, such "culturally embedded ideas about language" as "correctness" and "beauty" are involved in the process of "political legitimation" which may result in self-censorship on the part of the translators.

Milroy (2001: 535) sees such discourses as belonging to "standard-language cultures" where "virtually everyone subscribes to the ideology of standard language", one aspect of which is "correctness". In such cultures, "the canonical form of the language is a precious inheritance that has been built up over the generations (…) by a select few who have lavished loving care upon it, polishing, refining and enriching it until it has become a fine instrument of expression" (Milroy 2001: 537).

The battle to protect standard Turkish is fought in a wide variety of media including the internet. There are several non-governmental web-sites which argue for the protection and the cultivation of standard Turkish. Some of them are (i) "Lovers of Turkish" (http://www.turkcesevdalilari.com/), (ii) "Association of Revitalizing Our Turkish" (*http://www.turkcan.org/anasayfalist.asp*), and (iii) "The Denunciation Line of Language Gendarmeries" (*http://forum.antoloji.com/tahta/tahta.asp?tahta=10007*). Such web-sites intend to create room for cultivation of Turkish by means of reinforcing the standard.

In newspapers, citizens caring about their language write columns about the dissolution of the Turkish language. Thousands of complaints are made by the people about the misuse of Turkish. *Turkish Daily News* lists some of these complaints which stress that people should refrain from anything which debases and damages the Turkish language.[5] These discourses illustrate what Milroy (2001: 538) calls the "complaint tradition" which has an important role of standard-language maintenance.

All these discourses also interact to create what Fairclough (1989) calls "discoursal common sense" in which reality comes to appear to be natural and taken-for-granted. Reality is not neutral reality in this context; rather it

---

[4] http://www.sabah.com.tr/2003/12/16/yaz15-10-115.html
[5] http://www.turkishdailynews.com.tr/article.php?enewsid=15599

is the reality which differs according to the social ideologies underlying the different perceptions of reality. Discourses, by way of hegemonic closures, fix meanings in particular ways, and exclude all other meaning potentials; and the discursive practices of the translators appear as natural and delimited aspects of reality. In such a case, it is highly likely that the Turkish translators systematically stick to standard language that enjoys cultural and public prestige (i.e. symbolic capital) partly because the acceptance of their translations implies the perpetuation of their careers.

In such countries as Turkey where standardization is circulated through discourses as commonsensical, the taken-for-grantedness of standardization leads the translators to develop a linguistic habitus. That is, standardization is internalized by the translators who may then initiate self-censorship. In this way, standardization which is at first an external governing force becomes an internal governing agent. As time passes, the translators' linguistic habitus becomes a set of automatic responses that guides their decision-making process towards the politically correct linguistic choices.

In order to have a clear picture of linguistic standardization in the Turkish translations of heteroglossia, it is necessary to dwell on some concrete examples which illustrate the Turkish translators' approach to language variation in literature. It has been noted, up to this point, that the Turkish translators have been systematically standardizing literary heteroglossia. Even though very few translators have made a radical decision to break with the deeply-rooted tradition of standardization in the Turkish translations, they are not followed by the other translators or they are criticized by some literary critics.

A good example is the case of the Turkish translations of the Cockney dialect. The Thracian dialect of Turkish actually provides "satisfactory equivalence in the TL in terms of cultural, class-specific, lexical, and partly phonological features" in the translation of Cockney (Büyükkantarcıoğlu 1999: 80). The most striking characteristic of the Thracian dialect of Turkish is the dropped 'h' (e.g. 'em for *h*em), which is similar to the dropped 'h' of Cockney (e.g. 'ouse for *h*ouse). However, the Thracian dialect has, so far, only been used in Sevgi Sanlı's (1987) translation of Shaw's ([1916] 1999) *Pygmalion* which is famous for its Cockney dialect. Sevgi Sanlı's use of dialect in translation is an unprecedented example in the Turkish tradition of literary translation. No translator other than Sevgi Sanlı has used the Thracian dialect to translate the Cockney dialect in various English novels such as Dickens's novels although the Thracian dialect successfully reflects the social and class-related characteristics of Cockney. Sevgi Sanlı used the Thracian dialect in the translation of *Pygmalion* because translation of drama entails much more different aspects (e.g. performance) than translation of novels does. Therefore, the consideration of performance on stage is one of the reasons why a Turkish dialect has been used for the first time in a Turkish translation. Another possible reason for Sanlı's dialectal choice is that she might have wished to get away from standardization and to introduce a new norm of recreating the linguistic otherness of heteroglossia. However, the other Turkish translators who translate heteroglossic drama texts or novels have not followed Sanlı in this radical choice. Such dialectal drama texts as Shakespeare's (1982) *Henry V* are all translated into standard Turkish without the consideration of performance on stage.

Another example is the Turkish translation of the Scottish novel, *Trainspotting*. The heteroglossic style in Irvine Welsh's (1993) *Trainspotting* is parodic: it enters into a polemic with Standard English. *Trainspotting* criticizes the standard middle-class way of life in Britain in addition to the middle-class attitude towards non-standard language and its resulting moral distinction between individuals. Afflicted by the psychological influence of a "divided linguistic inheritance" (Craig 1999: 15), the Scottish characters in the novel resist the uniformity of a homogenous standard language. The Turkish translator (Sabri Kaliç), however, refrains from reproducing the effect of a "divided linguistic inheritance" in the Turkish translation by standardising the dialectal voices.

Trainspotting mixes "patois with Standard English to disrupt and stretch English" for its purpose of colonial resistance (Aegerter 1997: 902). To "stretch" English is carried out in the novel by moving beyond its symbolic power and keeping away from the norms of Standard English. *Trainspotting* illustrates what Deleuze and Guattari (1986: 23) call the traits of the "tensor": "the incorrect use of prepositions", "the abuse of the pronominal", "the importance of accent as a tension internal to the word", and "the distribution of consonants and vowels as part of an internal discordance". However, the Turkish reader of *Trainspotting* does not see such instances of what Deleuze and Guattari call "tensors" or "nodes of pain" because the Turkish translator systematically avoids disrupting standard Turkish by sticking to its syntactic and lexical correctness notions.

On the other hand, given that heteroglossia is itself a message in *Trainspotting*, Sabri Kaliç had to make some sound elisions (in a very inconsistent and an extremely restricted way, though) in an attempt to give the Turkish reader a sense of variation in language. Therefore, at certain parts of the Turkish translation, the translator resorted to the strategy of eliding some sounds—a strategy that created colloquial Turkish but not a heteroglossic style. Even this is criticized by a critic, Anil Gökpek (2006), who accuses Sabri Kaliç of making certain "linguistic mistakes which can infuriate even a primary-school student".[6] Obviously, Kaliç's partial attempt to reflect the original novel's heteroglossic style is seen as an annoying linguistic error. Gökpek's criticism shows us the Turkish reader's intolerance to any attempt that breaks the norms of written standard Turkish in literature.

5. Conclusion

The use of heteroglossia in literature (thereby, in literary translation) is a strategy of struggle not only with the hegemony of legitimate language and proper writing, but also with the knowledge and the beliefs valorized and circulated by the upstanding discourses of dominant ideologies.

Since the habitus of the Turkish translators ensures the perpetuation of the dominant discourses on standard language, they have long refrained from opposing the discourses of dominant language ideologies. In this way, standard Turkish has become common-sense; and the translators have acted consciously or unconsciously under the influence of linguistic correctness which has systematically closed off the Turkish translations to non-standard language varieties. To apply Mey's (1985: 250) words to our context, this has given rise to "idealization or standardization of language-in-use which always turns out to be one of the most powerful means to maintain the 'given' linguistic order". In other words, standard Turkish has been maintained in the translations of heteroglossia through legitimacy which is conferred on it by public opinions and discourses.

In instances where such metalinguistic discourses marginalize all variants as impurities, the translator might hesitate to place himself/herself in a counter-cultural position that implies radical marginality. Throughout this article, various discourses have shown the canonical nature and the unquestioned status of standard Turkish. They have also shown why the unifying power of standard Turkish remains potent in the cultural formation and in the ideological institutions.

The taken-for-grantedness of standard language emerges when heteroglossic varieties are pushed out of our vision not only in official settings but also in literary translations. Here the critical project for translation studies is a matter of denaturalizing the taken-for-granted understanding of language. This paper concludes that in such cases where

---

[6] http://www.izedebiyat.com/yazi.asp?id=20861

censorship is implicitly spoken in the practical use of language in translation and is hidden from the public consciousness, it is necessary to engage with a critical approach to translation by piercing the opacity of censorship.

References

Primary Sources

Kaliç, Sabri (2001) *Trainspotting*, İstanbul: Stüdyo İmge Books.
Sanlı, Sevgi (1987) *Pygmalion*, Ankara: Devlet Tiyatroları Genel Müdürlüğü.
Shakespeare, William (1982) *Henry V*, Oxford: Clarendon.
Shaw, Bernard (1999) (1st ed. 1916) *Pygmalion*, at *http://www.bartleby.com/138/* (24.05.2004).
Welsh, Irvine (1993) *Trainspotting*, London: Minerva.
http://www.byegm.gov.tr/constitution.htm
http://www.meb.gov.tr/stats/apk2001ing/section_0/preface.htm
http://www.rtuk.org.tr/ying3984.htm

Secondary Sources

Aegerter, Lindsay (1997) 'Michelle Cliff and the Paradox of Privilege', in *College English*, vol. 59, 898-915.
Akbayır, Sıddık (2003) *Language and Diction*, İstanbul: Akçay.
Bakhtin, Mikhail (2001) "Unitary Language", in L. Burke, T. Crowley & A. Girvin (eds.) *The Routledge Language and Cultural Theory Reader*, London and New York: Routledge, 269-279.
Blommaert, Jan (1999) "The debate is open", in J. Blommaert (ed.) *Language Ideological Debates*, Berlin, New York: Mouton de Gruyter, 1-38.
Bourdieu, Pierre (1991) *Language and Symbolic Power*. J. B. Thompson (ed.), and G. Raymond and M. Adamson (trans.), Cambridge: Polity in association with Basil Blackwell.
Büyükkantarcıoğlu, Nalan (1999) "Language Varieties and Translation: A Sociolinguistic Perspective", in *Çeviribilim ve Uygulamaları Dergisi*, vol. 5, 65-85.
Craig, Cairns (1999) *The Modern Scottish Novel: Narrative and the National Imagination*, Edinburgh: Edinburgh University Press.

Deleuze, Gilles & Guattari, Felix (1986) *Kafka: Toward a Minor Literature* (translated by D. Polan), Minneapolis: University of Minnesota Press.

Fairclough, Norman (1989) *Language and Power*, London: Longman.

Gal, S. (1998) "Multiplicity and Contention among Language Ideologies: A Commentary", in B. B. Schieffelin, K. A. Woolard & P. V. Kroskrity (eds.), *Language Ideologies: Practice and Theory*, Oxford: Oxford University Press, 317-332.

Gerdener, Wilhelm (1986) *Purism in Nynorsk*, Münster: Kleinheinrich.

Hall, Robert Anderson (1942) "The Italian questione della lingua: an interpretive essay", in *University of North Carolina Studies in Romance Languages and Literatures*, North Carolina: Chapell Hill.

Merkle, Denise (2002) "External and Internal Pressures on the Translator: Relationship to Censorship" at http://www.ln.edu.hk/eng/staff/eoyang/icla/Denise%20Merkle.doc (17.10.2006).

Mey, Jacob (1985) *Whose language? A Study in Linguistic Pragmatics*, Amsterdam, Philadelphia: John Benjamins Publishing Company.

Milroy, Lesley (2001) "Language ideologies and the consequences of standardization", in *Journal of Sociolinguistics*, vol. 5, no. 4, 530-555.

Toury, Gideon (1995) *Descriptive Translation Studies–and Beyond*. Amsterdam and Philadelphia: John Benjamins.

—. (1999) "Translation as a Means of Planning and the Planning of Translation: A Theoretical Framework and an Exemplary Case" at http://www.tau.ac.il/~toury/works/plan-tr.htm (17.10.2006).

Venuti, Lawrence (1998) *The Scandals of Translation: Towards an Ethics of Difference*, London and New York: Routledge.

Wober, Mallory (1990) "Language and Television", in H. Giles & W. P. Robinson (eds.) *Handbook of Social Psychology*, Chichester: John Wiley & Sons Ltd, 561-582.

Woolard, Kathryn (1998) "Introduction: Language Ideology as a Field of Inquiry", in B. B. Schieffelin, K. A. Woolard & P. V. Kroskrity (eds.) *Language Ideologies: Practice and Theory*, Oxford: Oxford University Press, 3-50.

http://forum.antoloji.com/tahta/tahta.asp?tahta=10007
http://www.izedebiyat.com/yazi.asp?id=20861
http://www.sabah.com.tr/2003/12/16/yaz15-10-115.html
http://www.turkcan.org/anasayfalist.asp
http://www.turkcesevdalilari.com
http://www.turkishdailynews.com.tr/article.php?enewsid=15599

UKRAINE: TRANSLATING THE WARS

NATALIA OLSHANSKAYA,
KENYON COLLEGE - GAMBIER, OH, USA

Abstract: The paper discusses censorship in translating newspaper articles on military conflicts in a Ukrainian newspaper published in three languages, Ukrainian, Russian, and English. The article links translation strategies to cultural and ideological contexts and shows how in today's world of globalization, censorial mechanisms can be exercised across borders.

An attempt is made to identify dominant discursive norms which have influenced specific translation practices. The author shows how the application of these norms affects the transferring of sensitive information from the East to the West and from the West to the East.

Translation and interpreting are permanently involved in various stages of military operations: from the declaration of war to final attempts to resolve military conflicts. All these stages of warfare are communicated verbally, and have to be transferred into many languages in order to reach the international community. As Mona Baker wrote in her book *Translation and Conflict*, "Contemporary wars have to be sold to international and not just domestic audiences, and translation is a major variable influencing the circulation and legitimation of the narratives that sustain these activities." (Baker 2006: 2). The interplay between reality and its representations during the time of conflict is an interesting area for semiotic study; polarization of these representations becomes especially evident in translation, and is revealed in all aspects of censorship.

In today's world, mass media in general, and hard-copy or internet versions of newspapers in particular, are the main channels of communicating information about military conflicts around the globe, and it is only to be expected that newspapers "package" their ideological product depending upon the markets. Original articles devoted to the description and analysis of warfare differ in translation, and are tailored to meet the discursive and ideological requirements of the new reading audiences. In this article, I will try to show how numerous changes in the relationship between power and ideology in today's globalized world have affected censorship, and how censorship is now exercised across borders. Consequently, the traditional definition of censorship as an "officially authorised" state action "to examine printed matter, films, news, etc. before public release, and to suppress any parts on the grounds of obscenity, a threat to security, etc." (Allen 1991: 181) has to be revisited and re-evaluated. The notion of censorship can no longer be limited to repressive (administrative) or consensual (self-censorship) control intended to silence radical opinions. The traditional binary model of censorship, that is the understanding of censorship as repression versus freedom, should be replaced by an approach which allows us to view censorship as a combination of two discursive practices: the legitimation of certain points of view alongside the delegitimation of others.[1]

In his analysis of censorship, sociologist Pierre Bourdieu states that during periods of political stability, when the dominant discourse feels less threatened, suppression of information is less common than during times of political instability and change (Bourdieu 1980: 91) Indeed, it is obvious that during wartime, mass media becomes more state controlled. These censorial impulses of governments, which are publicly justified by fear of disclosure of sensitive information, have been exercised most recently throughout the world in a variety of ways: from public reprimands of journalists by the US government for the negative portrayal of the war in Iraq to such extremes as the assassination of several Russian journalists for their reports on the war in Chechnya. Even in the so-called "free democracies," mass media seem to be controlled by special interest groups which censor the coverage of events in an attempt to legitimize certain discourses, and some very reputable newspapers of the "free world" have been accused of presenting biased information about the military conflicts in which their countries have been engaged.[2]

In an attempt to obtain a more impartial point of view on recent military conflicts, I have chosen to analyze articles published by a newspaper in Ukraine, one of the countries which has not been directly involved in any recent major armed conflicts. My initial assumption was

---

[1] See Foucault's understanding of power as a combination of fields and forces, a network of relations, a process rather than a static form (Foucault 1979: 215-216).

[2] For example, in their recent book *The Record of the Paper*, Howard Friel and Richard Falk claim that the *New York Times* did not live up to its reputation of impartiality in providing advocacy for the current invasion of Iraq. Having analyzed the editorials of this most influential newspaper for the past fifty years, the authors argue that it has often failed to present dissenting views and on more than one occasion has neglected international law in its reports on armed conflicts around the globe (Friel & Falk 2005).

that their coverage of events, both in the original and translations, would be less affected by censorship. Articles on military conflicts from the Ukrainian newspaper *Dzerkalo tyzhnia* [*Weekly Mirror*] were analyzed; thirty two issues of the weekly covering the last two and a half years were randomly selected from the archives. *Weekly Mirror* is published in three languages (Ukrainian, Russian, and English), and it is reputed to be one of the more progressive, independent, and objective sources of information in the country.

By definition, mass media seek to appeal to a broad audience; they also communicate information which is ideologically charged, and consequently may be censored by political, economic, and social groups in power or seeking some sort of influence or power. Variations in methods used to win this public appeal were evidenced in the analyzed original newspaper texts and their translations. These differences were most noticeable between translations from Ukrainian into Russian and translations from Ukrainian into English, that is, between texts targeting the East and the West.

There were twenty-nine articles on armed conflicts published in the 32 original Ukrainian issues of the *Weekly Mirror*. The articles under review were not limited to military operations proper, but included those discussing war-games, the planning of war, potential military actions, and what has become known as "the war on terror." Almost no changes were introduced into the Russian translations, but more than half of the "war" articles–17 out of 29–were eliminated from the English version. It is hard to imagine that they were suppressed in the English translation for reasons other than ideology.

For example, out of the three articles missing in the English language September 2006 issue, one dealt with the American position on the enrichment of uranium in Iran and possible war actions, the second discussed the Israeli-Lebanese war, the third was devoted to the war in Iraq in the context of the general situation in the Middle East. The article on the war in Iraq *"Chy vidpovidal'na zovnishnia polityka zahidnyh krain za global'nyj teroryzm?"* ["Should the Foreign Policy of Western Countries Be Held Responsible for Global Terror?"] appeared in issue 32 of the newspaper, and was authored by Kim Howells, the British Minister of State in the Commonwealth Office. Apparently it had been written in English, but then appeared in the Ukrainian and Russian versions of the newspaper, but not in the English version. Kim Howells, who prior to becoming minister had a career in mass media and knows too well how to use censorial mechanisms, publicly acknowledged on British TV in March of 2006 that "Iraq is a mess." Yet in the September issue of the Ukrainian newspaper in question he gives a much more positive portrayal of the events, saying "I sincerely continue to believe that it had been the right course of actions" (my translation). He then explains how "for the first time in Iraq's history, the country is governed by a truly elected government," and that in some regions of Iraq the British troops have successfully handed over the control of security to the Iraqis. This kind of self-censorship clearly reflects the position of a politician who does not want to be identified as a supporter of the war, overwhelmingly unpopular in the West, and who consequently suppresses the text in the English language press, but chooses to support his government's official policy in the articles translated for Eastern European consumption. This special example of censorship, when the original was suppressed and the text appeared only in translations, was exhibited in two other similar cases within the relatively modest corpus that I analyzed.

One cannot underestimate the recent efforts of many Eastern European countries to appeal to the sentiments of Western European governments in the hope of being accepted into the EU or of gaining some other more immediate advantages, and consequently their attempts to exercise self-censorship in communicating with the West. The following example that can explain, if not justify, such caution has been taken from a March 2004 issue of the *Weekly Mirror* which had published an article by a British political analyst James Sherr. The author examined the outcome of the 2004 elections in Spain and directly linked the results of the elections to the bombings in Madrid, also suggesting that the withdrawal of the Spanish troops from Iraq carried out under this newly elected government could have a larger negative impact on the war on terror all over the world. The article was carefully translated into Ukrainian and Russian, and published in all the three versions of the newspaper. In the Ukrainian and Russian versions of the newspaper, the political message of the spreading danger of terrorism was intensified by the image of a giant dragon snake spreading its claws all over Europe, but in the English version, it was toned down by the image of a mourning person with a candle lit in commemoration of the victims of the Madrid bombings. By itself, this manipulative change of meaning through images is an interesting mechanism of censorship in translation, widely employed by mass media. The article was not well received in Spanish diplomatic circles, and a week later, issue 12 of the *Mirror* had to publish an angry letter from the Spanish Ambassador to Ukraine who claimed that Sherr's article had disrespected the dignity of the Spanish people and "their proven resolve against terrorism." Both Ukrainian and Russian translations of this letter were introduced with an extensive four-paragraph forward in which the editorial board stated that the opinion of James Sherr did not reflect their position, and that it was not uncommon for the newspaper to publish controversial opinions on various matters. The editorial board also thanked European diplomats for their attention to the discussion of international affairs in the Ukrainian press. This highly apologetic reaction of the Ukrainian newspaper would have seemed exaggerated to the Western English-language readership, not to mention any newspaper editorial board in the West, and consequently it was not introduced into the English language version.

This exchange exemplifies a more or less successful attempt by an influential state, a member of the EU, to suppress an undesirable point of view expressed by the mass media of another, less powerful, country. This particular example also shows how mechanisms of censorship have become more intricate and complex in our globalized world, and how they can be triggered across borders. It also eloquently reveals changes in the censorship of translated texts: many articles devoted to sensitive international matters are differently censored depending on whether the translations are packaged for American and Western European audiences or for the Eastern European readers.

In the previous example, censorship was exercised through the addition of new segments of text from one language to another; other translated articles revealed a more common censorial mechanism–intentional deletion of parts of narratives. Several translations from Ukrainian into English were heavily edited, while again preserved almost intact in the translations into Russian. The comparison of the Ukrainian originals with the English translations shows that it was a common practice to delete phrases, sentences, paragraphs, and even blocks (up to three paragraphs) from the target text. For example, in issue 26 from July 2006, the article "Iraq Behind, New Mission Ahead" devoted to anti-NATO protests in Ukraine, which had stopped the Ukrainian fleet from participation in military training operations, was abridged in a way that toned down the emphatic rhetoric of the original through the restructuring of paragraphs, the shortening or exclusion of sentences, and numerous other changes in syntax (elimination of rhetorical questions, substitution of inverted word order by stylistically neutral structures, etc.). These systematic changes manipulated the meaning of the original text, and consequently affected the clarity of the discourse and its interpretation by the new potential readers.

The theory of implicature, developed about forty years ago by the philosopher H. Paul Grice (Grice 1975: 3:53-54), has been applied by discourse analysts and stylisticians to the study of extended sequences of speech, but its possibilities have not been sufficiently explored in studying the fluctuations and manipulation of meaning in translation. Grice's concept of implicature accounts for the gap between the literal meaning of an utterance and the way it functions in specific contexts; it stresses the decoding process in which interlocutors routinely form a conclusion from premises in order to interpret each other's discourse as coherent and relevant. It relies on the participants' observance of what Grice called, "the cooperative principle," that is a set of discursive rules, or a set of maxims different for various languages, cultures, and ideologies. Grice's "maxim of quality," which is concerned with truthfulness and demands that the participants of a discourse not communicate anything for which they do not have sufficient evidence, is easily linked to more recent discussions of translation ethics and obvious instances of ideological manipulations (or censorship) in translation. Naturally, his "maxim of quantity," which deals with the amount of information required to provide a meaningful exchange, can be related to censorship and suppression of information in translation. The previously described three types of censorship, that is (a) the total suppression of the source text, (b) the total or partial deletion of translated texts, and (c) the introduction of new sizable elements into the narrative, exemplify the violation of "the maxims of quality and quantity," and consequently result in the general misrepresentation of the discourse. Less evident, but similarly important for identifying instances of censorship, is Grice's "maxim of manner," which stresses the style and clarity of discourse.

It seems that manipulations in translation based on change regarding the maxims of quantity and quality from the source to the target texts result in obvious, explicit instances of censorship, while censorship in translation based on changes with respect to the maxim of manner is no less pervasive, and yet more difficult to detect. My further analysis will be devoted to violations of the maxim of manner and their impact on the meaning of target texts. Examples will be drawn from one particular article which seemed to represent most typical censorial mechanisms used in translation.

The article "Iraq and the Impermissibility of Failure" was originally written in English by a British political analyst for the October 2003 issue and then translated into Russian and Ukrainian. In general, translations from English have been executed very carefully without any deletions or major changes, probably because the editorial board of the *Weekly Mirror* cannot censor its Western authors for fear of losing them. The author in question is a regular contributor to the weekly, and judging by his comments, he is an obvious supporter of the war in Iraq. Hesitating to censor the contents of the source text, the newspaper introduces a "disclaimer" at the end of the English language text: "The article expresses the opinions and viewpoints of its author alone, which may not coincide with the official position of the Defence Ministry of the UK".

On the other hand, the Ukrainian translation promotes the war even more strongly than the original, since in 2003 the war in Iraq was widely supported in Ukraine. And though in Russia the reaction to this war was much less enthusiastic, the Russian version of the article is identical to the Ukrainian version, which is further evidence of the current strained relations between the two former allies. The changes in both the Ukrainian and Russian target texts are similar and consistent, which allows us to assume that either the translations into both Slavic languages were executed by the same person, or one of these target texts is a re-translation from the other. Through subtle changes in the vocabulary and grammar, the translations intensify the positive image of the war by toning down the mention of the controversy about it in the West.

The source text (English)	**The target texts** (Ukrainian/Russian)
implacable enemies	*neprymyrenni oponenty/ neprimirimye opponenty* [implacable opponents]
for these enemies	*dlia nyh/ dlia nih* [for them]
misgivings	*poboiuvannia/ opaseniia* [concerns]
the force of that condemnation	*intensyvnost' takoi krytyky/ intensivnost' takoj kritiki* [the intensity of this criticism]
tension	*superechky/ spory* [arguments]
overwrought atmosphere	*napruzhena atmosfera/ napriazhennaia atmosfera* [tense atmosphere]
mighty phalanx of politicians	*chyslenni polityky i komentatory/ mnogochislennye politiki i kommentatory* [numerous politicians and commentators]

On the other hand, when the original text mentions the success of the coalition forces, the translations tend to introduce substitutions which exaggerate it (e.g., "coalition forces recovered"–in the source text, "coalition sources achieved success"–in the target texts; "relatively swift victory"–"swift victory"). Grice's "maxim of manner" is obviously violated by the translator(s) either through the replacement of stylistically neutral vocabulary with words with explicitly strong negative connotation, or through the substitution of less commonly used epithets for the ones which would be normally used and anticipated in this context ("overwrought atmosphere"–"tense atmosphere", "implacable enemies"–"opponents"). Small, yet systematic modifications in the grammar only intensify this effect through changes in (1) the modality and (2) the grammatical tense of sentences:

> (1) Today, demoralization and its allies–recrimination, opportunism and cynicism–**could prove** even more damaging to the future of Iraq ... (ST)
> *Siogodni demoralizatsiia ta vzaemni obvynuvachennia [...] bil'sh rujnivni dlia majbutniogo Iraku.* [Today, demoralization and allies-recriminations [....] **are** even more detrimental to the future of Iraq.] (TT)
>
> (2) The failure **was** evident at all levels. (ST)
> *Tsej proval ochevydnyj na vsih rivniah* [There **is** failure at all levels] (TT)

The change of the grammatical tense in example (2) downplays the fault of the US officials at the planning stage of the war.

Similar changes in syntax occur in other instances. For example, the original text makes it clear that mistakes in war planning have happened before, comparing the types of misjudgements made by the Bush administration in Iraq to "the types of misjudgements (over Kosovo) to which the Clinton administration was also prone."(ST) The translator introduces a separate sentence, thus pushing into prominence the military mistakes of the previous administration:

> Po-druge, prychyny provaliv polityky administratsii Busha ne lyshe v zazrozumilosti, scho zasudzhuetsia vsima. Tsi provaly dopuscheni vnaslidok vplyvu politychnogo protsesu, nepravyl'nyh sudzhen' (iak u vupadku z Kosovo), do iakyh bula shyl'na administratsiia Klintona."
> [These failures are the result of the negative effect of the political process and wrong assumptions (as in Kosovo) which had been implemented under Clinton.]

The introduction of a new sentence paired with the omission of the adverb "also" result in the violation of Grice's "maxim of manner", and lead to a change in the meaning of the statement. Instead of the comparison (between two misjudgements) in the source text, the reader of the target text is now presented with what can be interpreted as a causal relationship: misjudgements of Clinton's administration have caused recent mistakes in war planning.

From our observations, we can draw some general conclusions:

1. In today's world of globalization, social and political changes have affected the very nature of censorship, which is now often not administered by a state or government. The boarders and sources of political pressure have become more and more blurred, and often cannot be examined within a single country. These changes in censorial mechanisms are most explicitly exercised in translation.

2. The officially authorized censorship of autocratic regimes seems to have given way (at least in most of Europe and North America) to slightly different censorial mechanisms that suppress information potentially damaging to the interests of specific parties and groups which aim at winning mass public appeal and support. In this case, the norms of discourse developed and supported by these groups in control of the access to the means and the form of expression are not legal entities, which potentially gives more power to the translator.

3. In translation, the implementation of these norms varies from one socio-economic, political, and cultural environment to another; most differences in the application of censorial mechanisms occur in the transferring of the information from the East to the West and from the West to the East.

4. Censorship in journalism is most obviously revealed in the violation of "the maxims of quality and quantity" which is exercised through: a) total suppression of either the source or the target texts; b) partial suppression of the source or target texts; c) changes in the graphic representation and/or the introduction of new images.

5. Rhetoric plays a crucial part in censorship. The violation of "the maxim of manner" in translated texts may result in covert instances of censorship which often occur in the so-called "free democracies". They are pervasive and yet more difficult to detect than the cases of the violation of "the maxims of quantity and quality"

References

Allen, R. E., (ed.) (1991) *The Concise Oxford Dictionary of Current English*, Oxford & New York: Oxford Univ. Press.

Baker, Mona (2006) *Translation and Conflict. A Narrative Account*, London & New York: Routledge.

Bourdieu, Pierre (1980) *Le sens pratique*, Paris: Minuit.

Foucault, Michel (1970) *Discipline and Punish: The Birth of the Prison*, New York: Vintage.

Friel, Howard & Richard Falk (2005) *The Record of the Paper: How the New York Times Misreports US Foreign Policy.* London: Verso.

Grice, H. P. (1975) "Logic and Conversation", in P. Cole and J. L. Morgan (eds.) *Syntax and Semantics. Speech Act*, New York: Academic Press.

Chapter Four

Translation & Censorship: Revisiting Past Constraints and Assumptions

Morality and Poetic Theorizing as Censorship Strategies: In the Translation of *Heroides* by Miguel do Couto Guerreiro (1720 - 1793)

Maria dos Anjos Guincho,
ESSS / CECC-Univ. Católica Portuguesa de Lisboa, Portugal

Abstract: The fact that the Portuguese culture was often historically constrained by ecclesiastical, royal, moral or civil censorship did not prevent it from taking an interest in other cultures, especially those that enjoyed greater international prestige. To understand the stakes more fully, it might be useful to look back on the 18th century, a period which witnessed an increase both in the number of translations produced and in the translation strategies undertaken by translators at that time (word for word translation, imitation, paraphrasing or conversion).

A case particularly representative of this issue is the first complete Portuguese translation of Ovid's *Heroides* by Miguel do Couto Guerreiro in 1778: *"Ovid's Letters–Epistulae Heroidum, Purged of all obscenity and translated in regular rhyme (...)"*. Bearing in mind the suggestive title of the translation, this paper aims to discuss the socio-political manipulative tendencies of Couto Guerreiro's text, as understood in modern-day Translation Studies. In the course of this undertaking the following steps will be taken:
- analysis of the context in which the translation was produced;
- interpretation of the messages on translation and censorship contained in paratextual elements;
- interconnection of these principles with the translation, taking into special consideration the comparison of linguistic puns between the original text and the translated text. We will devote our attention on this matter entirely to the 13th Epistle, *From Laodamia to Protesilau;*
- consideration of the poetic creativity of literary "imitation";
- discussion of how the translated text was received in the target culture and literary system.

We ought to imitate the ancients: these are the teachings of Horace, those dictated by reason and acknowledged by the entire literary world. But this doctrine, this good advice, should be embraced and followed in such a way that it appears to be rejected, imitating and not translating. Poets ought to be imitators in fables, in images, in thoughts, in style; but those who imitate must make their imitations their own.[1]
—Correia Garção, *Obras Completas*, p. XXXVIII

The epigraph alludes to the conditional adaptation of literary values that have been handed down from the past and presents one method of viewing the act of translation in the eighteenth century: imitation, a common practice continuing along the lines of intertextuality maintained throughout the history of Translation, in terms of theory and pragmatics. In fact, continued use of ancient models as tools for a range of purposes, from pedagogic to political, has led to a number of forms of translation, from word for word translation to conversion, paraphrasing and imitation, which all have as a common denominator the desire to adapt to the moral and aesthetic rules of readers of different periods. Continually announcing cultural changes, "imitation" implies creativity, and is generally applied to that which nowadays is considered to be "literary translation" (Hermans 1993: 102). Indeed, this form of translation is in tandem with the increasing demand for a critical spirit and the consequent bourgeois transformation of literature in Western culture. These phenomena, which gradually developed in line with the social and political conditions particularly from the time of the Renaissance on, emerge in the eighteenth century, at a time when the occupation of writer and the art of translation, both intimately linked, would necessarily be privileged by the rationalism and enlightenment of the period.

Encompassing this new spirit, the world vision of eighteenth-century Portugal engages in

> the permanent exercise of reasoning related to common sense, fearful of old delusions, and a universal curiosity that in literature extends beyond the Pyrenees and the Alps and in philosophy and science leaves behind the

---

[1] "Devemos imitar os antigos: assim no-lo ensina Horácio, no-lo dita a razão e o confessa todo o mundo literário. Mas esta doutrina, este bom conselho, devem abraçá-lo e segui-lo de modo que mais pareça que o rejeitamos, isto é, imitando e não traduzindo. Os poetas devem ser imitadores nas fábulas, nas imagens, nos pensamentos, no estilo; mas quem imita deve fazer seu o que imita."

All translations from the Portuguese are mine. For the sake of readability, English glosses will be used in the text and the majority of Portuguese quotes will be included in footnotes.

constraints of the library and the conventional cloisters, and all the goalposts erected by the absolute letter of Aristotle and Saint Thomas, and by the *Ratio Studiorum* and even by the Censorship Boards. (Cidade 2005: 12)[2]

This reasoning outlines the notions at the heart of this paper. The first is linked to the idea that Portuguese culture has been conditioned throughout most of its history by ecclesiastical or civil censorship. The second notion relates to the fact that during the period under study here, Portuguese interest in the culture of Europe took a number of forms and that there were "always people who, by means of translation or imitation, made this contact as close and as fruitful as possible" (Cidade, 2005: 161).[3]

Looking beyond our current time frame, in order to gain a better understanding of our train of thought, it could be said that from the beginning of the Portuguese monarchy and the acceptance of the Holy See, censorship had been a traditional practice in the fight against heretic thinking or thinking that was "simply disrespectful" (Rodrigues 1980: 16), but that the forms it took became more severe and better organized (including preventive and repressive censorship) following the cultural revolution that went hand in hand with the invention of the printing press, and which obviously led to the increased circulation of translations. The first Portuguese list of prohibited books dates back to 1547 and amongst the criteria for prohibition, suppression or printing, we can highlight, for obvious reasons, those which caution the reader against false gods and worldly love, texts which at the time were considered to be both sensual and dishonest.[4] It is also relevant to note–if we consider that there is no need to stress the importance of works "in language" for the development of national cultures–the Inquisition's opposition to texts in the vernacular. Although any type of book or document in Latin was theoretically subject to prohibition, there were works that could be read in Latin but not in the

---

[2] "permanente exercício duma razão regressada ao bom senso, receosa de delírios antigos, e uma curiosidade universalista, que indo, em literatura, para além dos Pirinéus e dos Alpes, em filosofia e em ciência deixa muito longe a estreiteza da biblioteca e claustro conventuais, todas as balizas postas pela letra morta de Aristóteles e São Tomás, pela Ratio Studiorum, e até pelas Mesas Censórias."

[3] "a cada passo quem, pela tradução ou pela imitação, torne esse contacto o mais estreito e fecundo possível"

[4] On this point, it is important to remember the purges of "profane immoralities" made to the post 1572 editions of *The Lusiadas*, and to other classic works. For more information on this issue, see, among others, the study by Graça Almeida Rodrigues, in *Breve História da Censura Literária em Portugal*, p. 25.

vernacular. For example, there are indications that the Ovidian *Heroides* was prohibited in Portuguese in the censorship period between 1660 and 1697 (Rodrigues 1980: 30), despite a partial translation of it appearing for the first time in the *Cancioneiro Geral* by Garcia de Resende–an anthology representing the linguistic development during the period of Humanism and the interest in the Classics. However, it might be reasonable to assume that the aforementioned *Heroides* had already been subjected to censorship and editing.[5] *Mutatis mutandis*, various models of censorship were constantly active, and during the second half of the eighteenth century, the law courts of the Royal Censorship Board, the *Real Mesa,* which had substituted the Inquisition, set up the *Novo Índice Expurgatório* (1768), a newly created set of criteria for suppression, and adopted seventeen rules to be followed in the selection of books, including rules which would safeguard the church, and more importantly, royal power. During the time of Prime Minister Marquis of Pombal, the Censorship Board was unmistakably supported by the creation of the Régia Oficina Tipográfica [Royal Printing Press] that printed legal documents and books for the large bookstore adjacent to it. Aware of the cultural novelties of the period and the reorganization of public education, and therefore interested in the new political thinking, the censors of the *Real Mesa* were now more concerned with reading material of a political nature that might jeopardize the right of the ruling sovereign. Nonetheless, this did not stop them from prohibiting the works of the Jesuits and, following tradition, "obscene books that corrupt the habits and the morals of the country"[6] (rule 6) (Guedes, 1987: 77).[7] Moreover, many foreign works produced in the new European spirit of the eighteenth century were also prohibited, with the exception of some books that could be read by privileged readers, to whom a special license was issued. Nevertheless, it should be noted that aside from the fact that "forbidden fruit is always more tempting," and in spite of the strictness of the censorship boards, be they the Inquisition, the Royal Censorship Boards–*Real Mesa Censória*, the *Mesa da Comissão Geral sobre o Exame e Censura dos Livros* (1787-

---

[5] Based on a study by Anselmo Braancamp Freire, "*A Censura e o Cancioneiro Geral*", Graça A. Rodrigues notes that the index referring to the *Cancioneiro Geral* dictated cuts on 70 of the 227 folios that make up the work.

[6] "os livros obscenos que corrompessem os costumes e a moral do país"

[7] In relation to the history of books and book stores in eighteenth-century Portugal, namely on the merits and the spread of French culture and the merits of bookstore owners, such as Bertrand, Férin or Chardron, see the study by Fernando Guedes, *O Livro e a Leitura em Portugal, Subsídios para a sua História-Séculos XVIII-XIX*, p. 15 ff.

1794),[8] or other censors of the time, prohibited books were always able to penetrate Portugal, particularly during that period. It was thus that "throughout the whole of the eighteenth century, the activity of the clandestine press was intense, without which the surprising spread of Enlightenment in Portugal could never have been anticipated" (Rodrigues 1980: 45).[9]

Thus, restrained by the aforementioned limitations, yet nevertheless anxiously awaiting intellectual novelties, the fact is that, as is to be expected in a period of neoclassicism, "the merits of the *Arcades* were numerous, not only in the renewal of literary genres, but also in the perfecting of the language" (Rocha Pereira 1988: 170).[10] As was previously stated, when quoting Hernâni Cidade, the development of the areas mentioned in this reference owes much to the effort devoted to translations, which were not only a useful language teaching tool (for both source and target languages), but also allowed for a wider and more educated public to gain access to texts from other cultures and to satisfy a taste for the Classics (some via texts/foreign translations), which, in one way or another "conveyed" the meaning and the style of the major cultural trends, even if that meant resorting to different guises.

In this linguistic and literary context, the position of translation became so well-renowned that it gave rise to the concept of the *República Literária* (*apud* Pinilla and Sánchez 1998: 36). The reflections of the intellectual community were particularly centred on the practice of translation, demonstrated in movements that, at different times, agreed that the letter of the source text should be faithfully followed, or that the choice of the meaning was more important. Since knowledge of languages was becoming more commonplace and there were more authors, those movements even at times revealed a certain lack of appreciation for the act of translation, except in the case of literary translation (imitation), since this presupposed the notion of a "second original" and of a "text", which was thought best to be left exclusively to writers.[11] As a result, the Royal

---

[8] Another branch of censorship.
[9] "por todo o século XVIII a actividade da imprensa clandestina foi vigorosa e, sem ela, não se poderia esperar o surpreendente surto do Iluminismo em Portugal"
[10] "foram numerosos os méritos dos Árcades, não só na renovação dos géneros literários, mas também no apuramento da linguagem"
[11] In relation to the set of thoughts on translation, from the end of the seventeenth century to the end of the eighteenth century, that aside from French influences, usually follow Quintillion in the area of prose and Horace in poetry, there are various views as to how to approach the issue. Of the thinkers who are chronologically closer to Miguel do Couto Guerreiro and between views on

Press catalogue of 1777 already included long lists of books which could be purchased, and in the Philology section, devoted to a large number of classical authors, the name of the Latin poet, Ovid, now appeared, amongst other prestigious names. [12]

However, this issue shall be analyzed here from a particular, albeit significant, angle, which is bound up with the epigraph. Returning our attention to the writer, translator and physician, Miguel do Couto Guerreiro, one could ask whether his translation of *Heroides* could be seen as one of the paradigms of the different methods of understanding translation in the eighteenth century. Was his translation produced, in the Classic/Renaissance sense of *election,* as an embellishment of the Latin model, more or less connected to the original linguistic procedures? Or was it an imitation with a certain amount of freedom in relation to the source text? Or could the source text have been altered, in the political sense of manipulation, since this was a time when censorship prevailed?[13] Could censorship have influenced the concept of translation and the procedures that Miguel do Couto Guerreiro undertook in relation to the Ovidian text?

Using this text and its "translation/imitation" as a starting point, I will attempt to outline one of the responses to translation in this historical period. Having already clarified the context in which the translation arose, I will now focus on the way in which it was absorbed into the culture and

---

literalism and literary-literalism, the different discourses included in the preliminary texts of Luís António Verney (1746), Cândido Lusitano (1758), Custódio José de Oliveira (1771), Vicente Lisbonense (1777), Jerónimo Soares Barbosa (1788), Joaquim José da Costa e Sá (1788). Pedro José da Fonseca (1790), among others, are all worthy of a mention. For a detailed study of the different positions, from which the idea becomes clear that "the writer is to work on literary translation, and other translations can be worked on by others," see Castilho Pais, *Teoria Diacrónica da Tradução Portuguesa*, pp. 34-35 ff. and also Pinilla e Sánchez, *O Discurso sobre a Tradução em Portugal*, pp. 35-154.

[12] During the last quarter of the eighteenth century, there are numerous titles of original texts as well as the constant inclusion of translations in the catalogues of bookstore owners: see Guedes, *idem*, pp. 94-116. As to the abundance of Portuguese translations under the auspices of Humanism see Fidelino de Figueiredo, *Bibliografia de Traduções* and Gonçalves Rodrigues, *A Tradução em Portugal*, vol. I, II, III.

[13] The aforementioned epigraph allows for a certain openness and creativity in translations; aspects that are in keeping with current theories: "from the point of view of the target literature, all translation implies a degree of manipulation of the source text for a certain purpose", Hermans (1985) "Introduction: Translation Studies as a new paradigm", p. 11.

the receiving literary system, and compare the linguistic elements of the source and target texts, and, insofar as the theory and practice of literary translation is concerned, its poetics.
The translation will be analyzed according to the following two levels of methodology:
- The set of messages regarding translation and censorship found in the paratextual elements;
- The differences between the source text and the translation, with regard to the 13th epistle: *From Laodamia to Protesilaus*.[14]

1. Prior censorship, self-censorship and anticipation of critical reception: peritexts and epitexts

Within the framework of the "enlightened" spirit of the *República Literária*, and respectful of aesthetic criteria already established by Horace, Du Bellay, Beauzée, Correia Garção and Verney the latter seeking "to balance artistry with common sense (...) and embracing in the Old only that which does not offend moral reasoning" (*apud* Cidade 2005: 36),[15] Miguel do Couto Guerreiro immediately provides clues in the title of his translation regarding the changes made to the older text. These modifications based on truth and intelligent imitation are explained throughout his long preface, "Prefação", which includes a set of rhetorical restrictions applied to the translation of poetry, governed by the criteria of usefulness, enjoyment and efficiency, and which precedes his translation of *Heroides*, published in 1789.

Thus, at the peritextual level, the title of the work, ***Ovid's Letters–Epistulae Heroidum, Purged of all obscenity and translated in regular rhyme: with the letters of reply, some by Ovid himself, others by Sabini and Sidronius and most by the Translator; and an Epilogue at the end of each one, revealing the doctrine therein: and an Analysis of what the good imitator must observe in them–Added to which are a few short Notes for a***

---

[14] The choice of this epistle is based on the fact that it is included in the translations of *Cancioneiro Geral* of 1516. Having already analyzed the letter *From Dido to Eneias*, (which is also included in this compendium of translations), in a paper in 2000, it would be interesting to set up a comparative study of the translations of the letter *From Laodamia to Protesilaus;* two translations produced in different literary periods.

[15] "moderar o engenho pelo bom juízo (...) e a abraçar nos Antigos apenas o que não repugna à boa razão"

better understanding,[16] reveals the need to control the content of each of the epistles, injecting them with moral content, as well as setting out the structure applied to the discourse. In fact, given Ovid's standing in the *Who's Who* of ancient mythology, and that much of the success of his works can be attributed to the themes of love and the eroticism contained therein, it is only natural that because of censorship the translator would have had to adopt preventative strategies in his literary work. Within this context, it is a well-known fact that Ovid's work had already been subjected to the imperial censorship of Augustus; it is therefore only natural that the works would have been continually monitored in Portugal during the time of imposed censorship.

In keeping with the "purges" and "moralizations" patent in the title is the editorial information on the first page, which is clearly in line with the alterations proposed in the subtitles: the work of the author and translator, Miguel do Couto Guerreiro, was published in Lisbon by the Oficina Patriarcal de Francisco Luiz Ameno, *With the permission* of the *Real Mesa da Comissão Geral sobre o Exame, e Censura dos Livros*. In this way, the additional content in the title not only points to the fact that the work was submitted to the censor, but also allows for the inference that the method of translation, similarly to literary practice, was closer to creative activity, which yet again consolidates the idea that the status of the translator was becoming increasingly important and accepted (see Susan Bassnett 1980: 7). In this respect and on the first page of the work– these being aspects that we consider to be dependent on the will of the translator, and probably the censor or the editor – it is worth noting the coexistence of the names of the author and translator, which in itself reinforces a more auspicious view of translation.

All of these intermediary spaces between the texts and the reader, which are theoretically considered to be important research models in the History of Translation, generally provide information about many aspects which are present (or silenced) in the translation. In this case, the *Prefação* reveals some processes of self-censorship and the defence mechanisms to be adopted prior to external censorship, both at the level of the literary reception of the work and at that of the official censor. In this area, the translator provides information which assesses the writing of other

---

[16] **Cartas de Ovidio**, *chamadas Heroides–Expurgadas de toda a obscenidade e traduzidas em rima vulgar: com as suas respostas, escriptas umas pelo mesmo Ovídio; outras por Sabino, e Sidronio, e a maior parte d'ellas pelo traductor; e hum Epilogo no fim de cada Huma, em que se mostra a doutrina que della se póde tirar: e huma Analyse do que nas mesmas deve observer o bom imitador.– Ajuntam-se algumas breves Notas para sua melhor intelligencia*

scholars and he points out the reasoning behind the prescriptive and descriptive aspects of his own work, and also behind the copious explanatory notes which permeate the whole translation.

In fact, it is within this literary and poetic exuberance that Miguel do Couto Guerreiro, at times juxtaposing issues of genre and style and of literary critique, and at others justifying his self-censorship by means of Christian-based reasoning, discusses the significance of his "analysis" and the best way of conveying his message for the pleasure of the "curious and cautious" public reader, to whom he presents himself in the familiar tone, as

a) The author, the source and the translator

Miguel do Couto Guerreiro begins by praising the work he will translate, "Amongst the literary monuments of Antiquity that have survived (…) the most ingenious poetic composition" (1789: 2 ff.),[17] and minimizes his own self-worth by suggesting that he has neither the spirit nor the hope of ever perfectly imitating the poet's *opus major*, *Metamorphoses*,[18] which he considers unique, yet "barren and sterile, absolutely implausible"[19] and the allegories of which require allegoric interpretations (on the part of the translator and the reader) which, although they may be arbitrary, are able to ascribe to the meaning of the Author. Although he is seemingly in agreement with Verney, who considered this work to be puerile, he refutes him with regard to the allegation that the Poet lacked a sense of reflection. Despite the fact that some Portuguese translations of parts of the *Metamorphoses* were already available at the time, Miguel do Couto Guerreiro recommends *Heroides* to the reading public, namely because no "guesswork is necessary to

---

[17] "Entre todos os monumentos literários da Antiguidade, que nos restam (…), a composição poética mais engenhosa"

[18] The presence of the *Metamorphoses* by Ovid has always been a part of Portuguese literary history–a reminder that Camões made many references to Ovid, as did António Vieira–in the eighteenth century there are at least partial translations of this work, (José António da Silva Rego, for example, produced the *Compêndio das Metamorfoses* in 1772) and there are other translations, versions or commentaries of *Tristia, Ibis, Fasti* and *Ars Amatoria*. The observations in reference to the Latin work, made by Miguel do Couto Guerreiro, seem to follow those of Verney (see Cidade, *idem*: 36), whereas not when referring to what is said about the author. This difference in opinion is in harmony with the various translation concepts of the time.

[19] "infructuosa, e estéril, absolutamente inverosímil"

understand it"[20] besides the fact that, in comparison to the works of Homer and Virgil, it constitutes "the greatest work of one of the greatest poets."[21]

It should be noted at this point that although the high moral standard of Portuguese culture had not been favourable to the translation of poets such as Virgil or Ovid in the past, in the translator's lifetime they would serve as models of rhetoric and skill, only to be imitated by those who "hear of them in such places or read of their invention".[22]

b) The genre, style and translation

Applying the principles established in Horace's *Ars Poetica* that specify the imitation of good examples for the perfection of Poetry,[23] the translator adopts a eulogistic attitude in relation to himself and the Latin poet (echoing D'Ablancourt), and in the same manner, regarding problems related to literary aesthetics and poetic creation, he reflects on the epistolary genre, which he considers exemplary of "strange taste", yet the best of the lower Poetry.

Subsequently, since he reveals his knowledge of other cultures "Letters held in such high esteem in all the civilized Nations of Europe, that there is no language that they have not been translated into"[24] the translator might be expected to shed light on these editions, but he makes no reference to any comments or earlier translations, not even indirectly, and there is also no indication of the source he used.

However, he states that he is hopeful of being listed in the *República Literária*, if not as a writer, at least as a translator (note the recurrent theme of humility), an idea that is subsequently discredited when he declares that he is the first to have translated Sabini and Sidronius.[25] He also explains to his readers that he belongs to the populace, but not being "without invention and education", he prepared himself for the great task "out of patriotic zeal", which, suggests on the one hand, that he is up to

---

[20] "necessário adivinhar para as entender"
[21] "a máxima obra de um dos poetas máximos"
[22] "ouviram falar em tais lugares ou leram a respeito da invenção"
[23] The eighteenth-century cult for Horace led to the publishing of at least seven translations of *Ars Poetica*, one of which was translated by Miguel do Couto Guerreiro. There are also allusions to Horace in his *Tratado da Versificação Portuguesa, dividido em três partes*, as well as in his *Epigramas Portugueses*.
[24] "Cartas tão estimáveis em todas as Nações cultas da Europa, que nenhuma há, em cuja límgua elas não andem traduzidas"
[25] Sabini and Sidronius are considered by some to be the authors of several epistles found in the Ovidian *Heroides*.

date in terms of his thoughts on a new image of scholars on the social scale, and on the other, the continuity of the functional aspects of translation, grounded at the level of utility and devised to enrich the language and to culturally expand the nation.

Confirming this idea, the translator focuses on the specific elements of translating texts in rhymed verse, and states that he almost lost his senses in his efforts to avoid producing "an enormous monster" when translating the meaning of the Letters. Following this, justifying the alterations by means of numerous quotes from Horace's *Ars Poetica*–also demonstrating his understanding of the translation ideas of the era–he calls for a translation that is more faithful to the meaning, even though the two meanings are not always in harmony: "as happens every time that he [the Author] becomes unworthy of this harmony", given that "good practice requires that what the Author says in these passages be totally omitted or replaced by honest and decent thoughts".[26]

Interestingly enough, in the case of these passages, the translator had initially thought of having them printed with a different typeset, so that those who were interested could read them in the original, but eventually chose infidelity over imitation in this case, so as to save the readers "this work."

Advocating the theory that what is to be expected from translation is "the concept that the words and sentences mean, expressed with energy and elegance",[27] Miguel do Couto Guerreiro refers to the style of other editions and to earlier comments, displaying knowledge of the problems of translation that result from the different language structures, and that the reception of the translated text depends on the requirements of the context in which it was produced.

Along this line, he takes a defensive tone in condemning the translators of Latin or French works who "were fixated with clinging to the words and phrases"[28] (Dolet, D'Ablancourt) of the authors, inventing a Lusitanian-Latin or Galician-Lusitanian language," which makes it almost "as difficult to understand the translation as the original".[29] In this manner, between respect for the integrity of the author and the desire to eternalize his own name, between betrayals, explanations, recommendations and

---

[26] "assim sucede todas as vezes que ele (o Autor) se faz indigno dessa concórdia" / " os bons costumes clamavam que ou omitisse totalmente o que o Autor dizia nesses lugares, ou os suprisse com pensamentos honestos e decentes"

[27] "o conceito que as palavras e as frases significam, expresso com energia e elegância"

[28] "viciados em se aferrar às palavras e frases"

[29] "tão dificultosa de entender a tradução como o original"

criticism, the translator alludes negatively to the puns, acrostics, and pleonastic circumlocutions of "depraved taste" of the poets of the "Reborn Phoenix", stressing at this point the need for a new form of writing literature that may be observed so as to avoid "scholastic terms" in favour of others that are more "commonly known". Thus, regarding the choice of vocabulary, criticizing those who merely appreciated the academic style, Couto Guerreiro exemplifies a modern taste, that was predominantly concerned with searching for reality:

> (...) in poetry one should not speak of the donkey; but if the forbidden animal should have to be spoken of, it should be called a *simple four-legged, long-eared beast of burden.* Speaking of a horse is a capital offence: *wild beast* should be used, or *Andalusian.* Such that, when it is stated that someone is mounted upon a wild beast, one does not understand whether it is a horse or an ox; and stating that someone is mounted on an Andalusian, that which first comes to mind is a man rather than a horse; and such is the case of '*Algaravio*', normally understood to be a man, rather than a dried fig.[30]

This method of translation, one of the styles in the French practice, consisted of suppressing or replacing some passages with others that were more in keeping with the tastes of the new reading public, which led to freedom of choice of forms in translation. Thus, falling back on the authority of Horace, Claudian Claudianus and Metius to justify the rhythm and the "consonance" of his verses, the translator states that he is confident in the method chosen to present the work to readers, but that his work will inevitably fall into the hands of critics of "good or bad will, of bad and good results"[31] to whom he pays as much attention as does "the Moon to dogs that bark at it".[32]

c) Self-censorship and literary censorship

Justifying translation options based on didactic objectives, and this time insinuating that the pre-existing source text merely served as raw

---

[30] "na poesia se não deve falar em burro; mas que havendo de entrar nela o interdito animal se deve chamar, por exemplo, *Simples bruto de balão, Quadrúpede, grande orelha.* Falar-se em cavalo é crime de primeira cabeça: deve dizer-se *bruto*, ou *Andaluz.* De modo que dizendo-se, que ia um sujeito montado em um bruto, não ficamos entendendo, se ia em cavalo, se em boi; e dizendo-se, que ia montado em um Andaluz, mais depressa entendemos homem que figo"
[31] "boa ou má vontade, de efeito e de bom efeito"
[32] "a lua dos cães que lhe ladram"

material for a new text, the translator displays attitudes of reverence toward the censors (and editors) saying "that they are not obliged to rack their brains over the work of others",[33] and he expresses concerns as to the commercial book circuits. However, he states that he will continue to defend his work energetically against critics who are unfair "simply in order to show off their knowledge".[34]

After the explanations for the formal and moral reasons that led him to transform the source text, the translator's anticipation of possible censorship on receipt of the work appears to have been opportune, since he received some negative criticism from his contemporary Costa e Silva.[35]

Other peritextual components linked to the preliminary text and to the context of the translation include concerns regarding the price of the translated book, so that everyone could benefit from it at moderate expense,[36] the explanation of gaps, and the texts attached to the translations in the form of catalogues, where excellence was required, yet with the fear of complaints that they would not account for themselves. In this area, explicitly developing strategies of self-censorship and defence, Miguel do Couto Guerreiro takes great care at the end of every translated story to analyze the principles that a good imitator can take advantage of from these analyses. It is, in fact, in these textual spaces that the moralization becomes evident, as is the case of the fable chosen for this paper, in which, by using persuasive arguments and pleading causes with its rhyming tercets, the author sets out teachings for married women, who, in the absence of their husbands, ought to behave with modesty and honesty.

In this case, despite being restricted by the ethical and moral values of the royal censorship board, *Real Mesa da Comissão Geral sobre o Exame e Censura dos Livros*, and reshaping his translation with original moralities and unique responses, also in the form of epistles given to the

---

[33] "que não têm obrigação de quebrar a cabeça com trabalhos alheios"
[34] "puramente para mostrar que sabem"
[35] The indications and excerpts are based on information found in Inocêncio, *op. cit*: 232-234 and in Pinilla and Sánchez, *op. cit*: 106. A few of the expressions include: "verbose translation," "tercets well-conceived," "ruinous teaching principles on the part of the author (translation)," "lack of classical studies," "crude phrases," etc.
[36] It is interesting to note that, the information preceding the index of the translation informs the reader as to one of the aspects related to the commercial circulation of books: "The first and third tomes were each taxed for the amount of three hundred and fifty *reis*, paper currency. The Royal Censor board, *Meza*, 16th of March, 1789. It includes three signatures."

heroines, is there not an idea in this *Prefação* that it could be regarded as literary work, an idea of the translation as re-creation, i.e. the brightening in the literary system of the concept of originality?

It is also possible within the *Protestação* to confirm that the processes of "imitation" are coherent with the exposed paratextual guidelines and to find elements that reveal the reasons for the censure of the ideological and ethical contents of the Latin *Heroides*. In fact, demonstrating that he does not recognize Ovid as an unquestionable authority in the perception of the marvellous pagan, on the last page of Tome II:

> The Translator protests that, if in what he wrote as an Author, he uses some terms that only belong to Gentile Theology, he uses them as supposition and not as belief in the doctrine of the Gentiles; because he is truly Roman Catholic.[37]

This declaration is once again obvious evidence of the strictness imposed by the censorship board, to which the translator would submit his work, or which he would comply with in advance, with a view to the legal circulation of the work, but which he also benefited from to produce his own personal work.

However, it should be made clear that, on the whole, in relation to the paratexts (and even on the front and inside covers), "the opinions printed give rise to the misleading conclusion that the examiner limited himself to approving or rejecting the books presented" (Saraiva 1950-1962: 139).[38] Thus, even though it has not been possible to ascertain whether there was direct censorship of this translation, or whether the alterations and suppressions to "purge the evil" were of the translator's own doing, the fact is that "the most perfect example suggesting that the author (and translator) were subject to censorship is found in the form of a protest, the *Protestação*" (Martins 2005:798),[39] which is formulated in a similar way to the example to which we refer. It can also be argued that, as a rule,

> the forced docile obedience of the authors was compensated for, in part, through the publication of the texts, the opinions and the licenses, without cuts and reformulations imposed by the censorship authorities, and in this

---

[37] "Protesta o Traductor, que se no que escreveu, como Author, usa de alguns termos só próprios da Teologia Gentílica, os usa, supondo, e não crendo a doutrina dos Gentios; porque é verdadeiro Católico Romano"

[38] "os pareceres impressos levam à enganadora conclusão de que o revedor se limitava a provar ou a reprovar os livros apresentados"

[39] "o exemplo mais perfeito da declaração de sujeição de um autor (e tradutor) ao poder censório encontra-se sob a forma de *Protestação*"

manner allowing the self-esteem of the authors/translators to be restored (Martins 2005:799).[40]

Meanwhile, it would seem pertinent to recall that all these textual materials are dependent on the translated text, while at the same time guiding its reception and the actual writings of the translation, revealing information regarding both the cultural context of the era and the type of discussion in relation to translation norms.

Whichever is the case, in addition to the compliance with the set of norms to which he was subjected, or which he imposed on himself, other attitudes of censorship are contained within this translation which, given their relatively subtle nature, can only be understood by means of a more detailed study of the micro and macro structural aspects of the translated text.

2. Translation differences in *Laodomia e Protesilau*

Regarding the various versions of the story concerning the love between Laodamia and Protesilaus, *Heroides* presents a letter supposedly written by the desperate heroine to her new husband, persuading him to have some compassion for the great love that she has nurtured for him and advising him to leave the war in Troy.

Having handled the "accessories" so well, the poet-translator could not, as he himself states, leave the original totally intact. By incorporating the material borrowed from the Ovidian text, we are faced with a text which is cohesive, but which, in relation to the source text, is full of gaps, rejection or replacement of words. Moreover, while a number of elements have been changed for reasons of style, or to accommodate the Portuguese rhyme, there are others that are clearly and necessarily related to the inevitable duty to moralize.

At this point a question arises: what forms of immorality were there in *Heroides* that need to be purged? In order to answer this question it is necessary to look at several sections of the source and target texts so as to gain a better understanding of the strategies used by the translator or by the official censor. After an initial reading, it becomes very clear that the aesthetic attributes of the production of verse are enhanced to the detriment of the erotic elements. The choice of texts under study will be

---

[40] " a docilidade forçada dos autores era compensada, em parte, pela publicação dos textos dos pareceres e das licenças, omitindo a existência de cortes e de reformulações impostas pelas autoridades censórias, vendo assim os autores / tradutores reparada a sua auto-estima"

looked at from three perspectives: a) the text as poem, b) the "training of the translator" and c) the occlusion of obscenities.

a) Complying with rule XXV, amongst others, of the *Tratado da Versificação Portuguesa* (1984),[41] "In lengthy poems there is beauty / If there is variety in the consonants; / Yet it is less of a shortcoming to repeat them / Than to compose inaudible sentences", Miguel do Couto Guerreiro converted the Latin couplets to rhyming tercets, a difficult task, but which, according to Costa e Silva,[42] sometimes resulted in verses that were truly poetic, in terms of images and also in relation to the echoes of Camões evoked:

Latin Text[43]	Eighteenth-century Portuguese translation
Hectore nescio quem timeo; Paris Hectore dixit/ Ferrea sanguinea belle mouere manu.	Não sei, que Heitor me cerca de cuidados,/ Um, de quem Paris disse, que em peleja/ sangue verte com braços bronzeados.
Hectora, quisquis is est, si sum tibi cara, caueto;/ Signatum memori pectore nomen habe	Se te lembras de mim, qualquer que seja, / Este Heitor, anda dele acautelado, / Seu nome na lembrança, sempre esteja.

Literal translation of Portuguese translation:

I know not which Hector encircles me with care / One of whom Paris spoke, who in battle / blood gushes from tanned arms.

If you remember me, however that may be / This Hector knowest that / His name in memory, will always remain.

Even though the rhyme and the metre are maintained in the Portuguese translation, insofar as the poetic development of the translation is not aesthetically even, this raises the question as to whether this is not part of a strategy to draw the attention of the censor to the merits of the expression, to the consent based on the beauty of the poetry.

---

[41] Page 20.
[42] See Inocêncio, *op . cit:* 234.
[43] The Latin text is found in Letter XIII, *Laodamia Protesilao*, from the lesson of *Les Belles Lettres*, 1965, pp. 79- 85.

For a more complete answer, it would be interesting to check other translations and works by the author/translator, a task that will have to be left for a future research project.

b) The criticism that Costa e Silva levels at the translator/poet,[44] accusing him of being unenlightened, seems to be unfounded. The suggestion that he left the profession of shoemaker in order to pursue a course in medicine is a rather dubious assertion: according to research carried out by Inocêncio, it is completely devoid of all truth (Inocêncio *idem*: 234). In the midst of the epithets of "a simple rhymester of prose" and "one of the best amongst our poets of satire, not only for the number of poems of this genre published, but also for the morality and decency that prevail therein" (*Ibidem*: 232-233),[45] the critics remain hesitant. As to his bibliography, it can be noted that his three books of "useful" satire are followed by eight books of elegies, from which he also removed the erotic elements that they generally contained, replacing them with themes on human misery. A more scholarly or Latinized choice of expressions might be expected from such a gifted poet and mediator with a strong religious disposition, were it not necessary to take into consideration the fact that the translator was aware that the language might offend some people, but that it surely would serve those readers who possessed insufficient "intelligence" in Latin. Thus, having openly declared his commitment to spreading culture, the use of older or more popular words might reflect an anti-scholarly attitude, which would much please the governmental authorities and the Royal censorship board. The translation reveals the translator's struggle between translating the semantic aspect of the words and retaining their meaning. It could be argued that the authority of reason during the Neo-classical period would have invalidated any artistic expression which did not clearly present the ideas contained within it (Terry Cochran 1984: 8).

---

[44] See footnote 12.
[45] "um dos primeiros lugares entre os nossos poetas satíricos, não só pelo número de poemas deste género que publicou, mas pela moralidade e decência que publicou"

Latin text	Eighteenth-century Portuguese translation
…Et quia tua uela uocaret, …uentus erat.	. Bom vento…vento malvado.
gélida maesta refecit aqua.	. Fazem que eu a mim torne borrifada
. Pectora legitimus casta momordit amor.	. Este meu peito casto anda roído
. Classe uiuisque potens, per quae fera bella geruntur; / Et sequitur regni pars quota quemque sui?	. Na armada, que faz guerra, e grande parte / Dos seus fortes vassalos o seguia.
. Pees tuus offenso limine signa dedit.	. Que saindo da porta tropeçaste
. remoque moue ueloque carinam	. Mete remo, mete vela
. Vestras quisque redite domos	. arribai às consortes, mães e manos.

Literal translation of Portuguese translation:

Gentle wind ... malevolent wind.
Covers mine own with mist
This my chaste heart aches
In the armada that wages war, and a large part / Of their strong vassals follow with them.
When you crossed the doorway, you stumbled
Position oars, position sail
seek comfort in your consorts, mothers and siblings.

c) The allusions to eroticism or the broaching of themes linked to sex in national literature were continually one of the major obstacles that intellectuals had to face in the light of censorship in Portugal. Thus, it is logical that a close eye would have been kept on the maintenance of social order and good habits. In a society where behaviour that was against public morals was prohibited, would it have been possible to allow the work of an erotic Latin poet from a distant and immoral society to go unpunished?

Latin text	Eighteenth-century Portuguese translation
. Oscula plura uiro mandataque plura dedissem, / Et suntquae uolui dicere multa tibi.	. Então me despedira, então te dera / mil conselhos; e o que hoje está guardado, / E não pude dizer então dissera.
. amanti	. Amorosos companheiros
. Officium fecere pium	. Obra pia
. malus hospes	. hóspede aleivoso
. Tu mihi luce dolor, tu mihi nocte uenis. / Nocte tamen quam luce magis ; nox grata puellis, / Quarum suppositus colla lacertus habet. / Aucupor in lecto mendaces caelibe somnos; / Dum careo ueris, gaudia falsa luuant.	. Sobre as terras, ou seja noite, ou dia, / Tu és a qualquer hora o meu cuidado. / Há nas horas diurnas companhia; / Divirto-me com ela; e não é tanta / dessa tua saudade a tirania. / Chega a noite, o cuidado o sonho espanta; mal pelo sono passo; e tal é esse, / .Que em vez de controlar-me, me quebranta.
. Quae mihi dum referes, quamuis audire iuuabit, / Multa tamen capies oscula, multa dabis;	. Talvez te interrompesse com meiguices; / Talvez tu em igual correspondência / Da tua te distraísses.
. adultera	. adúltera malvada.
. Arma dabit, dumque arma dabit, simul oscula sumet / (Hoc genus officit).	. Dando as armas também estarão dando / Sinais dos seus amores: que prazeres / Para os dois será este afecto brando!
. Crede mihi, plus est quam quod uideatur, imago; / Adde sonum cerae, Protesilaus erit. / Hanc specto teneoque sinu pró cônjuge uero / Et, tam quam possit uerba referre, queror.	. Digo-lhe o que presente te diria; / E por vezes nos braços o sustenho. / Crê-me, que este retrato se avalia / em mais do que parece; / Se falasse o meu Proteselau. / Nele pasmada estou, qual se pasmasse / em ti; com muitas culpas o censuro, / Como se ele resposta me tornasse.

Literal translation of Portuguese translation:

I bid you farewell, a thousand recommendations / advising you a thousand ways; and that which today is kept [silent], / What I couldn't say, I shall now say.

> Loving companions
> Good work
> disloyal host
> Over the lands, be it night or day, / At all hours you are my concern. / There is company during the daylight hours; / I enjoy the company; and my melancholy for you is not so tyrannical. / Night falls, concern distances the dream; I hardly sleep; and it is such, / That instead of controlling me, it breaks me.
> I might interrupt you with my tenderness; / You might in turn / Be distracted from yours.
> Wicked adulteress
> Giving the arms is also giving / Signs of your love: what pleasure / For both of us shall be this mild affection!
> I tell you what I would say in your presence; / And often times hold in my arms. / Believe me, that this portrait is more than it seems; / If my Protesilaus could speak. / I am fixated on him, as if I were fixated / on you; with my blame I censor him, / As though he considers me the answer.

Apart from some excerpts containing missing words and changes in word order in relation to the classical Latin rhetoric, the translated text does not contain any infidelities in terms of meaning. In relation to the choice of words, there are various disparities that are often due to limitations imposed by the need for correct pronunciation and for prosody or speech-rhythms. It is clear that the preference for rhyme, with the aim of rendering elasticity at the levels of syntax and vocabulary in the target language, the purification and simplification of the language and the speed of the rhythm reduce the local colour and the seriousness of the tone of the pre-existing work. Nonetheless, the adoption of this poetic form, frequent in eighteenth-century translations,[46] fits within the parameters of a new literary dynamic, where once again translation in rhyme becomes an efficient resource that provokes alterations in the canons of the linguistic and literary systems. Among other modifications to be highlighted in the text, we can point to the addition of qualifiers to emphasize the sensual meaning of certain nouns, as in the case of "wicked adulteress", and also, the omission of expressions semantically linked to the intimacy of the characters.

---

[46] The reference made is to various translations and other texts that include rhymed compositions, among others those published by the translator Miguel do Couto Guerreiro. Aside from a general theoretical view of the problem presented in *Arte Poética* by Francisco José Freire in 1748, the more technical points related to poetry, such as metrification and versification were broached by Pedro José da Fonseca in the Prologue of his translation of *Ars Poetica* by Horace (1790) and by Miguel do Couto Guerreiro (1784), in the aforementioned work.

On the other hand, the intertextual handling of the mythological characters is achieved successfully, such that the alternation of the original discourse registers remains. Traces of oral register, as well as a number of incursions on the part of the translator, underscore the dramatic shades of the epistle, and the expressions of religious temperament, such as, "the good works," are literally preserved.

In this re-working, "purged of obscenities", there appears to be a concern on the part of the translator to present his first readers, the *Real Mesa da Comissão Geral sobre o Exame e Censura dos Livros,* with a text that has been intentionally and explicitly manipulated, so that a moralized edition could circulate amongst his readers, one that would not only revive a seldom-read classical author, but also one that would instil in them the need to uphold the Portuguese language and its literature, while consolidating and spreading the taste for classics.

Thus, Miguel do Couto Guerreiro's imitation lies somewhere between translation and literary worth, or even between interpretation and rhyming translation. If the translation of poetry, with its linguistic challenges has always been considered a prime example of complex reading, then this particular work reveals him as a neo-classical translator, who has managed to present and interpret subjects imagined by a prestigious author, in another language. In other words, the translator neither attains perfection, the sublime of which he speaks in his introduction, nor does he faithfully follow the expressions and phrases that give life to the discourse. Instead, he applies a "genological and individual transformation" to his translation, which is governed by literary and censorship codes, by his own subjective idiolect and by his ideology,[47] presenting us with a text of creative character that is not difficult to read. This effort to retain an individual identity while translating gains relevance if we consider some of his other theoretical reflections on translation, such as the one included in the advice "To the Reader" of *Ars Poetica by Horace Translated in Rhyme*. In this work the translation is characterized as having been a "difficult undertaking because it depends on two conditions: one, myself in Horace via thoughts; and the other, Horace in myself via expression" (*apud* Sibilla 1995: 105).[48] This insight demonstrates the idea of applying the writing processes and the dominant mentality of the time to the source text, so that the translation can be integrated into the receiving culture. With regards to its acceptance, there is evidence that the reading public had a strong desire

---

[47] Based on Popovic, Bassnett distinguishes five types of expressive transformation: constitutive, genological, individual, negative and topic.

[48] "empresa dificultosa porque depende de duas situações: uma, de mim em Horácio pelos pensamentos; outra de Horácio em mim pela expressão"

to read *Heroides* in the Portuguese language. What is demonstrated, therefore, is translation as an activity which ensures the survival of a text, by giving it a new form in a new culture. In other words, the self-controlling of the poetic norms and the manipulation requirements performed confirm that Miguel do Couto Guerreiro was a censor and editor of his own work, that he was an incorporated translator, who incorporated this new cultural atmosphere to which he contributed with his moral obligations both to the original author and to the readers of the translation, or rather, the analysed translation, which "represents the cultural ideology toward which the authorities had hoped that Portuguese society would incline" (Guedes 1987: 106).[49] Furthermore, considering the choice of the text by Ovid, the title of the translation itself, "in rhyme", and the options taken in the act of translation, and therefore, in the order of discourse, could these not all be signs that the translator not only interpreted the source, but also manipulated it and imposed self-censorship? In response to this question, we can only state that "as Susan Bassnett noted, due to the fact that we are human beings it is impossible not to interpret, and for that reason, several translations of one same text are different. In fact, in cases where a choice is given, does not the simple choice of text to be translated reveal a preference, an ideology and a certain world vision?" (África and Claramonte 1995: 84).

As can be seen, this type of censorship which is imposed or "voluntarily" adopted by the translator throughout the translation process shares some similarities with modern trends in the politics of Translation Studies. That is to say that parallels can be established regarding the idea of manipulation, and how and to what extent ideology moulds texts and translations (Bassnett 1980: 9-10), and the way in which relationships between discourse and power are continually altered and/or energized, as in the case of royal and religious authority that, incidentally, the translator made use of to creatively expand his model. In fact, by comparing this translation with the *Heroides* found in the *Cancioneiro Geral* of 1516, it can be concluded that both were translatable, acceptable and valid, yet both were produced according to different norms from different historical periods.

In conclusion, suffice to say that, in the same way that many translators of the eighteenth century did, Miguel do Couto Guerreiro not only created a text which was somewhat different from the original, since by imitating he had to make the imitation his own, but he was also an agent for

---

[49] "representa o ideal cultural para onde o Poder desejaria que a sociedade portuguesa pendesse"

Reading, since through him questions of a literary, editorial, translation and censorship nature arise.

References

Primary sources

Guerreiro, Miguel do Couto (1789) *Cartas de Ovídio chamadas Heroides, expurgadas de toda a obscenidade, e traduzidas em Rima vulgar*, 2 vol., Lisboa: Oficina Patriarcal de Francisco Luiz Ameno.

—. (1784) *Tratado da Versificação Portuguesa, dividido em três partes"*, Lisboa: Oficina Patriarcal de Francisco Luiz Ameno.

—. (1793) *Epigramas Portugueses*, Lisboa, Oficina Patriarcal.

Ovídio (1965) *Heroïdes* (texte établi par Henri Bornecque et traduit par Marcel Prévost), Paris: Les Belles Lettres.

Secondary sources

África, Maria Cármen/ Claramonte, Vidal (1995) *Traducción, manipulación, desconstrucción*, Salamanca: Biblioteca Filológica, Ed. Colegio de España.

Bassnett, Susan (1980) *Translation Studies*, London and New York: Methuen.

Carneiro, Manuel Cerejeira (1985) "Versão Portuguesa de Três cartas de Ovídio por João Roiz de Sá Meneses", in *Letras/Revista da Universidade de Aveiro*, nº 2.

Cidade, Hernâni (2005) *Ensaio sobre a Crise Cultural do Século XVIII*, Lisboa: Editorial Presença [1st ed: Coimbra, 1929].

Cochran, Terry (1984), *O Século XVIII Português*, www.Mapageweb.Umontreal.ca/cochran/ecrits/pdf/século.pdf. 5/jun/05.

Figueiredo, Fidelino de Souza (1921-1922) "Para a História do Humanismo em Portugal (Bibliographia de Traducções", in *Estudos de Litteratura. Artigos Vários*, 4ª Série, Lisboa: Portugalia, 217-245.

Freire, Anselmo Braancamp (1922) "A Censura e o Cancioneiro Geral", in *Boletim da Classe de Letras,* Coimbra: Imprensa da Universidade.

Garção, Pedro António Joaquim Correia (1958) *Obras Completas*, vol. I, Lisboa: Sá da Costa.

Guedes, Fernando (1987) *O Livro e a Leitura em Portugal–Subsídios para a sua História, Séculos XVIII e XIX*, Lisboa e São Paulo: Editorial Verbo.

Hermans, Theo (1985) "Introduction: Translation Studies as a New Paradigm" in *The Manipulation of Literature. Studies in Literary Translation*, London & Sidney: Croom Helm.

—. (1999) *Translation in Systems, Descriptive and System-Oriented Approaches Explained*, Manchester: St Jerome Publishing.

—. (1993), "Literary Translation: The Birth of a Concept", in José Lambert and André Lefevere (eds.), *La traduction dans le développement des littératures/Translation in the Development of Literatures*, Leuven: Leuven University Press, Peter Lang.

Hulpke, Erika (1991) "Cultural Constraints: A Case of Political Censorship", in Harald Kittel and Paul Frank (eds.) *Interculturality and the Historical Study of Literary Translations*, Berlin: Erich Schmith Verlag.

Martins, Maria Teresa Esteves Payan (2005) *A Censura Literária em Portugal nos Séculos XVII e XVIII*, Lisboa: FCG/FCT.

Pais, Carlos Castilho (1997) *Teoria Diacrónica da Tradução Portuguesa/Antologia (Séc. XV-XX)*, Lisboa: Universidade Aberta.

Pereira, Maria Helena da Rocha (1988) *Novos Ensaios sobre Temas Clássicos na Poesia Portuguesa*, Lisboa: Imprensa Nacional-Casa da Moeda.

Pinilla, José A./ Sánchez, Maria Manuela (1998) *O Discurso Sobre a Tradução em Portugal*, Lisboa: Colibri.

Rodrigues, A. A. Gonçalves (1992) *A Tradução em Portugal, Volume Primeiro: 1495-1834*, Lisboa: Imprensa Nacional-Casa da Moeda.

Rodrigues, Graça Almeida (1980) *Breve História da Censura Literária em Portugal*, Lisboa: Biblioteca Breve.

Saraiva, António José (1950-1962) *História da Cultura em Portugal*, 3 vol, Lisboa: Jornal do Foro.

Tahir-Cürçaglar, Sehnaz (2002) "What Texts Don't Tell–The Uses of Paratexts in Translation Research", in Theo Hermans (ed.), *Crosscultural Transgressions–Research Models in Translation Studies, Historical and Ideological Issues*, Manchester UK & Northampton MA: St. Jerome Publishing.

CENSORSHIP AND SELF-CENSORSHIP IN ENGLISH NARRATIVE FICTION TRANSLATED INTO SPANISH DURING THE EIGHTEENTH CENTURY

ETERIO PAJARES,
UNIVERSITY OF THE BASQUE COUNTRY, SPAIN

Abstract: Censorship played an important role in the cultural transfer of English fiction translated into Spanish in the Enlightenment. Translations were subjected to a double filter: one imposed by the government and the control of the Inquisition, this last one especially being stringent. Foreign works–and translations belong to that category–were particularly subject to inspection and the novel was considered as a minor and wasteful entertainment. In spite of this, the English novel of the 18th century was to become in time the model, par excellence, for modern fiction. The significant advance which came about in means of communication throughout that century favored the exchange of ideas and knowledge, despite the impediments imposed by those in power, unable to see anything in this exchange but the corruption of customs and a foreign-based "invasion".

There were numerous translations and the translators manipulated the texts in order to guarantee the publication of their efforts. Another important fact is that France, through its language and culture, becomes the medium through which eighteenth century Spaniards met the world beyond their shores. The translation of England's language and culture into Spanish is totally and completely mediated through the language and culture of France, a social and cultural phenomenon of no small moment. It could be said that every English novel translated into Spanish during the 18th century was done not through a source text (ST) but by means of a target text (TT) which has previously modified the ST. My purpose in this essay is to show the reader how censorship worked and in which way translators pre-filtered translations.

1. Censorship

Censorship played an important role in the intercultural transfer of English narrative fiction during the Enlightenment in Spain. Novels were submitted to a double filter: one by the government and another by the Inquisition. Foreign translated texts, and novels in particular, were a special target for censors, since they were unable to see anything in this genre but the corruption of customs and a foreign-based "invasion". Censorship was institutionalized for the first time in Spain in 1502. The application of censorship criteria would vary from government to government and, in spite of its harshness and the fact that the death penalty was one of the threats, the real truth is, as Defourneaux points out, that

> No theologian, no philosopher, no thinker, poet, humanist or scientist, perished in the flames of the Inquisition. Sentences of the court were generally mild during the eighteenth century and very rarely implied grievous punishment. (Defourneaux 1963: 165)[1]

One peculiarity of Spanish censorship, compared to other European countries–France, for example–was that while in those countries the Inquisition had no other power than spiritual punishment, in Spain, and in alliance with the State, it could inflict pecuniary and even physical affliction.

But what was censored? Rumeu de Armas gives us the answer:

> The perusal of these works and their censorship must not only examine whether they contain anything against Religion, good manners or the prerogatives of His Majesty, but if they are spurious, superstitious, reprobate or deal with things vain and useless, or if they contain any offence against the community, or private individuals, or against the honour and decorum of the Nation; and although the censor's judgement must extend to all these in order to form a decision, the censorship will suffice if it indicates whether there is anything against religion, good manners or the prerogatives of His Majesty, and if they are appropriate for publication. (Rumeu de Armas 1940: 45)[2]

---

[1] "Sans doute l'Inquisition espagnole n'a brûlé sur ses bûchers aucun penseur, aucun intellectuel. Les sentences du Saint Tribunal furent au XVIIIe siècle généralement douces et n'entraînèrent qu'assez rarement des peines afflictives."
[2] "El examen de estas obras y su censura no sólo ha de ser sobre si contienen algo contra la Religión, contra las buenas costumbres o contra las regalías de Su Majestad, sino también si son apócrifas, supersticiosas, reprobadas o de cosas

This is precisely what we have noticed in several of the official censorship reports studied and our procedure in this article is to examine the role of censorship and self-censorship in real practice. In this connection, the application made by José González de Francia for permission to print the Spanish translation of Fielding's *Joseph Andrews* states that "there is nothing in the translation contrary to the doctrine of our religion, nothing against the customs of a Christian country" (Archivo Histórico Nacional:[3] Consejos. Leg. 5562-77). A similar comment appears in the application formulated by Juan de Escoiquiz (AHN: Consejos. Leg. 51640- 36) for permission to print his translation of Edward Young's *Selected Works*. Among other things, this application states very clearly that the translation does not go against a) our holy faith; b) good manners; c) royal prerogatives; or d) the Laws of the country. A good job was done by the translator since the censor declares the translation: "expurgada de todo error" [free from errors] and it is authorised with certain corrections.

From time to time, the quality of the translation is judged, particularly when the censor is a qualified member of the literary establishment. Josef Baucis requests permission to print a translation of *Le commerce et le gouvernement considérés relativement l'un à l'autre* [*Trade and Government relatively considered to each other*] by the Abbot de Condillac (AHN: Consejos. Leg. 5550-58). The assigned censor is Jovellanos and though he praises the fidelity of the translation, he also observes that sometimes the TL lacks propriety. When Father Estala evaluates the translation *El comercio y gobierno considerado uno a otro relativamente* [*Trade and Government relatively considered to each other*] by Sir George Stanton and rendered into Spanish by María Josefa Luzuriaga, he points out:

> The translation shows extensive knowledge, accuracy, clarity and purity in its use of Spanish and I observe the translator has been skilful enough to omit or tone down certain expressions which would not be socially correct among us. (AHN: Consejos. Leg. 5562-63) [4]

---

vanas o sin provecho, o si contienen alguna ofensa a Comunidad o a particular o en agravio del honor y decoro de la Nación; y aunque el juicio y el dictamen del censor deba extenderse a todos estos respectos para formar su resolución, en la censura bastará que diga si contienen o no algo contra la Religión, buenas costumbres y regalía de Su Majestad, y si son o no dignas de la luz pública."

[3] From now on: AHN

[4] La traducción está hecha con mucho conocimiento, con exactitud, claridad y pureza de la lengua castellana y noto que el traductor ha tenido la destreza de omitir o suavizar algunas expresiones que entre nosotros serían malsonantes.

These comments allude not only to the phenomenon of translation but to self- censorship as we will see later on.

Censorship by the Church, or the Inquisition, hindered cultural transfer from other languages into Spanish and retarded the cultural development of the Enlightenment. There are reports in which works of fiction, and works in general, were authorised by the State but came up against an immense obstacle in the hands of the Inquisition. One is tempted to consider what is so harmful in that charitable comedy *Joseph Andrews* that it be blocked by the censor three times and in three different translations during the eighteenth century. In José González de Francia's version the state censor declares: "no hallar nada en ella contrario a los dogmas, la religión o las costumbres" [There is nothing in it against dogmas, religion or customs]. And he goes on to say: "está mejor hecha que lo que acostumbra la caterva de traductores de que estamos inundados" [It is better rendered than what is usual by the host of translators swamping us] and he is favourable to giving it the *plácet*. But the Church representative, the Vicario Eclesiástico de Madrid, finds the novel noxious and, without providing further reasons, passes judgment: "No ha lugar" [it is not proper], thus destroying the great effort of the translator and editor at a time when texts were handwritten and considering the reader, as part of the process of censorship, a Lilliputian.

But sometimes clergymen were victims of their own rapacious desire for prohibition. The careful reading of several reports of the time, worthy of a psychological study, show the frequent contradictions of this social class, never free from errors. Once D. Manuel de Araoz proposed, in 1791, the translation of a book written in French under the Spanish title of *El Onanismo. Disertación sobre las enfermedades producidas por los excesos venéreos y principalmente por la masturbación. [Onanism. Dissertation on diseases produced by venereal excesses, mainly by masturbation]*. Contrary to what one may think, the translation was not only authorised (in spite of "masturbation"), but judged to be "convenient". But, in order to save the souls of those readers incapable of understanding the frequent examples of bad behaviour provided in the translation, the Vicar imposed on the author the condition that it be published in Latin instead of Spanish. Who could speak Latin at the end of the eighteenth century when the language of diplomacy was mainly French? Only academics and seminary students. It seems that the unborn Freud, and the unconscious of course, played a shabby trick on the Vicario Eclesiástico here.

When the translated texts were about religion censors used a powerful magnifying glass, as can be observed in the translation of George Campbell's *Dissertation on Miracles* rendered into Spanish, directly from

English, by Cesáreo de Nava Palacio under the title *Defensa de los milagros del Pentateuco* [*A defence of the miracles of the Pentateuch*] (which implies harsh self-censorship). One of the greatest paradoxes of ecclesiastical censors is admitting that there is nothing really serious to be condemned in a particular piece of translated work and, almost immediately and without a convincing explanation, denying permission to print the work, as stated in this report:

> Concerning the main substance of the work there is no proposition in it against our faith, sane doctrine, good customs, and Royal Law, and its reading does not lead true wise people into error... / But among the ignorant and little cultivated faithful, among Catholics not very deeply rooted in their faith, and among Enlightenment intellectuals, who abound in present-day Spain, it is our understanding that the reading of this work, as it is translated, may cause great harm. (AHN: Consejos, Leg. 5559-30)[5]

2. Self-censorship

Censorship implies a certain degree of self-censorship, both in its conscious and unconscious variants. For this reason it seems obvious that following the struggles involved in translating a text, more difficult in the past than nowadays, the translator works hard in order to be successful in the publication of the target text (TT). Translators, on the other hand, were familiar with the legal legislation concerning their job. When they presented their work before the censors it was usually asserted that there was nothing in the translation that infringed the rules and that the source text (ST) had been conveniently purged. They went on to request that they kindly be notified if censors found any faults in order to modify the text according to the requirements. So the translator is a conscious/unconscious collaborator with the repressive machinery of censorship in order to achieve the final goal of the *imprimátur*. As we have seen in the TT of George Stanton's *Viaje al interior de la China y Tartaria* [*A Journey to the inside of China and Tartaria*], these amendments to the applications appear mostly in the paratext, in the foreword preceding the translation. These ideas emphasise the differences between catholic Spain and other,

---

[5] "en lo substancial a la obra ni se contiene proposición alguna contra la Fé, sana doctrina, buenas costumbres, y Pragmática Real, ni su leyenda induce, o da ocasion á los verdaderamente sabios para error alguno.../ Mas á los fieles ignorantes, o poco doctos, á los Católicos no mui arraigados en la fé, y á los Sabios del Siglo, sujetos de que abunda en el dia nuestra España, nos parece que la leyenda de esta Obra según que se halla traducida, puede ocasionar mucho perjuicio..."

particularly non-catholic, countries. One cannot yet sense here the perverted idea that English customs are deviant and immoral. For example, Ignacio García Malo says in his translation of Richardson's *Pamela*:

> Whether because English customs are more corrupt than ours, or because the English language admits certain expressions and idiomatic sayings which would would sound bad in ours, we have thought it convenient to reform or omit them, without in this way taking anything from the main plot or the background of the narrative. (Richardson 1793, I: III)[6]

It is true that most of these observations do not belong to the Spanish translators but to the French. Being especially sensitive about the point of good taste, there are many situations which they would consider should not be reflected on the printed page. English novels were always[7] translated from an intermediate text–French mostly–or "texto derivado" (Rabadán 2001) in a kind of mediated translation or "traducción mediada" (Merino 2004). Spaniards knew nothing about English life and customs. They closely followed the French *belles infidèles* and the norms of *bon goût* which were in favour of suppressions and changes to render the TT acceptable to the customs of the target culture. Be as it may, some of the changes can be attributed to the Spanish translator as can be seen in the rendering of *Pamela* in which García Malo transforms the wife of an English clergyman into an aunt and his daughter into his niece. That same year, 1794, the translator of *Clarissa,* in a similar situation, does not make any amendments; he simply includes a note stating that English clergymen are permitted to marry. Both novels were authorised. Similarly, Goldsmith's *The Vicar of Wakefield* could not be published in Spanish in the eighteenth century; it had to wait until 1833. The paratext advises the reader of the married condition of the protagonist in accord with the rules of the Anglican Church. At the same time, and after establishing the superiority of Catholicism as the only true faith, the translators speak so negatively of Anglican clergymen that it is a contradiction to present this novel (with such a paratext) as a model of "pure moral".

---

[6] "sea porque las costumbres de Inglaterra estan mas corrompidas que las nuestras, ó porque la índole de la lengua inglesa admite ciertas expresiones é idiotismos que sonarian mal en la nuestra, hemos juzgado oportuno reformarlas ó suprimirlas, sin que por esto falte nada á la accion principal, ó al fondo de la historia."
[7] Of all the novels we have studied only the TT of *Rasselas* by Samuel Johnson, translated by Inés Joyes y Blake in 1798, took English as a ST (Pajares 2000) and even here with the possibility of a consultation of a French version (Stone 2006).

> The clergy of the Church of England is not in any way as praiseworthy as ours. In all truth, it can and must be said that compared with the catholic clergy they are completely despicable. They separated from the Church of Rome under the pretext of reforming certain abuses, and if the truth be told there is no abuse from which the Anglican ministers can be said to be free..., but what worse abuse than their acceptance of matrimony? (Goldsmith 1833: 25)[8]

Félix Enciso Castrillón, himself a writer as well as a translator, says in his version of a novel by Elizabeth Helmet:[9]

> It is rare to find an English work in which we do not find portrayed the most ferocious acts, beyond the limits of human malice. This happens in the original of the text I present to the public; so I have been forced to translate it not literally, but giving it a new form and a new dénouement more proper to our character (Enciso 1808: 374). [10]

It is not easy to understand our early translators but it seems evident that in relation to the issue of conscious self-censorship they tried to influence ecclesiastical censors in order to win a favourable verdict. But what about unconscious self-censorship? To what extent were these translators inclined to believe that the job of the Inquisition was absolutely necessary and that it contributed to the salvation of their souls? Self-censorship and censorship will always be linked; they go hand in hand and cannot be understood separately. The human condition reveals that sometimes we are both tormentors and victims of our own existence. True to heart, and in spite of the zeal of censors, foreign ideas did penetrate the Peninsula and avoided the complete alienation of the spirit of the people of the time.[11] As the quick-witted Mariano José de Larra said, "ideas travel in

---

[8] "El clero de la iglesia Anglicana no es tan apreciable como el nuestro, en ningun sentido. Se puede y debe decir en obsequio de la verdad, que comparado con el clero católico es enteramente despreciable. Se separó de la iglesia de Roma con el pretesto de reformar abusos, y no hay abuso á decir verdad de que los ministros anglicanos no sean víctimas... pero ¿qué mas abuso que el de su pretenso matrimonial?"

[9] *Historia de Bruce y Emilia o el Quixote de la amistad*. Taken from García & Lafarga 2004.

[10] "Es rara la obra inglesa donde no se noten los actos más feroces y más fuera de los límites de la malicia humana. Esto sucede en el original de la obra que presento al público; y así me he visto precisado a no traducirla literalmente, sino antes bien a darla una nueva forma y un desenlace más propio de nuestro carácter"

[11] Due to the lack of space we do not focus on the consequences the practice of translation under the rules of censorship had in the target culture. Most of these can

stagecoaches together with parcels". Or, if you like, in the words of the French critic Marcelin Defourneaux,

> the Inquisition could not, in fact, separate Spain from European culture. Eighteenth century Spanish history shows the opposite. But some people living within its frontiers had the feeling of being confined in an "intellectual prison" through the bars of which freedom could be perceived. (Defourneaux 1963: 166)[12]

References

Primary sources

AHN, Consejos, Leg. 5562 (77) [*Las Aventuras de Joseph Andrews...*]
AHN, Estado, Leg. 3234 (37) [*Historia de las Aventuras de Joseph Andrews*]
AHN, Consejos, Leg. 5562 (68) [*Victorina ó la joven desconocida entre sus mismos padres*]
—. 5532-II (17) [*El pleito sin fin ó la Historia de Juan Bull*]
—. 11283 (7) [*Pamela Andrews ó la virtud recompensada*]
—. 51640 (36) [*Obras selectas de Eduardo Young*]
—. 5551 (9) [*El último día del mundo*]
—. 5 550 (58) [*El comercio y gobierno considerado uno á otro relativamente*]
—. 5562 (63) [*Viaje al interior de la China... recopilado por Sir Jorge Stanton*]
—. 5547 (14) [*Observaciones sobre la curación de la gonorrea*]
—. 5559 (30) [*Defensa de los Milagros del Pentateuco*]
—. 5561 (27) [*Educación de los niños*]
—. 3238 (6) [*Dedicatoria de El Paraíso Perdido*]
—. 5562 (12) [*Historia del Caballero Carlos Grandison*]
—. 5560 [*Historia del Caballero Carlos Grandison*]

---

be seen in the series of essays written by Eterio Pajares on English novels rendered into Spanish.

[12] "l' Inquisition n'a pas, en fait, fermé l'Espagne à la culture européenne; toute l'histoire du XVIIIe siècle espagnol démontre le contraire. Mais elle a donné à certains de ceux qui vivaient à l'intérieur de ses frontières l'impression d'être enfermés dans une 'prison intellectuelle' à travers les barreaux de laquelle ils pouvaient entrevoir la liberté."

Secondary sources

Defourneaux, Marcelin (1963) *L'Inquisition espagnole et les livres français au XVIIIe siècle*, Paris: Presses Universitaires de France.

García, María Jesús & Lafarga, Francisco (2004) *El discurso sobre la traducción en la España del siglo XVIII. Estudio y antología*, Kassel: Reichenberger.

Goldsmith, Oliver (1833) *La familia de Primrose. Novela moral escrita en Ingles por el celebre O. Goldsmith con el título de The Vicar of Wakefield y traducida al castellano por D. A. B. y L. D. C.*, Barcelona: Imprenta de A. Bergnes.

Merino, Raquel (2004) "Progresión metodológica en un estudio descriptivo de traducciones", in José Maria Bravo (ed.) *A New Spectrum of Translations Studies*, Valladolid: Universidad de Valladolid, 231-264.

Pajares, Eterio (2000) "Contra las 'Belles infidèles': la primera traducción al español del *Rasselas* de Samuel Jonson". *Trans. Revista de traductología*, 4: 89-99.

Rabadán, Rosa (2001) "Las cadenas intertextuales inglés-español: traducciones y otras interferencias (inter)semióticas", in Eterio Pajares, Raquel Merino & José Miguel Santamaría (eds.) *Trasvases culturales: literatura, cine y traducción*, Bilbao: Universidad del País Vasco 3, 29-42.

Rabadán, Rosa & Merino, Raquel (2004) "Introducción", in Gideon Toury *Los estudios descriptivos de traducción, y más allá. Metodología de la investigación en estudios de traducción. (Descriptive Translation Studies and beyond)*. Translation, forewords and notes by Raquel Merino & Rosa Rabadán, Madrid: Cátedra.

Richardson, Samuel (1793) *Pamela Andrews ó la virtud premiada*, Madrid: Imprenta Real, I: III.

Rumeu de Armas, Antonio (1940) *Historia de la censura literaria gubernativa en España*, Madrid: M. Aguilar.

Stone, John (2006) *Samuel Johnson as Linguist, Critic, Essayist, and Writer of Narrative Fiction: Literary Historiography and Reception*, Diss. Barcelona: Universidad de Barcelona.

IBERIAN CENSORSHIP AND THE READING OF *LAZARILLO* IN 19TH CENTURY PORTUGAL[1]

RITA BUENO MAIA, UNIVERSIDADE DE LISBOA, PORTUGAL

Abstract: Hendrik van Gorp (1981) in his pioneer work on the European translations of the Spanish picaresque canon concludes that pilot translations have a key role in the modulation of the later translations and, consequently, in the construction of the national picaresque literatures.

La vida de Lazarillo de Tormes y de sus fortunas y adversidades, the first picaresque novel, was forbidden by the Spanish Inquisition a few years after its first edition (?), while an expurgated version by Juan López de Velasco could be printed and read. Portuguese Indexes were inspired by the Spanish ones. The original *Lazarillo* was banned in 1581, while the censored one was allowed in 1624.

This present essay shall focus on the possible influence of Velasco's 1599 version, *Lazarillo Castigado*, on the first Portuguese translation of Lazarillo de Tormes and, based on van Gorp's hypothesis, explore the possibility that the first translation influenced a later one. Finally, it will reflect on the consequences of the interference of the censors in the external structure of this novel and its influence in the understanding of the Portuguese readership of the picaresque genre.

1. Introduction

If we wished to define the latest study trends in the picaresque, we could well begin with the greater attention given to the reception of these novels in their original context and in the different target contexts that have imported them. For example, Hendrik van Gorp dedicates a few pages of *Poetics Today* (1979) to the study of the first European translations of picaresque novels, justifying it with the belief that the pilot translations

---

[1] I wish to thank Mick Greer for kindly revising this text.

were those "that drove the later versions and contributed to the creation of a picaresque literature in the different literary systems" (209).[2]

Supposing it possible that the pilot translations were a main source in the construction and modulation of the picaresque genre in the different European contexts, this paper shall focus on the possible influence of the Spanish censured version on the first Portuguese translation of *La vida de Lazarillo de Tormes y de sus fortunas y adversidades* and then explore the possibility that the first translation influenced a later one.

2. *Lazarillo* and the Iberian censorship

We don't know the exact date of *Lazarillo*'s first edition, but the oldest four editions still available are from 1554. In 1559, only five years later, it was banned in the *Cathalogues librorum qui prohibentur mandato Fernadi de Valdes* published in Valladolid. The reasons for this ban are the same ones used by Bataillon to justify the book's great success: "the popular anti-clericalism present in the picaresque novel and its lack of respect for the powerful were supported, after all, by the new anti-clerical attitude of the men of literature" (Bataillon, 1968: 71).[3] The anonymity aroused the Inquisition's suspicions as well.

In 1573, Juan López de Velasco, a man of literature, offered the censors an expurgated version of *Lazarillo*, entitled *Lazarillo Castigado*, where all the passages considered offensive to the Christian faith and the established order were suppressed. Perceiving a non-correspondence between the titles of the chapters and their content,[4] he modifies the book segmentation and the titles of the different *tratados*. In 1583, in the *Index et catalogues librorum prohibentorum*, responsible for censorship, Gaspar Quiroga restored the ban on the original *Lazarillo*: "Lazarillo de Tormes, parts one and two, except the ones corrected and printed after 1573".[5]

In Portugal the picaresque novel was first banned in the 1581 Index, printed by order of Dom Jorge de Almeida, the Lisbon archbishop and general inquisitor; although the section dedicated to books in the

---

[2] "qui ont dirigé les versions ultérieures et qui ont même contribué a créer une literature picaresque dans les différents systèmes littéraires."
[3] "anticlericalismo popular de la novela picaresca, su falta de respeto para con los poderosos, encontraban apoyo, en fin de cuentas, en el nuevo anticlericalismo de los letrados (…)"
[4] It's now consensually accepted that the division of chapters was made by the first editor, probably against the author's wish.
[5] "Lazarillo de Tormes, primera y segunda parte: no siendo de los corregidos, e impressos de 1573 á esta parte"

Portuguese language was under the responsibility of Fr. Bartolomeu Ferreira. This fact proves the beginning of *Lazarillo*'s diffusion through the Portuguese readership, as the bans on vernacular books present in the Portuguese 1564 Index had their origin in the Valdés 1559 Index. Nevertheless, Ferreira decided not to include the ban on *Lazarillo* at that point.

In the large 1624 Index, the responsibility of the Jesuit priest Baltazar Álvares, *Lazarillo de Tormes* is, once again, present: "This book printed before the year of 1559 is totally forbidden, but that printed in the same year in Madrid, or a similar one, is allowed with the following changes".[6] The demand of these eight textual modifications would remain till 1768.

The two earlier Portuguese editions of *Lazarillo de Tormes*, the one published in 1626, in Lisbon by Antonio Alvarez and the one printed at Domingos Carneiro's bookbinder (Lisbon) in 1660, reproduce the censored version of the picaresque novel.

3. The 1786 re-edition of the first Portuguese translation of *Lazarillo*

In 1721, António Faria Barreiros, a typographic corrector, published *Vida de Lazarilho de Tormes: historia entretenida e traduzida do castelhano* [*The Life of Lazarilho de Tormes: a pleasing story and translated from Castilian*] in Bernardo da Costa Carvalho's Lisbon workshop. Martino (1999) had access to this damaged book present in the Biblioteca Municipal do Porto and, through an exhaustive textual analysis, he identified Domingos Carneiro's 1660 edition as its source text. This edition has a particularity with important consequences in the configuration of the picaresque genre in the Portuguese target context.

The interference of Juan Velasco in the external structure of the novel can be summarised as follows: he suppresses the fourth chapter, the shortest and the most suggestive of all, where the author uses the metaphor "romper los zapatos" [tear the shoes] as an allusion to the sexual initiation of the child, victim of the master's sodomy (a friar). He suppresses the fifth as well, which narrates Lázaro's astonishing discovery of the lies and trickery used by his master to lead the *believers* to buy his bulls. The title "Prólogo" [Prologue] is modified to "Prólogo del autor a un amigo suyo"[Author's prologue to a friend of his], creating a contrast between the form of address that figures in the title and the one used in the text

---

[6] "Esta obra impressa antes do ano de 1599 de todo se proíbe, mas a impressa no dito ano em Madrid, ou outra como ela, se permite com as seguintes emendas"

(*vuestra merced*). The first *tratado* ("Cuenta Lázaro su vida y cúyo hijo fue" [Lázaro tells about his life and his parents]) is divided in two: "Lázaro cuenta su linaje y nacimiento" [Lázaro tells about his genealogy and birth] and "Assiento de Lázaro con el ciego" [Lázaro settles with a blind man], the second and the third ("Cómo Lázaro se assentó con un Clérigo y de las cosas que con él pasó" [How Lázaro took up with a priest and the things that happened to him with that man] and "Cómo Lázaro se assentó con un Escudero y de lo que acaeció con él" [How Lázaro took up with a Squire and what happened then) are maintained, with the suppression of these passages judged offensive or heretical, as well as the modification of its titles: "Assiento de Lázaro con un clérigo" [Lázaro settles with a Priest] and "Assiento de Lázaro con un Escudero" [Lázaro settles with a Squire]. Finally, *tratados* six and seven are combined: "Lázaro assenta con un capellán y un alguazil y despues toma manera de biuir" [Lázaro settles with a Chaplain and a Constable and then finds his way to settle down].

As we can see in the table, the Portuguese translation of 1721 reproduces Velasco's modifications of the external structure of *Lazarillo*.

Title in *Lazarillo Castigado*	*Vida de Lazarillo de Tormes, história entretenida e novamente feita...*
"Prólogo del autor a un amigo suyo"	
"Lázaro cuenta su linaje y nacimiento"	"Conta Lazarilho sua jeração, e seu nascimento" [Lázaro tells about his genealogy and birth]
"Assiento de Lázaro con el Ciego"	"Assento de Lazarilho con un Cégo" [Lazarilho settles with a blind man]
"Assiento de Lázaro con un clérigo"	"Como Lazarilho se pôs a servir a hum Clérigo" [How Lazarilho was on a Priest's duty]
"Assiento de Lázaro con un Escudero"	"Morada de Lazarilho com um Escudeiro" [Lazarillo dwells with a Squire]
"Lazaro assenta com un capellán y un alguazil, y despues toma manera de biuir"	"Acomoda-se Lazarillo com Hum Capellão, e hum Meirinho, e depois toma modo de viver" [Lázaro settles with a Chaplain and a Constable and then finds his way to settle down]

Table 4-1

Despite noticing the substitution of the repeated word "assiento" (settlement) for "se pôs a servir" (to be on duty), "morada" (dwelling) and "accomoda-se" (*accommodates*), we shouldn't forget that the suppression of repetitions is one of the most persistent universals of translation.[7] But there is an important difference between the Portuguese translation and the expurgated Castilian text: the absence of the prologue.

There is a reason why certain chapters are longer than others or why they occupy a particular position in the novel: the purpose of the autobiography. The prologue presents *Lazarillo de Tormes* as an accomplishment of an epistolary debt to a *vuestra merced* who has demanded the complete narration of the *caso*. This structure, similar to the public confession letters of 16th century Humanism, becomes one of the most realistic features in the novel. This subject, too plain at first glance, needed a good reason to claim, for the first time in history, a literary status. The justification of a *marido consentidor* [consenting husband] to a superior *vuestra merced* seemed a fair one. To fulfil his purpose, Lázaro decides to reveal everything about himself and, because he decides to explain the case from its beginning (as the prologue tells us), he eventually composes his autobiography. The traditional episodic structure of the *sarta* is thus replaced by a motivated disposition of the narrated material, as Lázaro Carreter explains: "making a hierarchy of the events that are not mere cases, but disposed causes of only one case".[8]

In addition, the protagonist leaves the temporal immobility he lived in to become a substance shaped by past experiences, which makes this novel an ancestor of the *Bildungsroman*. Once again, Lázaro Carreter's words are highly elucidating:

> The epic hero had been, till then, a character not modified nor shaped by his own adventures (…). Whereas in *Lazarillo*, the main character is not a cause, but a result; (…). Thus, the town crier that tolerates the dishonour in his marriage is a man shaped to accept it by his genealogy and his different life lessons. (Lázaro Carreter 1978: 66)[9]

---

[7] See Laviosa-Braithwaite 1998: 288-291.

[8] "jerarquizando los sucesos que no son sólo casos, sino causas ordenadas de un caso único"

[9] "El héroe épico era, hasta entonces, un personaje no modificado ni moldado por sus propias aventuras (…). En el *Lazarillo*, al contrario, el protagonista es resultado y no la causa; (…). Y, de este modo, el pregonero que suporta la deshonra conyugal es un hombre estrenado para aceptarlo por herencia y por sus aprendizajes variados."

Changing the title of the prologue was not a random decision. By adding "del autor a un amigo suyo" [from the author to a friend of his], Velasco removed the confusion between the barriers of fiction and reality into which the empirical author immersed, to his own great amusement I believe, a world of readers, for, as Francisco Rico explains about 16th century culture, "The willing suspension of disbelief took place only (…) when the fiction signs, i.e., the reasons for the disbelief, were ostentatiously noticeable" (2000: 164).[10] The new game of verisimilitude would surely be a threat to the believers of a book religion. Following the 1660 edition, the pilot-translation of 1721, its 1786 revised re-edition and the 1838 translations suppress the prologue.

The modern structure of the novel was reduced by the conservative attitude of the target culture into a well known model based on comic episodes, similar to the Italian *novella*, whereas the fictional traits were affirmed. The titles of the translations reflect these manipulations. While the Spanish title uses the word *vida* [life] as a unifying narrative element and specifies the material as his fortunes and misfortunes; in the first Portuguese translation, the comical factor is reiterated and the misfortunes are replaced by roguery, *Vida de Lazarosinho de Tormes. Historia Entretenida (…) na qual conta as suas ditas e subtilezas* [*The Life of Lazarosinho de Tormes. An entertaining story (…) in which he tells of his fortunes and subtleties*]. In 1838, the titles of the two translations promise the narration of marvellous adventures instead of a life story: *Aventuras Maravilhosas de Lazarilho de Tormes* [*The Marvellous Adventures of Lazarilho de Tormes*] and *Aventuras e astúcias de Lazarinho de Tormes escritas por elle mesmo e traduzidas por José da Fonseca* [*Adventures and Crafts of Lazarinho de Tormes written by himself and translated by José da Fonseca*].

4. The 1838 António José Vilale's translation

Whereas each cover of the three parts of the 1786 António Faria Barreiros's translation of *Lazarillo de Tormes* states "Com licença da Real Mesa Censória" [With the permission of the Royal Censoring Board], António José Vilale could publish his translation of the 1554 novel attached to the *Segunda Parte de la Vida de Lazarillo de Tormes sacada de las Chronicas Antiguas de Toledo* [*Second Part of the Life of Lazarillo*

---

[10] "La *willing suspension of disbelief* se producía únicamente (…) si los signos de los artificios, y con ellos las razones para el *disbelief*, para la incredulidad, estaban resaltados con toda ostentación."

de Tormes drawn out of the Old Chronicles of Toledo] (the responsibility of Juan de Luna) which is characterized by Laurenti (1979) as a manifestation of extreme anticlericalism.

Although *Aventuras Maravilhosas de Lazarilho de Tormes* does not contain the prologue, the addressee of the epistolary narrative is named throughout the novel as "amigo leitor" [The equivalent of the English 'Gentle Reader' (Lit. 'friendly reader')].

The last two chapters are fused into the single "Lazarilho passa ao serviço de hum capellão" [Lazarilho enters the service of a chaplain], recalling the expurgated version. Neither the fourth nor fifth chapters are suppressed, although the revealing of the bull seller's dishonesty seems to offend the more sensitive and devoted readers. Thus, the translator chooses to mark his presence and defend himself from possible accusations in a single translator's note on page 157:

> Nowhere in this narrative is there the aim of derogating the earned respect of the authentic bulls published in the legal forms, neither should we ridicule true devotion, but only protect the simple souls and simple-minded people against hypocrisy and imposture.[11]

The source text language is expressed on the cover: "Traduzidas da lingua francesa" [Translated from the French language] and the name Juan de Luna is substituted by a French author and translator, Grandmaison y Bruno. It's the year of 1838, after the suppression of the previous press censorship by the Constitutive Court in 1822, but the Marquis of Pombal's severe control over importing French revolutionary ideas and the presence of a group of booksellers in Portugal,[12] as well as the exile experience of some liberals in France, have contributed to the greater valuing of the French source context.

17th and 18th century French translation trend is known as *les belles infidèles*, characterized by Laviosa in these words: "[a translator] adapted classical texts to current canons and genres (through omissions and improvements) to such an extent that some of his translations are considered travesties of their originals" (1988: 411). It is probable that the French modifications of the picaresque could have influenced the Portuguese reading and the understanding of the picaresque genre.

---

[11] "Em toda esta narração não se tem em vista derogar ao respeito devido ás bullas authenticas e publicadas nas formas legaes, nem tão pouco ridicularizar a verdadeira piedade, senão precaver os ânimos simples e miniamente credulos contra os embustes da hypocrisia e da impostura."

[12] Such as "Rolland, Aillaud, Borel, Bertrand, Meaussé, Loup, Dubié, Dubeaux"

Hendrik van Gorp draws a list of the main shifts present in the European translations of the *novela picaresca española*, due to the use of the French as source texts since the 18th century. One of them is the denial of the original open ending full of *desengaño* [deception] and the preference for a happy bourgeois ending present in *Gil Blas de Santillane* (1715-1735, by Lesage). Van Gorp describes this fact as "typical of the impact of an aesthetic code (the French classical 17th century code) on a foreign genre" (van Gorp 1981: 214).[13]

With the Portuguese case, in the place once occupied by a Lázaro de Tormes who knows his "prosperidad y (…) cumbre de toda buena fortuna" [prosperity and at the height of all good fortune living] in a rented appendage of his master, sharing his wife with him and taking advantage of some of his old clothes, we have, instead, an avenged Lázaro. In the 1838 António Vilale's version, Lázaro's friends, who already figured in the original picaresque, talking quite wickedly about the *ménage à trois* in the archpriest's house, become the true reason for the happiness of the ex-rogue, who now lives a bohemian life as a wealthy man. Here is an illustrative piece:

> In fact, thanks to my friend's protection and to some lords that gave me the honour of their benevolence, I found myself indemnified from all the works and fatigues that I had suffered till that moment. (…) Thus, my gratitude was beyond limits: (…) we ate and drank with abundance. (…) But the best of all was that Lazarilho de Tormes spent not a single nickel on those feasts. At that time, I wasn't allowed to pay anything.[14]

5. Conclusion

Future works on the possible existence of a Portuguese picaresque literature should take into account not only the European history of the picaresque genre, but also the Portuguese context: the fact that the translations of the Spanish picaresque novels appeared only in the 19th century.

---

[13] "typique pour l'impact d'un code esthétique (le code classique du 17ème siècle français) sur un genre étranger"

[14] "Com effeito mediante a protecção de meus amigos, e de alguns senhores, que me honravão com a sua benevolencia, fiquei indemnizado de todos os trabalhos e fadigas que até alli tinha soffrido. (…) Assim a minha gratidão não tinha limites: (…) comiamos e bebiamos á farta. (…). Mas o melhor de tudo era que naquella epoca Lazarilho de Tormes gastou em taes comezainas hum único seitil. Não me deixavão nunca pagar."

It is now clear that censorship modulated the Portuguese reading of *Lazarillo de Tormes*. But we cannot forget the words of Harry Sieber about the major role that translators assumed in the construction of the picaresque genre, which is present in the studied case: "The translations of Spanish picaresque novels are the key to an understanding of the European history of the genre. Translators were readers who not only injected their own tastes and attitudes in their translations, but also assessed and attempted to include the sensibilities of a wider invisible reading public." (1977: 59)

References

Primary Sources

Grandmaison y Bruno (1838) *Aventuras Maravilhosas de Lazarilho de Tormes*, Paris: Pillet Aîné.

—. (1992) *The Life oF Lazarillo of Tormes, parts one and two* (translated and edited by Robert S. Rudder and Carmen Criado de Rodriguez Puertolas), Project Guttemberg, E-book available on http://www.gutenberg.org/etext/437.

Luna, Juan de (1979) *Segunda Parte de la Vida de Lazarillo de Tormes: Sacada de las Crónicas Antiguas de Toledo* (edition, prologue and notes by Joseph L. Laurenti), Madrid: Calpe, S.A.

—. (1786) *Vida de Lazarosinho de Tormes, historia entretenida, novamente feita e traduzida de castellano para português por António de Faria Barreiros*, Lisboa: Officina José da Silva Nazaré.

—. (1989) *La Vida de Lazarillo de Tormes* (edition, prologue and notes by Antonio Rey Hazas), Madrid: Editorial Castalia.

Secondary sources

Bataillon, Marcel (1968) *Novedad y fecundidad del "Lazarillo de Tormes"* (translated by Luis Cortés Vázquez), Barcelona, Salamanca and Madrid: Ediciones Alaya, S.A.

Laurenti, Joseph L. (1979). "Prólogo" in Juan de Luna (ed.), *Segunda parte de la vida de Lazarillo de Tormes sacada de las crónicas antiguas de Toledo* (prólogo y notas de Joseph L. Laurenti), Madrid: Espasa-Calpe, 6-89.

Laviosa-Braithwaite, Sara (1998) "Universals of Translation", in Mona Baker (ed.) *Routledge Encyclopedia of Translation Studies*, London, New York: Routledge, 288-291.

Lázaro Carreter, Fernando (1978) *"Lazarillo de Tormes" en la Picaresca* (2nd edition), Barcelona: Editorial Ariel.

Martino, Aldo (1999) *Il* Lazarillo de Tormes *e la sua ricezione in Europa (1554-1753)*, 2 vol., Pisa/Rome: Instituti Editoriali and Poligrafici Internazionali.

Rego, Raul (1982) *Os Índices Expurgatórios e a Cultura Portuguesa*, Lisboa: Instituto de Língua e Cultura Portuguesa.

Rico, Francisco (2001) *La novela picaresca y el punto de vista* (4th edition corrected and enlarged), Barcelona: Seix Barral Biblioteca Breve.

Sieber, Harry (1977) "The picaresque novel in Europe: a literary itinerary of the pícaro" in: *The Picaresque*, London: Methuen, 37-62.

Van Gorp, H. (1979). "Traductions et évolution d'un genre litteraire : Le roman picaresque en Europe au 17ème et 18ème siècles", in *Poetics Today*. Vol. 2: 4, 209-219.

SELF-CENSORSHIP IN VICTORIAN TRANSLATIONS OF HANS CHRISTIAN ANDERSEN

VIGGO HJØRNAGER PEDERSEN,
UNIVERSITY OF COPENHAGEN, DENMARK

Abstract: Books were not censored in Victorian England. But all the same there were fairly strict rules governing what might and might not be published, especially for children. As Hans Christian Andersen was generally perceived as a children's writer pure and simple rather than as a writer for both adults and children, such rules were also applied to translations of his stories.

This paper will examine Andersen's own ideas about censorship, and briefly discuss the literary climate in Britain in the early decades of the 19th century, up to the 1840s when the first translations appeared. This discussion will be followed by examples from Andersen tales in Victorian translation where there is clear evidence of (self)censorship from the publisher and/or the translator.

Most examples are from the work of Caroline Peachey, one of the first translators, and Dr. Dulcken, by far the most productive of the 19th century translators of Andersen. It is my contention that with experienced writers like these, censorship was not really needed: they knew what was expected of them, and translated accordingly.

1. Introduction

Unlike plays, books were not censored in Victorian England, censorship having been abolished in 1695. But that does not mean that there were not fairly strict rules governing what might and might not be published, especially for children. As Hans Christian Andersen was generally perceived as a children's writer pure and simple rather than as a writer for both adults and children, such rules were also applied to translations of his stories.

This paper will examine Andersen's own ideas about censorship, and briefly discuss the literary climate in Britain in the early decades of the

19th century, up to the 1840s when the first translations appeared. This discussion will be followed by examples from Andersen tales in Victorian translation where there is clear evidence of departures from the text that must be due to the publisher's and/or the translator's ideas about decorum where children were concerned.

Most of the examples will be taken from the work of Caroline Peachey, one of the first translators, and that of Dr. Dulcken, by far the most productive of the 19th century translators of Andersen. It is my contention that with experienced writers like these, censorship was not really needed: they knew what was expected of them, and translated accordingly.

2. Children's literature before 1840

Children's literature in the form of mass produced books aimed at a child audience developed earlier in England than in other countries because England was the first country to have a fairly numerous, reading middle class. Books tended to be religious, and as the 18th century drew to a close, increasingly moralizing: emphasis shifted from developing piety with a view to the hereafter, to cultivating more secular qualities in the young readers, such as would, in the words of Newbery, a pioneer within children's literature, make everybody love them.

The prevailing climate in children's literature in the first decades of the 19th century was conservative, a feature which was somehow bound up with a fear of supposedly revolutionary French ideas. Many educators thought that the distance between Rousseau and Robespierre was not very great. So, although the ideals of Romanticism had been current for four decades by the time the first translations of Andersen appeared in English, many providers and critics of children's literature still regarded its ideas with suspicion, preferring the utilitarian and moralizing approach of an earlier age, frequently with the further demand that children's reading should inculcate religion. A prime exponent of these views was Sarah Trimmer (1741-1810), whose work is discussed in Hjørnager Pedersen (2004). She frowned on imaginative literature, and wanted above all children's literature to be didactic, an attitude which she was certainly not alone in having, and which frequently led to the inclusion in children's books of geographical and historical information. So relatively late a text as Andrew Lang's version of "The Ugly Duckling" (1907) adds information about the appearance of cygnets which is not in Andersen's original (see Hjørnager Pedersen 2006). She also preferred original

English writing to translations of French writers, who tended to be republican, and, if not, Papists.

3. Exclusion of tales

This is indeed a point to be noted about the transfer of children's literature from one language to another: that many books and stories never reach the translation stage, but are simply left alone as unsuitable. This is not quite the case with Andersen; but many of his late tales with social criticism or religious doubt in them were translated much less than the early a-political ones, and many were not reprinted. This applies e.g. to "The Gardener and the Family", which satirizes over social stratification, and "Auntie Toothache", a great satirical tale full of nihilism.

4. Andersen and Revolution

There are remarkably few statements about politics in Andersen's fiction, and not many in his letters and diaries, either. The reason, I think, is twofold. In the first place, Andersen, throughout most of his life, considered politics to be of secondary importance when compared with other aspects of human life. But in addition to Andersen's general disinclination to indulge in political speculation, meddling in politics was dangerous during the last decades of absolute monarchy in Denmark, and extremely unlikely to further a career within the arts. Although detention, as in the case of the revolutionary writer Dr. Dampe (1790-1867), who spent 20 years in a state prison for advocating revolution, was exceptional, the authorities, frightened by the French Revolution in 1789 and its sequel in 1830, took a very dim view of any manifestation of radical sympathies.

That Andersen, at an early age, was very well aware of this appears from the following quotation (in my translation) from his *Skyggebilleder*, published in 1831, the year after the revolution of 1830, when Andersen was 26. Ostensibly, this is about Prussia, but it is very easy to apply the wisdom of it to Denmark.

> The prime minister, von Klewitz, has circulated a Government order to all newspapers in Prussia, recommending respect not only for the letter of the laws of censorship, but also for their spirit. The editors may report historical facts, but not describe revolutionary activities in detail, let alone seem to applaud them. ... Editors are recommended at all times to describe or from other papers to quote examples of zeal for the upholding of law

and order, etc., and to show the sad consequences dissidence may have for personal safety, commerce, and industry etc etc. (Andersen 181: 85-86)[1]

An extreme case of censorship is included in one of his tales, "The Shadow"; in it, a learned man is put to death after having been declared insane because he threatens to reveal the true nature of his shadow, who has not only acquired independence and wealth, but is about to be married to the crown princess and thus to become the heir to the throne. Though this is fiction, it is unfortunately only too easy to find parallels from the real world, and it shows Andersen's awareness of some of the brutal facts underlying contemporary politics.

5. Victorian Andersen translations: Caroline Peachey and Henry Dulcken

On the basis of my investigation (Hjørnager Pedersen 2004) it seems reasonable to assume that Caroline Peachey saw it as her task to provide good, entertaining, but also educational and edifying stories for children, and that she saw Andersen's tales as providing her with the raw material for that. About some Spanish folktales she had translated, she admitted that she had edited erotic situations and allusions out. We should not be surprised, therefore, that she also "improved" Andersen's tales, regarding him mainly as a writer for children, and translating accordingly.

Peachey's most explicit comment on her attitude to Andersen's art is to be found at the end of her memoir of his life, based on his autobiography and prefaced to the second edition of her Andersen translations:

> ... surely it may safely be asserted, that Andersen's Tales chime in harmoniously, both with our Christmas hymns, and our Christmas games; they are diverting enough to be the companions of our holiday; and have, for the most part, a healthful, religious feeling, which may well accord with the more serious thoughts of our holy-day. (Andersen 1852: xxxix-xl)

---

[1] "Geheimestatsminister v. Klewitz har ladet omsende en lithographeret Circulaire til Redacteurerne af de offentlige Blade i Preussen, og anbefaler disse, ei allene at opfatte Censurlovenes Bogstav, men ogsaa deres Aand Redacteurerne maae nok fortcelle historiske Facta, men de maae ikke ved Fortællinger af revolutionaire Begivenheder, paa en omstændelig, eller vel endog paa en lovprisende Maade fremstille Oprørs- og Opstands-Scener. ... Redacteurerne anbefales stedse, at fremstille, eller optage fra andre Tidsskrifter, Exempel paa Hengivenhed for Ordens Vedligeholdelse etc, urolige Bevægelsers sørgelige Følger for personlig Sikkerhed, Handel og Handtering o.s.v. o.s.v."

"Healthful religious feeling" to Peachey seems to imply a respect for decorum and an absence of material which might bring a blush to the cheek of a young person, or simply describe ordinary sinful mortals rather than (more or less) respectable models for the young readers; and if Andersen should neglect his duties in this department, Peachey is ready to help him. Here are a few examples.

5a. Not in front of the children

In "The Top and the Ball" the top says to the ball:

> Skulle vi ikke være Kjærestefolk, **siden vi dog ligge i Skuffe sammen** (A: II, 27) [2]

> ... since we are thrown so much together (P: 146)

Literally the Danish means "since we are lying in the same drawer", and the connotations of the original are clearly sexual (see a phrase like "ligge i seng sammen" [lie in (one) bed together].

Later in the same story the ball, who had rejected the top, meets him again many years later in the rubbish bin, and tells her story: she never married the swallow she imagined to be in love with her, but fell into the roof gutter, where she has been till recently:

> ... saa faldt jeg i Tagrenden, og der har jeg ligget i fem Aar og sivet! Det er en lang Tid, kan De troe, for en Jomfru! (A: II, 29)

A literal translation of the text is "... there I have lain five years, soaking! That is a long time, believe me, for a maid!" (Danish "Jomfru" means both "young woman" and "virgin").

This is toned down a little by Dulcken, who translates as follows:

> I fell into the gutter on the roof, and have lain there full five years, and become quite wet through. You may believe me, that's a long time for a young girl. (D: 216)

But Peachey's translation, by introducing the idea of a fatigued young lady, tries to avoid the obvious connotations of "gutter":[3]

---

[2] In the following A. = Andersen (1963 ff.), D. = Dulcken (1889), H. = Hersholt (1942-47), and P. = Peachey (1852), from the list of primary sources.

I fell into the gutter, and there I have lain five years, and am now wet through. Only think, what a wearisome time for a young lady to be in such a situation! (P: 148)

In "The Tinder-Box", Peachey changes direct reference to the fact that the soldier is a hot-blooded young man, who has a lovely girl brought to him at night, into a harmless situation that respects both sexual taboo and class difference:

... det var en virkelig Prindsesse; Soldaten kunne slet ikke lade være, han maatte kysse hende, for det var en rigtig Soldat. (A: I, 27)
[it was a real princess; the soldier could not help himself, he had to kiss her, for he was a true soldier (my translation)].

A real princess was this! so beautiful, so enchantingly beautiful! the Soldier could not help himself, he knelt down and kissed her hand. (P: 361)

But it is not only sexual references that are toned down. References to violence and death, which indeed are very frequent in Andersen, suffer the same fate, even in an innocent example from "Little Ida's Flowers", where Andersen has "Blomsterne ere ganske døde" (the flowers are quite dead) which Peachey changes to "... are quite faded".

In his detailed discussion of "Great Claus and Little Claus", Bredsdorff (1954) emphasizes that in Peachey's "Great Claus", people are not killed as in Andersen's; that the farmer's wife is visited by her cousin, in all innocence, not by a sexton up to no good, and that that unhappy gentleman is presented to the farmer as a magician, not as the Devil.

The toning down of the underlying brutality of the original folktale means that a point about conventional piety is missed. In Andersen's version, Little Claus is not only liberated by the cattle drover from the sack into which he has been put to be drowned, but replaced by him, because the drover wants to go to heaven quickly.

So when Great Claus comes out of church, he can comment on the lightness of the sack, which he puts down to the good effects of Sunday worship, and in this pious mood he goes on, as he believes, to drown his enemy. All this is removed by Peachey, who obviously disapproves of this sort of piety, not reflecting or caring that it is a true picture of life, and also very funny; the passage is translated by Dulcken, but changed by Peachey:

---

[3] Danish "tagrende" (roof gutter) does not have the negative associations of English "gutter"; on the other hand the idea that the ball has "ligget i fem år og sivet" (been soaking for five years) reminds us that Andersen seems to associate forbidden female sexuality with (dirty) water,

Soon afterwards Great Claus came out of the church. He took the sack on his shoulders again, although it seemed to him as if the sack had become lighter; for the old drover was only half as heavy as Little Claus.

"How light he is to carry now! Yes, that is because I have heard a psalm."

So he went to the river, which was deep and broad, threw the sack with the old drover in it into the water, and called after him, thinking that it was little Claus, "You lie there! Now you shan't trick me any more!" (D: 32)

Presently Great Claus came running back again,[4] he took up the sack, and again flung it over his shoulders, thinking, "How much lighter the burden seems now, it always does one good to rest for ever so short a time". So on he trudged to the river, flung the sack out into the water, and shouted after it "There now, Little Claus, You shall never cheat me any more!" (P: 285)

5b. Religious taboo

It is perhaps not so strange that references to sex and violence should be considered undesirable in stories intended for children, and as demonstrated above, this is indeed frequently the case in translations of Andersen. The same situation applies to socially unacceptable phenomena, especially references to objects and situations which Victorian ladies considered indelicate. For instance, Howitt transforms "Spyttebakke" (spittoon) into "door mat".

However, I shall here concentrate on a seemingly innocent area which was (and, surprisingly, still is) problematical, that of religion. We are not only concerned with ideas–the fact that references to religion are frequently toned down or omitted, like Great Claus's visit to the church in Peachey's translation just mentioned–but with the question of words like God and the Devil being found undesirable, together with collocations where such words occur.

The reason for my surprise is the fact that English critics and biographers of Andersen frequently mention his piety as positive, and underline the Christian message which his stories contain; Peachey is not alone in praising Andersen's "healthful, religious feeling". Still, according to many translators, there is a time and a place for everything, and whereas references to God and to immortality may be in order in "The Story of a

---

[4] In Peachey's version, Great Claus has not been to church, but merely called a man back into the porch because he wanted to speak to him; moreover, the content of the sack is not the cattle drover, but "the withered stump of a tree which stood by the roadside". Little Claus still makes off with the old man's cattle; but he does not cause his death.

Mother", many translators seem to believe that there can be too many references to such matters, and that some should be left out. Thus the intimacy with God in the following passage from "Reisekammeraten" is modified considerably by Dulcken, and completely left out by Peachey.

De kom saa høit op, at Kirketaarnene dybt under dem tilsidst saae ud som smaa røde Bær, nede i alt det Grønne, og de kunde see saa langt bort, mange, mange Mile, hvor de aldrig havde været! saameget smukt af den deilige Verden havde *Johannes* aldrig før seet paa eengang, og Solen skinnede saa varmt fra den friske blaa Luft, han hørte ogsaa Jægerne blæse paa Valdhorn inde mellem Bjergene, saa smukt og velsignet, at han fik Vandet i Øinene af Glæde, og kunde ikke lade være at sige: "Du gode vor Herre! jeg kunde kysse Dig, fordi Du er saa god mod os allesammen, og har givet os al den Deilighed, der er i Verden!" (A: I, 74) [the last sentence means: Good God, I could kiss you because you are so good to all of us and have given us all the loveliness in the world]

They had clambered up so high that the church-towers far beneath them showed like little red berries scattered among the green of the landscape, and they could see over so many, many miles of country! So much of the beauty of this fair world Hans had never before seen, and the sun shone warmly amid the blue vault of heaven, and the wind bore to him the notes of hunters' bugle-horns from various quarters - so sweet and wild were those notes!–and the tears stood in his eyes with transport and gratitude. (P: 387)

They came so high up that the church steeples under them looked at last like little blueberries among all the green; and they could see very far, many, many miles away, where they had never been. So much splendour in the lovely world John had never seen at one time before. And the sun shone warm in the fresh blue air, and among the mountains he could hear the huntsmen blowing their horns so gaily and sweetly that tears came into his eyes, and he could not help calling out, "How kind has Heaven been to us all, to give us all the splendour that is in this world!" (D: 51).

This inhibition applies even more in the case of references to the Devil, of which, by the way there are not many. There are no fewer than 57 occurrences of "Djævel", "Dævel" and their derivatives in the *Magnus* corpus, but only 17 of them are from the tales: such references are far more common in the novels. But the prominent position of "Dævel" in the opening section of "The Snow Queen" is frequently considered undesirable, and the Devil is edited out or changed into a demon, a goblin or a wicked magician: P.: magician; D.: goblin and demon.

The examples so far refer to cases where the "depth of intention"[5] is considerable. However, Andersen, like other Copenhageners of his time, also habitually "took the Lord's name in vain" in colloquial phrases which were considered unexceptionable by contemporary Danes. We are not here concerned with swearing–"Pokker" [pox], a frequent swearword, is not found in the corpus at all, and oaths derived from "Fanden", "Satan" or other names for the Devil are very rare indeed. But the adjective "velsignet" [blessed] is of frequent occurrence as an intensifier, and if there are more than 600 occurrences of "Gud" and derivatives, many of these serve a similar purpose:

"Great Claus and Little Claus":
Gud, hvilken deilig Kage, han kunde see staae derinde! (A: I, 32)
Heavens! what a glorious cake he saw standing there! (D: 26)
... he caught sight of a great, appetizing cake. (H.)[6]

In many cases we have more or less fixed phrases like "Gud bevares", "Herre Gud", "Gud skee Lov", which are toned down or left out in translation:

"The Tinder-Box":
Nei Gud bevares! hvor der var meget Guld! (A: I, 25)
Mercy! what a quantity of gold was there! (D: 20)
What a sight! Here was gold and to spare. (H)[7]

It is apparent that, while Dulcken and Hersholt follow Andersen some of the way, both show a distinct tendency to avoid direct translation of these expressions, and this is even more true of other translators.[8]

---

[5] By depth of intention Arne Thing Mortensen implies the degree of literalness with which an utterance should be understood. Do you really die if you do not respect a deadline? The correct interpretation of this will depend on the language and culture involved. "Direction of intention" means implication. If somebody says "It's hot in here," is this then a statement of fact, or do they want you to open the window?
[6] Quoted from Magnus, no pagination.
[7] Cf. footnote 5.
[8] It appears from Glyn Jones (1993: 76-77), as well as from my own observation, that religious taboo is still a very active force.

6. Conclusion

Compared to the brutal forms of repression mentioned in other conference papers, Andersen and his translators did not encounter any persecution from public authorities. But I think that we would do well to remember that repression of free speech is not only a question of mobilizing the law and the bailiffs. In 19th century Britain–as well as in Denmark–a literary climate was created in which certain things simply were not expressed; to a large extent the norms of the two countries coincided; but all in all the religious as well as social taboos were stronger in the English-speaking world than in Denmark, and this undoubtedly influenced the English translations of Andersen, just as it influences the production of children's literature to this very day.

References

Primary Sources

Andersen, H.C. (1963-90) *Eventyr og Historier*, Vols. I-VII (ed. by Erik Dal & Erling Nielsen), Copenhagen: Hans Reitzel.

—. (1852) *Danish Fairy Legends and Tales* (translated by Caroline Peachey, 2nd ed.), London: Addey & Co. (1st ed.: 1846, 3rd ed.: 1861).

—. (1889) *Stories for the Household* (translated by H.W. Dulcken), London: George Routledge and Sons. Rpt. as *The Complete Illustrated Stories of Hans Christian Andersen*. London: Chancellor Press, 1983ff.

—. (1942-47) *The Complete Andersen* (translated by Jean Hersholt), New York: Heritage Press.

—. (1831) S*kyggebilleder*, Copenhagen: Reitzel.

Secondary Sources

Bredsdorff, Elias (1954) *H.C. Andersen og England*, Copenhagen: Rosenkilde og Bagger.

Hjørnager Pedersen, Viggo (2004) *Ugly Ducklings? Studies in the English Translations of Hans Christian Andersen's Tales and Stories*, Odense: University Press of Southern Denmark.

—. (2006) "Translation or Paraphrase?", in V. Hjørnager Pedersen *Essays on Literature and Translation, POET* no. 30, Copenhagen: Dept. of English, Germanic and Romance Studies.

Jones, W. Glyn (1993) "Hvad har de dog gjort ved Andersen - en historie til skræk og advarsel", DAO 4, Copenhagen: Centre for Translation Studies, 67-80.

Magnus (1992) A CD-Rom made available through CD-Danmark, Copenhagen. Contains all Andersen Tales in English and Danish, and five more works by Andersen in Danish.

CONTRIBUTORS

Glòria **Barbal** - *gloria7@ozu.es*
Has a degree in Didactics, Philology and Journalism (Universidad Autonoma, Barcelona) and a post-graduation in Translation by the University of London. She has worked as a teacher, film translator and journalist. She is now preparing her PhD about the Ingmar Bergman's films at Universidad Pompeu Fabra, Barcelona.

Maria del Cármen **Camus Camus** - *camusc@unican.es*
Lecturer at the University of Cantabria (Spain), where she teaches Syntax and Didactics at the Teacher Training School and ESP courses for students of Medicine and Physical Education. She is a member of the TRACE Group and is currently working on her thesis in Translation Studies and Censorship (*Traducciones censuradas de novelas y películas del oeste en la España de Franco*) at the University of the Basque Country.

Olga **Castro Vázquez** - *olgacastro@uvigo.es*
A graduate in Journalism at the University of Santiago de Compostela (2002), and in Translation and Interpreting at the University of Vigo (2004). Awarded the DAS (Diploma of Advanced Studies) in the PhD programme "Translation and Paratranslation: Cultural Trends and Translation Policies" (2006) with a research project on *Translation and Social Change: Analytical Elements for a Non-Sexist Translation*. Member of the research group *Feminar: Feminism and Resistances (theory and practice)*, and is currently preparing her doctoral thesis on the interactions between Feminism and Translation. She combines her research projects with her job as a translator and interpreter, as well as being a journalist in charge of the press office of the NGO *Implicadas no desenvolvemento*. She has also published different articles in the *Yearbook of Literary Galician Studies*, in the *Journal of Translation Viceversa*, in the portal *Women's Internetwork*, and also in *Lectora, Journal of Women and Textuality*.

Nam Fung **Chang** - *changnf@ln.edu.hk*
Professor in the Department of Translation, Lingnan University, Hong Kong. PhD in Translation Studies (Warwick University). Has translated into Chinese Oscar Wilde's four comedies, and Jonathan Lynn and Antony Jay's *Yes Prime Minister*. Academic works include *Yes Prime Manipulator*, *Criticism of Chinese and Western Translation Theories* (in Chinese), and papers in *Babel*, *The Translator*, *Perspectives*, and *Target*.

Rui Pina **Coelho** - *ruipinacoelho@gmail.com*
Has a degree in Modern Languages and Literature and a MA in Theatre Studies (University of Lisbon). He is a member of the Centre for Theatre Studies of the Faculty of Letters (University of Lisbon), and teaches at the High School for Theatre and Cinema. He writes as a theatre critic for *Público*, a national daily newspaper. He was a founding member of Trimagisto, an experimental theatre company in Évora, where he works as an actor and stage director.

Hilal **Erkazanci** - *hilalerkazanci@yahoo.co.uk*
Lecturer in Translation and Interpretation Studies at Hacettepe University, Ankara. She has a BA and MA from Hacettepe University. She has received her PhD from Univesity of East Anglia, Norwich. The title of her MA thesis is "Effect of lexical and syntactic strategies on simultaneous interpreting". Her PhD thesis is about "Heteroglossia in Turkish translations: locating the style of literary translation in an audience-design perspective". Her research interests include pragma-stylistics in translation, language and identity in translation and interpretation, critical sociolinguistics, and critical language awareness in translation and interpretation. She is a translator into Turkish and English.

Cristina **Gómez Castro** - *cristina.gomez@unican.es*
PhD student and researcher in Translation Studies. Her main interests are the theory and methodology of translation, the study of the interaction between ideology and translation and the way (self)censorship is present in the rewritings of texts.

Currently she is preparing her PhD on translation and censorship under Franco's Spain.

Research stays at the Catholic University of Leuven, Belgium and the University of Aston, Birmingham, Great Britain. She has published case studies on censorship during the Francoist regime.

Maria dos Anjos **Guincho** – *mariabmg@gmail.com*
Teacher of French Culture and Literary Translation at the Catholic University of Portugal (Lisbon) and at a Secondary School in Oeiras. She has an MA in Comparative Literature (Portuguese and French) and is currently preparing her PhD on the translations of Ovid in Portugal. She was a member of the research project "Literary History and Translations. Representations of the Other in the Portuguese Culture" (1998-2005) and is now participating in the new project "Intercultural Literature in Portugal 1930-2000: a Critical Bibliography" led by Prof. Seruya. Her main interests are Translation Studies, Cultural Studies and Medieval Literature.

Viggo **Hjørnager Pedersen** - *vhp@get2net.dk*
MA, PhD, Dr. Phil., associate professor at Copenhagen University (English). Has published on Translation Studies and Literature. Most recent book (2004), *Ugly Ducklings?*, is a monograph on the English translations of Hans Christian Andersen's tales. Also editor of the 3rd and 4th editons of the Vinterberg & Bodelsen Danish-English dictionary (1990 and 1998). Among his literary translations are two novels by E. M. Forster and three by William Golding.

Patrícia López **López Gay** - *lespaul26@yahoo.com*
She has three degrees: in Translation and Interpretation (University of Granada), Modern Languages (University John Moores, Liverpool) and Applied European Languages (University of Provence). She has published *(Auto)traducción y (re)creación. Un pájaro quemado vivo, de Agustín Gómez Arcos*, in 2005, and several articles in European journals on her main research area – literary self-translation. Her research activity is currently carried out at the University of Paris 7 and at the Autonomous University of Barcelona, as a member of the AUTOTRAD research team.

Rita Bueno **Maia** - *ritabmaia@gmail.com*
Has a degree in Modern Languages and Literatures (French and Spanish) by the University of Lisbon. She is currently preparing her MA on the translation of the picaresque novel in Portugal and its importance for the Portuguese literary history. As a result of her activity in associations concerning Hispanic Studies, she won a scholarship for the University of Navarra, where she attended lectures by famous Spanish experts in the *Siglo de Oro*.

John **Milton** - *jmilton@usp.br*
Full professor of English Literature and Translation Studies at the University of São Paulo, Brazil. He is the author of *O Poder da Tradução [The Power of Translation]* (Ars Poética 1993), later published as *Translation: Theory and Practice* (Martins Fontes 1998) and *O Clube do Livro e a Tradução [The Book Club and Translation]* (EDUSC 2002). He translated the well known book by João Cabral Melo Neto, *Morte e Vida Severina* into English (*Death and Life of Severino*, Pleiade 2003) and is currently studying the relationship among politics, economy and translation.

Maria Lin **Moniz** – *lin.moniz@gmail.com*
Teacher of English and German at Escola Secundária de Palmela (Secondary School) with a post-graduation course of Translation - English and German (1990-1992).

She was a member of the research team working on "Literary History and Translations", led by Prof. Seruya (1998-2005).

PhD in Translation Studies (2006). Title of thesis: "On the narratives of World War I in Portuguese translations".

She was a member of the organising committee of the international conference on "Translation and Censorship – from the 18th Century to the Present Day", Lisbon, 27-28 November 2006.

She is currently working on Translation and Censorship in Portugal as a member of the research team supervised by Prof. Seruya. Ongoing project: "Intercultural Literature in Portugal 1930-2000: a Critical Bibliography".

She translated Kafka (*Brief an den Vater*) and Thomas Mann (some short stories) into Portuguese.

Natalia **Olshanskaya** - *olshanskayan@kenyon.edu*
Associate Professor of Russian in the Department of Modern Languages and Literatures at Kenyon College, USA. She has taught courses in translation studies at the Odessa State University (Ukraine), at the University of St. Andrews (Scotland), and at the College of William and Mary (USA). She has worked as interpreter and translator, and has published numerous articles on the theory and practice of translation.

Eterio **Pajares** - *fippaine@ehu.es*
Doctor in English Philology. He worked in Secondary Education for several years and he has taught English Literature to undergraduate students, and translation to postgraduates at the University of the Basque

Country for sixteen years. He has published several articles on Translation and Comparative Literature, particularly in the field of the eighteenth century cultural studies. He has also undertaken some translations, in collaboration, of authors such as Washington Irving and Henry James. He has worked in some I+D Research Projects on Translation and Censorship. He is one of the co-organizers of scientific events related with translation such as the International Congress "Cultural Transfers: Literature, Cinema and Translation", which is held in the University of the Basque Country triannually.

Fran **Rayner** - *frayner@ilch.uminho.pt*
Teaches undergraduate courses in Dramatic Literature and post-graduate courses in Dramatic Literature and Performance at the Universidade do Minho (Portugal). Her doctoral thesis, entitled "Caught in the Act: The Representation of Sexual Transgression in Three Portuguese Productions of Shakespeare," analysed contemporary performances of Shakespeare and was published by the University's Centro de Estudos Humanísticos in 2006. Her published research is in the areas of Shakespearean performance, gender and queer theory.

Alexandra Assis **Rosa** - *a.assis.rosa@netcabo.pt*
Professor at the Faculty of Letters, University of Lisbon (Portugal), where she teaches Media Translation, English Linguistics and Discourse Analysis, at graduate level, as well as Translation and Text Linguistics, Translation and Applied Linguistics, at post-graduate level. She is also a member of the University of Lisbon Centre for English Studies, and her main areas of research are translation and applied linguistics, and translational norms in both literary and media translation. She has published on the translation of forms of address and linguistic variation in fiction, as well as on reader profiling.

José **Santaemilia** - *jose.santaemilia@uv.es*
He is Associate Professor of English Language and Linguistics at the University of Valencia, as well as a legal and literary translator. His main research interests are gender and language, sexual language and legal translation (English-Spanish). He is the author of *Género como conflicto discursivo: La sexualización de los personajes cómicos* (2000) and has also edited several books (*Sexe i llenguatge: La construcció lingüística de les identitats de gènere* (2002) and *Género, lenguaje y traducción* (2003)) and published (with José Pruñonosa) the first critical edition and translation of *Fanny Hill* into Spanish (Editorial Cátedra 2000).

Ana Teresa **Santos** - *a.briziomarquesdoss@bham.ac.uk*
Took her first degree in Modern Languages and Literatures in the University of Coimbra. She has taught Portuguese Language in the Departament of Hispanic Studies of the University of Birmingham, U.K., where she was also the Portuguese Studies Coordinator. She is preparing an MPhil on the Portuguese translations of William Faulkner's *Sanctuary*. Her research has included the study of the Portuguese reception of Faulkner. She has published articles on the reception of Faulkner in Portugal. She is translating the book *The Case of Lima Barreto and Realism in the Brazilian "Belle Époque"*, by Dr. Robert Oakley and she is part of the team of translators of Heaventree Press for the project of translation of Lusophone African poetry.

Teresa **Seruya** – *tmseruya@gmail.com*
Full professor in the Department of Germanic Studies at the Arts Faculty of the University of Lisbon, teaching literature and culture in the German language. She also teaches History of Translation and Translation Theory. She works with the Catholic University of Portugal, as head of a research project on "Literary History and Translations" (1998-2005). Her main research area in the present is the history of translation in Portugal in the 20th century, leading another research project on "Intercultural Literature in Portugal 1930-2000: a Critical Bibliography".

She has published on literature and culture in the German language, particularly from the 20th century, the history of Germanic Studies in Portugal and the history of translation in Portugal.

She has organized four national conferences on Translation Studies in Portugal and two international EST (European Society for Translation Studies) conferences since 1998.

She is a literary translator of the following German authors: Goethe, Kleist, Leopold von Sacher-Masoch, Döblin and Thomas Mann.

Full professor in the Department of Germanic Studies at the Arts Faculty of the University of Lisbon, teaching literature and culture in the German language. She also teaches History of Translation and Translation Theory. She works with the Catholic University of Portugal, as head of a research project on "Literary History and Translations" (1998-2005). Her main research area in the present is the history of translation in Portugal in the 20th century, leading another research project on "Intercultural Literature in Portugal 1930-2000: a Critical Bibliography".

She has published on literature and culture in the German language, particularly from the 20th century, the history of Germanic Studies in Portugal and the history of translation in Portugal.

She has organized four national conferences on Translation Studies in Portugal and two international EST (European Society for Translation Studies) conferences since 1998. She is a literary translator of the following German authors: Goethe, Kleist, Leopold von Sacher-Masoch, Döblin and Thomas Mann.

Jaroslav **Spirk** - *Jaroslav.S@gmx.de*
Has a degree by the Institute of Translation and Interpreting Studies, Faculty of Philosophy and Arts, Charles University, Prague, Czech Republic. Has an MA in the subjects of Translation and Interpreting: English AND Translation and Interpreting: German. His MA thesis dealt with the Theory of Literary Translation by the Slovak scholar Anton Popovič. In October 2006, he was accepted as a PhD student of Translation Studies at the same Institute. He is now in Lisbon conducting his doctoral research on the cultural relations between Portugal and Czechoslovakia through translations.

Helena **Tanqueiro** - *helena.tanqueiro@uab.es*
Has a degree in Romanic Philology by the University of Lisbon and a PhD in Translation Theory by the Autonomous University of Barcelona, where she has been teaching since 1999. She has been Head of the Centre for the Portuguese Language/ Camões Institute at the same University since 2001. She is currently the main researcher of the AUTOTRAD project concerning self-translation within the theory of literary translation.

Gabriela Gândara **Terenas** - *ggandarat@netcabo.pt*
Took a degree in Modern Languages and Literatures, later specialising in Anglo-Portuguese Studies. She has been a lecturer at Universidade Nova de Lisboa since 1993, where she has taught a range of courses, particularly in areas of British and North American Cultures and also Translation Studies. Amongst her principal works are: *O Portugal da Guerra Peninsular. A visão dos militares britânicos (1808-1812)* (2000) and *Diagnoses Especulares: imagens da Grã-Bretanha na imprensa periódica portuguesa (1865-1890)*, her Doctoral Thesis, 2004. She also published several articles on subjects such as Anglo-Portuguese relations in Africa, the influence of Herbert Spencer's thought in Portugal, Catholicism in Britain and its relation with the Portuguese social and cultural context, the reception of the British political thought in Portugal, the images of the English woman and the reception of British painters in the Portuguese press during the second half of the 19th century.

Ibon **Uribarri Zenekorta** - *fipurzei@ehu.es*
After studying philosophy and media studies, he spent around five years in Germany (Mainz, Marburg) researching on philosophy (PhD in 1996) and translating German philosophy into Basque language. He has written several books on German philosophy in Basque language. He spent one more year abroad in Oxford (Basque Visiting Fellow at St. Antony's College), and then he returned to the University of the Basque Country. Since 2002 he teaches German to Basque/Spanish translation in Vitoria-Gasteiz. His research work moves in two directions: German to Basque translation and German philosophy in Spanish translation. He has translated works by Immanuel Kant, G.W.F. Hegel, Charles S. Peirce, Sigmund Freud and others.

Christine **Zurbach** - *zurbach@mail.telepac.pt*
Full Professor at the University of Évora (Portugal). PhD in Comparative Literature/ Translation Studies. Title of thesis: "Theatre Translation and Practice in Portugal, 1975-1988" (2002). She is currently director of the degree in Translation at the University of Évora, where she teaches undergraduate and post-graduation courses both in the area of Translators Training and in Comparative Literatures and Poetics. She has published on her main research interest–Theatre Studies.

INDEX

08/15 17
1984 219
50 Nursery Rhymes 8
A Arte em Portugal no Século XX (1911-1961) 6
A Capital 201
A Fera Amansada 51, 69
A Gathering of Bald Men .. 230, 232, 234, 235, 238
A Metade Arrancada de Mim 202
A Midsummer Night's Dream .49, 50
A Mulher de Trinta Anos 199
A Reabertura do Paraíso Terrestre 12
A Salvação do Mundo 76
A Small Village Called Lidice 16
A Tradução em Portugal 270
A Tragédia de Macbeth 53, 54
Aaltonen, Sirkku 61, 73
Abellán, Manuel Luis 117, 185, 186, 188, 194
addresser 86, 88, 90, 91, 92
Adolescência 208
Aegerter, Lindsay 248, 250
África, Maria Cármen 286, 287
AGA (Archivo General de la Administración) ... 104, 105, 149, 150
Agirbiceanu, Ion 212
agnosticismo 121
AHN (Archivo Histórico Nacional) 291
Ainsi fut assassiné Trotsky 11
Aixelá, Javier Franco 234, 240
Akbayır, Sıddık 245, 246, 250
Albornoz, Raquel 191, 193
Alden, Dauril 34, 37, 45
Alencar, José de 200, 223
Alexandre, Valentim 37, 45
Alfonsina 137

Allan, Keith 164, 172
Allen, R. E. 99, 253, 260
Almada, Izaías 202
Almeida, António Vitorino de 66
Almeida, Dom Jorge de 299
Álvares, Baltazar 300
Alvarez, Antonio 300
Alvarez, F. L. 112
Alvarez, Raquel 194
Amado, Jorge 201, 223
Amell, Samuel 186, 188, 194
Amicis, Edmundo de 209, 213
Amis, Sir Kingsley W. 218
Amorim, Francisco Gomes de 76, 80
Amorim, Sônia Maria 200, 213
Anacreonte 8
Anatomia de Uma História de Amor 55, 59
Anatomy of a Love Story 57
Andersen, Hans Christian. 308, 309, 310, 311, 312, 313, 314, 316, 317
Anderson, Maxwell 55
Anderson, Perry 42
Andrade, Carlos Drummond de. 201
Animal Farm 219
anti-theatricalism 63
Antolín Rato, Mariano 188
Appia, Adolphe 53
Aragon, Louis 10, 17
Araoz, D. Manuel de 292
Arcades 269
Archivo General de la Administración 103, 148
Arias Salgado, Rafael 120, 125
Aristocles 148
Arnau, A. 190, 193
Ars Poetica 274, 275
Artaud, Antonin 79
As Velhas 212

Index

Ash, Timothy Garton.................. 97
Assis, Machado de 8, 200, 223
Astrín Bada, Miguel Maria........ 157
Asturias, Miguel Angel............ 222
Au pays de Staline....................... 7
Auclert, Hubertine.................... 135
Augustus 272
Auntie Toothache 310
author-translator 175, 178, 179, 180, 181
Autobiografía de Federico Sánchez 177
AUTOTRAD............................. 174
Aventuras e astúcias de Lazarinho de Tormes escritas por elle mesmo e traduzidas por José da Fonseca 303
Aventuras Maravilhosas de Lazarilho de Tormes 303, 304
Ávila, Norberto 51
Azevedo, Aluísio...................... 223
Azevedo, Cândido de ..4, 20, 22, 23, 29
Azevedo, Manuela de............59, 60
Azurara, Gomes Eannes de 222
Babeuf, François Noël................ 16
Babo, Alexandre........................ 82
Bair, Deirdre...............133, 135, 145
Baker, Mona...............182, 252, 260
Bakhtin, Mikhail 242, 243, 250
Balzac, Honoré de ..10, 18, 199, 219
Bantam Books....................133, 134
Barber, Benjamin R...............97, 99
Barnes, Peter 55
Baroja, Pio............................... 108
Barradas, Mário....................65, 72
Barreiros, António Faria.....300, 303
Barreto, L. 223
Bassnett, Susan..132, 145, 272, 285, 286, 287
Bataillon, Georges.................... 299
Bataillon, Marcel..................... 306
Baucis, Josef............................ 291
Bayle, Jean 16

Beauvoir, Simone de 130, 131, 133, 134, 135, 137, 138, 139, 141, 142, 143, 145, 219
Beauvoir, Sylvie Le Bon de....... 140
Beauzée, Nicolas 271
Becher, Johannes R. 220
Becker, John 220
Beckett, Samuel........................ 219
Belden, Jack 7
belles infidèles 294, 304
Bennet, Alan.............................. 55
Bensiliman, Raquel 213
Bensoussan, Albert............ 175, 182
Benthall, Michael 53
Beobachtungen......................... 111
Bergman, Ingmar...... 119, 120, 121, 128, 129
Bergson, Henri.......................... 108
Bergua, José 111, 112, 117
Bernardo da Costa Carvalho (typographic workshop) 300
Bernhardt, Sarah........................ 49
Bertelsmann............................. 202
Besteiro, Julián 108, 109
Biblioteca dos Séculos 200
Biblioteca Tempo Universitário .. 39
Bildungsroman 302
Bioy Casares, Adolfo................ 149
Bissaya Barreto, Fernando........... 84
Blasco Ibáñez, Vicente 222
Blatty, William Peter. 190, 191, 193
Blommaert, Jan.......... 241, 243, 250
Boito, Arrigo 49
Böll, Heinrich 221
Bolshevism 11
Bolt, Robert 55
Bond, Edward 55
bookshops
    legal bookshops 237
    licensed bookshops 237
    underground bookstalls....... 237
Borges, Jorge Luís 24, 149, 222
Bost, Jacques 134, 136
Bou, Patricia 164, 172
Bourdeille, Pierre de (see Brantôme) 13

Bourdieu, Pierre 62, 96, 242, 250, 253, 260
Boxer, Charles Ralph 30, 31, 32, 33, 34, 36, 37, 38, 39, 40, 42, 43, 44, 45
Branco, Cassiano 84
Brand, Max 156
Brantôme, seigneur de (i.e. Pierre de Bourdeille) 13
Bravo, Maria Elena 24, 29
Brazão, Eduardo 49
Brecht, Bertolt 10, 47, 50, 55, 57, 59, 63, 79, 220
Bredel, Willi 220
Bredsdorff, Elias 313, 317
Brentano, Franz Clemens 108
Breton, André 10
Breve História da Censura Literária em Portugal 267
Brezhnev, Leonid 222
Brezhnevization........................ 216
Bridget Jones: The Edge of Reason 163, 165
Bridget Jones's Diary.........163, 165
Brock, Timothy C...........96, 97, 100
Brod, Max 220
Broeck, Raymond van den 224
Brontë sisters (Anne, Charlotte, Emily) 186
Brontë, Charlotte 199, 209, 210, 213
Brown, Calvin S. 26, 29
Brulin, Tone 79
Bueno, Gustavo 104
Buffalo Bill 159
Burridge, Kate 164, 172
Burton, Deirdre 86, 88, 99
Buruma, Ian............................... 97
Bush, Niven............................... 13
Bushnell, Candace 165
Busquets, Néstor 172
Bussy, Dorothy............................ 8
Büyükkantarcıoğlu, Nalan..247, 250
C.I.T.A.C. (Círculo de Iniciação Teatral da Academia de Coimbra) 51, 54
Cabot, Meg............................... 165

Cabral, Carlos 53
Caetano, Marcelo.20, 29, 30, 31, 48, 50, 55
Calinesco, George 212
Camões, Luís de ..30, 208, 222, 273, 280
Campbell, George..................... 292
Camus, Albert............................. 10
Cancioneiro Geral..... 268, 271, 286
Capanema, Gustavo.................. 201
Capaz ou Incapaz para o Casamento............................ 13
Caras Pintadas 12
Carel, Christian.......................... 14
Carmona, General Óscar 5
Carnation Revolution 1974.... 54, 95
Carneiro, Mário de Sá................ 222
Carpentier, Alejo 222
Carreter, Lázaro........................ 302
Carrión-Cervera, Jesús Navarro. 157
Carroll, Lewis............................ 200
Carvalho, Arons de 95, 99
Carvalho, Bessa de 52
Carvalho, Rui de 65, 71
Casanova, Giovanni Giacomo 13
Casson, Lewis............................. 49
Castillejos Osuna, Andrés.......... 157
Castro, Francisco Lyon de 23
Cátedra 137, 139, 142
Cathalogues librorum qui prohibentur mandato Fernadi de Valdes................................. 299
Catholicism....................... 105, 294
Cela, Camilo José 222
Cellule 2455. Couloir de la mort. 19
Cénico de Direito........................ 49
censoring apparatus ... 241, 242, 245
Censoring Commission 3, 4, 6, 7, 8, 10, 18, 19, 20, 56, 75, 78
censorship3, 4, 5, 7, 8, 9, 10, 17, 20, 21, 40, 117, 147, 149, 176, 219, 252, 293
  a posteriori censorship .. 36, 43
  a priori censorship......... 34, 43
  censorial mechanisms252, 254, 257, 260

de facto censorship 97
ecclesiastic censorship 108
economic censorship 158
implicit censorship 244
legal censorship 166
media censorship 95
naturalized censorship 242
official censorship 184, 187
opaque censorship 242
overt censorship 229, 230
political censorship 238
post-publication censorship 96, 97, 236
pre-publication censorship.. 95, 96, 97, 236
pre-publication self-censorship 236
preventive censorship.185, 267
prior censorship 48, 95
private censorship 97, 120
propaganda censorship 34
public censorship 163, 172
religious censorship 211
repressive censorship 267
self-censorship28, 43, 65, 97, 105, 111, 114, 147, 148, 149, 157, 161, 163, 164, 171, 172, 174, 176, 177, 179, 180, 181, 182, 184, 187, 201, 228, 241, 242, 244, 246, 247, 253, 255, 272, 273, 277, 286, 291, 292, 293, 295
silencio administrativo 187
socially-enforced censorship 97
soft censorship 97
state censorship120, 159, 164, 185
transparent censorship 242
Censorship: a World Encyclopedia 95
Cervantes, Miguel de 208, 212
Chacon, Vamireh.36, 39, 40, 41, 42, 43, 44
Chagas, Manuel Pinheiro 213
Chaves, Ana Maria 21, 29
Che Guevara 201
Chekhov, Anton 76, 80, 221

Chéri 10
Chessman, Caryl 19
Chesterton, G. K. 199
chick lit 165
children's literature 309, 310, 317
Chinese translation tradition 238
Chitarrori, Luis 141
Christie, Agatha 187, 199
Cidade, Hernâni.267, 269, 271, 273, 287
Círculo do Livro 202
Claramonte, Vidal 286, 287
Clarendon Press 30
Clarissa 294
Claudio, Jean 12
Clinton, Hillary 230, 232, 239
Clube do Livro ..199, 200, 201, 202, 203, 205, 207, 209, 211, 212
Coccioli, Carlo...174, 179, 180, 181, 182
Cochran, Terry 281, 287
coherencia textual 121
Coleção Amarela 199
Coleção Nobel 199
Colette 10
colonialism
    aggressive colonialism 32
    colonial war 6, 33, 95
    Portuguese colonial empire. 32, 84, 85
    Portuguese colonial world ... 36
Comédia Humana 200
Comissão de Exame e Classificação de Espectáculos 54
communicative strategy 144
communism 215
Communism 215, 216, 217, 222
Communist Manifesto 113
Como en un espejo 128
Companhia de Teatro da RTP 51
Companhia Nacional de Teatro ... 53
Companhia Rey Colaço-Robles Monteiro 50, 52, 53, 54
Company, Juan Miguel. 50, 53, 120, 129
Comparative Literature 174

Condillac, Étienne Bonnot de.... 291
Constant, Benjamin 8
consumer fiction 156
cooperative principle 257
correct language 242
Cortázar, Julio 222
Cortesão, Armando ...33, 34, 36, 37, 38, 45
Costa, Lúcio 201
Craig, Cairns 248, 250
Craig, Gordon.............................. 53
Critique of Practical Reason 107
Critique of Pure Reason 107, 108, 109, 111
Cronin, Michael 131, 145
Crossland, Margaret 134
CTT (Correios, Telégrafos e Telefones) .4, 7, 8, 17, 18, 22, 24
Cuenca Granch, Enrique 159
Cummins, J. S. 34, 45
Customs Services 8, 22
Da esencia da verdade 114
Dampe, Jacob Jacobsen.............. 310
Darío, Ruben 222
Das Wesen der Wahrheit........... 114
David Campbell Publishers 134
Defensa de los milagros del Pentateuco 293
Defourneaux, Marcelin......290, 296, 297
Deleuze, Pilles 248, 251
Delgado, Humberto 6, 7
Delibes, Miguel 222
Dente por Dente ...53, 61, 63, 64, 71
Departamento de Imprensa e Propaganda 201
Departamento Nacional de Propaganda e Difusão Cultural
.... 201
Der Panzer zielte auf Kafka 221
Descartes, René 108
de-semantization 166
de-sensitization.......................... 166
de-Stalinization 216
Deux essais sur le marxisme 14
Dias, Anderson Fernandes 202

Diccionario de seudónimos literarios españoles 149
Dickens, Charles199, 205, 206, 207, 209, 213, 218, 247
dictatorship 3, 62
  Dita branda 38
  Dita dura 38
  sham dictatorship 38
Die Religion innerhalb der Grenzen der blossen Vernunft 110
dime novels 157
discoursal common sense 246
Dissertation on Miracles 292
distribuidora Chamartín 121
doblaje 120, 127
Dolores, Carmen 64, 65, 72
dominant culture 243
Domingos Carneiro 300
Dos Passos, John 17, 18, 188, 218
Dostoievsky, Fiodor 10, 199, 200
Dreiser, Theodore 218
Du Bellay, Joachim 271
Duelo ao Sol 13
Dulcinea operation 6
Dulcken, Henry .308, 309, 312, 313, 315, 316, 317
Duras, Marguerite 220
Durbaş, Refik 246
Dürrenmatt, Friedrich 221
Dzerkalo tyzhnia 254
Eco, Umberto 97
Edipe 143
Editora Abril 202
Editora Ática 202
Editora Globo de Porto Alegre .. 199
Editora José Olympio 199
Editora Martins 200, 201
Editora Saraiva 200, 202
Editora Tempo Brasileiro 42
Editorial Minerva 21, 28, 29
El comercio y gobierno considerado uno a otro relativamente 291
El Onanismo. Disertación sobre las enfermedades producidas por los excesos venéreos y

principalmente por la masturbación 292
El Padrino 190
El segundo sexo.130, 135, 136, 137, 138, 139, 141, 142
El séptimo sello ..119, 120, 121, 128
Ellis, Havelock 19
Éluard, Paul 11
Em Busca do Tempo Perdido 200
Empresa Vasco Morgado 51
Enciso Castrillón, Félix 295
Encyclopedia of Sociology 96
English narrative fiction 290
English Old Vic Theatre 49
Enlightenment ...269, 289, 290, 292, 293
Ensayos sobre el movimiento intelectual en Alemania 108
Epic Theatre 47, 55, 59
epitext 133
Escoiquiz, Juan de 291
Estado Novo ..20, 21, 31, 36, 37, 43, 44, 91, 95, 200, 201, 211
Estala, Father Pedro 291
Euripedes 8
Even-Zohar, Itamar 182, 224
Everyman's Library 134, 140
Existentialism 114, 219
expurgations 235
Fairclough, Norman 246, 251
faithfulness 229, 230, 237
Falk, Richard 253, 261
Faria, Isabel Hub 33, 88, 99
Fascism 17, 75, 113
Faulkner, William 21, 22, 23, 24, 25, 27, 28, 29, 199, 218
Fawcett, Peter 28, 29
Federico Sánchez se despide de ustedes 174, 176
Federico Sanchez vous salue bien 174, 176
Feliz Ano Novo 202
feminism 39, 131
feminist translators 132
Fernández Núñez, Manuel.111, 112, 117

Ferrari, Angelo 49
Ferreira, Fr. Bartolomeu 300
Ferro, António 4, 5, 51
Feuerbach, Ludwig 105
Fichte, Johann Gottlieb 104
Fielding, Helen ..163, 165, 169, 171, 172
Fielding, Henry 291
Fígados de Tigre 76
Figueiredo, António de 85, 95, 99
Figueiredo, Guilherme 223
Filosofía pura. Anejo a mi folleto "Kant" 108
First Republic 7
Fitzgerald, F. Scott 218
Flaubert, Gustave 200
Flotow, Luise von 134, 139, 145
Fogos Cruzados 199
Fonseca, Rubem 202
formalism 220
Foucault, Michel 253, 260
Four Screenplays of Ingmar Bergman 121
França, José Augusto 5, 6, 20
France, Anatole 219
Franc-Maçonnerie et Catholicisme 15
Franco, General Francisco .. 23, 103, 104, 107, 108, 109, 111, 112, 114, 119, 136, 147, 148, 149, 150, 158, 160, 161, 164, 177, 184, 186, 188
French Revolution 16, 310
French Women's Suffrage Organization 135
Fresas salvajes 128
Freyre, Gilberto ...36, 37, 38, 39, 40, 43, 45, 201
Friel, Howard 253, 261
Frisch, Max 221
From Laodamia to Protesilaus. 265, 271
Fuentes, Carlos 222
Fühmann, Franz 220
Fürnberg, Louis 220
Fyfield, Charles 50

Gabeira, Fernando 202
Gal, Susan 152, 246, 251
Gallegos, Rómulo 222
Gallimard 130, 141
Galvão, Henrique 7
Gaos, José 109
Garção, P. A. Correia .266, 271, 287
García Hortelano, Juan 222
García Lorca, Federico 59, 222
García Malo, Ignacio 294
García Márquez, Gabriel 222
García Morente, Manuel ... 108, 111, 112
García-Alas Ureña, Leopoldo Enrique 148
García-Puente, Juan ... 136, 137, 141, 143
Gardner, Erle Stanley 187
Gargantua 199, 209, 211
Garnier, Christine 5
Garrett, Almeida 222
Garrido Vilariño, Xoán Manuel 133, 145
Gaspari, Elio 38, 45
gender approach 132, 135
gender bias 169
gender politics 72
Genette, Gérard 132, 133, 145
Geração de 70 41
Gerdener, Wilhelm 243, 251
Gide, André 199
Gil Blas de Santillane 305
Gill, Peter 55
glasnost 217
Glazer, Sarah 135, 141, 145
Gogol, Nikolai Vasilievich 221
Gökpek, Anil 249
Goldsmith, Oliver 294, 295
Gómez Arcos, Agustín 179, 183
Gómez Ortiz, Tomás .. 156, 159, 161
González de Francia, José .. 291, 292
González Ledesma, Francisco .. 158, 161
González, Cardinal Zeferino 106
Gorbachev, Mikhail ... 216, 217, 222, 227

Gorki, Maxim .10, 79, 200, 208, 213
Gorkin, Julien 11
Gorp, Hendrik van 298, 305, 307
Goytisolo, Juan 222
Graciotti, Mario 200, 202, 208
Gracq, Julien 219
Grandes Esperanças 200
Grandmaison y Bruno, Félix de 304, 306
Grass, Günter 221
Great Claus and Little Claus 313, 316
Green, Melanie C. 96, 97, 100
Greene, Graham 218
Greenpeace: Verde Guerrilha da Paz 202
Grenier, Fernand 8
Grice, H. Paul 256, 257, 259, 261
Grutman, Rainer 175, 182
Guattari, Félix 248, 251
Guedes, Fernando 268, 286
Guedes, João 53
Guerra e Paz 200
Guerreiro, Miguel do Couto 265, 270, 271, 272, 273, 274, 275, 276, 277, 280, 284, 285, 286, 287
Guide international de l'amour ... 12
Guirao Hernández, Pedro 157
Gusmão, Fernando 65, 71, 72
Gutiérrez Lanza, Maria del Camino 119, 120, 129
Guzmán, Eduardo de 158
Hall, Robert Anderson 243, 251
Hallewell, Laurence ... 201, 207, 214
Halliday, Michael 88, 99
Hamlet 49, 53
Hammett, Dashiel 199
Hamsun, Knut 209, 213
Hard Times .199, 205, 206, 211, 213
Hardy, Thomas 186
Harte, Bret 200
Has Democracy Collapsed? 16
hate speech 97
Hegel, G. W. F. 104

Heidegger, Martin 39, 104, 111, 113, 114
Heindel, Max 15
Helmet, Elizabeth 295
Hemingway, Ernest 10, 18, 188, 218
Henderson, Diana 69, 73
Henry IV 54
Henry V 49, 54, 248
Henry, O. 200
Henry, the Navigator 85
Hermans, Theo 266, 270, 288
Heroides 265, 268, 270, 271, 274, 278, 279, 286
Hersholt, Jean 312, 316, 317
heteroglossia 242, 243, 247, 248, 249
heteroglossic texts 241, 242, 245, 248
Heym, Stefan 220
Hidalgo Martínez, Antonio 156
História do Teatro Português 77
Hitler, Adolf 201, 220, 233
Hjørnager Pedersen, Viggo 308, 309, 311, 317
Hochhuth, Rolf 221
Hoesenlaars, Ton 62, 73
Holden, Wendy 165
Holmes, James Stratton 224
Homage to Catalonia 189
Homer 274
Horace 271, 274, 275
Howells, Kim 254
Howitt, Mary 314
Hrala, Milan 218, 219, 220, 221, 222, 228
Hugo, Victor 208, 209, 212, 219
Humilhados e Ofendidos 199
Hunan People's Publishing House 236
Hunter, Tod 156
Huxley, Aldous 199
IAN/TT (Instituto dos Arquivos Nacionais/ Torre do Tombo) 7
Icaza, Jorge 222
ideology 131, 132, 144, 158, 174, 182, 252, 254, 286, 320

cultural ideology 286
dominant ideology 139, 140
ideology of standard language 246
ideology of the consumers . 237
ideology of the translator ... 285
official ideology 233, 237
patriarchal ideology 132
Il-lusitania 20
Imaz, Eugenio 109
imitation 266, 269
implicature 256, 257
Index 299, 300
Index et catalogues librorum prohibentorum 299
Innerarity, Daniel 98
Inquisition .. 108, 268, 269, 289, 290, 292, 295, 296, 297, 298, 299
Inspecção Geral dos Teatros 47
Instituto Nacional do Livro 201
Instituto Progresso Editorial, S.A. 22
Instrucciones y Normas para la Censura Moral de Espectáculos 126
Intercultural Literature in Portugal (1930-2000): A Critical Bibliography 4
Introduction to the Theory of Pure Form in Theatre 79
Ionesco, Eugène 219
James, Henry 200
Jardiel Poncella, Enrique 14
Jianu, Nicolae 207, 208, 212, 213
Jolicoeur, Louis 175, 182
Jonathan Cape 134
Joseph Andrews 291, 292
Jovellanos, Gaspar Melchor de .. 291
Joyce, James 199
Judt, Tony 98
Julius Caesar 54, 63
Junta de Censura 121
Kafka, Franz 199, 202, 220, 221
Kaliç, Sabri 248, 249, 250
Kant, Immanuel .103, 104, 105, 106, 107, 108, 109, 110, 111, 114, 117, 118

Kant. *Reflexiones de centenario* 108
Kantianism 106
Kaputt 17
Kennedy, Dennis 55, 60
Keyes, Marian 165
Khrushchev, Nikita 216, 221
Kierkegaard, Sören 16, 134
kiosk fiction 148
Kipling, Rudyard 200
Kirst, Hans Hellmut 17
Kisch, Egon Ervin 220
Knopf, Alfred 133, 139
Knopf, Blanche 133
Kott, Jan 47, 55
Krause, Karl C. F. 104
Krausism 105, 106
Kreye, Adrian 98
Krich, Aron M. 15
Kritik der reinen Vernunft 111
Kundera, Ludvík 220
Kundera, Milan 220
Kunert, Günter 220
Kunze, Reiner 220
Kush, Celena E 135, 141, 146
L'écriture ou la vie 176
L'enseigne de Gersaint 17
L'univers concentrationnaire 16
La Chine ébranle le monde 7
*La ciencia española bajo la
  Inquisición* 108
La Ciociara 18
La Féria, Filipe 55
La filosofía de Kant 108
*La filosofía española actual.
  Indicaciones bibliográficas*.. 106
La maîtresse noire 11
*La paz perpetua (Zum ewigen
  Frieden)* 109
La saison chaude 12
La Selección en el Hombre 19
*La vida de Lazarillo de Tormes y de
  sus fortunas y adversidades* 298,
  299
*La vie économique de la Russie
  Soviétique* 14

Lady Chatterley's Lover ... 233, 235,
  236, 237
Lafuente Estefanía, Marcial 158
Lafuente, Felipe Antonio ... 149, 161
Lage, Francisco 52
Lambert, José 175, 182, 224, 288
Lane-Mercier, Gillian 132, 146
Lang, Andrew 309
Langa, Mandla 230, 232, 233, 239
language planning 241, 243, 244
language policies 244
LaPrade, Douglas Edward . 188, 194
Larra, Mariano José de 295
Laski, Harold J. 14
Laurenti, Joseph L. 304, 306
Lavios Angulo, Miguel 157
Laviosa-Braithwaite, Sara . 304, 306
Lawrence, D. H. 233
Lazarillo Castigado 298, 299
Lazarillo de Tormes .. 298, 299, 300,
  302, 303, 306
Lázaro Carreter, Fernando 307
Lázaro, Alberto 188, 189, 194
Le Clézio, Jean-Marie G 219
*Le commerce et le gouvernement
  considérés relativement l'un à
  l'autre* 291
Le deuxième sexe 130, 132, 133,
  135, 136, 138, 140, 142, 143,
  144
Le premier amour du monde 8
Lefevere, André 76, 83, 132, 145,
  224, 288
legitimate language 242, 244, 249
Lemos, Pedro 51
Lenin, Vladimir 148, 201
León, Víctor 172
Les dames galantes 13
Les Éditeurs Français Réunis 7
Les femmes que j'ai aimées 13
Les homosexuels 15
Lesage, Alain-René 305
Lessing, Gotthold E. 104
Lévi-Strauss, Claude 39
Levý, Jiří 215, 223, 224, 227, 228
libation 223

Liberalism 41
Life of Galileo 50
linguistic habitus 241, 244, 247
linguistic otherness 248
Lisbon Players............................ 50
Lispector, Clarice 223
literariness 176
literary canon............................ 243
literary system 82, 176, 271, 278, 284, 299
Little Ida's Flowers.................... 313
Lived Experience 134
Living History 230, 235, 237, 238
Livraria Bertrand 143
Lliró Olivé, José Maria.............. 156
Lobato, José Bento Monteiro 201
Lobtinière-Harwood, Susanne de 132, 135, 146
Lodge, David.......230, 234, 238, 239
Lolita .. 230, 233, 234, 235, 237, 238
López de Velasco, Juan 298, 299
López García, José 157
López Hipkiss, Guillermo 159
López López-Gay, Patricia 177, 179, 181, 183
López Pardina, Teresa 138
Los juicios sintéticos a priori desde el punto de vista lógico 108
Losada Martín, Juan 157
Luna, Juan de 304, 306
Luso-Tropicalism 37, 38, 43
Luzuriaga, María Josefa 291
Lyons, John 87, 99
Macbeth..............................53, 54
Macbeth–Que se Passa na Tua Cabeça? 54
Macedo, Diogo de 5
Machado, José Maria.203, 204, 206, 210, 211, 213
Macieira, Virgílio 51
Madame Bovary 202
Mãe Coragem e Os Seus Filhos .. 50
Maeztu, Ramiro de 108, 118
Mailer, Norman 218
Majerová, Marie........................ 221
major language 243

Malaparte, Curzio 17
Mallorquí, José 159
Malta, Eduardo 5
Mancisidor, José 222
Mandela, Nelson 233
Mandiargues, André Pieyre de .. 219
Manifesto (see *Communist Manifesto*) 113
manipulatory effects 244
manipulatory mechanisms 171
Mann, Thomas........................... 199
Manzanares, Alfonso 157
Mao Zedong 229
Marcelist period 74, 75
Marchal, Jean 14
Markham, James................ 184, 194
Martínez Orejón, Felix 157
Martino, Aldo 300, 307
Martins, Luzia Maria 47, 54, 55, 57, 58, 60
Martins, M. Teresa Payan .. 278, 279
Martins, Pedro 51
Martorell Linares, Alicia .. 137, 138, 142, 143, 145, 146
Marx, Karl 104, 113, 114, 201
Marxism-Leninism 216
mass fiction 148, 194
Massai, Sonia 62
mass-market fiction 156
Massot, Josep 188, 193, 194
Matos, General José Maria Norton de.. 5, 7
Matos, Ruy de 51
Mattoso, José...................... 98, 99
Maugham, Somerset 200
Maupassant, Guy de 13, 200, 219
Mauperrin, Margarida................. 55
maxim of manner....... 257, 259, 260
maxim of quality 257
maxim of quantity 257
McCullers, Carson 188
McEnery, Tom....165, 167, 170, 172
Measure for Measure 53, 61, 63, 64
Mein Kampf............................ 201
Meireles, Admiral Manuel C. Quintão.. 7

Meirelles, Cecília 201
Memorias Posthumas de Braz Cubas 8
Mendes, João Fragoso 81
Mercuri, Valentina 179, 180, 181, 183
Merimée, Prosper 200, 208, 212
Merino, Raquel..173, 185, 194, 294, 297
Meriwether, James 24, 29
Merkle, Denise 244, 251
Mesa da Comissão Geral sobre o Exame e Censura dos Livros 269
metalinguistic discourse 242, 244
Metamorphoses 273
Mey, Jacob 249, 251
Meyenburg, Erwin 50
Meyer, Augusto 201
microtextual analysis 105
Miguéis, José Rodrigues 223
Millgate, Michael 21
Milliet, Sérgio 143
Milroy, Leslie 244, 246, 251
Milton, John 156, 188, 194, 203, 214
Ministry of Information and Tourism 185
Miranda, Ana 223
miscegenation...........41, 94, 98, 209
Moi, Toril 135, 146
Molina Foix, Vicente................ 98
Monteiro, Luís de Sttau...51, 61, 63, 64, 69, 70, 71, 72
moralization 272, 277
Moravia, Alberto 18
Moreira, Adriano 37, 45
Moreno García, José.................. 157
Moreno, María 137, 141
Morgado, Vasco 69
Mota, Teresa.............................. 52
Munerato, Elice 38, 39, 44
Munteanu, Francisc 212
Murilo, Rubião 223
Nabokov, Vladimir....179, 230, 233, 239
Namora, Fernando 223
narrative of the West ..147, 148, 149

National Socialism 16, 17
naturalización pragmática.. 124, 126
Nava Palacio, Cesáreo 293
Negreiros, Joaquim Trigo de 6
Nekrassov 14
Neo-Kantianism................. 106, 108
Neo-Scholasticism............. 106, 109
Neruda, Pablo 11, 222
New Russian Short Story Writers 11
Newbery, Linda 309
Nick Carter 159
Niemeyer, Oscar....................... 201
Nietzsche, Friedrich... 104, 113, 114
nihilism.................... 121, 127, 310
nivel macrotextual 121
nivel microtextual 121, 126
nodes of pain 248
Nogueira, Goulart....................... 53
Noite de Reis.............................. 52
nom de plume 157, 158
Nord, Christiane 175, 183
normalization............................ 217
Normas de censura cinematográfica 128
norms.103, 120, 175, 248, 249, 286, 317
  discursive norms 252
  expectancy norms 229
  ideological norms 229
  language norms................. 225
  linguistic norms 242
  literary norms.................... 225
  market economic norms..... 237
  of bon goût....................... 294
  poetic norms 286
  posited norms 132
  social norms..................... 147
  translational norms 229,   236, 279, 323
Nos Bastidores da Censura 202
Nouss, Alexis 131, 146
nouveau roman 219, 220
novella 303
Novo Índice Expurgatório 268
Novosilzov, N................... 179, 183
Nunes, L. Bojunga.................... 223

Núñez, Toribio 109
O Amansar da Fera ...51, 61, 63, 69, 71, 72
O Caminho do Céu 207, 213
O Desconhecido 212
O Gigante Gargântua 203, 211
O Girassol 212
O Livro e a Leitura em Portugal, Subsídios para a sua História-Séculos XVIII-XIX 268
O Livro Vermelho da Igreja Perseguida 201
O Luso e o Trópico 36, 45
O Mercador de Veneza 53
O Pão 212
O Prazer 13
O Processo 202
O Professor 209, 211
O Romance de Maria Clara 209
O Segundo Sexo 143
O Tarado do Brás 202
O Vermelho e o Negro 200
Ó, Jorge Ramos do 5, 7, 20
O'Neill, Michael 55
Obras Completas 266
Odes 8
Oficina Patriarcal de Francisco Luiz Ameno 272
Olivares Leyva, Monica 186, 194
original text .43, 132, 137, 175, 176, 181, 182, 256
Ortega y Gasset, José 108
Orwell, George 189, 219
Os Mastins 207, 212
Osborne, John 55
Otello 49
Othello 49, 51
Othello ou o Moiro de Veneza 51
Ovid ...265, 270, 273, 274, 278, 286
Oviedo, Juan Carlos 51, 54
Oxford Playhouse Company 52
Pajares, Eterio 296
Palant, Pablo 135, 136, 137, 141, 143, 145
Palla e Carmo, José 74, 76

Palla, Maria Antónia. 74, 76, 94, 95, 99
Pamela 294
Pandolfi, Vito 79
Panova, Vera 7
Pantagruel 203
paratexts 130, 132, 140, 144, 278, 293, 294
  iconic paratexts.. 135, 137, 139
  linguistic paratexts 144
Parshley, Howard 134, 135, 139, 140, 144, 145, 146
patronage 76
Paulo, Rogério 51, 65
Peachey, Caroline 308, 309, 311, 312, 313, 314, 315, 317
Pedro, António 53, 64, 65, 71
Penguin Books 134, 140
Pennock, Barry 164, 172
Pequeño Karma 180
Pereira, Maria Helena da Rocha 269
Pereira, Pedro Luiz 202
perestroika 216, 217, 227
Pérez Galdós, Benito 222
Performance Studies 61, 72
peritext 133
Perojo, José 108, 109, 111, 112
Perry, João 52
Picador 134
picaresque 298, 304, 305, 306
Piccolo Karma 174, 179, 180, 181
PIDE (Polícia Internacional de Defesa do Estado) 4, 7, 8, 11, 18, 22, 24, 54
Piñeiro, Ramón 114
Pinilla, José A 269
Pinter, Harold 79
Pinto, Ângela 49
Pinto, Francisco Leite 5
Pirandello, Luigi 199
pirated copies 237
Pires, José Cardoso 223
Pitagoras 134
Pitigrilli 10, 12
Plato 147, 148
Platonov 76

Plinay/Plessey Automática Eléctrica Portuguesa.............................. 51
Poe, Edgar Allan 200
Poetics Today 298
Poetika umeleckého prekladu.... 225
political correctness..................... 97
Polysystem Theory.....131, 175, 238
Pombal, Marquis of............268, 304
Popesco, Dumitru Radu.............. 212
Popovič, Anton..215, 223, 224, 225, 226, 227, 228
popular narrative 147, 148, 149, 156
Portinari, Cândido 201
Porto, Carlos......................53, 59, 60
Portugália 18
Poulain de la Barre, François 134
Prague Spring............................. 216
Prelo publishers........................... 75
Prévert, Jacques......................... 219
propaganda.................................. 11
　　censorial propaganda........... 43
　　propaganda office.................. 5
Proscenium................................. 51
Proust, Marcel 145, 199
pseudonym 147, 148, 149, 150, 151, 153, 155, 156, 157, 158, 161
Psique........................136, 141, 143
Publicações Dom Quixote......21, 29
Publicações Europa-América 23
pulp fiction/ pulps 150, 156, 161
purism 241, 243
　　linguistic purism..........242, 243
Pushkin, Alexander 208, 212
Puzo, Mario........................190, 193
Pygmalion 247, 248
Pym, Anthony 75, 78, 83
Queen, Ellery 49, 199
Queirós, Eça de 201, 222
Queiroz, Rachel de 201
Queneau, Raymond 220
Quental, Antero de 40
Quiroga, Gaspar 299
Rabadán, Rosa...118, 119, 150, 156, 157, 161, 164, 173, 194, 294, 297

Rabelais, François.... 199, 203, 204, 205, 211, 213
Race Relations in the Portuguese Colonial Empire, 1415-1825. 30, 31, 33, 35, 36, 38, 39, 43, 44
Racine, Jean.................................. 8
racionalismo 107, 121, 127
Ramírez, Vera............................ 158
Ramos, Artur 59, 60, 80, 81
Ramos, Graciliano 201, 223
Ramos, Rui 34, 45
Random House 141
Random House Mondadori........ 136
Raposo, Hipólito......................... 20
Rattigan, Terence....................... 55
Real Mesa Censória... 268, 269, 303
Real Mesa da Comissão Geral sobre o Exame e Censura dos Livros 278, 285
Rebello, Luiz Francisco.. 53, 61, 63, 64, 65, 66, 69, 71, 72, 74, 75, 76, 77, 78, 79, 80, 81, 83
Rebelo, Luís de Sousa 34, 45
reception society....................... 144
Reflexões sobre a revolução da nossa época 14
Régia Oficina Tipográfica 268
Régio, José 76, 80
Rego, José Lins de..................... 201
Rego, Raul................................. 307
Rei Lear 51
Reisekammeraten....................... 315
Renn, Ludwig............................ 220
República Literária ... 269, 271, 274
Resende, Garcia de 268
retranslation................................ 22
Retrato Inacabado: Memórias..... 64
Revista Contemporánea............ 109
Revista de História 37
Revista de Occidente 104
Revista dos Tribunais 202
rewriting94, 141, 144, 164, 171, 178
　　as artistic practice 78
　　as linguistic practice 78
　　as textual practice 78
　　cultural rewriting 144

Rey Colaço, Amélia 50, 51, 55
Rey y Heredia, José............107, 111
Rhodes, Cecil 41
Ribas, Pedro 112
Ribeiro Neto, Agenor 209, 213
Ribeiro, Eurico Branco.......200, 209
Ribeiro, Francisco 51, 52
Richard III.................................... 54
Richardson, Samuel.................. 294
Richepin, Jean 208, 212
Rickert,Henrich 108
Rico, Francisco...................303, 307
Riera, Ernest.............................. 172
Roas Bastos, Augusto................ 222
Robbe-Grillet, Alain.................. 219
Robbins, Harold 201
Robespierre, Maximilian........... 309
Rodrigues, A. A. Gonçalves...... 270
Rodrigues, Fernanda Pinto 20, 21, 26, 28, 29
Rodrigues, Graça Almeida 7, 20, 267, 268, 269
Rodrigues, Urbano Tavares....... 223
Rodríguez Aroca, Luis 157
Rodríguez Espinosa, Marcos.... 188, 189, 194
Rodriguez Puertolas, Carmen Criado de.............................. 306
Rogers, Paul. Patrick. 149, 161
Rohmer, Sax............................... 199
Rolland, Romain 219, 304
romantic novel........................... 156
Romanticism 309
Romeo and Juliet.47, 52, 55, 57, 58, 59, 63
Romeu e Julieta........................... 52
Ronai, Paulo 200
Roque da Silva, Rolando 213
Rosa, João Guimarães 223
Rosa, Tomás Santa 201
Rosas, Fernando 5, 6, 20
Rossi, Ernesto.............................. 49
Rousseau, Jean-Jacques............. 309
Rousset, David 16
Rovira Armengol, José.............. 112
Royer, Louis-Charles 12

Rubiani, Ferruccio 209
Rudder, Robert S. 306
Ruiz Catarineu, Joaquín............. 157
Rulfo, Juan 222
Rumeu de Armas, Antonio 290, 297
Russel, Bertrand 10
Sagra, Ramón de la................... 104
Salazar, António de Oliveira 5, 6, 7, 11, 20, 29, 30, 31, 32, 33, 34, 40, 42, 47, 48, 51, 61, 62, 67, 143, 215
Salmerón, Nicolás 109
samizdat...................................... 219
Sanchez Salazar, General Leandro A... 11
Sánchez, Maria Manuela 269
Sanctuary................... 21, 24, 27, 29
Sanlı, Sevgi............... 247, 248, 250
Sanmartín, Júlia................. 168, 173
Santaemilia, José 163, 169, 171, 173
Santamaría, José Miguel... 156, 161, 297
Santos, Graça dos .48, 50, 60, 62, 72
Santuário 22, 24
Sanz del Río, Julián 104
Saraiva, António José 278
Saramago, José 17, 223
Sartre, Jean Paul 10, 14, 39, 79, 134, 139, 143, 219
saudade 114
Saviotti, Gino 70
Schell, Orville................... 237, 240
Schelling, F. W. J 104, 107
Schopenhauer, Arthur........ 105, 111
Schwarz, Roberto 38, 46
Seabrook, Jerry........................... 55
Seara Nova 60, 81, 83, 99
Seco, Manuel............. 168, 169, 173
second original 269
Seghers, Anna................... 220, 221
Selected Works of Edward Young 291
self-construction 147, 148, 156
self-reference........86, 87, 88, 90, 91
Semprún, Jorge..174, 176, 177, 178, 179, 182

Sena, Jorge de 52, 60
Serioja.. 7
Seruya, Teresa...................3, 20, 44
Shaffer, Peter............................... 55
Shakespeare Our Contemporary 47, 55
Shakespeare, William 47, 48, 49, 50, 51, 52, 53, 54, 55, 57, 59, 61, 62, 63, 64, 65, 70, 71, 72, 73, 79, 218, 248, 250
Shakespeare: Histories and Nations 55
Shaw, Bernard....................247, 250
Sheen, Fulton 8
Sherr, James 255, 256
Sieber, Harry 306, 307
Siglo Veinte........................136, 143
Silas Marner......................207, 213
Silva, Dionísio............................ 202
Silva, Domingos Carvalho da.... 203
Simenon, Georges 199
Simon & Schuster 121
Simon, Sherry....121, 129, 131, 146, 220
Simone de Beauvoir, her world-famous study of The Second Sex 134
Simons, Margaret A. ..134, 135, 146
Skyggebilleder............................ 310
Small World.......230, 234, 235, 236, 237, 238
Smith, Lígia Junqueira 22
Snell-Hornby, Mary 131, 146
SNI (Secretariado Nacional de Informação).......................... 5, 7
Sobre Dios y la Religión............ 110
Sobre la esencia 109
Social Criticism......................... 174
socialism with a human face 217
Sociedade de Instrução Tavaredense 53
Sociology of Literature.............. 174
Sofocles... 8
Sonho de Uma Noite de Verão 50

Spanish Civil War 103, 104, 106, 108, 109, 113, 114, 159, 188, 189
Spark, Muriel............................. 218
speech regularities 3, 4, 6
Spengler, Oswald....................... 108
Spirit Policy.................................. 4
Splendor in the Grass 188
Staehlin, Padre Carlos Maria.... 119, 121, 125
Stalin, Joseph..10, 11, 148, 217, 222
Stalinization...................... 216, 224
Stanco, Zaharia 207, 208, 212
standard dialect......................... 243
standard language..... 242, 243, 245, 247, 248, 249
standardization....241, 242, 243, 247
Stanton, Sir George 291, 293
state-owned publishing house.... 237
Steinbeck, John.................. 199, 218
Stendhal..................................... 219
Stevenson, Robert Louis............ 200
Storey, David............................... 55
Strange, Jeffrey J. 96, 97, 100
subliterature 149
Sudamericana 136, 137, 141, 143
Susu, Zhao................................. 239
symbolic capital........................ 247
T.E.L. (Teatro Estúdio de Lisboa) 55, 57
T.E.U.C. (Teatro dos Estudantes da Universidade de Coimbra) 53
T.M.L. (Teatro Moderno de Lisboa) 63, 64, 65
Ta Kung Pao............. 235, 237, 240
Tanqueiro, Helena 174, 175, 181, 183
Tanto Barulho por Nada 52
target audience.......................... 141
target literary system 175
target reader.............. 180, 182, 233
target society 139, 140, 144, 164
Teatro de Algibeira..................... 53
Teatro de Bolso 53
Teatro do Ateneu de Coimbra 54
Teatro do Povo 51

Teatro Experimental do Porto 53
Teatro Moderno de Lisboa 53, 61, 63
Teatro Monumental 61, 69
Teatro Municipal de São Luís 74, 75, 79, 80, 81
Teatro Nacional D. Maria II ...50, 54
Teatro Nacional Popular.........51, 52
Teatro Vasco Santana.................. 55
Tempos Difíceis 205, 206, 211
Tena, Cayetano Luca de 52
tensors 248
Teoría transcendental de las cantidades imaginarias 107
Teória umeleckého prekladu 225
Terre élue 17
texto derivado 294
Thackeray, William M. 186, 218
The Adventures of Tom Sawyer . 201
The Banquet 16
The Capital of the World 188
The Collected Works of Bertolt Brecht 220
The Exorcist 190, 191, 193
The Fifth Column and First 49 Stories 188
The Gardener and the Family ... 310
The Godfather 190, 193
The Homosexuals, as Seen by Themselves and Thirty Authorities 15
the Iron years................................. 4
the Lead years 4, 5
The Lord of the Rings 219
The Lusiadas 267
The Merchant of Venice 50
The Mother 74, 75, 76, 77, 79, 80, 81, 82
The New Shakespeare Festival Company 54
The Professor 199, 211
The Random House 134
The Second Sex ..130, 133, 134, 135, 139, 140, 141, 146
The Seventh Seal 119
The Shadow 311

The Snow Queen 315
The Story of a Mother 315
The Taming of the Shrew 51, 61, 63, 69
The Tinder-Box 313, 316
The Top and the Ball 312
The Ugly Duckling 309
The Vicar of Wakefield 294
The Wild Palms 24
theatrical system 76, 82
Theory of Literary Translation .. 174
Through a Glass Darkly 119
Tiananmen Square 230
Toledano, Carmen 171, 173
Tolkien, J. R. R.......................... 219
Torre, Manuel Gomes da 65
Toury, Gideon78, 83, 119, 150, 161, 175, 183, 224, 241, 243, 251
TRACE 103, 104, 149, 162
Traducción y censura de textos cinematográficos en la España de Franco: doblaje y subtitulado inglés-español (1951-1975) .. 120
Traducción y censura inglés-español: 1939-1985 Estudio preliminar 118
Trainspotting 248
translation 3, 13, 14, 16, 18
    and clarification 28
    and democratisation 18
    and explicitation 28
    as act of communication 131
    as cultural transfer 289, 292
    as process of mediation...... 131
    as re-creation 278
    as rewriting 86, 132
    audiovisual translation 119
    creative translation............. 176
    factory translation 211
    improved translation 311
    intralingual translation84, 86, 94
    literal translation 65, 181
    literary translation175, 223, 266
    mediated translation........... 294

paratranslation 130, 131, 133, 139, 144
   paratranslative behaviour... 140
   patriarchal translation 135
   praxeology of translation ... 225
   privileged translation 176
   professional translation 175
   prospective translation 4, 18
   pseudotranslation 147, 148, 149, 150, 151, 157
   retranslation 21
   self-translation 174, 175, 176, 177, 178, 179, 180, 181, 182
   sui generis translation. 176, 178
   traducción aceptable ... 124, 126
   translation commissioner 28
   translation ethics 257
   translation theory 215, 223, 228
   translational strategies 84, 86, 245
   translative behaviour 140
Translation and Conflict 252
Translation Studies 72, 74, 131, 174, 286
   cultural turn 131
   ideological turn 131
translator
   self-translator 174, 180
   translator's (in)visibility 131, 144
   translator-traitor 176
Tratado da Versificação Portuguesa 280
Trimmer, Sarah 309
Trinka, Zdena 16
Trotsky, Leon 11, 148
Tsinghua University Press 238
Turkish Daily News 246
Turkish Language Association. 244, 245
Twain, Mark 148, 200, 218
Twelfth Night 50
Uhse, Bodo 220
Ultimatum 41
Um Pedaço de Terra .. 207, 212, 213

Um Vagabundo Toca em Surdina 209
Umění překladu 224
Unamuno, Miguel de 108
Une femme à hommes 14
Uslar Pietri, Arturo 222
Vainer, Nelson 207, 208, 212, 213
Vallvé, Manuel 159
Varela, Alfredo 222
Vargas, Getúlio 200, 201, 211
Vasconcelos, Marília de . 21, 24, 25, 26, 27, 28, 29
Vasconcelos, Maurício de 80
Vautel, Clément 12
Vega, Miguel Ángel 164, 173
Velasco, Juan 300, 303
Velde, Th. H. van de 13
Velvet Revolution 216, 217, 222
Vencidos da Vida 41
Venuti, Lawrence 243, 251
Vera Ramírez, Antonio 156
verbs
   of action process 88
   of intention process 88
   of material process 88
Verdi, Giuseppe 49
Verney, Luís António 271, 273
Viagens de Gulliver 200
Viaje al interior de la China y Tartaria 293
Vian, Boris 219
Viana, António Manuel Couto 53
Vicente, Gil 222
Victorian England 308
Vida de Lazarilho de Tormes: historia entretenida e traduzida do castelhano 300
Vida de Lazarosinho de Tormes. Historia Entretenida (...) na qual conta as suas ditas e subtilezas 303
Vidart Schuch, Luís ... 106, 107, 117
Vieira, Padre António 273
Vilale, António José 303, 305
Vila-San Juan, Sergio 185, 194
Vintage 29, 134, 260

Virgil 274
Wallace, Edgar 199
Wallenstein, Carlos 48, 60
Waugh, Evelin 218
Weekly Mirror 254, 255, 257
Welsh, Irvine 248, 250
Wen Wei Po 235, 240
Werfel, Franz 220
Werther 202
Wesker, Arnold 55
Western 147, 149, 150, 156, 157, 158, 160, 161
White, Martin 49
Whitman, Walt 218
Wild Strawberries 119
Wilder, Dan 156
Wilder, Thornton 55
Willis, Ted 55
Wilson, Pedro 49
Witkiewicz, Stanislas 74, 75, 76, 79, 80, 83
Wober, Mallory 245, 251

Wolf, Christa 20, 220
Woman's Life Today 134
Women's Studies 135
Woolard, Kathryn 244, 251
Woolf, Virginia 199
World-Wide Shakespeares: Local Appropriations in Film and Performance 62
Wyler, Lia 199, 214
Xiao, Zhonghua .. 165, 167, 170, 172
Xinwen Wu Bao 233, 238, 240
Yilin 235, 237
Young, Edward 291
Zhao Susu 235
Zhdanov, Andrei A. 219
Zhong xi yixue piping 238
Zola, Émile 18
Zozaya, Antonio 108, 109
Zubiri, Xavier 109
Zum ewigen Frieden 111
Zweig, Arnold 220